Trade, Globalization and Sustainability Impact Assessment

To the late Konrad von Moltke

Trade, Globalization and Sustainability Impact Assessment

A Critical Look at Methods and Outcomes

Edited by Paul Ekins and Tancrède Voituriez

Routledge
Taylor & Francis Group
LONDON AND NEW YORK

First published 2009 by Earthscan

2 Park Square, Milton Park, Abingdon, Oxon OX14 4RN
711 Third Avenue, New York, NY 10017, USA

Routledge is an imprint of the Taylor & Francis Group, an informa business

First issued in paperback 2016

Typeset by MapSet Ltd, Gateshead, UK
Cover design by Susanne Harris

Earthscan publishes in association with the International Institute for Environment and Development

A catalogue record for this book is available from the British Library

Library of Congress Cataloging-in-Publication Data

Trade, globalization and sustainability impact assessment : a critical look at methods and outcomes / edited by Paul Ekins and Tancrède Voituriez. – 1st ed.
p.cm.
Includes bibliographical references and index.
ISBN 978-1-84407-661-1 (hardback)
1. Commerce. 2. Globalization. 3. Sustainable development. I. Ekins, Paul. II. Voituriez, Tancrède, 1968–
HF1008.T724 2009
382–dc22

2008051842

ISBN 978-1-84407-661-1 (hbk)
ISBN 978-1-138-99372-3 (pbk)

Contents

List of Figures, Tables and Boxes

Figures

Tables

Boxes

List of Contributors

Edward Anderson is a lecturer in the School of International Development at the University of East Anglia, UK. He has a PhD in economics from the University of Sussex. In recent years he has carried out research on the impacts of international trade and migration on the wages of skilled and unskilled labour, which has been published in *World Development, Oxford Economic Papers and European Review of Economic History.*

Ana Bachurova has an MSc in environmental governance from the University of Freiburg, Germany. Her latest research work was for her master's thesis on the topic 'The role of private actors as norm-entrepreneurs in water governance networks'. She continues to pursue her professional career in the area of analysing, planning and decision making for natural resources use and environmental protection in the broader context of aiming at sustainable development. Her special field of interest is water governance.

Hernan Blanco holds an MPhil in environment and development from Cambridge University. He founded and directed RIDES, a research centre on sustainable development policies in Chile, until 2008. He is an international fellow of IIED (UK) and works now as a freelance consultant on issues related to sustainability, social responsibility and public participation. He is a lecturer at the Universidad del Desarrollo in Chile.

Daniel Blobel studied geo-ecology at Karlsruhe University. He is a senior analyst at Ecologic Institute in Berlin. Among his areas of interest are climate policy, trade and sustainable development, as well as impact assessment and indicators.

Massimiliano Cali is a research officer with the Overseas Development Institute (based in Geneva). His research focuses on the relation between trade, development and growth, on the effects of migration on source countries, and on the determinants and implications of urbanization in developing countries. He is currently completing a PhD in economic geography at the London School of Economics.

Sylvain Chabe-Ferret has a PhD in economics from the University of Auvergne and is currently a research fellow at Cemagref, where he develops and implements econometric methods to evaluate the impact of public policies on development and/or the environment

Matthew Collins has an MSc in environmental policy from the Bard Center for Environmental Policy and a BA in German studies from Macalester College. He is currently serving as president and CEO of Integrated Ecosystem Market Services, a carbon consulting outfit based in Chicago, US.

Paul Ekins has a PhD in economics from the University of London and is professor of energy and environment policy at King's College London and a Co-Director of the UK Energy Research Centre. He was a Member of the Royal Commission on Environmental Pollution from 2002 to 2008. His academic work focuses on the conditions and policies for achieving an environmentally sustainable economy, with a special focus on energy policy, innovation, the role of economic instruments, sustainability assessment and environment and trade.

Clive George is a senior research fellow in the School of Environment and Development at the University of Manchester where he specializes in the development and application of impact assessment techniques. He was principal advisor to the World Bank on impact assessment systems in the Middle East and North Africa and has acted as a consultant to the European Commission, UNEP and other international agencies on the impacts of global and regional trade agreements.

Benjamin Görlach holds an MSc in international economic studies from the University of Maastricht. As a senior fellow with Ecologic Institute in Berlin, the main foci of his work are the evaluation of environmental policy instruments, particularly in economic terms, and the economic valuation of environmental goods and services. He is currently working at the German Emissions Trading Authority (DEHSt), Berlin, Germany.

Julien Gourdon has a PhD in economics from the CERDI, a joint research unit of the University of Auvergne and the CNRS. He was professor assistant at University of Auvergne from 2004 to 2006. In 2006 he joined the World Bank, Washington DC, working on aid effectiveness and Millennium Development Goals, and recently on trade issues in the Middle East and North Africa region.

Jesko Hirschfeld has a PhD in economics from the University of Göttingen, Germany. He is senior researcher in the field of Environmental Economics and Policy at the Institute for Ecological Economy Research (IÖW) in Berlin, which he joined in 2002. He is currently working on land and water management in the light of climate change and global economic development.

Wesley Ingwersen has an MSc in environmental engineering from the University of Florida where he is currently a PhD candidate working with LCA and other tools for quantifying sustainability of traded products. He was a transatlantic fellow at Ecologic in Berlin in 2006, during which time he began collaboration on the chapters herein.

Colin Kirkpatrick is emeritus professor of development economics at the University of Manchester, where he has been director of the Impact Assessment Research Centre and director of the Regulation Research Programme. He developed the Trade Sustainability Impact Assessment methodology for the Euopean Commission and has advised UNCTAD, ILO, UNDESA and OECD on sustainable development policy, monitoring and evaluation.

Clemens König is a PhD student at the Munich Graduate School of Economics and works as a research and teaching assistant at the Seminar for Economic Theory at LMU Munich. His research interests include game theory and mechanism design as well as institutional and environmental economics.

Tristan Le Cotty joined the International Research Center on Agriculture and Development (CIRAD), France, as an economist in 2007. His research works are on production economics, international economics and prospective. He has done his PhD on multifunctionality and international trade in Montpellier (LAMETA) and has worked with IDDRI for 18 months.

Mohamed Ali Marouani is associate professor in economics at Paris1 Panthéon Sorbonne University. He is a research fellow at ERF (Economic Research Forum, Cairo) and a research associate at DIAL (Development Institutions and Long Term Analysis, Paris). He also lectures at Sciences-Po Paris.

Dirk Scheer studied political science and literature in Heidelberg, Germany, and Seville, Spain. From 2001 until 2008, he worked as a research associate at IÖW. In November 2008 he joined the Interdisciplinary Research Unit on Risk Governance and Sustainable Development (ZIRN) at the University of Stuttgart dealing with potentials of simulation technologies at the science–policy interface.

Robin Vanner has an MSc in environmental technology from Imperial College London. He has been a research fellow at the Policy Studies Institute in London since 2003, focusing on cost assessment and behavioural economics. Since 2007, he has developed his own consultancy practice whilst remaining a visiting research fellow at the Policy Studies Institute.

Tancrède Voituriez has a PhD in economics from Paris I Panthéon Sorbonne University. He has carried out research on the impacts of international trade on world market price instability at the International Research Center on Agriculture and Development (CIRAD). He has been a lecturer at Sciences Po on trade and development since 2005, when he joined IDDRI as an associate researcher on trade and sustainable development.

Ingmar von Homeyer studied political science at Free University Berlin and holds a PhD (2002) in social and political sciences from the European University Institute, Florence. He is a senior fellow at Ecologic Institute for International and European Environmental Policy, Berlin and Brussels, working mainly on issues related to EU environmental governance.

Acknowledgements

Our main acknowledgement is of the person to whom this book is dedicated, the late Konrad von Moltke.

Konrad was the architect of the SIAMETHOD research project, which produced most of the papers on which this book is based. It was Konrad who persuaded the European Commission's Directorate General (DG) for Research that it needed to take a critical look at what its funding for Sustainability Impact Assessment (SIA) had, and had not, achieved, and it was a tragedy for all of us when he died, after the funding for the project had been agreed but before the project itself had got off the ground.

Clearly the project would have been different, and probably better, had Konrad survived to lead it. But we hope that he would not have been displeased by this output from it, because one of the things we have tried to express through it is Konrad's passionate but pragmatic concern for both development and environmental protection, and his belief that they could only be realized through the cooperative, enlightened action of multilateral institutions. This concern was a source of inspiration to all those who worked with Konrad during his most productive life, as well as to us working on the project and on this book to which it has given rise.

We would also like to acknowledge the efforts of the contributors to this book, whose attention to deadlines meant that the book was much less painful to produce than many of its kind, and express our gratitude to DG Research of the European Commission, which funded the SIAMETHOD project through its Framework 6 Programme. We hope the European Commission will find useful our conclusions about how its SIA processes might be developed. Finally, we would like to thank our most efficient editors at Earthscan, particularly Jonathan Sinclair Wilson, Rob West and Alison Kuznets. We hope that this book will prove to be a worthy addition to their incomparable list that, like the work of Konrad von Moltke, is so clearly focused on increasing understanding of that difficult but most important concept of our times, sustainable development.

List of Acronyms and Abbreviations

ABCDE	Annual World Bank Conference on Development Economics
ACP	African, Caribbean and Pacific
AFTA	ASEAN Free Trade Area
BCA	border carbon adjustment
BEET	balance of emissions embodied in trade
BIC	Brazil, India, China
BIT	bilateral investment treaty
BTA	border tax adjustment
CAFTA	Free Trade Agreement with Central American States
CAFTA-DR	Free Trade Agreement with Central American States and the Dominican Republic
CAP	Common Agricultural Policy
CBD	Convention on Biological Diversity
CCA	causal chain analysis
CCFF	Compensatory and Contingency Financing Facility
CDM	computable disequilibrium model
CEC	Council for Environmental Cooperation
CGE	computable general equilibrium
CIRAD	International Research Center on Agriculture and Development
CITES	Convention on International Trade in Endangered Species
CSO	civil society organization
CSR	corporate social responsibility
CTE	Committee on Trade and Environment
CTESS	Committee on Trade and Environment Special Session
DCAP	developed countries' agricultural policies
DEHSt	German Emissions Trading Authority
DSB	Dispute Settlement Body
EA	Environmental Assessment
EBA	Everything But Arms
EC	European Commission
ECPAT	End Child Prostitution, Child Pornography and the Trafficking of Children for Sexual Purposes

EEA	European Economic Area
EFTA	European Free Trade Association
EIA	Environmental Impact Assessment
EKC	Environmental Kuznets Curve
EL	export liberalization
EMFTA	Euro-Mediterranean Free Trade Area
EMP	Euro–Mediterranean Partnership
EPFI	Equator Principles Financial Institution
ER	Environmental Review
ERF	Economic Research Forum
ETS	Emission Trading Scheme
EU	European Union
FAO	Food and Agriculture Association
FDI	foreign direct investment
FIPA	Foreign Investment Protection and Promotion Agreement
FLO	Fairtrade Labelling Organizations International
FSC	Forestry Stewardship Council
FTA	Free Trade Agreement
GATS	General Agreement on Trade in Services
GATT	General Agreement on Tariffs and Trade
GCC	Gulf Cooperation Council
GDP	gross domestic product
GHG	greenhouse gas
GMO	genetically modified organism
GSP	Generalized System of Preferences
GTAP	General Trade Analysis Project
GVC	global value chain
HO	Heckscher–Ohlin (model)
IA	Impact Assessment
ICA	International Commodity Agreement
ICAO	International Civil Aviation Organization
ICREA	International Commodity-Related Environmental Agreement
IDPM	Institute for Development Policy and Management
IFC	International Finance Corporation
IFOAM	International Federation of Organic Agricultural Movements
IIED	International Institute for Environment and Development
ILO	International Labour Organization
IMF	International Monetary Fund
IÖW	Institute for Ecological Research
ITO	International Trade Organization
ITS	international tax on support
IUU	illegal, unreported and unregulated
LCA	Life-Cycle Assessment
LDC	least developed country
LULUCF	land use, land use change and forestry

M&A	mergers and acquisitions
MAI	Multilateral Agreement on Investment
MCSD	Mediterranean Commission on Sustainable Development
MEA	multilateral environmental agreement
MFN	Most Favoured Nation
MMSD	Minerals, Mining and Sustainable Development
MPC	Mediterranean Partner Country
MSC	Marine Stewardship Council
NAFTA	North American Free Trade Agreement
NAMA	non-agricultural market access
NEG	new economic geography
NGO	non-governmental organization
OECD	Organisation for Economic Co-operation and Development
OEM	original equipment manufacturer
PPM	Process and Production Method
PPP	Polluter Pays Principle
PSIA	Poverty and Social Impact Assessment
PTA	Partnership Trade Agreement
RTA	Regional Trade Agreement
SADC	Southern Africa Development Community
SCA	Sustainable Commodity Agreement
SCM	subsidies and countervailing measures
SEA	Strategic Environmental Assessment
SIA	Sustainability Impact Assessment
SMEs	small and medium sized enterprises
SPS	Sanitary and Phytosanitary measures
SSM	Special Safeguard Mechanism
STE	State Trading Enterprise
TAA	Trade Adjustment Assistance Programme
TBT	Technical Barriers to Trade
TNC	Trans National Corporation
TLROW	trade liberalization in the rest of the world
TRIMS	Trade Related Investment Measures
TRIPS	Trade-Related Aspects of Intellectual Property Rights
TRQ	Tariff Rate Quota
TTA	Trade Adjustment Assistance
UL	unilateral liberalization
UNCED	United Nations Conference on Environment and Development
UNCTAD	United Nations Conference on Trade and Development
UNDP	United Nations Development Programme
UNEP	United Nations Environment Programme
UNFCCC	United Nations Framework Convention on Climate Change
UNIDO	United Nations Industrial Development Organization
USDA	United States Department of Agriculture
WES	World Earth Summit

WHO	World Health Organization
WSUP	Water & Sanitation for the Urban Poor
WTO	World Trade Organization

Overview and General Introduction

Paul Ekins and Tancrède Voituriez

Trade Sustainability Impact Assessments and the challenges of trade liberalization from 1999 to 2008

Trade Sustainability Impact Assessments (SIAs) originated in the particular context of the World Trade Organization (WTO) negotiations on trade liberalization, a few months before the WTO Ministerial Conference was convened in Seattle in November 1999. Rising concerns over the social and environmental impacts of the previous liberalization cycle (the Uruguay Round, 1986–1994), sharp criticism of the opacity of final decision making in the WTO, from which developing countries and non governmental organizations (NGOs) were excluded, plus the protracted and worrying difficulty for the European Union (EU) in defending its own preferences on particular issues such as agriculture, cultural goods and environmental standards, were all warning signals – much clearer now than they were at the time – that WTO trade negotiations were very likely to be disrupted and that the EU would be found guilty for such a disruption, along with a few other OECD (Organisation for Economic Co-operation and Development) countries. All these three signals turned to red a few weeks before Seattle, resulting in the Ministerial Conference's ultimate collapse.

Trade SIAs were only budding at this time and could not prevent the wreckage of the Seattle, and later on, the Cancun WTO Ministerial Conferences. However, they deserve undisputed merit for having anticipated and seriously considered the three warning signals aforementioned, through their bid to rebalance the outcomes of trade liberalization across the pillars of sustainable development, countries and stakeholders (Box 1).

Ten years later, what has been achieved? This is the triggering question of this book. Trade SIAs have benefited from substantial improvement over the

Table 1 *Issues at stake and achievements, from Seattle to Hong Kong and beyond*

1999, issues at stake	*'negotiation roller coaster' 1999–2005 achievements*	*2008, issues at stake*
Sustainable development three pillars	The 'institutionalization' of the environment: Doha Declaration on Trade and Environment; WTO Special Sessions of the Committee on Trade and Environment (CTE)[5] Focus on poverty: the UN Millennium Summit – the Millennium Development Goals[6]	Development (poverty and inequality) focus: Who gains, who loses? Dynamic effects of trade on growth and development
Participation	WTO public symposia and forums for NGOs Amicus curiae briefs from NGOs can be received by Panels (Dispute settlement) The 30 August 2003 WTO decision on the Implementation of Paragraph 6 of the Doha Declaration on the TRIPS Agreement and Public Health and the Cotton initiative exemplify NGOs' commitment and firmer grip on trade agenda	Weak states' participation Within-country participation Participation in standards setting, public/private partnership
Market access	'Will International Rules on Subsidies Disrupt The World Trading System?'[7] 'Debunking the fallacies on agricultural market access'[8] 'Own trade liberalization provides the highest gains'[9]	Collective preferences disclosure and compatibility across countries Reconsidering market access gains: long-term (productivity effects) gains; services and investment.
References/ benchmark: Uruguay Round, World Earth Summit	**References/benchmark:** Seattle collapse	**References/benchmark:** No reference: what should a fair development round look like?

Note: TRIPS, Trade-Related Aspects of Intellectual Property Rights.

overall effect of trade disciplines on the domestic policy space and the design of domestic subsidies – what Pascal Lamy called in 2004 the 'social fabric' or 'collective preferences', an issue that this book examines in some detail. Between these two columns, the second column displays some of the salient milestones that have paved the way from Seattle (1999) to Hong Kong (2005) and to today's situation. The final row in the table provides the implicit references or benchmarks against which the issues listed in each of the three columns are expressed. The 2008 column identifies many of the themes taken up in the chapters of this book.

Of course, the trade and sustainable development debate dates back to before 1999 (see Box 2). One can recall the growing international concern

Overview and General Introduction

Paul Ekins and Tancrède Voituriez

Trade Sustainability Impact Assessments and the challenges of trade liberalization from 1999 to 2008

Trade Sustainability Impact Assessments (SIAs) originated in the particular context of the World Trade Organization (WTO) negotiations on trade liberalization, a few months before the WTO Ministerial Conference was convened in Seattle in November 1999. Rising concerns over the social and environmental impacts of the previous liberalization cycle (the Uruguay Round, 1986–1994), sharp criticism of the opacity of final decision making in the WTO, from which developing countries and non-governmental organizations (NGOs) were excluded, plus the protracted and worrying difficulty for the European Union (EU) in defending its own preferences on particular issues such as agriculture, cultural goods and environmental standards, were all warning signals – much clearer now than they were at the time – that WTO trade negotiations were very likely to be disrupted and that the EU would be found guilty for such a disruption, along with a few other OECD (Organisation for Economic Co-operation and Development) countries. All these three signals turned to red a few weeks before Seattle, resulting in the Ministerial Conference's ultimate collapse.

Trade SIAs were only budding at this time and could not prevent the wreckage of the Seattle, and later on, the Cancun WTO Ministerial Conferences. However, they deserve undisputed merit for having anticipated and seriously considered the three warning signals aforementioned, through their bid to rebalance the outcomes of trade liberalization across the pillars of sustainable development, countries and stakeholders (Box 1).

Ten years later, what has been achieved? This is the triggering question of this book. Trade SIAs have benefited from substantial improvement over the

Box 1 What is a Trade SIA?

Trade Sustainability Impact Assessment (Trade SIA) is a process undertaken before and during a trade negotiation which seeks to identify economic, social and environmental impacts of a proposed trade agreement. The purpose of a Trade SIA is to integrate sustainability into trade policy by informing negotiators, and particularly EU negotiators, of the possible social, environmental and economic consequences of a trade agreement. The idea is to assess how best to define a full package of domestic policies and international initiatives to yield the best possible outcome, not just in terms of liberalisation and economic growth, but also of other components of sustainable development. A Trade SIA should also provide guidelines for the design of possible accompanying policy measures. Such measures may go beyond the field of trade as such, and may have implications for internal policy, capacity building or international regulation. Accompanying measures are intended to maximise the positive impacts of the trade negotiations in question, and to reduce any negative impacts.

Source: 'What is Sustainability Impact Assessment (SIA)?', http://ec.europa.eu/trade/issues/global/sia/faqs.htm

period, with numerous applications to both multilateral and bilateral trade liberalization agreements,[1] and a published handbook (EC, 2006), made possible through significant funding from the European Commission (EC). Meanwhile the multilateral trading system has found itself on a roller coaster ride, ending in a stalemate in July 2008 when WTO trade negotiations finally seem to have got stuck in the sand. The background of explanatory factors behind the postponement of the Doha Round achievement seems rather similar to what it was in 1999. Developing countries are still asking for a fairer agreement, one that gives them relatively more compared to developed economies – their voice is simply louder, the threat of a veto more seriously considered, than ten years ago. Transparency and participation, though improved since the Seattle Ministerial Conference, remain controversial issues. Finally the EU suffered throughout the Hong Kong Ministerial Conference in 2005 a sustained crossfire of complaints for its stringency on agricultural market access, despite its claim to be the most developing country-friendly among OECD economies.[2] This would suggest that Trade SIAs have not made the contribution to trade talks, and particularly to the EU's trade position, that might have been expected. This book makes the case that Trade SIAs have done little to benefit trade negotiations because the hurdles trade negotiations need to surmount have in fact changed over the 1999–2008 period, in spite of superficial similarities, and that Trade SIAs have failed to address a number of important factors that cause negotiators to resist free trade today.

A comparison between the context for trade negotiations of 1999 and 2008

Though any diagnosis on who is to blame for the deadlock of the Doha Development Round is politically sensitive, a reasonable reading of the current crisis in the WTO is that considerable misunderstanding prevails across member countries, a number of which relentlessly argue that they have already reached their break-even point and that they cannot concede more – in term of market access or subsidy cuts – without incurring net negative social returns to their concessions.[3]

This point is a major new development in the current period when compared to 1999. In 1999 it was certainly admitted that trade talks had to be rebalanced across sustainable development pillars, member countries and stakeholders; there was no misunderstanding about this point. The naming of the current Round as 'the Doha Development Round' acts as a kind of reminder of such imbalances. Efforts made ever since to rebalance the trade negotiation process have been substantial. Leading developing countries (Brazil and India) figured among the five interested parties who took the initiative in 2004 to relaunch trade talks and draft the July package – an initiative that would have been confined to Quad countries (EU, US, Canada, Japan) in the General Agreement on Tariffs and Trade (GATT) and during very early WTO times.

Yet if enough efforts were made for the EU and US to claim that the playing field was now adequately level for reciprocal concessions to occur on a fair basis, the development objective of the Doha Round creates the seemingly intractable situation whereby developing countries are entitled to ask for more, while developed countries claim they have already made substantial concessions. And whereas a 'sustainable development round' was called for by vocal NGOs in 1999, with consensual reference to the three pillars of sustainable development pillars, now a 'fair development round' is the priority, with no consensual idea of what such a fairness should be.

The paradigmatic shift from 'sustainable development' to 'development' and 'fairness' is not a purely semantic issue.[4] It raises the point that should a Trade SIA be created from scratch against the new background given by 'development' and 'fairness' priorities, while keeping the similar 1999 objective of helping negotiators improve trade sustainability, then the information such a Trade SIA should convey would be a bit different from that based on the earlier perspective.

Table 1 captures the salient features of the contexts for the trade negotiations in 1999 and 2008, when it became obvious that the Doha Round was in trouble. The first column recalls what the issues at stake were in 1999, during the take-off period of Trade SIAs. It singles out as of key importance the three sustainable development pillars, and issues of participation and market access, as briefly outlined above. The third column does the same with the 2008 context. A development focus (e.g. inequality and poverty reduction) has replaced the sustainable development focus that prevailed in 1999. Participation issues have somehow been detached from WTO itself (1999 situation), with the focus shifting towards the participation of third countries, particularly 'weak' or 'poor' states, and towards domestic participation for the definition of negotiators' position within countries. Finally, debates about impediments to market access are now accompanied by concerns about the

Table 1 *Issues at stake and achievements, from Seattle to Hong Kong and beyond*

1999, issues at stake	*'negotiation roller coaster' 1999–2005 achievements*	*2008, issues at stake*
Sustainable development three pillars	The 'institutionalization' of the environment: Doha Declaration on Trade and Environment; WTO Special Sessions of the Committee on Trade and Environment (CTE)[5] Focus on poverty: the UN Millennium Summit – the Millennium Development Goals[6]	Development (poverty and inequality) focus: Who gains, who loses? Dynamic effects of trade on growth and development
Participation	WTO public symposia and forums for NGOs Amicus curiae briefs from NGOs can be received by Panels (Dispute settlement) The 30 August 2003 WTO decision on the Implementation of Paragraph 6 of the Doha Declaration on the TRIPS Agreement and Public Health and the Cotton initiative exemplify NGOs' commitment and firmer grip on trade agenda	Weak states' participation Within-country participation Participation in standards setting, public/private partnership
Market access	'Will International Rules on Subsidies Disrupt The World Trading System?'[7] 'Debunking the fallacies on agricultural market access'[8] 'Own trade liberalization provides the highest gains'[9]	Collective preferences disclosure and compatibility across countries Reconsidering market access gains: long-term (productivity effects) gains; services and investment.
References/ benchmark:	**References/benchmark:**	**References/benchmark:**
Uruguay Round, World Earth Summit	Seattle collapse	No reference: what should a fair development round look like?

Note: TRIPS, Trade-Related Aspects of Intellectual Property Rights.

overall effect of trade disciplines on the domestic policy space and the design of domestic subsidies – what Pascal Lamy called in 2004 the 'social fabric' or 'collective preferences', an issue that this book examines in some detail. Between these two columns, the second column displays some of the salient milestones that have paved the way from Seattle (1999) to Hong Kong (2005) and to today's situation. The final row in the table provides the implicit references or benchmarks against which the issues listed in each of the three columns are expressed. The 2008 column identifies many of the themes taken up in the chapters of this book.

Of course, the trade and sustainable development debate dates back to before 1999 (see Box 2). One can recall the growing international concern regarding the impact of economic growth on social development and the environment in the early 1970s, leading in 1972 to the Club of Rome's report *The Limits of Growth* (Meadows et al, 1972), the Stockholm Conference on the Human Environment and, ultimately, the creation of a Secretariat in the United Nations – the United Nations Environment Programme (UNEP) the same year.

What emerged as a novelty in the 1990s is twofold. First, the 1992 World Earth Summit (WES), when giving its political birth to 'sustainable development', ranked environmental issues at the top of the agenda – suffice it to recall the three international conventions the WES led to: biological diversity, climate change and desertification. Sustainability meant implicitly environmental sustainability (Sampson, 2005). The second novelty lies in the convergence of ideas after the WES took place, stemming from UN bodies (UNEP, Committee on Trade and Environment (CTE) and the GATT/WTO), towards the common belief that trade and environment could work hand in hand, or to turn it in another way, that trade liberalization should be compatible with environmental protection provided that flanking measures targeted on the environmental impacts of trade accompanied trade liberalization. The so-called 'win–win' scenarios (freer trade, better environmental protection) quickly flourished in the academic literature following the creation of the WTO. 'Win–win' solutions were and still are a common objective of UN environmental bodies and the WTO.

Ten years after the WES, the Plan of Implementation adopted at the World Summit on Sustainable Development in Johannesburg in 2002 reiterated the need to 'promote open, equitable, rules-based, predictable and non-discriminatory multilateral trading and financial systems that benefit all countries in the pursuit of sustainable development [and] support the successful completion of the work program contained in the Doha Ministerial Declaration' (WTO, 2002). Conversely, WTO integrated explicit references to sustainable development in its various texts, which was not the case at all within GATT. GATT-think originally rested upon the assumption that environmental policies could distort and hamper trade, exemplified by the fact that the Director-General of the GATT Secretariat submitted to the 1972 Stockholm Conference a document warning of the 'real danger that in attempting to combat pollution, governments may unwittingly introduce new barriers to trade' (GATT, 1971). But the WTO made a significant shift and adopted a more balanced approach to sustainable development issues. First 'sustainable development' appears as an objective of the Organization in the Preamble to the founding document of the WTO (see Box 2). This objective was reiterated in the 2001 Doha Declaration whereby trade ministers told the world:

> *We strongly reaffirm our commitment to the objective of sustainable development... We are convinced that the aims of upholding and safeguarding an open and non-discriminatory multilateral trading system, and acting for the protection of the environment*

Box 2 The institutionalization of the environment within GATT and the WTO

At the **November 1971** meeting of the GATT Council of Representatives, it was agreed that a Group on Environmental Measures and International Trade (the 'EMIT Group') be established.

1972 Stockholm Conference on the Human Environment

In 1987, the World Commission on Environment and Development produced a report entitled *Our Common Future* (WCED, 1987, also known as the Brundtland Report), in which the term 'sustainable development' first came to political prominence. The report identified poverty as one of the most important causes of environmental degradation, and argued that greater economic growth, fuelled in part by increased international trade, could generate the necessary resources to combat what had become known as the 'pollution of poverty'.

In 1991, members of the European Free Trade Association (EFTA) requested the Director-General of GATT to convene the EMIT group as soon as possible. Its activation was necessary, they stated, in order to create a forum within which trade-related environmental issues could be addressed. Reference was made to the upcoming 1992 United Nations Conference on Environment and Development (UNCED), and to the need for GATT to contribute in this regard.

In 1992, the UNCED, also known as the 'World Earth Summit', drew attention to the role of international trade in poverty alleviation and in combating environmental degradation. Agenda 21, the programme of action adopted at the conference, addressed the importance of promoting sustainable development through, amongst other means, international trade. The concept of 'sustainable development' had established a link between environmental protection and development at large.

In 1994, WTO Members recognized in the Preamble establishing the WTO that:

> *their relations in the field of trade and economic endeavour should be conducted with a view to raising standards of living ... while allowing for the optimal use of the world's resources in accordance with the objective of sustainable development, seeking both to protect and preserve the environment and to enhance the means for doing so in a manner consistent with their respective needs and concerns at different levels of economic development.*

In **April 1994**, a Ministerial Decision on Trade and Environment was adopted, calling for the establishment of a Committee on Trade and Environment (CTE).

In **November 2001**, at the Doha Ministerial Conference, it was agreed to launch negotiations on certain issues related to trade and environment. The CTE and the Committee on Trade and Development were asked to act as a forum in which the environmental and developmental aspects of the negotiations launched at Doha could be debated. The Doha Ministerial Declaration contains a paragraph that encourages Members to share their experience and expertise with others on how national environmental reviews can be performed.

Source: WTO, various pages, www.wto.org/english/tratop_e/envir_e/envir_e.htm

> *and the promotion of sustainable development can and must be mutually supportive.* (WTO, 2001)

Hence within WTO, sustainable development no longer (or not only) was a suspicious pretext governments could use to escape trade liberalization, but it became also an objective that trade could help them reach. In this regard, the

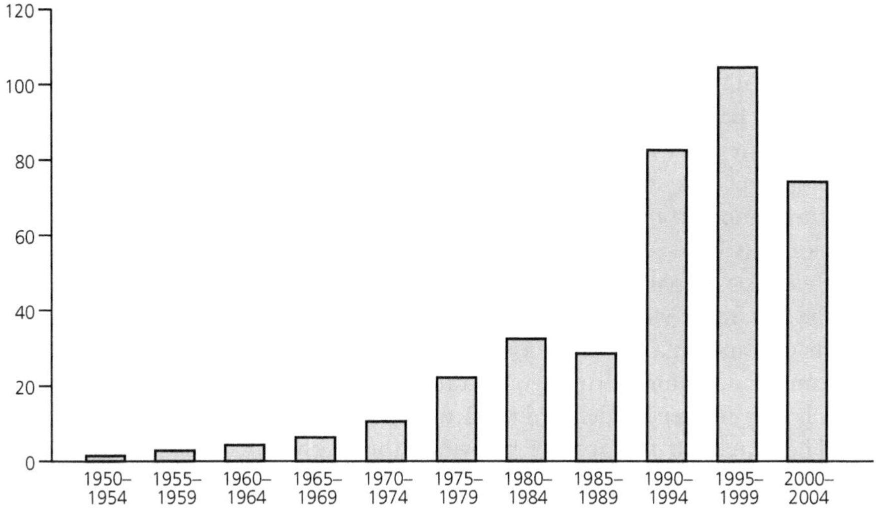

Source: authors, JSTOR Database

Figure 1 *'Trade' and 'Environment' in academic literature, a statistical overview*

2001 Doha Conference, with the launching of negotiations on issues related to trade and environment, marked the ultimate culmination of the institutionalization of the environment (under the rubric of sustainable development) into the world trading system.

When looking at ideas and knowledge, and not only at institutions, one would observe a similar shift towards a focus on environment and trade issues (important contributions were Bhagwati and Hudec, 1996; Antweiler et al, 2001; Copeland and Taylor, 2003) while attempting to demonstrate in line with earlier arguments (e.g. Bhagwati and Ramaswami, 1963) that undistorted trade was compatible with sound and efficient environmental national policies.

When focusing on methodological aspects, it is striking to see that most of the breakthroughs in SIA occurred in the 1990s, during the institutionalization phase of the environment within the world trading system, with the founding contributions of the OECD (2000, 2002), UNEP (2001),[10] the EU (Kirkpatrick et al, 2002),[11] the North American Commission for Environmental Cooperation (CEC, 2000), most of them dealing first and foremost with environmental issues. A retrospective and chronological look at the academic contributions on 'trade and the environment' since the 1950s strikingly reveals how the institutionalization of the environment in the world trading system aforementioned was accompanied by – and indeed partly caused – a rising trend in academic papers on the subject that peaked around the time of Seattle (1999), and then declined in the years round Doha (2001) (Figure 1). Then the tide flowed back, as did the momentum on environmental issues within the WTO.

Conversely, the literature on trade, poverty and inequality, experienced in the wake of Seattle and Doha a fascinating expansion, with institutional bodies such as DFID (2000), UNDP (Rodrik, 2001; UNDP, 2001), UNCTAD (2004), the World Bank (2000, 2001) and the IMF (Bannister and Thugge, 2001) issuing their own reports on this issue, first because (thanks to the Doha Development Round) poverty and inequality reached the top of the agenda at this time, and second because the available evidence on the supposed positive relationship between trade and reduced inequality had been made on too rough a basis, in particular relying on cross-national regressions of weak validity, the lessons of which could no longer hold when considering disaggregated effects of trade on a country, case-by-case basis (Rodrigues and Rodrik, 1999). Transmission channels from world trade down to poverty and inequality have since been a matter for detailed research (e.g. Winters, 2000).

The gear shift toward the prioritization of the assessment of the social impacts of trade liberalization does not mean of course that nothing any longer happens on the environment front. It nonetheless stresses the nerve centre of today's negotiations and methodological agitation, which seeks to bring into a single frame of reference both the 'social impact' of sustainable development literature (which is different from the environmental and economic impacts) and the 'social' cost of welfare economics. It is also now clear that the priority set today on poverty and inequality reduction – namely 'development' – closes the circle opened by the Brundtland report (WCED, 1987) when its new term 'sustainable development' drew attention to the link between the environment and development by identifying poverty as a principal cause of environmental degradation – the pollution of poverty.

Overview and structure of this book

These developments provide the context and rationale for this book. It proceeds from the now widespread recognition that globalization driven entirely by trade liberalization and market processes will deliver neither sustainable environmental outcomes nor the development of those low-income countries that have fewest market advantages. In other words, such globalization is inconsistent with any notion of 'sustainable development', the aspiration for which has now been expressed (as noted above) many times in many international forums by senior representatives of practically all countries, and which, in the trade context, is enshrined in the Preamble to the Constitution of the World Trade Organisation (WTO). The demonstrations that halted the WTO Ministerial Conference in Seattle in 1999 arose out of this recognition of, and were protesting against, this situation.

The book takes as its starting point the two developments in relation to trade negotiations that, following the demonstrations, have sought to remedy, or at least ameliorate, the situation that gave rise to them. The first was the initiation of the Doha Round of WTO negotiations, which was dubbed the Doha Development Round, because it was intended to give a special profile to development issues, and which was the first ever WTO negotiation round explicitly to include environmental issues. The second has been the vigorous development and promotion, especially by the European Commission, of SIAs of trade negotiations.

Neither development has been particularly successful. At the time of writing this book, it seems, with the failure of the Geneva negotiations in July 2008, that the Doha Development Round has run into the sand with no obvious motor for its resumption in the immediate future. SIAs for their part, while generating much interesting and potentially useful information, have failed to have a significant impact on either the course or outcomes of trade negotiations.

There is no obvious reason why it has proved so far impossible to bring the Doha Round to a conclusion. The economics of trade would suggest that, while trade negotiations may be tough, as every party strives to get as much as possible, while giving away as little as possible, in the end a deal will be struck, because there exists a deal that is to the benefit of all parties. The expectation of Trade SIAs was that they would facilitate the process of deal-making by bringing more evidence of diverse kinds to the negotiating table, which negotiators could use both to arrive at their overall assessments of the net benefits to be derived from trade, and to put in place where necessary the measures of mitigation to increase the net benefits from liberalization, and compensation to cushion the losers from it, which would make agreement easier to reach. So far, Trade SIAs have manifestly failed to deliver on this expectation.

This book assesses the experience of Trade SIAs, exploring why they have so far proved marginal to trade negotiations. It also analyses the factors and arguments, sometimes revealed or illuminated through Trade SIAs, sometimes not, that hamper the conclusion of trade liberalization agreements. Linking the impulses to set up a development round and undertake Trade SIAs, it basically asks: what are the explanations for the failure of trade negotiations and what new policy approaches, taking account of these explanations, might be able to reconcile multilateral trade and sustainable development. Thus it analyses, and makes proposals for breaking the current impasse between the desires in some quarters for further trade liberalization, and the determination in others that any such liberalization should generate real gains for environment and development as well as for market traders.

The book is structured in four parts. The first sets out the current context for issues of trade liberalization, development and environment, and how they are assessed through Trade SIAs. The second examines some of the new challenges for trade liberalization, arising from the post-Uruguay Round agenda, including the issues of investment, services and commodities. It also identifies the arguments against trade liberalization, in particular the threat to culturally valued collective preferences, that are often among the contextual realities of, but which may not be made explicit in, trade negotiations, but which need to be addressed if such negotiations are to succeed. Part 3 makes proposals for policies at the national level that could both lead to improved identification of problems arising from trade liberalization and enable these problems to be more successfully resolved. Part 4 identifies the progress in international cooperation that will also need to be made for freer trade and sustainable development to be reconciled.

Thus, in Part 1 of the book, Chapter 1 examines the likelihood that trade liberalization through WTO negotiations would make gains for development, in respect of three different interpretations of 'fairness', which was the motivation for setting up a 'development round': the correction of past unfairness in the trade regime; poverty reduction; and the generation of economic growth. The chapter concludes that trade liberalization could not realistically have been expected to make substantial gains in terms of any of these interpretations of development. Chapter 2 goes further. It shows how seeking to promote development goes against some of the most fundamental dynamics and processes of trade negotiations, such as making deals based on reciprocity, and that in any case knowledge of the causal links between trade liberalization and development are simply not adequate to engage in the former with the objective of promoting the later. The whole idea of a 'development round' of trade negotiations was fundamentally misconceived.

Chapter 3 describes the processes, objectives and achievements of Trade SIAs. It examines the question of whether an SIA process that assesses impacts in all trading partners is capable of going beyond the promotion of European collective preferences, to promote the interests of all affected citizens and contribute to stronger global or regional governance. It makes use of the experience that has been accumulated during the EC Trade SIA programme, and draws on work undertaken for the European Commission by many individuals and organizations, with particular reference to the studies that have been undertaken for the multilateral WTO negotiations and for the SIA of the Euro-Mediterranean Free Trade Area (EMFTA).

In Part 2, Chapter 4 explains why Trade SIAs carried out to date have had little impact on the trade negotiations themselves. Essentially Trade SIAs have not managed to illuminate the underlying reasons why countries might seek to resist trade liberalization, which are an important part of the contextual realities of trade negotiations. Four such reasons are identified in the chapter: a desire to protect vested interests; a desire to avoid potentially painful adjustment costs; a desire to prevent the amplification of negative, especially environmental, externalities; and a desire not to go against collective social preferences in relation to important social or cultural values. If impact assessments became able to shed explicit light on these matters, they might be of more help to negotiators whose negotiating agendas inevitably, though perhaps not explicitly, seek to take them into account. A number of the subsequent chapters assess in relation to the issues on which they are focusing the significance of these desires to resist trade liberalization, and the arguments which they invoke.

Chapter 5 goes beyond trade in goods and examines the case of investment. Investment has proven to be a highly controversial issue in the context of international trade negotiations and globalization more broadly. Attempts to negotiate a Multilateral Agreement on Investment (MAI) within the OECD ended in failure in 1998, and negotiations about an investment agreement within the WTO seem to have been suspended indefinitely. Chapter 5 shows that the implications for development of foreign direct investment and investment agreements are difficult to quantify, due to a lack of statistical data as well as the complex network of influencing factors. Even where forecasts can be generated from economic models, assessments have mostly failed to connect this data to social and environmental indicators. It is consequently argued that rather than predicting a specific outcome of investment liberalization, a sustainability assessment should focus on what conditions need to be met in order to ensure additional investment will occur and render sustainable development benefits.

Chapter 6 investigates available examples of SIAs of trade in services liberalization. It summarizes empirical findings focusing on three specific service sectors (environmental services, tourism and transport services). The case studies show that the extent to which trade in services liberalization can boost or hamper the development process (in the direction of the UN Millennium Development Goals) strongly depends on domestic regulatory capacities. This conclusion corroborates and even reinforces similar conclusions established for trade in goods in Chapter 1.

In the following chapter, the familiar issue of governing trade in commodities is re-examined in the light of the most recent findings of Trade SIAs. SIAs have been successful in revealing how the impacts of commodity trade may turn negative and serious in respect of sustainable development, including the depletion of non-renewable resources, the unsustainable exploitation of renewable resources, overproduction, price volatility, declining terms of trade in relation to manufactures, and the potential to disrupt communities, undermine good governance and stimulate corruption. These negative impacts of commodity trade relate closely to reasons why countries might seek to resist trade liberalization, which are described in Chapter 4. Because they may be exacerbated by simple trade liberalization, they may therefore intensify opposition to such liberalization unless they are addressed. However, SIAs have so far proved ineffective in encouraging negotiators to pay adequate attention to the impacts and to acknowledge the extent to which they affect the negotiating position of other countries, especially, but not only, in respect of agricultural commodities.

The last chapter of this part explores the implications for trade of 'collective preferences', a concept that originated in a speech of Pascal Lamy at a time when he was European Commission Directorate General for External Trade Commissioner, and which has ever since pervaded trade policy debates, in spite of its differing, sometimes controversial interpretations. Trade rules can interfere very differently with collective preferences depending on the type of public goods at stake. To analyse this interference, three types of collective preferences are distinguished:

1 a society's collective preferences for non-market goods affecting its own living conditions (for example, health or, in trade parlance, sanitary and phyosanitary [SPS] standards, domestic labour standards, local environmental standards, and all national public goods and services);
2 a society's collective preferences for non-market goods affecting other societies' living conditions (child labour or the depletion of local resources in trading partner countries, etc.);
3 a society's collective preferences for global public goods (such as the prevention of climate change or ocean pollution, global security, etc.). (These preferences could theoretically be interpreted as affecting domestic living conditions, but their fulfilment depends on other countries' choices.)

Clarifying the various interpretations of the concept, this chapter suggests that collective preferences are one of the key reasons why countries seek to resist trade liberalization. The various disputes over such matters that have arisen give indications about the way the WTO deals with policies in favour of such non-trade concerns, which can be used to interpret WTO practices regarding collective preferences. It appears that the content of the preferences itself is not challenged, but the defendant country's ability to make a proper assessment of its needs for the challenged policy is crucial to the dispute panel's decision.

Chapter 9 begins Part 3 by noting that public participation in policy making is increasingly recognized not only as an extension of democratic ideals, but also as a means to improve policy performance. Approaches to participation in impact assessment have co-evolved with impact assessment methodology and benefited from both knowledge gained from inclusion of participation in broader policy and management and growing recognition of its utility. But inclusion of public participation in SIAs of EU trade agreements is challenging because of many factors, including the privacy of the negotiation process, multinational participants and the general complexity of the consequences of trade agreements. Drawing on previous experience in SIAs of trade agreements as well as the wider body of participation literature and expert consultation, the chapter suggests improvements to the methodology and integration of public participation in SIAs so that SIA may become able to meet participation objectives in the demanding context of international trade negotiations.

A reasonable hypothesis explaining why Trade SIAs seem of so limited interest in negotiations for trade liberalization lies in the limited information Trade SIAs have conveyed so far on the distribution of the impacts of trade liberalization among the population – that is, who are the gainers and the losers from trade policy reforms. Chapter 10 addresses the issue of how to increase knowledge on the determining factors making some households or individuals losers, while others are gainers, from the trade liberalization process in the context of developing countries. It finds that the assessment of the distributional outcomes of trade reforms is difficult, and recommends going beyond the analyses of computable general equilibrium (CGE) models to use more micro-simulations and sectoral analyses, based on an initial identification of the price effects of the trade reform. A further challenge is to ensure that sufficient attention is given to social as well as economic impacts across different groupings of households.

Chapter 11 continues the theme of identifying the distributional impacts of trade liberalization, noting that in the past, trade liberalization has produced winners and losers in the labour market, and will in all likelihood continue to do so in future. It finds that there are arguments for and against government intervention to transfer some of the benefits of trade enjoyed by the winners to offset some of the costs incurred by the losers; these arguments should be assessed on a case-by-case basis. Deciding the appropriate level and form of any transfer is not easy, but there are lessons from the experience of OECD countries that can be used to design good policy in this area.

Finally in Part 3, Chapter 12 explores product, or value, chain assessment, an emerging methodology for a better understanding of the dynamics of global economic transformation processes. Instead of focusing on countries and their level of economic development as the ultimate units of account, product chain assessment takes economic actors, markets, products and substance flows as a starting point. In this manner product chain assessment offers the prospect of reflecting more accurately the dynamics of markets subject to liberalization and the relationship between producers and consumers. The methodological basis for product chain assessment is, however, still rudimentary. A significant effort to develop this methodology appears particularly promising from the perspective of analysing the sustainability impacts of globalized and fragmented product chains, which are themselves an outcome of trade liberalization.

The concept of collective preferences explored in Chapter 8 introduces special challenges for the international trading system. Chapter 13, the first chapter in Part 4 on international cooperation examines how collective preferences for non-trade concerns of exporting and importing countries can be reconciled. Focusing on agriculture, the chapter shows that, in some cases, tariff barriers that could help satisfy collective preferences for non-trade concerns in a given country may generate a net cumulative welfare that exceeds the level created through free trade. However, unlike free trade that theoretically only creates winners at country level, protectionism arising from the desire to protect collective preferences creates both winners and losers in comparison with free trade. Net cumulative welfare may be positive while domestic welfare is declining in one country. An international compensation mechanism is sketched out to address this issue, which could help reconcile both efficiency and cooperation and confirm the real value of collective preferences in any given country.

Chapter 14 returns to the commodities theme of Chapter 7. Given the lack of success of SIAs so far to persuade negotiators of commodity trade liberalization to pay adequate attention to its potential negative impacts on important (especially environmental) aspects of sustainable development, this chapter investigates how else these impacts might be mitigated, both through the rules of the world trade system itself, and through various government, producer and consumer initiatives that have already sought to mitigate the impacts, but with limited success. The chapter proposes that elements of these initiatives should be combined into a new kind of Sustainable Commodity Agreement (SCA), which could ensure that further liberalization of commodity trade was politically easier to achieve because it made a contribution to sustainable development rather than compromising it. SIAs could propose SCAs as measures to mitigate negative impacts of trade liberalization.

Finally, Chapter 15 seeks to create a framework that can address jointly two of the greatest challenges facing the world today: climate change and the 'bottom billion' poverty issue. These issues cut across each other logically, and if countries are to find global deals, they have to make compromises and find incentives to get other countries into the negotiation process. For example, one of the ways to promote a deal on climate change with major developing countries, such as China, India and Brazil, might be to give them a much better deal on trade. This chapter explores how to help governments arrive at a global deal on these two big issues by developing issue linkages. Focusing on possible negotiation linkages between climate change and trade liberalization, the chapter derives implications for the design of climate change and trade policies in a multilateral framework.

As noted in the Acknowledgements, this book arose from a project, SIAMETHOD, financed by DG Research of the European Commission in its Framework 6 research programme, which concluded early in 2007.[12] Most of the papers on which the chapters are based therefore date from the previous year, and use data from a year or two earlier than that. We have only sought to bring this data up to date where it seemed materially to affect the relevant analysis or conclusions. Most of the SIAMETHOD papers are derived from much longer working papers, which can be consulted on the SIAMETHOD website by readers who wish the explore in greater depth the issues that they cover.

The book is for the general reader, who will find readily accessible the SIAMETHOD papers. However, we have added to the papers arising from the project, especially to illuminate the development dimension of the book. One result is that the papers in the book now cover a range of styles, from the fairly general to those that are clearly rooted in economic analysis. We hope that non-economists will not be put off by the papers of this latter kind, and that their efforts will be rewarded by giving them greater understanding of how economists think about and seek to analyse these issues.

Notes

1 One of the most recent and notable achievements is 'Sustainability impact assessment of proposed WTO negotiations. Final global overview trade SIA of the Doha development agenda' (Kirkpatrick et al, 2002). Readers interested in particular applications of Trade SIA methodology are invited to consult the Trade SIA EU website: http://ec.europa.eu/trade/issues/global/sia/index_en.htm.

2 The EU, and France in particular, were deemed to be 'excessively defensive on agricultural issues', according to Pascal Lamy in an interview given to *Le Monde*, 24 February 2006.
3 See Voituriez (2007). See also 'The Doha Development Agenda: Sweet Dreams or Slip Slidin' away?', Pascal Lamy Speech, International Institute of Economics, Washington, 17 February 2006, available at www.wto.org/english/news_e/sppl_e/sppl19_e.htm.
4 Emblematic of this paradigmatic shift is the book from Joe Stiglitz and Andrew Charlton, *Fair Trade for All*, issued in December 2005 during the WTO Hong Kong Ministerial Conference.
5 'With its broad based mandate, the CTE has contributed to bring environmental and sustainable development issues into the mainstream of WTO's work.' WTO official webpage, www.wto.org/english/tratop_e/envir_e/wrk_committee_e.htm.
6 The first goal is 'to eradicate extreme poverty and hunger', while 'ensuring environmental sustainability' ranks only 7 out of 8.
7 Bagwell and Staiger (2005).
8 Panagariya (2004).
9 Anderson and Martin (2006).
10 See also United Nations Environment Programme (UNEP), *Integrated Assessment of Trade Liberalization and Trade-Related Policies, Country Studies* – Round II, available at www.unep.ch/etu/publications/Ctry_studies_2.htm. An ongoing series of studies is available in draft form, for example: United Nations Environment Programme (UNEP), *Handbook on Integrated Assessment of Agriculture*. Draft prepared for the meeting Geneva, 17/18 November.
11 See http://europa.eu.int/comm/trade/issues/global/sia/index_en.htm.
12 The final report and policy brief of the project may be found at www.iddri.org/L'iddri/SIAMethod.The editors would like to acknowledge the support from DG Research for the SIAMETHOD project.

References

Anderson, K. and Martin, W. (eds) (2006) *Agricultural Trade Reform and The Doha Development Agenda*, The World Bank, Washington DC and Palgrave Macmillan, Basingstoke

Antweiler, W., Copeland, B. R. and Taylor, M. S. (2001) 'Is free trade good for the environment', *The American Economic Review*, vol 91, no 4, pp877–908

Bagwell, K. and Staiger, R. W. (2005) 'Will international rules on subsidies disrupt the world trading system?', Mimeo, Columbia University, New York

Bannister, G. and Thugge, K. (2001) 'International trade and poverty alleviation', IMF Working Paper No. 01/54, International Monetary Fund, Washington DC

Bhagwati, J. and Hudec, R. (eds) (1996) *Fair Trade and Harmonization: Prerequisites for Free Trade?*, MIT Press, Cambridge, MA

Bhagwati, J. and Ramaswami, V. K. (1963) 'Domestic distortions, tariffs, and the theory of optimal subsidy', *Journal of Political Economy*, vol 71, pp44–50

CEC (2000) 'The environmental effects of free trade' and 'Assessing environmental effects of the North American Free Trade Agreement (NAFTA)', Papers presented at the North American Symposium, Assessing the Linkages between Trade and Environment, October 2000, North American Commission for Environmental Cooperation, www.cec.org/pubs_docs/scope/index.cfm?varlan=english&ID=14

Copeland, B. R. and Taylor, M. S. (2003) *Trade and the Environment*, Princeton University Press, Princeton

DFID (2000) 'Eliminating world poverty: Making globalization work for the poor', White Paper on international development, www.dfid.gov.uk/Pubs/files/whitepaper2000.pdf

EC (2006) *Handbook For Trade Sustainability Impact Assessment*, March, European Commission, Brussels, available at http://trade.ec.europa.eu/doclib/docs/2006/march/tradoc_127974.pdf

GATT (1971) *Industrial Pollution Control and International Trade*, GATT studies in International Trade, GATT Secretariat, Geneva

Kirkpatrick, C., George, C. and Scrieciu, S. (2002) *Further Development of the Methodology for a Sustainability Impact Assessment of Proposed WTO Negotiations*, University of Manchester, Institute for Development Policy and Management, 5 April, http://europa.eu.int/comm/trade/issues/global/sia/past.htm

Meadows, D. H., Meadows, D. L., Randers, J. and Behrens, W. H. (1972) *The Limits to Growth*, Universe Books, New York

OECD (2000) *Assessing the Environmental Effects of Trade Liberalization Agreements: Methodologies*, Organization for Economic Co-operation and Development, Paris, http://oecdpublications.gfi-nb.com/cgi-bin/OECDBookShop.storefront/EN/product/222000011P1

OECD (2002) *Assessing the Environmental Effects of Services Trade Liberalization: A Methodology*, Organisation for Economic Co-operation and Development, Paris, www.olis.oecd.org/olis/2000doc.nsf/LinkTo/com-td-env(2000)123-final

Panagariya, A. (2004) 'Agricultural liberalization and the developing countries: Debunking the fallacies', Mimeo, Columbia University, New York

Rodriguez, F. and Rodrik, D. (1999) 'Trade policy and economic growth: A skeptic's guide to cross-national evidence', NBER Working Paper No. W7081, NBER, Cambridge, MA

Rodrik, D. (2001) 'The global governance of trade as if development really mattered', Report for the United Nations Development Programme, New York

Sampson, G. P. (2005) *The WTO and Sustainable Development*, United Nations University Press, Tokyo

Stiglitz, J. and Charlton, A. (2005) *Fair Trade for All*, Oxford University Press, New York

UNCTAD (2004) 'Policy coherence, development strategies and integration into the world economy', Trade and Development Report (also others in this annual series)

UNDP (2001) 'Making global trade work for people', United Nations Environment Programme, Earthscan Publications Limited, London and Sterling, Virginia

UNEP (2001) *Reference Manual for Integrated Assessment of Trade Related Policies*, UNEP, Geneva, www.unep.ch/etu/etp/acts/manpols/rmia.htm.

Voituriez, T. (2007) 'Soyons généreux, soyons égoïstes: Le Cycle du Développement à l'OMC' [Be generous, be selfish: The Doha Development Round at the WTO] *Economie Rurale*, vol 291, January/February, pp11–17

WCED (1987) *Our Common Future*, Oxford University Press, Oxford

Winters, L. A. (2000) 'Trade liberalization and poverty', Paper prepared for the Department for International Development, University of Sussex, Brighton

World Bank (2000) World Development Report

World Bank (2001) World Development Report

WTO (2001) *Doha Declarations: The Doha Development Agenda*, WTO Secretariat, Geneva

WTO (2002) *Report of the World Summit on Sustainable Development*, WT/CTE/W/220/Rev.1, WTO Secretariat, Geneva

Part 1
The Context: Trade, SIAs and Development

1
Trade-induced Changes in Economic Inequality: Assessment Issues and Policy Implications for Developing Countries

Sylvain Chabe-Ferret, Julien Gourdon,
Mohamed Ali Marouani and Tancrède Voituriez

Introduction

The Doha Development Round stresses the need to rebalance the expected gains from freer trade toward developing countries. The development dimension given to the round echoes a double-meaning acceptation of fairness in the trade liberalization process. First, World Trade Organization (WTO) member countries are now committed to design trade liberalization agreements such as to correct past unfairness, according to which developing countries were prevented from developing as much as they ought to through effective trade openness among their partner countries. Secondly, trade liberalization should be fair according to the consensual meaning given to 'development' by international aid agencies and UN bodies for about the last ten years, which equates development with poverty reduction. A fair trade liberalization round should hence equally reduced poverty.

Trade economists have spared no effort to check that under the various scenarios on the table before the WTO Hong-Kong Ministerial in December 2005, expected gains from freer trade provided by trade models actually matched the expectation of fairness placed on the round in progress (Anderson and Martin, 2006; Hertel and Winters, 2006; Polaski, 2006). Computable general equilibrium (CGE) models highlighted the cost of protection and of distorting supports for the very countries that did resort to such policies, making the most protectionist countries the most beneficiaries from trade liberalization. Countries or regions such as the EU, Japan and the US hence came first out of the hat, which was not the kind of fairness or rebalancing effect one would have expected from a genuine development round. Estimates of possible changes in poverty headcounts induced by trade liberalization gave such tiny figures on their side – particularly when compared with the first assessments made about five years ago – that taunting comments began to appear, mocking the Doha pro-development posture, when 'much ado about nothing' would have conferred indeed a more appropriate title on it (Ackerman, 2005; CEPR, 2005). Ironically, because of the wide-scale implication of trade modellers in the advocacy of trade liberalization since the onset of the development round, the uneasiness and awkwardness of the Doha Round in fulfilling its development mandate seem to pervade the modellers' work, suggesting at least possible fallacies in the message conveyed by their estimates to trade negotiators, non-governmental organizations (NGOs) and the media (Panagariya, 2004).

What indeed came out of nearly a decade of debate on the trade-growth-poverty-inequality nexus? Ex-post evaluations based on cross-country studies fuelled harsh methodological controversy; they displayed weak evidence of a positive trade-and-growth linkage (Rodriguez and Rodrik, 1999), while the estimated impact of trade opening on income inequality turns out to be small because trade liberalization seems to favour the relative demand for skilled labour (Anderson, 2005). On the ex-ante modelling side, estimates of aggregate welfare changes from trade liberalization produced by static CGE models nourished blunt criticism for ignoring most – not to say all – market failures crippling developing economies (Stiglitz and Charlton, 2005).

Another sharp criticism of standard CGEs is their reliance on the representative agent hypothesis that impedes them from analysing the impact of trade liberalization on income distribution. Bourguignon et al (1991) and Cogneau et al (2003) proposed new methodologies, taking into account households' behaviour, to analyse the impact of policies on households. By linking CGEs with microsimulation models, such methodologies permit the analysis of the impact of trade liberalization on income distribution and poverty.

As a result, trade liberalization could be poverty-alleviating in the long run and on average, while it is acknowledged that trade liberalization brings about distributional changes that may make the poor even worse off in the short term in particular countries, and, notably, in the poorest ones (Winters et al, 2004). Then there is a third dimension of fairness in the trade liberalization process: according to whether a country faces short-term or long-term gains, its political capability to rally the support of its population for joining the liberalization project – and hence benefit in due time from effective gains from freer trade – will differ dramatically. A fair liberalization round should place them on an equal footing and hence take into account not only the distribution of gains and losses among countries and among households, but as well its distribution over time. This raises the issue of dynamic modelling and its weaknesses, especially in the way expectations are treated.

The starting point of this paper is given by country situations where trade liberalization is expected to be poverty- and inequality-alleviating in the long run while inducing a short run increase in poverty or in inequality. We hence focus on a trade-induced social injustice case, which is a different animal from the 'loud losers', lobby-based explanation of government reluctance to move down the liberalization road we are used to finding in political economy analyses. In this latter case, short-term gains do exist but they are politically risky to tap, which is not the case we embrace here. The question we ask is what are the distributive aspects of trade that are worth documenting to help governments better integrate trade policies within a global policy framework so as to enhance growth and reduce poverty and inequality. The method followed is a literature review, organized according to three different interpretations of fairness implied by the 'development' objective of the world trade liberalization agenda. Because a 'pro-development' trade liberalization agenda should first correct past unfairness in the trade regime, which raises the broad issue of country-level trade liberalization's ex-post impact assessment, we start in the next section with the review of the main findings of country-level ex-post assessments. But a 'pro-development' trade liberalization agenda should also reduce poverty at household level, a point we address in the third section. Last, because development is basically a dynamic process, the distributive-dynamic effects of trade liberalization are also considered. Across all these three definitions of fairness, the development objective of the Doha Round proves to be an objective that trade liberalization cannot systematically achieve. A synthesis of our ten main results concludes the paper.

Fairness interpretation one: Country-level ex-post assessment

The 'ex-post' empirical evaluation of trade liberalization's impact on inequality over the last decade provides interesting but no clear-cut results. Two main approaches have been followed, assessing:

1 wage inequality in the manufacturing industry between unskilled and skilled labour, using time series analysis;
2 aggregate inequality, measured by the Gini coefficient on various sources of revenue (land, capital, wages) on a cross-country basis.

These two approaches build upon the Heckscher–Ohlin (HO) model to test predictions of changes in income inequality among developing countries. Assuming that unskilled labour is the relative abundant factor in developing countries, trade liberalization should increase its relative returns when compared to capital and skilled labour, and hence reduce inequality. The results of studies on wage inequality reject HO predictions for developing countries in Latin America in the process of trade reform. Results in Asia are more heterogeneous. Concerning aggregate inequality, the first studies on global inequality that basically test the impact of openness in developing countries do not exhibit robust results either, producing insignificant effects, or rejecting the prediction, except in Calderon and Chong (2001). With both approaches, initial tests did not conform to the theory: namely the wage premium for skilled workers and overall inequality often increase in developing countries when trade is liberalized.[1]

Faced with this puzzle, authors have improved their theoretical approach and empirical assessment methods.[2] Several routes are liable to explain the increase of the skill premium and the widening of global inequality. All deal with heterogeneity among developing countries, be it heterogeneity in human capital endowment, heterogeneity in natural resources endowment, heterogeneity in outsourcing and foreign direct investment (FDI), or heterogeneity in technology. For each of them, outcomes and salient results are listed below. Unaddressed issues complete our review.

Heterogeneity in human capital endowment

We briefly review explanatory arguments as well as some test results that such arguments might have led to.

Argument one: One should consider heterogeneity in developing countries' human capital endowment, on the ground that some developing countries may not actually display a comparative advantage in unskilled-labour-intensive goods.

Wage studies: To explain the difference of liberalization's impact on wage inequality between Latin American and Asian countries, a possible candidate seems indeed the timing of trade policy reform. At the time when Latin American countries started to liberalize, they were no longer unskilled-labour abundant, contrary to East Asian countries that liberalized at a time when they were unskilled-labour abundant (Wood, 1997). Several studies (Harrison and Hanson, 1999) on wage inequality in Latin America provide evidence that unskilled-labour-intensive sectors were protected with the highest tariffs prior to trade reform. Such industries have experienced the largest tariff reductions in the process of trade reform. Hence 'the increase in the skill premium' matches trade theory predictions: provided that trade liberalization focused on unskilled-labour-intensive sectors, the economy-wide return to unskilled labour predictably shrank.

Gini studies: When testing the impact of trade openness accounting for human capital endowment, Spilimbergo et al (1999) and Fischer (2001) show that developing countries that were relatively less endowed in human capital experienced a lower increase in inequality after trade liberalization. Gourdon et al (2008) do not reproduce these results when taking into account heterogeneity in data sources and using different indexes of trade liberalization.[3] Nonlinearities in the relationship between human capital and inequality during trade liberalization seem to prevail.

To summarize, studies accounting for heterogeneity in human capital endowment do not refute the fact that trade liberalization benefits the relatively abundant factor in developing countries. They basically argue instead that all developing countries do not display a comparative advantage in unskilled labour, contrary to a widespread assumption.

Argument two: Different types of unskilled labour coexist in developing countries (basically educated and uneducated), which requires detailed assessment of trade impacts along them.

Wage studies: Wood (1994) argues that North–South manufacturing trade not only raises the wage of workers with basic education level relative to that of uneducated workers, but that it also raises the wage of skilled workers with basic education relative to uneducated skilled workers. This is mainly due to the impossibility for uneducated workers to be hired in export-oriented manufacturing activities.

Gini studies: Milanovic (2005) shows that trade liberalization increases income inequality in low-income countries but decreases inequality among middle-income economies. Milanovic interprets this result as a trade-off between liberalization and education: openness in developing countries might increase inequality by helping those with basic education, and leaving even further behind those with no education. The lowest income deciles begin to benefit from increased labour demand only when the poor become reasonably skilled. Gourdon et al (2008) differs from Spilimbergo et al (1999), by showing that (relative) abundant endowment in uneducated labour increases inequality when a country opens to trade whereas (relative) abundant endowment in basically educated labour significantly reduces it.

To summarize, taking into account heterogeneity in human capital endowment across developing countries explains that increased openness will only lead to an increase in basically educated labour demand, and in turn in its remuneration, while the demand for uneducated labour will fall, magnifying the skill premium effect.

Heterogeneity in natural resources endowment

In the literature on inequality, natural resource endowment is viewed as a possible factor that inverts the basic HO prediction.

Wage studies: Abundant endowment in natural resources may lead to wage inequality in manufacturing since processing industries of primary goods are more skill- and capital-intensive than low-skill manufactures. Bourguignon and Morrisson (1990) corroborate this intuition on a set of countries from Asia, Latin America and Africa.

Gini studies: Theory suggests that openness should lead to an increase in natural resource returns in countries where this factor is relatively abundant.

Leamer et al (1999) show that an increase in exports of primary commodities is positively correlated with income inequality, but they do not control for a country's relative abundance in natural resources. Large export volumes in primary commodities may indeed reflect high endowment in unequally distributed natural resources and cause inequality upsurge independently of trade openness. Spilimbergo et al (1999) and Fischer (2001) control for relative abundance in natural resource endowments. Their results indicate that while natural resources significantly increase inequality, trade liberalization in a land-abundant country has no clear effect. The fact is that the distribution of natural resources is as important as their relative abundance. For instance, in a country like Brazil where land is unequally distributed, openness might lead to an increase in inequality. Such a phenomenon is much less likely to occur in countries where land was equally distributed at the onset of liberalization (South Korea for example). So if one wishes to determine the impact of natural resources endowment on inequality under the process of trade reform, one has to account for inequality in the distribution of this asset.[4] When properly taken into account, inequality in land distribution seems to lead to unequalizing effects. This result is confirmed by Gourdon et al (2008) who test the impact of endowment in mining and fuel, which are often unequally distributed. They find that endowment in mining and fuel increases inequality, as does trade liberalization, in mining and fuel-abundant countries.

To summarize, the studies accounting for heterogeneity in natural resources endowment do not refute the fact that trade liberalization benefits the relatively abundant factor in developing countries. They basically argue instead that some developing countries display a comparative advantage in natural resources that might be unequally distributed among individuals. Whereas the effect concerning arable land (land for agriculture) is not clear and depends on the distribution of land, the effect of mining and fuel endowment leans towards increasing inequality during trade liberalization.

Outsourcing and FDI

Trade liberalization is expected to benefit unskilled-labour-intensive industries in developing countries. In the meantime, it is likely to lead to a move of unskilled labour industry from North to South, notably through outsourcing and FDI, which in turn should affect inequality.

Wage studies: Two effects are to be considered, which could cause an increase in the demand for skilled labour in developing countries. The *Industry effect* deals with the shift of skill-intensive intermediate goods production from developed to developing countries. Such products can be characterized as unskilled-labour-intensive from a developed country perspective, but they appear to be skilled-labour-intensive when considered from a developing country's point of view.[5] The *Occupation effect* deals with the fact that the rapid pace of change in an economy under reform increases the demand for individuals capable to enact change, such as managers and professionals, whatever sectoral shifts may be taking place. Cragg and Epelbaum (1996) report that the occupation effect seems more relevant than the industry effect to explain wage inequality in Mexico.

In brief, studies on outsourcing and FDI (Feenstra and Hanson, 1996) assume that trade liberalization leads to a shift of unskilled intensive industries from developed to developing countries, though such industries are not unskilled intensive from a developing country perspective and/or require skilled workers to manage the liberalization process.

Heterogeneity in technology

Last, trade patterns do not only depend on differences in factor endowment but also on differences in factor productivity, amounting to difference in technology. The inclusion of differences in technology and the appearance of technological change seriously complicates the prediction of trade-induced inequality.

Wage studies: In the literature on wages, technological differences lead to skilled-biased technological change. As different recent models show, skill-biased technological change can be indirectly and partly induced by trade policy.[6] Many authors argue that trade liberalization can increase wage inequality through capital goods imports. These imports raise the demand for skilled labour capable to use imported capital goods (machines for instance), thereby improving the productivity of skilled workers. Such an outcome is comparable to what occurs with skill-biased technical change (Harrison and Hanson, 1999; Gindling and Robbins, 2001; Pavcnik, 2003; Attanasio et al, 2004). Zhu and Trefler (2005) show that the technological catch up (measured by an increase in labour productivity) does not directly affect wage inequality but by allowing developing countries to specialize in more skill-intensive products, it nonetheless leads to an upsurge in wage inequality.

Gini studies: Easterly (2004) tried to explain global income inequality by differences in productivity. He shows that the predictions regarding the impact of trade openness on inequality are unclear once technological differences have been taken into account. If the relative labour scarcity of rich countries is sufficiently offset by higher relative productivity, then rich countries can be considered as 'labour abundant', exporting thus 'labour-intensive' goods. Liberalization in such a setting can generate an increase in inequality in developing countries. Heterogeneity in technological achievements among developing countries then affects the relative abundance of factors, causing some developing countries not to display comparative advantages in labour-intensive goods.

To summarize, studies stress basically two points. First, technological differences change the relative abundance of factors, causing some developing countries not to display the otherwise expected comparative advantage in labour. Secondly, trade liberalization changes the use of technology in a way that favours skilled labour.

Summary of issues

The developing country puzzle, according to which inequality increases with trade liberalization in spite of relatively abundant unskilled labour, has received renewed attention over the last decade. Explanatory factors mostly revolve around heterogeneity in factor endowments taken in a broad sense (e.g. human capital and natural resources included). A cycle of empirical studies aiming at reconciling HO predictions with (controlled) facts seems now to be ending, from which a list of issues can be outlined.

Examining and controlling for changes in endowment heterogeneity in one single model reduces the magnitude of the developing country puzzle to the poorest deciles of developing countries' populations, which are the most likely to incur significant losses either in income or wage. This is an issue as such.

A second issue pertains to the mapping of the different types of unskilled labour in developing countries and, accordingly, to the respective contribution of educated and uneducated workers' wage changes to changes in inequality.

Third, controlling for technological change leaves room for further work. Understanding trade's contribution to technological change, and in turn, the effect of trade-induced technological change on the demand for labour (either for intermediate goods or final goods provision) is of prime importance to predict possible changes in trade-induced inequality.

Last, identifying and comparing South–South trade inequality channels with North–South trade inequality channels, and then assessing the impact of South–South trade liberalization on inequality, would be two complementary issues, South–South trade liberalization being promoted as the most promising vehicle for trade-induced efficiency gains and possible growth.

Fairness interpretation two: Household level ex-ante assessment

At the household level, the consequences of trade liberalization are very difficult to disentangle from other sources of variation of income. That is why the micro studies of trade liberalization often rely on ex-ante evaluations. They model explicitly what would have been the consequences of trade liberalization on household welfare using pre-liberalization samples and hypotheses linking price and wage variations to trade reforms. This renders the results of these studies dependent upon these hypotheses and on a relevant modelling of household decisions.

Some studies try to overcome this difficulty by directly linking household welfare (approximated by hourly wage) to tariff variation at the industry level. Results from these studies have been described in the preceding section. A related approach is to approximate trade reform by time variation. When a country experienced dramatic changes in trade policy through time, along with a relative stability in the rest of its economy, this approach remains valid. Litchfield et al (2003) study the extent to which people escaped poverty in Vietnam between 1992 and 1998, based on their 1992 characteristics. Between these two periods Vietnam undertook dramatic trade reforms, including liberalization in rice and coffee prices. Farmers producing coffee and rice in 1992 escaped poverty at a much higher rate than the rest of the population. But these results are of limited scope and validity. First, McCulloch, Winters and Cirera (2002) cannot separate the consequences of trade liberalization per se from that of the bulk of reforms that Vietnam experienced between the two surveys (land reallocation, price and investment liberalization). Secondly, they cannot interconnect their measure of liberalization with household characteristics that changed between the two dates, because such a change is likely to be endogenous.

We report here the results from ex-ante studies trying to infer the consequences of trade liberalization on household welfare, using micro data.

Theoretical channels and methodological options

There are different kinds of trade liberalization, and they each have different consequences on domestic prices. We shall refer below to the following types:

- Unilateral liberalization (UL): removal of tariff barriers (non-tariff barriers are not studied in the literature dealing with developing countries) or export subsidies. UL implies a decrease in domestic prices in the small country case, which is the case we shall consider throughout the paper.
- Export liberalization (EL): removal of export taxes. EL implies an increase in domestic prices.
- Trade liberalization in the rest of the world (TLROW): mainly removal of developed countries' agricultural policies (DCAP). TLROW implies an increase in domestic prices.

The domestic price variation induced by trade liberalization has short run and long run effects.

1 Short run consequences: an increase in domestic prices implies a short run increase in the welfare of net producers of the good affected by trade liberalization, and conversely, a short run decrease in the welfare of net consumers (Deaton, 1989). To infer the distributional consequences of trade liberalization, one has then to locate net producers and net consumers on a real income scale (Deaton, 1997).
2 Longer run consequences: a price increase implies an increased demand for the mobile factor used in the production of the good (Ricardo–Viner effect), mainly labour, or for the factor intensively used in the production of the good (Stolper–Samuelson effect). This change in factor returns can magnify or counter the direct welfare impact of the price change (Porto, 2004).

The short run effect (1) on welfare of UL is positive for every good that is only consumed by the household. For goods both consumed and produced by the household (mainly agricultural goods, where domestic production is an important part of the household's consumption), one has to locate net producers and net consumers on an income scale. The total welfare effect of liberalization is measured by the sum of the net marketed surpluses of each good weighted by the expected price variation due to liberalization.

Longer run effects (2) can only be measured by assessing the consequences of trade liberalization on factor returns (mainly wages). Two techniques have been proposed: linking household micro models to computable general equilibrium models; or estimating directly the general equilibrium relationships linking factor returns to border prices.

For a typical poor rural household that is a net consumer of agricultural products, and that derives income from agricultural wages, the net welfare effect of UL is ambiguous. The decrease in prices increases its welfare as a consumer. Meanwhile it decreases demand for agricultural labour, decreases agricultural wages and thus rural households' income.

The net effect of liberalization for a typical poor household hinges on the relative magnitude of these two opposite effects. These, in turn, critically depend on empirical estimates of the following quantities and elasticities:

1 The direct price effect depends on the size of the household's marketed surplus and on the magnitude of the price changes due to trade liberalization.
2 The indirect factor returns effect depends on the elasticity of the agricultural wage with respect to border prices and on the share of the wage component in the household's income.

Determining which of these two effects dominates is thus an empirical matter.

Empirical evidence

An overview of empirical results is given in Table 1.1.

Direct price effect (1): The studies mentioned in Table 1.1 document that all around the world, the poor are mainly net consumers of goods that are protected by tariff barriers. Thus, UL would be beneficial to them and on the contrary, TLROW would be detrimental. As for taxed exported goods (cocoa, cotton, coffee), the poor do not consume them. EL would not increase poverty, and could decrease poverty in some cases.

Indirect price effect (2): The poor are mainly net sellers of agricultural labour. UL, decreasing agricultural prices, would decrease wages and thus the poor's income. The evidence is scarce (Porto, 2004), but this income effect seems to dominate the direct price effect. There is a magnifying effect: the elasticity of wages with respect to the prices of tradable goods is superior to one.

As a conclusion, if the existence of a magnifying effect is confirmed in other countries and studies, UL would be poverty increasing, while TLROW would be poverty decreasing. A less controversial result is that EL would be poverty decreasing, as both direct and indirect effects go the same way.

Table 1.1 *List of papers studying the distributional consequences of trade liberalization*

Authors	*Country*	*Products*	*Distributional impact of a price decrease*
Short run effects (1)			
Deaton (1989)	Thailand	Rice	Slight decrease in poverty The income of intermediate households decreases
Ravallion and van de Walle (1991)	Indonesia	Rice	Decrease in poverty
Budd (1993)	Côte d'Ivoire	Rice	Decrease in poverty
Porto (2004)	Argentina	Agricultural products	Decrease in poverty
Porto (2005)	Mexico	Maize	Decrease in poverty
Nicita (2005)	Mexico	Agricultural products	Decrease in poverty
Chabe-Ferret (2005)	Brazil	Maize and rice	Decrease in poverty
Benjamin and Deaton (1993)	Côte d'Ivoire	Coffee and cocoa	No impact on extreme poverty Decrease in the income of intermediate households
Rapsomanikis and Sarris (2005)	Ghana	Cocoa	No impact on extreme poverty Decrease in the income of intermediate households
Balat and Porto (2005)	Zambia	Cotton	Increase in poverty
Long run effects (1) + (2) (Estimated wage/price elasticities)			
Porto (2004)	Argentina	Agricultural goods and clothing	Increase in poverty (the negative wage effect dominates negative price effect)
Porto (2005)	Mexico	Maize	Increase in poverty (the negative wage effect dominates negative price effect)
Nicita (2004)	Mexico	Agricultural goods and clothing	Decrease in poverty (the negative wage effect is dominated by the positive price effect) Increase in inequality
Long run effects (1) + (2) (Combining CGEs to household surveys)			
Ianchovichina et al (2001)	Mexico	All products	Slight decrease in poverty (the negative wage effect is dominated by the positive price effect) Increase in inequality
Arndt (2005)	Mozambique	All products	Increase in poverty (the wage effect dominates)

Source: Authors

Remaining gaps

We review in this section the main knowledge gaps to be filled in order to provide a better and clearer overview of the poverty consequences of trade liberalization.

The importance of imported inputs: An often overlooked consequence of UL is cheaper access to imported inputs for agricultural households. Litchfield et al (2003) document that trade liberalization in Vietnam induced a decrease in input prices that contributed to poverty alleviation.

The extent of the pass-through from tariffs to producer and consumer prices: Much of the literature reviewed here hypotheses a perfect pass-through from border prices to producer and consumer prices. Nicita (2004) shows that transaction costs are high, and that the farther the border, the thinner the impact of border prices on producer and consumer prices.

The problem of missing markets: Much of the literature reviewed hinges on the hypothesis of perfectly functioning markets. But developing countries are characterized by highly imperfect markets (de Janvry et al, 1991). In the long run, failure to access the market for inputs, outputs or labour can prevent the households from grasping the benefits of trade liberalization. A thorough study of the transaction costs faced by the households is needed to conclude that they will benefit from liberalization in the longer run. In the short run, because in developing countries many households face high transaction costs so that they do not perceive the price change liberalization implies, they are neither harmed nor favoured by liberalization (Singh et al, 1986). But when adjusting to the price change, the additional constraint of missing markets reduces welfare impact. As the poorest households are the most likely to face transaction costs and imperfect markets, improving our knowledge on these topics is crucial in assessing the poverty consequences of trade liberalization.

Is there a magnifying effect of trade liberalization? Mixing various kinds of studies to accurately evaluate the impact of trade liberalization on wages and factor returns would add valuable information. The impact of trade liberalization on the poor critically hinges on the size of the wage effect relative to the direct price effect. The elasticity of wages to border prices is thus critical to evaluate the poverty consequences of trade liberalization. This is very difficult to measure, and has only been estimated by Porto (2003) for Argentina and Porto (2005) in Mexico. Porto estimates a reduced form linking border prices to wages, at a very aggregated level. Estimates of these effects could also come from studies using variation in protection across sectors to estimate the elasticity of wages to trade liberalization.

Are corner outcomes important? This question raises the issue of the impact of trade liberalization on unemployment and entry and exit into the informal sector. To assess the poverty consequences of trade liberalization, it is critical to consider the existence of unemployment. Price variations could induce a shift in or out of the labour force. That is documented by Krivonos and Olarreaga (2006): in Brazil, an increase in the price of sugar increases the likelihood that an individual works. Thus, an increase in sugar prices due to TLROW would increase the welfare of the poor mainly by increasing their participation in the labour market. Their gain through an increase in wages is less important. On the contrary, UL would decrease prices and deter entry into the labour force, thus decreasing the poor's welfare. A general modelling of the household's work allocation decision is thus needed to adequately infer the consequences of trade liberalization.

Fairness interpretation three: Market failures, adjustment costs and intertemporal dynamics

Market failures have a long record in development economics, though their emergence in policy makers' and policy advisers' discourses is fairly recent, dating back to the lukewarm performance of the structural adjustment programmes in developing countries in the 1980s. Market failures crippling developing economies have provided a renewed interest for targeted intervention by donor agencies ever since, with a marked focus in aid programmes for the financing of public goods or public-good-like services such as education, health and infrastructure. The World Bank's Poverty Reduction Strategic Programmes epitomize this focus. Incompleteness in factor markets (e.g. related to risk in labour and capital markets) gained a more measured momentum, though it was directly linked to imperfect information problems that made the core of the market failure literature at this time (Stiglitz, 1986; Greenwald and Stiglitz, 1988). Imperfect competition and externality issues lagged far behind, such market failures being of much higher concern in transition and industrialized economies. Ironically, and as shown below, trade liberalization impact models, when considering market failures, mainly restrict their consideration to imperfect competition and externalities, seldom exploring the basic features of developing economies.

The connection between market failures and trade is not that obvious yet. The Bhagwati and Ramaswami (1963) argument for free trade in the presence of market failure should have kept the two strands of literature separated, enabling developing governments to pursue the free trade objective while correcting for market failures at home. Unless market failures occur in international markets, the nexus between market failure and trade hence is weak. However, it gained a high profile after poverty reduction and development got into the picture and became key objectives of developing countries, donor agencies and WTO members all together. The connection followed two different directions, depending on whether market failures were considered as perennial or amendable features of developing economies.

In the first case, the efficiency losses induced by perennial market failures, superimposing on the distortions generated by trade protection, blurred the expected gains from freer trade in a second-best world (Stiglitz and Charlton, 2005). In this strand of literature, perennial market failures in developing countries relate mostly to factors and information markets, possibly degenerating into Pareto-inferior trade (Newbery and Stiglitz, 1984). Trade liberalization may not be the right question, or the right answer for such countries. Selective and temporary protectionism can be part of the second-best policy set (Greenwald and Stiglitz, 2006). Policy consequences can be summarized as market-failure-correction-before-liberalization, the magnitude and sequencing of trade liberalization depending on the second-best policies available to mitigate the market failures at stake.

On the second case, correcting for amendable market failures leaves room for the so-called efficient redistributive policies, namely policies reducing inequality while improving market efficiency, provided that existing market failures were discriminatory against the poor (Piketty, 1997). Public-good-like services (education, health, infrastructure) rank first in this respect, their provision increasing presumably both the aggregated gains from freer trade and the income share captured by the poorest. Own-trade liberalization remains in this case a priority objective. Policy consequences can be summarized as market-failure-correction-cum-liberalization. To benefit the poorest, trade liberalization is to be accompanied indeed by 'complementary policies' (Hertel and Winters, 2006) and 'flanking measures' (EC, 2006), which all would help turn short-term losses into long-term gains. A pure redistributive version of the argument substitutes lump-sum transfers (cash compensations) for policies to correct market failure among the complementary measures to be implemented.

At first glance, these two directions seem reasonably compatible and convergent towards the same long-run development target. They moreover share the same rationale, according to which adjustment costs induced by trade liberalization do exist and require compensating mechanisms for trade to benefit the poor – as long as these bear such costs. They differ, however, on one single point that relates to the inclusion of dynamic and time in the adjustment of economies. In the perennial market failures case, adjustment is not a temporary shift of the economy toward a long-run, steady-state equilibrium, but a permanent feature of development – recall that they single out developing countries among other countries. There are costs to trade-liberalization induced adjustment. These costs are created by market failures, notably on capital and labour markets. These being unlikely to vanish, adjustment costs remain as long as the economy develops. Assessing who bears the cost over time, and whether this cost can be mitigated and/or shifted towards the wealthiest or towards the future, turn market failures into a genuine political economy issue. The case is different for amendable market failures. The adjustment costs they involve are transitory and likely to vanish once the market failures have been overcome. Development means moving from one production frontier to a broader and encompassing one. Adjustment costs provide there a rather static idea of the path involved in between.

In the following subsections, we dwell upon the adjustment cost literature, before turning to methodological issues raised by the dynamic adjustment of developing economies characterized by perennial market failure.

Adjustment costs and inequality in developing countries

Trade liberalization causes the previously protected sector of a country to shrink and thereby causes reallocation of resources between industries. Owners of resources initially employed in the protected sectors may hence incur income and wealth losses, depending on real price changes of the factors they are endowed with. In a static view of the economy, and with perfectly competitive markets, no adjustment cost occurs as such, except those induced by the transfer and compensation schemes – if any – set by the government to compensate losers. The distributive consequences of trade liberalization at country level are not altered by any hypothetical cost incurred by such a country's move toward free trade. Market failures in labour and capital markets, causing workers and capital to lie idle for a period, create two kinds of problems. They generate supplementary costs (when compared to the perfect markets situation) the magnitude of which will affect the net gains from trade. The distribution of such costs among households will in turn dramatically affect the distribution of trade-induced inequality.

The literature on trade liberalization with costs of adjustment has mainly focused on the optimal path of liberalization, gradual liberalization being presented as a reasonable means for government captured by 'loud' losers to ease their pain, win political support for reform and tap long-term (e.g. post-adjustment) gains. Gradualism was moreover the proof that adjustment costs did exist, governments being otherwise expected to move more quickly towards free trade (Furusawa and Lai, 1999).

Existence of adjustment costs in the process of trade reform is not disputed. Several empirical studies attempting to define and quantify them have been reviewed by international organizations such as WTO or United Nations Conference on Trade and Development (UNCTAD) over the last couple of years.[7] A critical review of major findings provides the following results:

- No single economic definition of adjustment cost prevails. There is similarly no consensus on what adjustment costs are expected to be in a purely competitive economy.
- In spite of loose definitions, consensus emerges to isolate unemployment, e.g. market failure, as a primary source of adjustment costs. Interestingly, adjustment cost pervades the discourses of government and policy makers, providing a comfortable and serious-sounding catch word substituting for 'unemployment' in trade liberalization debates.
- A second consensus seems to arises over the fact that adjustment costs – whatever their definition – are short term. As a consequence, they are likely to become another comfortable catch word, substituting this time to what turns out to be short-term welfare net losses for particular countries.
- Whatever their magnitude and distribution among income groups, adjustment costs lead to policy recommendations broadly in line with Bhagwati and Ramaswami (1963) recommendations:

> *trade liberalization may lead to adjustment costs and may affect domestic income distribution. But we do not believe that concerns about adjustment costs and income distribution are meaningful arguments against trade liberalization. We do believe that with appropriate domestic policies and institutions in place, everyone can gain from trade liberalization.* (WTO DG Mike Moore, Geneva, 18 March 2002)

- Concession of *possible* short-term losses are accompanied with marked assertion on *certain* long-term gains. The conclusion of de Cordoba et al (2006) is representative of such a line of thought:

> *Finally, addressing adjustment problems directly, by making markets work better and through redistributive mechanisms as well as by providing adequate, well directed finances and transition periods, would enable developing countries to opt for policies that would allow them to capture the larger long-term gain from trade.* (p73)

Readers will have recognized the common belief stated by Samuelson (2004):

> *Yes, good jobs may be lost here in the short run. But still total U.S. net national product* must, by the economic laws of comparative advantage, be raised in the long run (and in China, too). *The gains of the winners from free trade, properly measured, work out to exceed the losses of the losers. This is not by mysterious fuzzy magic, but rather comes from a sharing of the trade-induced rise in total global vectors of the goods and services that people in a democracy want. Never forget to tally the real gains of consumers alongside admitted possible losses of some producers in this working out of what Schumpeter called 'creative capitalist destruction.' Correct economic law recognizes that some American groups can be hurt by dynamic free trade. But correct economic law vindicates the word 'creative' destruction by its proof that the gains of the American winners are big enough to more than compensate the losers'.* (p135, emphasis in the original)

In his paper, Samuelson demonstrates that

> *sometimes free trade globalization can convert a technical change abroad into a benefit for both regions; but sometimes a productivity gain in one country can benefit that country alone, while permanently hurting the other country by reducing the gains from trade that are possible between the two countries. All of this constitutes long-run Schumpeterian effects, quite aside from and different from transitory short-run harms traceable to short run adjustment costs or to temporary rents from patents and from eroding monopolies on knowledge. (p142)*

When admitting short run losses and ascertaining for long-term gains, one takes for granted the systematic and positive impact of trade openness on productivity and growth. Such a relationship is not supported either by economic theory, as reminded by Samuelson, nor by empirical evidence. Weaknesses in the positive relationship between trade and growth hence makes dubious any assertion on the systematic mitigation of adjustment costs by opened economies and on 'the larger long-term gains from trade'.

Modelling liberalization's dynamic effects

One of the most popular tools for trade liberalization impact assessment undoubtedly is CGE models. We review in this section their performance in accounting for the various adjustment costs issues mentioned above and, particularly, market failures and dynamic effects.

Since the first generation of CGE models developed in the 1970s, modellers have amended the basic Walrasian framework to introduce imperfect competition and increasing returns to scale, dynamics and imperfect factor markets (especially labour) and heterogeneous household behaviour (mainly through microsimulation techniques). These improvements are, however, still far from being satisfactory to allow for a relevant analysis of the impact of trade liberalization on income distribution.

Imperfect competition and increasing returns to scale issues

Harris (1984) has been the first to model imperfect competition and increasing returns to scale within CGE models, while the first applications on developing countries are those of Devarajan and Rodrik (1989, 1991). The main criticism addressed to these models is that they overestimate the positive impact of trade liberalization. Indeed, the rationale behind these models is that when a country reduces its trade barriers, competition with foreign firms induces a lower mark-up, which means lower prices and higher supply by local firms, and thus an increase of domestic welfare. This phenomenon is called the pro-competitive effect of trade liberalization. However, there is no empirical evidence supporting the existence of such an effect. Moreover, as stressed by Slaughter (2000), if the labour-intensive industries are the most protected in a given developing country, the pro-competitive effect could induce an increase of inequality and poverty, as outlined in the earlier section above.

Are the links between trade liberalization and imperfect competition reduced to a lower mark-up? And are we really sure that mark-ups will be lower? If the product differentiation increases, mark-up could actually increase. Should we not instead focus on how product market imperfections impede small firms in developing countries from taking advantage of trade liberalization? Indeed, we see in many developing countries the constitution of new joint-ventures between big local firms and multinational corporations that allow the former to strengthen their domination on the domestic market with trade liberalization. We could better capture the consequences of trade liberalization on income distribution if we were able to model in a more relevant way markets functioning in developing countries.

Imperfect factor markets issues

CGE models that do not take into account imperfect capital and labour markets are irrelevant for analysing the economic and distributional impact of trade liberalization. The absence of these market failures is certainly one of the main reasons explaining the gap between models' predictions and observed outcomes. Indeed, one of the main issues of trade liberalization is the inter-sectoral reallocation of resources. The more segmented and inefficient factor markets are, the more costly this reallocation is.

Concerning capital markets, the distributional consequence of credit rationing is very important. Small firms and informal entrepreneurs have very difficult access to credit markets, which reduces significantly their capacity of intertemporal arbitrage. Decaluwe and Nsengiyumva (1994) have shown in the case of Rwanda how the policy impact is modified when taking into account credit rationing. This feature should be included systematically in any model dealing with trade liberalization in developing countries.

Labour market imperfections have been more often included in CGE models, even if the most influential ones in international trade negotiations still represent labour markets as working perfectly. Labour market imperfections could be divided in two categories: those linked to wage setting mechanisms and those dealing with firing/hiring mechanisms. The literature has mainly focused on the former (Marouani, 2002). The first generation of imperfect labour market CGE models have introduced labour market imperfections through minimum wages. The second generation of models relied on wage curves (De Santis, 1998), labour union behaviour modelling (Devarajan et al, 1997), matching models (Maechler and Roland-Host, 1995), or efficiency wage theory (Thierfelder and Shiells, 1997; Marouani, 2000, 2005). The presence of these imperfections allows for tackling the issue of unemployment but they also give different results in terms of income distribution.

However, even if these models are often built on solid theoretical foundations, their empirical validation is still weak, because it is a very difficult task. How would one estimate empirically the power of negotiation of a trade union or the probability for a shirker to be caught by his supervisor?

Finally, the last issue we would like to raise is labour mobility. In CGE models, inter-sectoral labour mobility is costless. CGE models in their current design do not have the possibility to analyse labour mobility. They just give the stock of labour demand of each sector, without looking at if the employees were formerly unemployed or working in other sectors. As we said previously, trade liberalization involves significant resource reallocation, and the cost of labour mobility (training, assistance programmes, etc.) should be one of the main factors taken into account to analyse the impact of trade liberalization.

Dynamics issues

The first generation of dynamic CGE models are called recursive or sequential. These models are actually static models linked by jumping variables (mainly capital accumulation). Households are characterized by myopic expectations, which is obviously unrealistic. However, these models are popular (especially within policy research circles) because they at the same time give the impression of tackling the issue of dynamics (since they explicitly model the evolution of variables from one period to another) and are very easy to handle.

The second generation of dynamic CGEs, namely intertemporal general equilibrium models, are more popular within academic circles. They rely on a truly dynamic framework: households maximize their intertemporal utility given their intertemporal budget constraint and firms maximize their discounted value given their capital accumulation constraint. However, the main shortcoming of such models is their treatment of expectations. Most of them rely on the rational expectations perfect foresight behaviour. The absence of uncertainty is unrealistic and induces an overestimation of the positive impact (or a minimization of the negative impact) of trade liberalization because households and firms are omniscient and are thus able to adapt their behaviour to any future shock in an optimal way. Ballard and Goulder (1985) and Ballard (1987) have shown the impact of the adoption of different expectation models. However, given the difficulty of the task, this direction of research seems to have been abandoned.

An exception may be found in Boussard et al (2004) and in Boussard et al (2006), who explicitly model expectations in a dynamic world CGE-model with imperfect information and incomplete risk market. The authors try to evaluate changes in welfare gains and their distribution due to trade liberalization with two versions of their model. In the first version, a standard world CGE approach is followed. In the second version, risk aversion, imperfect information and production lag in the agricultural sector are included. Impacts on agricultural production and income as well as on household welfare and gross domestic product (GDP) performance for selected countries are simulated. It appears that in case of imperfect information most of the gains related to comparative advantages vanish. The authors emphasize that their results are very sensitive to the way expectations are formalized. Because the imperfection information assumption relaxes the rational expectation hypothesis in its most restrictive form (whereby prices are anticipated perfectly), price expectation has to be formalized in an ad hoc fashion (naive, adaptive, etc.). The consequences of the formalization of price expectations on price behaviour are spectacular, price motion being random-like, chaotic or periodic according to the formalization selected. Such a model, which should preferably be called a computational general *dis*equilibrium model, provides a first insight of adjustments involved by trade liberalization over time in a global framework, from one disequilibrium position to another.

Another shortcoming of intertemporal models, especially those dealing with developing countries, is the hypothesis of a steady state growth. François et al (1999) note that this hypothesis is not acceptable, especially for countries facing a significant shock like trade liberalization. Dynamic models need to deal with transitional dynamics, not only at the macro but also at the sectoral level.

Finally, intertemporal CGE models usually include a dynamic optimization programme for capital accumulation, but labour demand is modelled in a static way. Thus, adjustment costs on capital accumulation are taken into account but not those on labour demand. In other words it is implicitly assumed that firms plan their investments in the long run to minimize capital adjustment costs and that labour demand adjusts to minimize the intra-period production costs. In reality firms plan both. Researchers should thus think of a way to model the demand of permanent workers in a dynamic setting, and temporary workers could be the adjusting variable. The distributional consequences of trade liberalization would be different if we take into account the fact that temporary workers could be more affected by a negative shock, since those are often more vulnerable than permanent employees.

Conclusion

The starting point of this paper is given by country situations where trade liberalization is expected to be poverty- and inequality-alleviating in the long run while inducing a short run increase in poverty or in inequality. The question we ask is what are the distributive aspects of trade that are worth documenting to help governments better integrate trade policies within a global policy framework so as to enhance growth and reduce poverty and inequality.

The method followed is a literature review, organized according to salient issues given by the three interpretations of fairness implied by the inclusion of the 'development' objective in the world trade liberalization agenda. A 'pro-development' trade liberalization agenda should correct past unfairness in the trade regime, which raises the broad issue of country level ex-post assessment. It should equally reduce poverty, which points towards household level ex-ante assessment. Last, because development is basically a dynamic process, the distributive-dynamic effects of trade liberalization are also considered.

A ten-point summary of the conclusions of this chapter follows:

1 Empirical evidence shows that inequality rises when developing countries open up their trade. Hence the poor get poorer, in relative terms. Simple HO predictions do not hold and the beautiful story the Doha Development Round should tell is likely to be wishful thinking unless trade-induced inequality is anticipated and corrected from the onset.
2 Such empirical findings are based on ex-post analysis. For this reason, they have a much more powerful and persuasive effect than ex-ante assessment results that are based upon numerical simulations.
3 Most of the knowledge gaps derived from such evidence are not new. The wage premium puzzle, technological-change induced inequality, the effects of missing markets on inequality, the impact assessment of dynamic adjustments, all these date back to the early structural adjustment periods.
4 Most methodological gaps are not new either. Macro–micro models received renewed interest and technical improvement in the second half of

the 1990s (with microsimulation, labour market imperfection modelling) but the basis dates back to the late 1980s. This said, the development and refinement of models, although insufficient, is not fully grasped by policy analysts who on average resort to static, perfectly competitive simulation models to derive policy recommendations.

5 The development goal stresses the shortcomings of available tools. Shortcomings are known: no market failure, no dynamics. Because development *is* dynamic *with* market failures, correcting for such shortcomings should be gaining momentum. We have to correct for such shortcomings, not for technical reasons, but on development grounds.

6 Disputed evidence arises: long-term gains may not be 'automatically' tapped and could vanish because of market failures. Evidence on long-term gains remains elusive, though forcefully asserted.

7 Policy recommendations could follow three directions: education investment, correction of failures in factor markets, and market access. Still one cross-cutting recommendation – or issue – prevails, namely to identify losers.

8 How to identify losers? The task is difficult, because we have to disentangle at the micro level the impacts of trade openness on a wide array of channels: relative demand for skilled labour through induced technical change or import of new technologies, imperfect access to markets (credit, labour, inputs, education). This cannot be done by investigating only the macro consequences of trade openness (total factor productivity, sector allocation).

9 Methods have to be implemented to investigate at the micro level how these macro changes interact to determine household welfare. Such contributions as those of Duflo and Banerjee (2005) or Fafchamps et al (2006) improve our understanding of micro determinants of growth and exports, and of the reactions of firms to trade openness. Such improvements, in the long run, help us to understand which variables drive factor demands and relative factor returns.

10 Without such a thorough micro analysis, the study of the distributional consequences of trade liberalization may not deliver usable results. This is a wide opened array of research, to guide Alice-WTO out of Doha's Wonderland.

Notes

1 This result is a generalization of salient outcomes of both approaches (Chabe-Ferret, 2005). Differences of course arise when looking at particular studies. The reason for difference between studies on wage and on income may be formulated as follows: the supply of skilled labour is much more inelastic than the supply of unskilled labour, which is more likely to be forced into unemployment. This is what the evidence from Krivonos and Olarreaga (2006) shows in the Brazilian sugar sector. When the price of sugar goes up, wage inequality increases, but once employment effects are accounted for, income inequality decreases or at least

remains stable. Thus, a large share of the gains accruing to unskilled workers comes from the move out of unemployment and not necessarily from higher wages.

2 For an excellent review of findings, see Anderson (2005).

3 Some Gini coefficients come from surveys on consumption or expenditure, other from surveys on revenue.

4 Using, for example, the Gini on land as in Lundberg and Squire (2003) and in Rama (2002).

5 See Hanson (2003) on North American Free Trade Agreement (NAFTA).

6 See for instance Thoenig and Verdier (2003).

7 Bachetta and Jansen (2003) for empirical studies on developed countries, published by the WTO. De Cordoba et al (2006) for UNCTAD on developing economies.

References

Ackerman, F. (2005) 'The shrinking gains from trade: A critical assessment of Doha Round projections', Global Developement and Environment Institute Working Paper 05-01, Tufts University

Anderson, E. (2005) 'Openness and inequality in developing countries: A review of theory and recent evidence', *World Development*, vol 33, no 7, pp1045–1063

Anderson, K. and Martin, W. (eds) (2006) *Agricultural Trade Reform and The Doha Development Agenda*, The World Bank, Washington DC, and Palgrave Macmillan, Basingstoke

Arndt, C. (2005) 'The Doha Trade Round and Mozambique', Policy Research Working Paper 3717, The World Bank, Washington DC

Attanasio, O., Goldberg, P. K. and Pavcnik, N. (2004) 'Trade reforms and wage inequality in Columbia', *Journal of Development Economic*, vol 74, pp331–366

Bacchetta, M. and Jansen, M. (2003) 'Adjusting to trade liberalization. The role of policy, institutions, and WTO disciplines', WTO Special Studies 7, WTO, Geneva

Balat, J. F. and Porto, G. (2005) 'The WTO Doha Round, cotton sector dynamics and poverty trends in Zambia', Policy Research Working Paper 3697, The World Bank, Washington DC

Ballard, C. L. (1987) 'Tax policy and consumer foresight: A general equilibrium analysis', *Economic Inquiry*, vol 25, pp267–284

Ballard, C. L. and Goulder, L. H. (1985) 'Consumption taxes, foresight and welfare: A computable general equilibrium analysis', in J. Piggott and J. Whalley (eds) *New Development in General Equilibrium Analysis*, Cambridge University Press, Cambridge, pp253–282

Benjamin, D. and Deaton, A. (1993) 'Household welfare and the pricing of cocoa and coffee in Côte d'Ivoire: Lessons from the Living Standards Surveys', *The World Bank Economic Review*, vol 7, no 3, pp293–318

Bhagwati, J. and Ramaswami, V. K. (1963) 'Domestic distortions, tariffs, and the theory of optimal subsidy', *Journal of Political Economy*, vol 71, pp44–50

Bourguignon, F. and Morrisson, C. (1990) 'Income distribution development and foreign trade', *European Economic Review*, vol 34, pp1113–1132

Bourguignon, F., De Melo, J. and Morrisson, C. (1991) 'Poverty and income distribution during adjustment', Policy Research Working Paper 810, The World Bank, Washington DC

Boussard, J. M., Gérard, F., Piketty, M. G., Ayouz, M. and Voituriez, T. (2006) 'Endogenous risk and long run effects of liberalization in a global analysis framework', *Economic Modelling*, vol 23, pp457–475

Boussard, J. M., Gérard, F., Piketty, M. G., Christensen, A. K. and Voituriez, T. (2004) 'May the pro-poor impact of trade liberalization vanish because of imperfect information?', *Agricultural Economics*, vol 31, pp297–305

Budd, J. W. (1993) 'Changing food prices and rural welfare: A nonparametric examination of the Côte d'Ivoire', *Economic Development and Cultural Change*, vol 41, no 3, pp587–603

Calderon, C. and Chong, A. (2001) 'External sector and income inequality in interdependent economies', *Economic Letters*, vol 71, no 2, pp225–231

CEPR (2005) press release, www.cepr.net/pressreleases/2005_11_22.htm

Chabe-Ferret, S. (2005) 'The distributional consequences of developed countries agricultural policies in Brazil: A non parametric analysis', Mimeo, contributed paper to the *Journées de l'économie du developpement de l'Association Française de Science Economique (AFSE)*, 19–20 May 2005, Clermont-Ferrand, France

Cogneau, D., Grimm, M. and Robilliard, A.-S. (2003) 'Evaluating poverty reduction policies: The contribution of microsimulation techniques', in J. P. Cling, M. Razafindrakoto and F. Roubaud (eds) *The New International Strategies for Poverty Reduction*, Routledge, London, New York

Cragg, M. I. and Epelbaum, M. (1996) 'Why has wage dispersion grown in Mexico? Is it the incidence of reforms or the growing demand for skills?' *Journal of Development Economics*, vol 51, no 1, pp99–116

Deaton, A. (1989) 'Rice prices and income distribution in Thailand: A non parametric analysis', *The Economic Journal*, vol 99, no 395, pp1–37

Deaton, A. (1997) *The Analysis of Household Surveys: A Microeconometric Approach to Development Policy*, John Hopkins University Press and The World Bank, Washington DC

Decaluwe, B. and Nsengiyumva, F. (1994) 'Policy impact under credit rationing: A real and financial CGE for Rwanda', *Journal of African Economies*, vol 3, pp268–308

De Janvry, A., Fafschamps, M. and Sadoulet, E. (1991) 'Peasant household behavior with missing markets: Some paradoxes explained', *The Economic Journal*, vol 120, no 409, pp1400–1417

Devarajan, S. and Rodrik, D. (1989) 'Trade liberalization in developing countries: Do imperfect competition and scale economies matter?', *American Economic Review*, vol 79, pp283–287

Devarajan, S. and Rodrik, D. (1991) 'Pro-competitive effects of trade reforms: Results from a CGE model of Cameroon', *European Economic Review*, vol 35, pp1157–1184

Devarajan, S., Ghanem, S. and Thierfelder, K. (1997) 'Economic reform and labor unions: A general-equilibrium analysis applied to Bangladesh and Indonesia', *The World Bank Economic Review*, vol 11, no 1, pp145–170

De Cordoba, S. F., Laird, S., Maur, J.-C. and Serena, J. M. (2006) 'Adjustment cost and trade liberalization', in S. Laird and S. F. de Cordoba (eds) *Coping with Trade Reforms. A Developing-Country Perspective on the WTO Industrial Tariffs Negotiations*, Palgrave Macmillan, Basingstoke

De Santis, R. A. (1998) 'The impact of a customs union with the EU on internal migration in Turkey under the two alternative Harris-Todaro and "Wage Curve" settings', Kiel Working Paper, N867

Duflo, E. and Banerjee, A. (2005) 'Growth theory through the lens of development economics?', *Handbook of Economic Growth*, vol 1, part A, pp473–552

Easterly, W. R. (2004) 'Globalization, inequality and development: The big picture', *Monetary and Economic Studies*, vol 22, pp57–87

EC (European Commission) (2006) *Handbook for Trade Sustainability Impact Assessment*, EC, External Trade, Brussels

Fafchamps, M., Zeufack A. and El Hamine, S. (2006) 'Learning to export: Evidence from Moroccan manufacturing', Mimeo, University of Oxford, Oxford

Feenstra, R. C. and Hanson, G. H. (1996) 'Globalization, outsourcing, and wage inequality', *American Economic Review*, vol 86, Cambridge University Press, Cambridge, pp240–245

Fischer, R. D. (2001) 'The evolution of inequality after trade liberalization', *Journal of Development Economics*, vol 66, pp555–579

François, J. F., Nordström, H. and Shiells, R. (1999) 'Transition dynamics and trade policy reform in developing countries', in R. E. Baldwin and J. F. François (eds) *Dynamic Issues in Commercial Policy Analysis*, Cambridge University Press, Cambridge, pp14–40

Furusawa, T. and Lai, E. L. C. (1999) 'Adjustment cost and gradual trade liberalization', *Journal of International Economics*, vol 49, pp333–361

Gindling, T.H. and Robbins, D. (2001) 'Patterns and sources of changing wage inequality in Chile and Costa Rica during structural adjustment', *World Development*, vol 29, no 4 (April), pp725–745

Gourdon, J., Maystre, N. and de Melo, J. (2008) 'Openness, inequality and poverty: Endowments matter', *Journal of International Trade and Economic Development*, forthcoming

Greenwald, B. C. and Stiglitz, J. E. (1988) 'Imperfect information, credit markets and unemployment', NBER Working Paper 2093, National Bureau of Economic Research, Inc., Cambridge, MA

Greenwald, B. C. and Stiglitz, J. E. (2006) 'Helping infant economies grow: Foundations of trade policies for developing countries', *The American Economic Review*, vol 96, no 2, pp141–146

Hanson, G. H. (2003) 'What has happened to wages in Mexico since NAFTA?' NBER Working Paper 9653, National Bureau of Economic Research, Inc., Cambridge, MA

Harris, R. (1984) 'Applied general equilibrium analysis of small open economies with scale economies and imperfect competition', *American Economic Review*, vol 74, pp1016–1033

Harrison, A. and Hanson, G. (1999) 'Who gains from trade reform? Some remaining puzzles', *Journal of Development Economics*, vol 59, pp125–144

Hertel, Th. and Winters, L. A. (eds) (2006) *Poverty and the WTO. Impacts of the Doha Development Agenda*, The World Bank, Washington DC, and Palgrave Macmillan, Houndmills, Basingstoke

Ianchovichina, E., Nicita, A. and Soloaga, I. (2001) 'Trade reform and household welfare: The case of Mexico', Policy Research Working Paper 2667, The World Bank, Washington DC

Krivonos, E. and Olarreaga, M. (2006) 'Sugar prices, labor income and poverty in Brazil', Policy Research Working Paper 3874, The World Bank, Washington DC

Leamer, E., Maul, H., Rodriguez, S. and Schott, P. K. (1999) 'Does natural resource abundance increase Latin American income inequality?', *Journal of Development Economics*, vol 59, no 1, pp3–42

Litchfield, J., McCulloch, N. and Winters, L. A. (2003) 'Agricultural trade liberalization and poverty dynamics in three developping countries', *American Journal of Agricultural Economics*, vol 85, no 5, pp1285–1291

Lundberg, M. and Squire, L. (2003) 'The simultaneous evolution of growth and inequality', *Economic Journal*, vol 113, no 487, pp326–344

McCulloch, N., Winters, A. and Cirera (2002) *Trade Liberalization and Poverty: A Handbook*, Centre for Economic Policy Research, London

Maechler, A. and Roland-Host, D. W. (1995) 'Empirical specifications for a general equilibrium analysis of labor market policies and adjustments', Document technique, N106, Centre de Développement, OECD, Paris

Marouani, M. A. (2000) 'Ouverture commerciale et emploi: Un modèle d'équilibre général avec salaires d'efficience appliqué à la Tunisie?', *Revue Economique*, vol 51, no 3, pp557–569

Marouani, M. A. (2002) 'Imperfections du marché du travail et modèles d'équilibre général calculables: Une revue de littérature', DIAL Working Paper DT/2002/16, Paris

Marouani, M. A. (2005) 'The Multi-Fiber Agreement phase out and unemployment in Tunisia', Göttingen, CEGE Discussion Paper 39, Göttingen University, Göttingen

Milanovic, B. (2005) 'Can we discern the effects of globalization on income distribution? Evidence from household surveys', *World Bank Economic Review,* vol 19, no 1, pp21-44

Newbery, D. M. G. and Stiglitz, J. E. (1984) 'Pareto-inferior trade', *Review of Economic Studies*, vol 51, pp1–12

Nicita, A. (2004) 'Who benefited from trade liberalization in Mexico? Measuring the effects on household welfare', Policy Research Working Paper 3265, The World Bank, Washington DC

Nicita, A. (2005) 'Multilateral trade liberalization and Mexican households: The effect of the Doha Development Agenda', Policy Research Working Paper 3707, The World Bank, Washington DC

Panagariya, A. (2004) 'Agricultural liberalization and the developing countries: Debunking fallacies', Mimeo, Columbia University, New York

Pavcnik, N. (2003) 'What explains skill upgrading in less developed countries?', *Journal of Development Economics*, vol 71, no 2, pp311–328

Piketty, Th. (1997) *L'Economie des Inégalités*, La Découverte, Paris

Polaski, S. (2006) *Winners and Losers. Impact of the Doha Round on Developing Countries*, Carnegie Endowment for International Peace, Washington DC

Porto, G. G. (2003) 'Trade reforms, market access, and poverty in Argentina', World Bank Policy Research Working Paper 3135, The World Bank, Washington, DC

Porto, G. G. (2004) 'Using survey data to assess the distributional effects of trade policy', Policy Research Working Paper 3137, The World Bank, Washington DC

Porto, G. G. (2005) 'Estimating household responses to trade reforms: Net consumers and net producers in rural Mexico', Policy Research Working Paper 3695, The World Bank, Washington DC

Rama, M. (2002) 'Globalization inequality and labor market policies', *Revue d'Economie du Développement*, vol 16, pp43–83

Rapsomanikis, G. and Sarris, A. (2005) 'The impact of domestic and international commodity price volatility on agricultural income instability in Ghana, Vietnam and Peru', Commodities and Trade Division Working Paper, Food and Agriculture Association (FAO), Rome

Ravallion, M. and van de Walle, D. (1991) 'The impact on poverty of food pricing reform: A welfare analysis for Indonesia', *Journal of Policy Modeling*, vol 13, no 2, pp281–299

Rodriguez, F. and Rodrik, D. (1999) 'Trade policy and economic growth: A skeptic's guide to cross-national evidence', NBER Working Paper W7081, National Bureau of Economic Research, Inc., Cambridge, MA

Samuelson, P. (2004) 'Where Ricardo and Mill rebut and confirm arguments of mainstream economists supporting globalization', *Journal of Economic Perspectives*, vol 18, no 3, pp135–146

Singh, I., Squire, L. and Strauss, J. (1986) *Agricultural Household Models: Extensions, Applications and Policy*, Johns Hopkins University Press, Baltimore

Slaughter, M. J. (2000) 'Trade and labor-market outcomes', *The Economic Journal*, vol 108, no 450, pp1452–1462

Spilimbergo, A., Londono, J. L. and Székely, M. (1999) 'Income distribution, factor endowments, and trade openness', *Journal of Development Economics*, vol 59, no 1, pp77–101

Stiglitz, J. E. (1986) 'Economics of information and the theory of economic development', NBER Working Paper 1566, National Bureau of Economic Research, Inc., Cambridge, MA

Stiglitz, J. E. and Charlton, A. (2005) *Fair Trade for All. How Trade Can Promote Development*, Oxford University Press, Oxford

Thierfelder, K. and Shiells, R. (1997) 'Trade and labor market behavior', in J. F. François and K. A. Reinert (eds) *Applied Methods for Trade Policy Analysis*, Cambridge University Press, Cambridge, pp435–478

Thoenig, M. and Verdier, Th. (2003) 'A theory of defensive skill-biased innovation and globalization', *American Economic Review*, vol 93, no 3, pp709–728

Winters, L. A., McCulloch, N. and McKay, A. (2004) 'Trade liberalization and poverty: The evidence so far', *Journal of Economic Literature*, vol 42, no 1, pp72–115

Wood, A. (1994) *North–South Trade Employment and Inequality*, Clarendon Press, Oxford

Wood, A. (1997) 'Openness and wage inequality in developing countries: The Latin American challenge to East Asia conventional wisdom', *World Bank Economic Review*, vol 11, no 1, pp33–57

Zhu, S. C. and Trefler, D. (2005) 'Trade and inequality in developing countries: A general equilibrium analysis', *Journal of International Economics*, vol 65, no 1, pp21–48

2
Why Did 'Development' Entrap the Doha Round?

Tancrède Voituriez

Introduction

'This meeting has collapsed. Members have simply not been able to bridge their differences' announced Pascal Lamy on Tuesday, 29 July 2008, after more than one week of negotiations on further trade liberalization by World Trade Organization (WTO) members. In particular, the Director General of the WTO said:

> *...there's no escaping the fact that the intensive efforts the whole membership has been putting in over the last days with the aim of establishing modalities in agricultural and NAMA [Non-agricultural market access – viz. industrial goods] have failed... Much has been achieved. Problems that had been intractable for years have been solved. [But] we have not been able to find convergence in the area of Special Safeguard Mechanism (SSM). And we did not even get around to discuss cotton.*[1]

WTO spokesman Keith Rockwell added, after a formal Trade Negotiation Committee (TNC) meeting the day after, that 'the common view all delegations expressed was that they were all disappointed. The common view was that this was going to be most difficult and painful for our poorest members. They all express the desire to preserve what has been achieved in the last 10 days and to build on that in a process for the coming months'. Rockwell adds: 'They really all said that which is quite interesting.'

What is interesting indeed is that an apparently technical issue – the SSM – made the talks collapse while 18 issues had been solved and only one was left to be discussed. More profoundly, it seems that the final disagreement in Geneva was not so much over SSM as over what 'development' actually meant for the negotiating countries. India for instance spoke of a development round as a means for developing countries to 'safeguard livelihood security', as Kamal Nath, the India's Minister of Commerce and Industry negotiator argued '[we, developing countries] need a safeguard mechanism in any event... But the negotiation of a SSM never came.' On the opposite, for developed countries such as the US, a development round rather meant more market openness: 'it would have been a very sad commentary if the conclusion of a development round ... resulted in higher barriers to trade', Susan Schwab, the US Trade Representative replied, 'a real development round involves trade liberalization, not market closing'. The development round was hence conceived as the right for developing countries to protect vulnerable people, with no possible trade-offs with commercial interests, on the one hand, and as the right to access other countries' markets, and especially developing countries markets, on the other. With such opposite targets, both hands could not join and applaud the happy conclusion of the development round.

The development issue facing the world trading system cannot be restricted, however, to the apparent divergence on SSM between US on one side, and India and the G33 group on the other.[2] As Pascal Lamy put it during the last press conference of the July 08 Ministerial, 'Ministers will as usual let you know the visible part of the iceberg. It is my responsibility not to tell you what the invisible part is all about. My experience is that the immersed part becomes visible the meeting after.' Cynics could easily argue that the July Conference failure epitomized the inherent flaw of this round. Nobody was ready to lose power, political credit, jobs and market share in particular sectors for an uncertain outcome amounting to a mere 0.1 per cent of world gross domestic product (GDP) in most estimates, goes the cynical view. And in spite of official regrets, most of the big players felt better off after the talks' failure. Negotiations went beyond the one week format to demonstrate, and pay tribute to, Pascal Lamy's impressive commitment, skill and talent, which were not in doubt. The US stood as a resisting power to emerging countries, and indeed put much of the blame on India and China. These two countries, and particularly the latter, are confirmed as new super trade and bargaining powers. Europe, and to a certain extent Brazil, are confirmed in their role of good-willing, middlemen countries or groups. And African countries are once again the main losers, but in the best position ever to ask for more aid and compensation, the cynic concludes.

An alternative and non-cynical view would support Lamy's conclusions that an agreement was really at hand and that the 'immersed part of the iceberg' temporarily postponed the conclusion of the round. In this line of thought, and beyond the immediate causes of trade talks collapse, we aim in this chapter to identify the root causes of a seemingly uncatchable Doha Round agreement, ever escaping the negotiators' voluntary chase, like the tortoise in Aristotle's fable racing ahead of Achilles' steps.

To do so, we try to answer the following question: What did a 'development round' possibly mean that a traditional round such as the Uruguay Round did not? We start by presenting the theoretical framework within which trade agreements are both needed and self-enforced, drawing on the classical and pioneer work of Bagwell and Staiger (1999). Whether or not the various meanings of development fit in their analytical framework is then addressed. We argue that because developing countries are overwhelmingly small countries, meaning price takers, because they relied extensively on non-reciprocity in deals making, because they tended to focus their demands on rich countries' agricultural subsidy cuts and, last, because of the absence of consensual knowledge on the link between trade liberalization and development, the 'development idea' in its various implications has made the talks collapse.

Some countries, more than others, need to negotiate a multilateral trade liberalization agreement: The Bagwell and Staiger framework

Understanding why countries need a multilateral setting to liberalize their own trade policy is beyond the reach of arguments based on either comparative advantage or protectionist bias. The former asserts that countries committing unilaterally to free trade will see their real income grow irrespective of what other countries do. It hence makes the very existence of the GATT/WTO unnecessary. The latter seeks to explain why some governments are so reluctant to listen to and apply the free trade tenet endorsed by trade economists.[3] The reason why the same governments might be both willing to protect their economy and make efforts to get rid of such protection indeed does not fit in such a framework.

The now well-diffused economic theory of the General Agreement on Tariffs and Trade (GATT) formulated by Bagwell and Staiger (1999) provides both a rationale for multilateral trade agreements such as those signed under the GATT and the WTO, and also for the core principles of the GATT/WTO, namely reciprocity and non-discrimination. Against the then-widespread arguments according to which GATT/WTO trade negotiations were driven by mercantilist interests and hinged hence on bad economics, they demonstrated 1) that the 'weight' given to exporters' interests in the negotiation process, coupled with the reciprocity principle allowed countries to maximize global welfare, and 2) that such a level of global welfare could not have been achieved without a multilateral bargaining process.

The argument goes like this. As we know since Torrens (1844), large countries face the incentive to set non-nil tariffs on imports for those products where they enjoy market power. When set at an appropriate level, large countries' import tariffs reduce import volumes, which in turn depresses world prices, and overall, when compared to the case of a small country whose

Table 2.1 *WTO as a means to escape the prisoners' dilemma situation of large protectionist countries*

		B	
		Free trade	*Protection*
A	Free trade	10\10	−10\20
	Protection	20\-10	−5\−5

import tariffs leave world price unchanged, switches part of the cost incurred by domestic consumers onto foreign exporters. When setting this 'optimal tariff', large countries benefit from an increase in national welfare, while hurting their trade partner whose export revenues decline. For a wide range of situations, the losses of exporters are greater than the gains reaped by the large country. Hence global welfare is hurt while one single country gains from its own protection. This is also called the terms-of-trade externality effect. Strong market positions are used to extract gains at a partner's expense. The external losses – which are nil in the case of a small country – induced by its own protection is simply not taken into account by the large country when setting its import tariff.

Adding up several large countries further worsens global welfare. Retaliation to one large country tariff by another large country leads to a super-tariff war for a wide range of products, to a decline in world prices overall, and to global welfare aggregate loss. It becomes then in the interest of every country to renounce their super tariffs; the problem is that the losses each country would face should the other ones renege on their promises to liberalize trade entrapped them all in a classical prisoners' dilemma situation. A third party is needed to overcome information asymmetries across countries and make them all stick to their commitment to cooperate and liberalize trade, which is in their own interest. Table 2.1 illustrates the different outcomes of the game.

Two countries, A and B, face two policy options: free trade; or optimal protection, that is, a tariff increasing its own welfare but reducing its trading partner's welfare. The first figure in the payoff matrix above is the payoff for country A, while the second is for country B. Each of the two countries can raise its welfare compared to free trade at the expense of its partner. Still, mutual protection is the worst, and most likely, situation. Cooperation toward free trade generates the higher global gains (WTO, 2007, p51).

Bringing large countries' tariffs to the level maximizing global welfare is basically what the multilateral trade liberalization game is all about. The Bagwell and Staiger argument ends like this. Pursuing their own interests, countries open up their market in exchange for reciprocal concessions from their large, trade partner countries. Thanks to the exporters and to their quest for market access, large countries do face incentives to get rid of their optimal tariff. Interestingly enough, the ultimate level of tariffs will not be systematically free trade. The game ends up when the mutual gains from the reciprocal exchange of market access are exhausted, which leaves room for small-country like tariffs – or 'distributive tariffs' –implemented as a means to switch toward producers some of the consumers' welfare without affecting world prices.[4]

Two sets of objections are brought to the Bagwell and Staiger economics of the GATT/WTO.[5] The former disputes the empirical validity of the theoretical framework they propose, and indeed there has been remarkable growth in the empirical testing of the Bagwell and Staiger position. Seminal work by Whalley (1985) showed that the tariff rates prevailing among major powers after the Smoot–Hawley Tariff Act was enacted in 1930 were close to those that would be predicted in the Nash non-cooperative equilibrium. But Regan (2006) contested this finding, interpreting the Smoot–Hawley tariffs as mere political protectionism. When surveying the empirical work, Bagwell and Staiger (2002) cautiously concluded that a 'strong affirmative presumption' existed in favour of the large country, terms-of-trade externality hypothesis. In their head-on empirical investigation of this issue, Bagwell and Staiger (2006) found estimates supporting their theory, but in light of the limitations of their study, they also concluded that it offered 'a first, albeit promising, glimpse at the empirical content of the terms-of-trade theory of trade agreements'. The same year, Broda et al (2006) found evidence that WTO non-member countries systematically set higher tariffs on goods with inelastic supply, from which they inferred that countries are motivated by optimum tariff considerations. But, here again, Regan (2006) contested the result, in particular for their relying on too small a sample of countries (only 15 countries).

The second set of objections put forward complementary, and in some cases substitute theories, to the Bagwell and Staiger framework, which was described as the 'traditional approach' in the WTO World Trade Development 2007 report. Three motives in this report are identified, which explain the commitment of countries toward multilateral trade liberalization. First, exchanging market access, which is the backbone of the Bagwell and Staiger approach. Second, capturing credit for the benefits of trade liberalization: the main argument here is that the market access conceded by trade partners provides a more visible signal (as the idea of 'concession' somehow conveys), and, consequently, a broad support from home exporters. Third, miscellaneous motives such as market size increase (enabling a small country to exploit economies of scale) and insurance provision (against the erosion of market access in a large market) complete the list. We start by applying the Bagwell and Staiger framework to the case of 'development' and 'developing countries', before extending it to issues or concerns not restricted to large countries and optimal tariffs per se.

Why 'development' does not fit in the Bagwell and Staiger framework

Adopted on 14 November 2001, the Doha WTO Ministerial Declaration defines the main objectives of the current trade liberalization negotiation round

– the 'Doha Round'. This round was renamed 'the Doha Development Round' because of the specific ambition pertaining to development and developing countries contained within it.[6] WTO members hence asserted in the introduction of the Declaration:

> 1 *We are determined ... to maintain the process of reform and liberalization of trade policies, thus ensuring that the system plays its full part in promoting recovery, growth and development.*
>
> 2 *International trade can play a major role in the promotion of economic development and the alleviation of poverty. We recognize the need for all our peoples to benefit from the increased opportunities and welfare gains that the multilateral trading system generates. The majority of WTO members are developing countries. We seek to place their needs and interests at the heart of the Work Programme adopted in this Declaration. Recalling the Preamble to the Marrakesh Agreement, we shall continue to make positive efforts designed to ensure that developing countries, and especially the least-developed among them, secure a share in the growth of world trade commensurate with the needs of their economic development.*
>
> 3 *We recognize the particular vulnerability of the least-developed countries and the special structural difficulties they face in the global economy. We are committed to addressing the marginalization of least-developed countries in international trade and to improving their effective participation in the multilateral trading system.*

The objective of harnessing trade for poverty alleviation and development promotion is distinguished from the broad goal of sustainable development found in the Preamble of the WTO. Paragraph 6 of the Declaration restates such a goal, anchoring sustainable development to the environment pillar.[7]

Noticeably, no clear and consensual criteria have been defined to assess whether or not the outcome of trade negotiations is 'favourable to development'. This inherent flaw actually weakened, not to say nullified, the self-enforcing character of trade agreements that arise from Bagwell and Staiger's rationale for the WTO. Oddly enough, neither the GATT nor the WTO has addressed the issue of benchmarking 'development' seriously, as shown by the fact that neither has bothered to define what a 'developing country' is. Any WTO member country can claim to be a developing country provided that no objection is raised by another member. In the negotiation process the lack of clear-cut definition of developing-country members has tremendous implications on the arguments and positions chosen by member states, and particularly by developed countries. While some support a broad definition of 'developing countries', others suggest differentiating emerging countries from lesser developed countries among the whole set of 'developing countries'. For instance, some among the French delegation were overheard questioning the agricultural trade negotiation package, insofar as European Union Common Agricultural Policy (CAP) tariffs would be drastically cut and would be unfair in benefiting primarily large land owners in emerging countries – with Brazil being the implicit case in point.

Defining development not on a country basis (level of income) but as an idea or a concept to which trade openness would be linked could have helped clarify expectations over the Doha Round; but as we see below, both on a country-definition basis and conceptually, the prior commitment to development put WTO negotiations in an awkward position.

Most developing countries are price takers – hence small countries in economic sense

In the Bagwell and Staiger framework, the rationale underlying the principle of reciprocity and justifying the very existence of the WTO is to be found in the inefficiency problem of international cost-shifting. WTO allows countries to escape the terms-of-trade driven prisoners' dilemma. This means that the global inefficiency problem induced by such cost-shifting (from domestic consumers to foreign exporters) arises because some countries are large enough in international markets to alter world prices at the expense of foreign exporters. In this framework, small countries in Staiger's own terms,

> *may not possess this power to any significant degree in most of the markets in which they operate. For these countries, an international trade negotiation may simply have little to offer in the way of the kind of efficiency gains that the larger countries can achieve because the governments of these small countries are already (unilaterally) making trade policy choices that, while potentially very trade-restrictive, are nevertheless efficient from an international perspective, since their choices can't possibly be motivated by international cost-shifting.* (Staiger, 2006, p432)

Hence the problem that international trade negotiations are expected to address may in fact *not* be a problem that the majority of WTO developing-country members face. As consequence, Staiger (2006) acknowledges, 'a central component of the benefit of trade negotiations may not be available to these countries'.[8]

The question then is whether developing countries, or at least part of them, are countries large enough to affect the prices of the products they trade. Evidence on this issue is limited and mixed. Thanks to differentiation, Daniel Gros (1987) observed, it remains possible that even very small countries have the power to alter their terms of trade. Broda et al (2006) inferred from non-WTO members' tariff levels (which are all developing countries) that trade policies were motivated by optimum tariff considerations. But as mentioned above, this study suffers from relying on a limited sample of countries. Until evidence of significant market power by developing countries becomes available, Staiger (2006) concedes, the majority of WTO developing-country members may not be part of the 'problem' that the WTO exists to solve. This said, he adds, 'does not of course by itself imply that they have nothing to gain from WTO negotiations: drawing that conclusion would be a bit like concluding that those who don't own guns have nothing to gain from gun control'.[9] As a conclusion, making an organization provide significant benefits to countries that are not part of the inefficiency problem such an organization exists to address looks overambitious within the Bagwell and Staiger framework.

Subsidy cuts may hurt while tariff cuts don't

Let's go on with the Bagwell and Staiger framework and try to understand how the subsidy cuts in OECD (Organisation for Economic Co-operation and Development) countries, called for by an overwhelming number of WTO developing-country members, became a bone of contention and, eventually, one of the main underlying causes of the July 08 Conference failure.

Subsidies have been a weight on WTO's shoulders from the very beginning of the Organisation. The creation of the WTO was nearly prevented by disputes in the Uruguay Round of GATT negotiations over the issue of negotiating disciplines on agricultural subsidies. The almost official motive behind the disruption of the WTO talks in July 2008 lies in the fact that the SSM flagged by India and other food-import dependent countries was justified – by such countries, and such countries only – to correct for *subsidized* food import surges. Prior to the July 08 Conference, disputes over subsidies that violate existing WTO rules have led to the largest amount of authorized retaliation in GATT/WTO history.

The common analysis over subsidies, Bagwell and Staiger (2004a) argue, was that the GATT subsidy rules were weak and inadequate, while the new disciplines on subsidies that were added to GATT rules with the creation of the WTO represent a significant strengthening of multilateral disciplines towards more global efficiency. This is particularly the case of the subsidies and countervailing measures (SCM) WTO agreement, as well as of rules governing domestic support in the WTO Agreement on Agriculture. Based upon the economic theory of decoupling and targeting, the latter sets apart distorting measures (e.g. coupled agricultural support) from least least-distorting subsidies (e.g. decoupled support). The former are bound and capped, while the latter are not. Even though objections have been made as to whether decoupled support actually had limited distortive effects in situations of market failures, the agricultural policy reforms triggered by WTO subsidy rules are directly inspired by neoclassical economics, and particularly the theoretical principle of targeting, which recommends policies directed toward specific objectives, more efficient than broad measures such as price support (Bureau, 2008). Should countries renounce their coupled support (like public intervention prices, deficiency payments and other output subsidies) and favour instead decoupled support, both national and global welfare should rise together (Dewbre et al, 2001). From this perspective, global efficiency enhancement can be considered as the bedrock of the Agreement on Agriculture subsidy rules.

Why then so much trouble when negotiating their cuts – for the distortive ones – and so many voices calling for their cap – for the decoupled ones? Subsidies, both substantially and procedurally, are different animals from tariffs. Contrary to tariffs, which are almost always 'least-best' policies even in situations of domestic market failures (Bhagwati and Ramaswami, 1963), subsidies are required to address market failures and make the economy get as close as possible to its efficiency frontier. According to the targeting principle indeed, production subsidies are hence almost always a preferred policy instrument to tariffs. As recalled by Bagwell and Staiger (2004a):

> *this is because a production subsidy distorts only one margin (i.e. producer decisions), and can therefore constitute a 'first-best' instrument of intervention in the presence of production distortions, whereas it is well-understood that a tariff distorts* two *margins (i.e. producer* and *consumer decisions) and therefore almost never corresponds to first-best intervention.*

In short, countries need subsidies on the ground of efficiency, they do not need tariffs.

Helping countries to get rid of their 'bad' subsidies may, however, look similar to the objective of trade agreements in Bagwell and Staiger's global efficiency framework, wherein countries through reciprocal market exchange face mutual incentive to eliminate the 'bad part' of their tariff (the part inducing terms-of-trade externality and hurting partners). Reciprocity was the principle allowing countries to give up this globally inefficient part of their protection. A procedural mechanism was hence the solution to the large country, super tariff problem, and this procedural device made market access opening self-enforcing in the Bagwell and Staiger framework. The case is different with subsidies. No reciprocal bargaining is set to help countries renounce their distortive (e.g. coupled) support. Instead, (apparently) substantial criteria such as 'least trade distortive', 'targeting' and 'decoupling' define a one-size-fits-all way of designing domestic subsidies, whatever the size of the country. The capacity of economic science to provide policy makers with uncontroversial criteria for the design of welfare-enhancing domestic subsidies proved crucial in this respect. In a way, both have failed. Doubts rapidly arise around the theoretical effectiveness of decoupling in situations of market failures, and particularly in situations of uncertainty and insurance market incompleteness that are fairly common in agriculture, all the more so in developing countries (Hennessy, 1998). On the other hand, policy makers also fell short of expectations, at least in the making of the 1996 US Farm Bill and the 2003 reform of the EU's CAP, because of their conservative, and partial, allocation of decoupled payments. Their intention to gain support from big farmers for their reforms somehow watered down the idea of decoupling, and by targeting large farms on average, left room for potentially significant cumulative distortive effects. 'Bad' subsidies may hence persist, particularly so among developed economies, stirring up anger from developing countries, whereas reciprocity in market access exchange led to the exhaustion of terms-of-trade externalities.

The 'subsidy problem' becomes even more serious when we contemplate negotiations on both tariff and subsidy cuts, and not on subsidy cuts only. A potential risk is then that misguided disciplines on subsidies would simply redirect public interventions toward the use of second-best instruments such as tariffs. How high such a risk is under WTO subsidy rules compared with GATT subsidy rules is the question Bagwell and Staiger (2004a) addressed. To start with, they recall that the effects of a tariff can be duplicated by a combination production subsidy/consumption tax, so that a government that has access to tariffs as well as a full set of production subsidies and consumption taxes enjoys a degree of policy redundancy. A central question behind the 'subsidy problem' is whether governments have access to a sufficiently rich set of domestic instruments, and therefore a degree of policy redundancy which can be exploited under tariff negotiations. Assuming that this rich set of domestic instruments is available, Bagwell and Staiger show that GATT subsidy rules are sufficient to ensure that an internationally efficient policy combination will be implemented under GATT tariff negotiations. They moreover find that efficiency under GATT tariff negotiations is attained even when responding to subsidies under GATT rules is allowed to be quite costly. Turning then to WTO subsidy rules, and to the SCM specifically, they first argue that the key innovation of the SCM agreement relative to the GATT is that WTO member countries now have the added right to challenge – and, in principle, force the removal of – any positive subsidy. They show that a range of efficient outcomes that were attainable under GATT subsidy rules are unattainable under the subsidy rules of the WTO. 'Intuitively', they write, the 'redundancy of policy instruments is utilized to achieve efficient outcomes through tariff negotiations under the institutional constraints of the GATT subsidy rules, and by introducing the potential that this redundancy will be removed, the WTO subsidy rules interfere with the ability of governments to structure their tariff negotiations so as to achieve efficient policy combinations' (Bagwell and Staiger, 2004a).

They conclude that the key changes introduced by the WTO subsidy rules may ultimately do more harm than good to the multilateral trading system, by undermining the ability of tariff negotiations to serve as the mechanism for expanding market access to more efficient levels. Too low a level of redundancy between subsidies and tariffs under WTO subsidy rules, when compared to the GATT, hampered the mere functioning of market access exchange and ultimately lead to inefficient level of protection and support. Flagged up by developing countries as a provocative anti-development long-lasting feature, too high a level of agricultural protection and subsidies among OECD countries have been relentlessly denounced as both unfair and globally inefficient. The 'subsidy (efficiency) problem' became a 'development problem'. Unsolvable within the current rules and negotiation process, this contributed to a deadlock.

The 'development' idea developed against the very idea of reciprocity

The agenda of developing countries during the GATT era explicitly infringes the reciprocity principle, established in the view of permitting mutually beneficial negotiations of market access exchange among equal (e.g. large) countries in the Bagwell and Staiger framework. This agenda can be typified, Narlikar (2005, p55) wrote, in the statement of the Indian representative in the early times of the GATT: 'Equality of treatment is equitable only among equals. A weakling cannot carry the burden of a giant'.[10] In practical terms, this view translated into the demand for preferential treatment by developing countries in the GATT, which took two forms – special market access for the products from developing countries, and exemptions from GATT obligations. Developing countries demands for preferential treatment generated some successes, Narlikar (2005) emphasizes (Box 2.1).

Let's recall after Staiger (2006) that it is possible that the ability of the WTO to deliver significant benefits for most of its developing-country members is severely limited. Should we consider, as in the Bagwell and Staiger framework, that the problem that the GATT/WTO exists to solve is a large-country problem and that most of the developing-country members of the WTO are small, then indeed 'even an idealized rules-based world trading system would offer little to most of the WTO's developing country members'. In this case, Staiger adds,

> *the exemption from policy commitments that developing country members were granted in the GATT era can be seen in effect as a form of 'benign neglect' granted to them by the developed-country GATT members.*

In this case, Staiger concludes:

> *the majority of developing country WTO members face a two-edged sword: they should resist attempts by the developed countries to get them to offer negotiated policy concessions of their own, but neither should they expect much out of the WTO. In this case, the role of small developing countries as WTO members is essentially to prevent the bigger countries from discriminating against them as these bigger countries use the WTO to find solutions to their problems.*

Box 2.1 The quest for non-reciprocity and exemptions, developing countries in the GATT

The only clause in the GATT that had allowed limited infant industry protection was Article XVIII. This was modified in 1954–55 to include XVIII*b* that allowed countries the use of Quantitative Restrictions for Balance of Payments purposes whenever foreign exchange reserves fell below the level they considered necessary for economic development.

In 1958, the Haberler report was issued to provide guidance for the work of the GATT, and recognized that 'prospects for exports of non-industrial countries in industrial countries, and on balance their development will probably fall short of the increase in world trade as a whole' (cited in Narlikar (2005, p57). As a result of the efforts of developing countries to bring development onto the agenda of the international economic organizations, the 1960s was designated as the UN Decade for Development. Dissatisfaction of developing countries also led to the formation of the UNCTAD in 1964 under the auspices of the UN General Assembly to address the trade and development concerns of developing countries, to correct, by implication, the failures of the GATT in this area.

GATT reacted by incorporating some changes. The Committee on Trade and Development was established in the GATT, and Part IV, devoted specifically to Trade and Development, was added on in 1965. While much of Part IV suggests good intentions rather than obligations, it recognized the principle of non-reciprocity for developing countries.

Institutionalizing this principle further, in 1968, the UNCTAD passed a resolution in favor of an early establishment of a 'generalized, non-reciprocal, non-discriminatory system of preferences'.

The GATT followed in 1971 with a waiver to the Most Favoured Nation (MFN) principle allowing the Generalized System of Preferences (GSP) for the next ten years.

The GSP was given a permanent and legal basis in the GATT in 1979 when the contracting parties agreed to pass the 'Enabling Clause'. The Enabling Clause was simply a waiver to the MFN and reciprocity rules and had been negotiated in the Tokyo Round, accompanied by an inclusion of the 'Graduation Principle'.

The Graduation Principle was an important qualification to the Enabling Clause that ensured that developing countries would be progressively taken off the GSP lists of particular developed countries as they began to show higher levels of development.

Source: Narlikar (2005)

This should not make trade talks collapse, however. What might have done so could instead stem from the fact that the demands of developing countries evolved noticeably during the Uruguay Round and the WTO era, moving from a position of seeking exceptions to their progressive integration as full-right members facing the rights and obligations of the other (large country) members. The case of least developed countries excepted, the Special and Differential Treatment negotiated during the Uruguay Round basically consists in longer implementation and reduced obligations conceded to developing countries, much more than the exceptions per se. 'The challenge of the developing world today seems to be much more nuanced', Narlikar (2005) acknowledges, 'which is based neither on an outright rejection of the reciprocal, multilateralism of the WTO nor a wholesale acceptance of it'. The Doha Round talks can be best characterized by a superimposition of two distinct types of demand – exemption (GATT era) and facilitation (Uruguay Round) –

largely because of the emergence of two main negotiating blocks between the Doha (2001) and Cancun (2003) Conferences, among the various overlapping coalitions of developing countries – namely the offensive exporters (G20) and the defensive importers (G33). The former, led by Brazil, seemed ready to move toward full reciprocity, conceding market access on NAMA against tariffs and subsidy cuts by OECD countries on agricultural products during the last days of the July 08 Conference. The latter somehow stood firm on its developing country status, arguing as India did that it was ready to negotiate commerce, but not livelihood and human security, whatever the imbalances such an exception would generate in the final package of modalities. 'I would like to emphasize the role of the G20', Brazilian negotiator Amorim said during the last G20 press conference at the end of the July 08 WTO Ministerial. 'It's an irony', he adds, that 'many of the achievements come from the G20, providing the main structures, ideas, formulas. The only issue on which the G20 was not able to agree inside the group was the one which took the round to a halt.' Exemption and facilitation-toward-reciprocity stances were not compatible across the 20 issues to be negotiated. Their superimposition mirrors the complexity of the 'developing country' group, which in itself actually does not exist. It lay at the heart of the complexities of the intertwined coalitions of developing countries and eventually prevented consensus.

The trade and development missing link

While all economists share Samuelson's (1939) view that some trade is better than no trade, no scientific statement, with scientific value on par with the comparative advantage theory, provides true and non-trivial predictions of the effects of trade openness on development. Admittedly this is largely because development remains a tricky concept to define and measure. Attempts to substitute 'growth' for 'development' have not proven decisive. Comparative advantages that predict instantaneous gains to any (small) country opening up its trade, say nothing about dynamic gains and growth. And growth theory, focusing on innovation, human capital or research and development, does not make either exports or imports enter its equations. Trade theory is silent about growth and conversely growth theory about trade. No consensual knowledge, liable to guide public policies toward a defined objective (Haas, 1992) – trade liberalization in this particular case – was available to make the trade and development linkage operational in WTO negotiations.[11]

Considering the absence of a theoretical link between trade and development, empirical studies and numerical simulations have multiplied over the last seven years. What has been observed from the launch of the Doha Round is increasing competition among economic research staffs over trade impact simulations according to various 'development' criteria such as country GDP, poverty headcount ratio or real wages in specific industries. OECD and World Bank trade models are no longer the main players in this field, their results being questioned and criticized (Bureau et al, 2006). And the gains from trade derived from competitive simulations and model refinements seem to shrink inexorably (Ackerman, 2005). What we know from all these studies on the impact of trade seems rather trivial: there are gainers and losers from trade liberalization; this is true at country level as well as household level; in some cases, the poorest are the losers, but in some cases only. Lastly, there should be gains for all, but some (households and countries) will have to wait a bit (see Chapter 1).

Strikingly, the indeterminacy of the (freer) trade-development relationship reinforced the pros and cons arguments over trade liberalization and provided a convenient vehicle for opposing ideologies, beyond what the empirical facts cautiously suggested. Some trade economists somehow oversold the benefits of the Doha Round accruing to developing countries, by publicizing free trade gains scenarios as partial trade liberalization scenarios as envisaged in the various WTO drafts.[12] The cheerleaders of globalization, as Rodrik (2007) called them in one of his papers, magnified the gains to be reaped by further liberalization of markets that are actually meagre for poor and rich countries alike. Overselling the pro-poor impact of trade liberalization did more harm than good to the negotiation process itself.

Rodrik (2007) asks:

> *Which is the greatest threat to globalisation: the protesters on the streets every time the International Monetary Fund or the World Trade Organisation meets, or globalisation's cheerleaders, who push for continued market opening while denying that the troubles surrounding globalisation are rooted in the policies they advocate?*

He answers that

> *a good case can be made that the latter camp presents the greater menace. Anti-globalisers are marginalised. But cheerleaders in Washington, London and the elite universities of North America and Europe shape the intellectual climate. If they get their way, they are more likely to put globalisation at risk than the protesters they condemn for ignorance of sound economics.*

Facing much uncertainty on the genuine contribution of further trade liberalization to development (when compared with more efficient domestic institutions and wider space to define, test for and implement *sui generis* policies), developing countries might hence have doubted what actual benefits they would gain from freer trade, while rich countries, even in the case of altruism and genuine interest in dealing a pro-development round, could have seen development gains shrink abroad in exchange for higher market access conceded at home. Acknowledging that 'a government can be expected to abide by commitments it negotiates within the GATT/WTO only if and for as long as it sees doing so to be in its self interest (i.e. GATT/WTO commitments are not meaningful unless they are self-enforcing)' (Bagwell and Staiger, 2004b), the lack of theoretical relationships between trade openness and development, along with the lack of empirical evidence of the significant impact of the former on the latter, made 'development' a political argument more than a sound and undisputable objective fitting the self-interest of WTO member countries.

Conclusion

Starting with the Bagwell and Staiger economics of the GATT, we have tried to look for reasons explaining how 'development' was transformed from a blessing to a curse during the Doha Round negotiation process. We have shortlisted four explanations and hence argued that because developing countries are overwhelmingly small countries, meaning price takers, because they relied extensively on non-reciprocity in deal-making, because they tended to focus their demands on rich countries agricultural subsidy cuts and, last, because consensual knowledge on the link between trade liberalization and development was lacking, the 'development idea' in its various implications has made the talks collapse.

Such hypotheses still need to be formalized in a general equilibrium setting such as in Bagwell and Staiger (1999), and ideally tested. Should they be validated, they provide some insight on the 'immersed part of the iceberg' Pascal Lamy mentioned in his final talk at the end of the July 08 Conference. Most of all, they stress the need either to forget about trade and development and leave it to dedicated UN agencies or Washington institution, or if development really matters, to reframe expectations on trade liberalization impacts on developing countries and adjust accordingly the necessary clarification and reform of the reciprocity principle in practice and of WTO subsidy rules – these two bones of contention – so as to keep WTO agreements both needed and self-enforced as they have proved to be thus far.

Notes

1 All the quotations from the final press conference of the July 2008 Package Conference of the WTO can be consulted on the WTO website, http://gaia.world-television.com/wto/20080721/meet08_webcasting_e.htm.

2 Developing countries are split across various coalitions and groups at the WTO, with some overlap. Brazil, India, South Africa and China headed the creation of the G20 a few weeks before the Cancun WTO Ministerial Conference in 2003, based around an alternative proposal for agriculture to the one put on the table by the US and the EU. Another group that had been set up earlier was the G33, led by Indonesia and which focused on proposals for special and differential treatment and special products. The least developed countries (LDCs) joined other countries from Africa, the Caribbean and Pacific during the Cancun Conference to form the G90. Some countries are members of two groups, hence China and India, which are both members of G20 and G33.

3 Or as Gregory Mankiw from Harvard putting in his *New York Times* Economic View, 13 July 2008: 'A majority of economists ... support free trade. Economists are nearly unanimous in their support for an unfettered system of world trade', Sunday Money, p4.
4 The 'distributive' part of tariffs may indeed remain, meaning tariffs set at such a level that they transfer part of consumer welfare to the producer without affecting world prices as in the classical small country case. As long as the remaining tariffs affect world prices, and as the same situation prevails for another country at least, there exists an opportunity of mutual gains through a further tariff cut. The 'large country' portion of tariffs is hence removed through the reciprocal exchange of market access, while the small country or 'distributive' part is left unchanged.
5 They are all wrapped up in the excellent 2007 WTO World Trade Report; see in particular pp53–64.
6 Panagariya (2002) noted that the main Ministerial Declaration itself uses the expressions 'least developed' countries 29 times, 'developing' countries 24 times and 'LDC' 19 times, while many of the annexes deal with issues of specific concern to developing countries.
7 See www.wto.org/english/thewto_e/minist_e/min01_e/mindecl_e.htm. Paragraph 6 goes like this:

We strongly reaffirm our commitment to the objective of sustainable development, as stated in the Preamble to the Marrakesh Agreement. We are convinced that the aims of upholding and safeguarding an open and non-discriminatory multilateral trading system, and acting for the protection of the environment and the promotion of sustainable development can and must be mutually supportive. We take note of the efforts by members to conduct national environmental assessments of trade policies on a voluntary basis. We recognize that under WTO rules no country should be prevented from taking measures for the protection of human, animal or plant life or health, or of the environment at the levels it considers appropriate, subject to the requirement that they are not applied in a manner which would constitute a means of arbitrary or unjustifiable discrimination between countries where the same conditions prevail, or a disguised restriction on international trade, and are otherwise in accordance with the provisions of the WTO Agreements.

8 Supporting this assertion, Staiger (2006) quotes a study by Subramanian and Shang-Jin Wei (2003), which indicates that membership in the GATT/WTO appears to have large positive and significant trade volume effects for developed countries but little if any systematic effect on the trade volumes of developing-country GATT/WTO members.
9 Details of small countries' motivations to access the WTO conclude Staiger's paper. A first potential role of the GATT/WTO is that of facilitating the *enforcement* of negotiated agreements. A second potential role of the GATT/WTO is that it may serve to provide an environment of reasonably stable and secure property rights over negotiated market access claims, thereby facilitating the negotiation of efficient agreements.
10 Quotation extracted from Narlikar (2005).
11 On this point see Stiglitz and Charlton, 2006; Rodrik, 2007.
12 See in particular the World Bank press presentation of the book *Agricultural Trade Reform and the Doha Development Agenda*, edited by Anderson and Martin (2005) on the World Bank website: 'Tariff reform could deliver annual global gains of $300 billion by 2015, says World Bank study',

http://web.worldbank.org/WBSITE/EXTERNAL/TOPICS/TRADE/0,,contentMDK%3A20716308~pagePK%3A64020865~piPK%3A149114~theSitePK%3A239071,00.html, and its comments by Mark Weisbrot, 'World Bank's claims on WTO Doha Round clarified', www.cepr.net/index.php/press-releases/press-releases/world-bank-s-claims-on-wto-doha-round-clarified/

References

Ackerman, F. (2005) 'The shrinking gains from trade: A critical assessment of Doha Round projections', Global Development and Environment Institute Working Paper 05-01

Anderson, K. and Martin, W. (2005) *Agricultural Trade Reform and the Doha Development Agenda*, The World Bank, Washington DC, and Palgrave MacMillan, Houndmills, Basingstoke

Bagwell, K. and Staiger, R. W. (1999) 'An economic theory of GATT', *American Economic Review*, vol 89, no 1, pp215–248

Bagwell, K. and Staiger, R. W. (2002) *The Economics of the World Trading System*, MIT Press, Cambridge, MA

Bagwell, K. and Staiger, R. W. (2004a) 'Subsidy agreement', National Bureau of Economic Research (NBER) Working Paper 10292, Cambridge, MA

Bagwell, K. and Staiger, R. W. (2004b) 'Enforcement, private policy pressure and the GATT/WTO escape clause', NBER Working Paper 10987, Cambridge, MA

Bagwell, K. and Staiger, R. W. (2006) 'What do trade negotiators negotiate about? Empirical evidence from the World Trade Organization', NBER Working Paper 12727, Cambridge, MA

Bhagwati, J. and Ramaswami, V. K. (1963) 'Domestic distortions, tariffs, and the theory of optimum subsidy', *Journal of Political Economy*, vol 71, no 1, pp44–50

Broda, C., Limao, N. and Weinstein, D. (2006) 'Optimal tariffs: The evidence', NBER Working Paper 12033, Cambridge, MA

Bureau, J.-C. (2008) *La Politique Agricole Commune*, La Découverte, Paris

Bureau, J.-C., Jean, S. and Matthews, A. (2006) 'The consequences of agricultural trade liberalization for developing countries: Distinguishing between genuine benefits and false hopes', *World Trade Review*, vol 5, no 2, pp225–249

Dewbre, J., Anton, J. and Thompson, W. (2001) 'Direct payments, safety nets and supply response: The transfer efficiency and trade effects of direct payments', *American Journal of Agricultural Economics*, vol 83, no 5, pp1204–1214

Gros, D. (1987) 'A note on the optimal tariff, retaliation and the welfare loss from tariff wars in a framework with intra-industry trade', *Journal of International Economics*, vol 23, nos 3–4, pp357–367

Haas, P. M. (1992) 'Introduction: Epistemic communities and international policy coordination', *International Organization*, vol 46, no 1, pp1–35

Hennessy, D. A. (1998) 'The production effects of agricultural income support policies under uncertainty', *American Journal of Agricultural Economics*, vol 80, no 1, pp46–57

Narlikar, A. (2005) *International Trade and Developing Countries: Bargaining Coalitions in the GATT/WTO*, RIPE Studies in Global Political Economy, Routledge, Taylor and Francis Group, London and New York

Panagariya, A. (2002) 'Developing countries at Doha: A political economy analysis', *World Economy*, vol 25, no 9, September, pp1205–1233

Regan, D. (2006) 'What are trade arguments for?: Two conflicting stories told by economists, with a lesson for lawyers', *Journal of International Economic Law*, vol 9, no 4, pp951–988

Rodrik, D. (2007) 'The cheerleaders' threat to global trade', *Financial Times*, 27 March 2007

Samuelson, P. A. (1939) 'The gains from international trade', *Canadian Journal of Economics and Political Science*, Vol V, pp195–205

Staiger, R. W. (2006) Review of *Behind the Scenes at the WTO: The Real World of International Trade Negotiations: Lessons of Cancun*, by Fatoumata Jawara and Aileen Kwa, in *Journal of Economic Literature*, vol 44, no 2, pp428–442

Stiglitz, J. and Charlton, A. (2006) *Fair Trade for All*, Oxford University Press, Oxford

Subramanian, A. and Shang-Jin Wei (2003) 'The WTO promotes trade, strongly but unevenly', NBER Working Paper 10024, Cambridge, MA

Torrens, R. (1844) *The Budget: On Commercial Policy and Colonial Policy*, Smith, Elder & Co, London

Whalley, J. (1985) *Trade liberalization Among Major World Trading Areas*, MIT Press, Cambridge, MA

WTO (2007) *World Development Report 2007*, WTO, Geneva

3

Have Sustainability Impact Assessments of Trade Agreements Delivered on Development Issues? A Reflexive Analysis of the Emergence and Main Contributions of Trade SIAs

Clive George and Colin Kirkpatrick

This chapter was previously published as 'Sustainability Impact Assessment of trade agreements: From public dialogue to international governance', George, C. and Kirkpatrick, C. (2008), *Journal of Environmental Assessment, Policy and Management*, vol 10, no 1, Imperial College Press/WSPC.

The chapter draws on work undertaken for the European Commission (EC) on the development and application of a methodology for assessing the impacts on sustainable development of trade negotiations and agreements. It reviews the work of many individuals and organizations engaged in the EC programme, whose contributions are gratefully acknowledged. The views and opinions expressed are, however, those of the authors alone.

Introduction

Policies for the ex-ante impact assessment of proposed trade agreements have been introduced in Canada, the US and the European Union (EU), following principles for transparency and public involvement established in national legislation for environmental impact assessment (George and Goldsmith, 2006).

These intiatives draw on the experience accumulated for ex-post assessments of the North American Free Trade Agreement (NAFTA) undertaken through the Council for Environmental Cooperation (CEC). For ex-ante assessments of proposed agreements the EU's approach is more complex than its North American equivalents (Kirkpatrick and George, 2006). In the US and Canada Strategic Environmental Assessments (SEA) of trade policy aim to identify potential environmental impacts in the home country, and to a lesser extent in other countries if domestic interests may be affected. This provides trade negotiators with additional information that can be taken into account in developing the country's negotiating position, alongside that available for economic and social issues. The EU's Sustainability Impact Assessments (SIA) extend the scope of the assessment to the EU's trading partners as well as Europe itself, and to economic and social impacts as well as environmental ones. This adds extra complexity to the assessment, and presents extra challenges for its integration into policy formulation. The assessment of impacts in other countries may conflict with a policy process that promotes the European interest in negotiation with those other countries, while the assessment of economic and social impacts may challenge the validity of separate analyses that are carried out as an integral part of preparing Europe's negotiating positions.

Europe's SIA programme was introduced at the initiative of Trade Commissioner Pascal Lamy (later to become Director General of the WTO) during the preparations for the 1999 World Trade Organization (WTO) inter-Ministerial Conference in Seattle. The decision to launch the programme was described by Commisioner Lamy as a response to concerns expressed by European citizens about 'the environmental and social impact of EU policies, globally as well as in Europe' (Lamy, 2003, p6). While accepting that other countries might see the SIA studies as an intrusion, he pointed out that the EC was simply trying to ensure that Europe's negotiators were sufficiently well-informed to take account of the collective preferences of European citizens, which 'place restraints on our negotiating positions'. The SIA studies were intended to contribute to 'greater dialogue between policy makers and civil society as a whole, from NGOs to private-interest lobbies'. The process informs the public dialogue that policy makers take into account when evaluating European collective preferences, alongside parallel economic assessments and direct consultation with key interest groups.

In contributing to the public dialogue the SIA studies aim to ensure that the public is well informed about the likely impacts of EU trade policy. By providing an objective analysis of the significance of potential impacts the studies aim to alleviate unwarranted concerns, while highlighting those of greater significance. Through the associated dialogue policy makers judge whether European collective preferences are sufficiently influenced by the assessed impacts to necessitate the 'restraints on our negotiating positions' envisaged by Commissioner Lamy.

Civil society representatives have expressed a degree of frustration when an impact that is assessed to be significantly adverse fails to stimulate a policy response (WWF, 2002; Birdlife International, 2003; SUSTRA, 2003; WIDE, 2004; RSPB and Solidar, 2005; CRBM et al, 2006). This is primarily a consequence of the role of SIA within the policy formulation process. The studies are not intended to influence policy making directly, but indirectly through their contribution to the public dialogue.

All of the SIA reports are available on the EC website and those of the organizations conducting the studies (see Box 3.1 for a list of the studies).[1] Their findings typically show that some public concerns are unwarranted but reinforce others, including potentially adverse environmental, social and economic impacts in Europe's trading partners and globally. However, it has to be accepted that European trade negotiators do not negotiate on behalf of other countries but on behalf of Europe. Responsibility for action to avoid adverse impacts in other countries rests with the governments of those countries themselves, either through policy measures adopted in parallel with a trade agreement, or through declining to enter into the agreement. Few European citizens express concerns about the impact of EU trade policy on the US. More serious concerns arise for countries that are less well placed to promote their own economic interests, to protect the poorer sections of their societies or to manage their natural environment effectively. A further concern arises when common global or regional interests are not fully recognized within the economic bargaining processes of trade negotiations.

This chapter examines the question of whether an SIA process that assesses impacts in all trading partners is capable of going beyond the promotion of European collective preferences, to promote the interests of all affected citizens and contribute to stronger global or regional governance. It makes use of the experience that has been accumulated during the SIA programme, with particular reference to the studies that have been undertaken for the multilateral WTO negotiations and for the SIA of the Euro-Mediterranean Free Trade Area (EMFTA). Similarities and differences at the global and regional level are identified, which offer pointers for how future SIA studies may be more fully integrated into the formulation of policy for sustainable global and regional development.

Trade liberalization and sustainable development

If the conventional economic argument in favour of free trade were the only consideration there would be no WTO and no trade negotiations (Krugman, 1997). Every country would gain economically from removing its import barriers and export subsidies unilaterally, whether or not other countries did the same. Greater economic efficiency would enable improved social conditions and higher levels of environmental protection. Any country that failed to open its borders would lose, prompting all countries to adopt free trade voluntarily.

Governments place restraints on imports and subsidize the production of tradeable products for a wide range of economic, social and environmental reasons. A country may wish to protect its agriculture and forgo the economic benefit of cheaper imports, in order to preserve the characteristics of rural areas and maintain food security in time of war. It may wish to promote the development of high added-value industries and protect them against imports until they are sufficiently well established to compete internationally. Removing such restrictions negates the benefits of introducing them, and is only done when an equivalent or greater benefit can be negotiated from other countries in return. The negotiating process can become highly political. Coalitions are formed, efforts to break them are made, strategies are revised and negotiating positions are changed, sometimes without opposing groups even noticing (Odell, 2006).

The conventional economic case for trade liberalization is based on the efficiency gains available if each country were to concentrate on producing those goods or services in which it has a comparative advantage. The comparative advantages of high income countries tend to be in high added-value products with high technology content and high skill levels, while those of low income countries are primarily in low wage products and commodities. High income countries benefit by reinforcing existing comparative advantages, while countering any erosion of them by further upgrading of technologies and skills. Developing countries develop by changing comparative advantages, through increasing their competitiveness in activities that earn high wages (Wade, 2003; Rodrik, 2004). Trade liberalization reinforces existing advantages, but may help to change them in the longer term by stimulating the introduction of new technologies and skills. Trade policy in developing countries must therefore draw a balance. Greater participation in international trade offers access to the technological and human capacities needed for development, but domestic industries may need a degree of protection if they are to survive for long enough to acquire those capacities.

The SIA studies show that the economic impacts of trade liberalization may be positive or negative, differing between countries and varying between the short term and the long term, depending on how the balances are drawn for any particular trade agreement. Most of the social and environmental effects occur as a result of the economic ones. These too vary between countries and between short-term and long-term effects, with some of the impacts positive and some negative. The net overall effect on sustainable development depends on how these impacts are weighed against each other, taking into account the different values of the different groups of people that are affected in different ways in different countries and the consequences for future generations. The SIA process contributes to the information on which such value judgements may be based, both in the development of a negotiating position and in the international negotiations.

Countries do not enter into trade negotiations in order to achieve economic efficiency gains. These are readily available from unilateral action, and influence the negotiations only in so far as each country attempts to persuade others that they would benefit from agreeing to its own requests. Those requests aim primarily at increasing export opportunities for the goods and services a country produces, with a focus on those that are of strategic importance for key interest groups or for the country's future development strategy. In return a country will be prepared to reduce import restrictions for goods or services whose importance has declined since the restrictions were introduced.

A country's initial negotiating position will normally aim for greater access to other countries' markets than is likely to be achieved in practice, and will offer less liberalization of its own markets than it may be prepared to accept. The negotiating mandate defines how far negotiators can go in the subsequent process of give and take. The analysis on which the mandate is based must be kept confidential, or the country's negotiating position would be weakened (European Commission, 2002a). The mandate cannot therefore be based on a publicly conducted SIA. It will instead be based on separate analyses and consultative processes whose findings must remain confidential. In Europe these have been formalized under the procedures introduced in 2003 for Impact Assessment (IA) of all major policy proposals (European Commission, 2002b, 2005).

The majority of impact assessments carried out under Europe's IA procedures are in the public domain. They inform policy making directly while also informing the associated public dialogue. For trade agreements, which entail negotiations with other countries, the IA informs policy directly but its analysis and findings are not publicly available (European Commission, 2006b). The separate SIA studies are carried out subsequently as part of the public dialogue. They aim to provide an objective assessment of effects in all three dimensions of sustainable development, in other countries as well as in Europe, in order to provide all sections of civil society with a better understanding of the issues and the potential impacts.

Coverage and content of the SIA studies

Some 20 SIA studies have been undertaken to date in the EU programme (Box 3.1). All of these have been conducted as independent assessments by a variety of external organizations. They include a series of studies for the WTO multilateral trade negotiations mandated by the WTO Ministerial Meeting in Doha in 2001, and SIAs for the EU's regional and bilateral trade negotiations. Further studies are currently being undertaken or are planned for other proposed trade agreements at the bilateral or regional level.

Through the regional and bilateral agreements listed in Box 3.1 the EU and specific countries grant each other lower restrictions on market access than have been agreed multilaterally through the WTO, and make additional commitments on trade-related issues that go beyond WTO requirements. These agreements have to comply with Article XXIV of the General Agreement on Tariffs and Trade (GATT), which defines the conditions under which regional trade agreements (RTA) may be established (WTO, 2007). The WTO defines a region as two or more countries, with no distinction between bilateral agreements and those between larger groups. The most-favoured nation

Box 3.1 European Union SIAs

Pre-Seattle SIAs

Initial development of SIA methodology

- Overview SIA

WTO Doha Development Agenda

Further development of SIA methodology

- Preliminary overview SIA
- Sector studies
  - Agriculture – major food crops
  - Non-agricultural market access – textiles and clothing, non-ferrous metals, pharmaceuticals
  - Competition policy
  - Environmental services
  - Distribution services
  - Forests
  - Agriculture
  - Fisheries
- Final overview SIA

Regional and bilateral SIAs

- EU-GCC (Gulf Cooperation Council)
- EU-ACP (African, Caribbean and Pacific)
  - overview SIA
  - sector/sub-region SIAs
- EU-Chile
- EU-Mercosur
  - preliminary overview SIA
  - sector studies
  - update of overview SIA
- Euro-Mediterranean Free Trade Area
  - overview SIA
  - sector/sub-region studies
- EU-Ukraine
  - global analysis
  - sector studies

Source: Information from www.europa.eu.int/comm/trade

(MFN) principle of the WTO requires that a product made in one member country be treated no less favourably than a similar one produced in another member. Article XXIV permits exceptions to this rule through the formation of a customs union or a free trade area, provided that the preferential treatment applies to 'substantially all trade' between the parties to the RTA, and that any interim arrangements for its establishment are completed within 'a reasonable

Box 3.2 The trade policy agenda

Market access for goods and services

- Agricultural tariffs
- Non-agricultural tariffs
- Trade in services

Rules-based measures

- Trade Facilitation
- Government Procurement*
- Trade and Investment*
- Competition Policy*
- Trade-Related Aspects of Intellectual Property Rights (TRIPS)
- Technical Barriers to Trade (TBT)
- Sanitary and Phytosanitary (SPS) measures
- Rules of Origin
- Subsidies, Anti-Dumping and Countervailing Measures
- Trade and Environment
- Dispute Settlement Mechanism

Removed from the WTO Doha agenda at the Cancun Ministerial meeting in 2003, but may be retained in regional or bilateral negotiations.

Source: Derived from IARC, 2006b

length of time'. All of the EU's regional and bilateral agreements are deemed to comply with these requirements.

Import duties or taxes (tariffs) are the most straightforward form of trade restriction and apply to both agricultural and non-agricultural goods. Services are not easily subjected to import duties, and other restrictions are applied. All forms of trade may also be restricted by other non-tariff measures, subject to WTO rules or to more stringent controls applied through a regional or bilateral agreement. Trade negotiations leading to a new or revised agreement generally cover both tariff reductions and revisions to these rules.

The principal measures for negotiation in the WTO Doha agenda are listed in Box 3.2. A regional or bilateral trade agreement may include the equivalents of any or all of these measures.

Revisions to any of the measures listed in Box 3.2 will have an economic impact, differing between countries. This includes the rules-based measures as well as the direct barriers to trade in goods and services. The economic impact may lead to significant social or environmental impacts. Some measures, such as those on trade and environment or changes to the rules on TRIPS, TBT or SPS, may also have direct environmental effects.

A comprehensive SIA study needs to assess the potential impacts of significant changes in any of these measures. The SIA studies for the WTO Doha agenda (IARC, 2006b) included an overview assessment of all the measures in

Box 3.2, and more detailed examination of those for which the impacts were assessed to be significant. The SIAs for regional and bilateral agreements have covered the market access provisions and any proposed rules-based measures of significant concern.

Two main types of economic effect can arise from any of these components of a trade agreement:

1 The balance of trade between countries is altered by a change in prices or other incentives, causing domestic production to increase for some goods and services and decrease for others, with consequent changes in overall economic efficiency (*static equilibrium effects*).
2 A country's rate of economic growth may be accelerated or decelerated by changes in opportunties and incentives for structural change and economic development (*dynamic development effects*).

Both types of economic effect result in economic, social and environmental impacts. Two further types of impact also occur:

1 The change from one trade equilibrium to another takes several years, with short to medium term economic, social and environmental impacts during the period of adjustment (*adjustment effects*).
2 The changes in economic structure may accelerate or decelerate existing processes of social transformation or environmental change (*social and environmental process effects*).

The SIA studies have assessed these various types of impact through a combination of theoretical analysis and empirical evidence from the literature. The assessment generally begins by evaluating the causal relationships for all aspects of the trade policy agenda. For the static equilibrium effects, particularly those associated with tariff changes, the causal relationships are fairly well understood and have been incorporated into economic models. These are particularly useful for providing quantitative estimates for some of the static equilibrium economic effects, and hence of the associated adjustment effects and their economic, social and environmental impacts. Some of the SIA projects have used the results of economic modelling studies available in the literature, while others have included a modelling analysis within the project. For the other types of impact the assessment is generally more qualitative, supported by quantitative information where available.

The assessment methodology and techniques have been broadly similar for all the studies, both at the multilateral level of the WTO negotiations and for Europe's regional and bilateral trade agreements. In broad terms the findings also tend to be similar, but with different implications for policy responses at the multilateral and regional level. Two of the SIA studies are examined in the next two sections, one at the multilateral level of the WTO negotiations, and the other at the regional level for the EMFTA.

SIA studies for the Doha Round of WTO negotiations

During the preparations for the 1999 WTO Conference in Seattle the EC initiated a preliminary assessment of the impacts on sustainable development of the proposed negotiations. The methodology was developed in early 1999 (Kirkpatrick et al, 1999), building on earlier North American experience of assessing the environmental impacts of trade policy (Government of Canada, 1992; USTR, 1993; OECD, 1994; CEC, 1999). An overview assessment of the Seattle agenda was undertaken prior to the WTO meeting (Kirkpatrick and Lee, 1999). This initial analysis indicated that while an overall economic benefit could be expected, many of the issues that had been raised were genuine cause for concern, and would need fuller investigation during the negotiations.

After the failure of the Seattle Conference, negotiations were subsequently mandated by the WTO Ministerial Meeting in Doha held in 2001. Following further development and refinement of the SIA methodology (Kirkpatrick and Lee, 2002), the EC launched more detailed assessments of all aspects of the Doha agenda.

As summarized in Box 3.1, the programme of studies for the Doha negotiations began with a preliminary overview SIA, proceeded through a series of more detailed sectoral studies, and concluded with a final overview SIA. The preliminary overview study gave an initial indication of the potential significance of likely impacts, which contributed to consultation on the choice of sectors for more detailed assessment. The final overview study drew together the findings of the other assessments and presented overall conclusions and recommendations.

Many economic modelling studies of multilateral trade liberalization had been undertaken before the Doha agenda was launched, using a wide range of approaches, assumptions and approximations. Many other modelling studies became available by the time of the final overview SIA. A comparative analysis of these studies was carried out rather than undertaking an additional modelling exercise specifically for the SIA. The comparative analysis provided quantitative information for the static equilibrium economic effects, covering both the welfare effect of changes in economic efficiency and the magnitude of the production changes occurring during the period of adjustment. These production changes are the principal source of environmental impacts and of short to medium term social impacts.

The key impacts and findings identified in the assessment are summarised in Box 3.3.

The sustainability impacts listed in Box 3.3 tend to confirm the concerns that have been expressed by civil society groups and by developing country governments during the preparations for the Seattle Conference and throughout the Doha negotiations. Since the negotiations were initiated at the end of 2001 they have achieved little progress, and reached an impasse at the Hong Kong Ministerial meeting at the end of 2006, which failed to be resolved at the Geneva meeting in July 2008 (see Chapter 2). Efforts to revive the process have

Box 3.3 WTO SIA programme: Key impacts and findings

Distributional issues

- Most countries experience beneficial impacts for some sections of society, but adverse short term impacts on others.
- Potential aggregate economic welfare gains are not necessarily shared by all countries or all socio-economic groups within these countries.
- The social and environmental impacts are similarly differentiated.

Economic benefits

- The global economic impact from static equilibrium effects is likely to be modest, and smaller than had been predicted in earlier years.
- The global impact on social welfare is modest, with a small reduction in absolute poverty levels in developing countries as a group.
- The potential economic benefits are likely to increase in the longer term, largely as a result of market adjustments to new conditions, productivity improvements and increased investment induced by greater trade openness.
- The impact on poverty reduction is expected to be favourable in some large developing countries, such as India and China.
- As a whole, developing countries are expected to experience an economic welfare gain from the Doha trade liberalization measures. Much of the gain is in large and newly industrializing countries.

Other economic and social issues

- Some countries, particularly in the least developed (LDC) group, are likely to experience an economic welfare loss, at least in the short term.
- The transition period may be associated with increased unemployment or underemployment as labour and capital move from less to more efficient uses.
- The adjustment costs can be severe in developing countries where social protection is weak or absent.
- The least developed countries, particularly in sub-Saharan Africa, are the least able to respond to market opportunities and the least likely to experience longer term economic gains.
- In some of the poorest countries, in sub-Saharan Africa for example, poverty may worsen as they stand to lose economically from trade liberalization and face severe supply side constraints.
- The adverse effects will be particularly severe in countries with high initial levels of protection and little or no comparative advantage in sectors where other countries' markets become more open.
- Most of the adverse effects are likely to be short to medium term, and may be highly significant if liberalization is rapid or not accompanied by effective social policies.
- These impacts may continue into the longer term in the absence of appropriate policies to support the creation of new employment opportunities.
- Countries with high initial protection may also experience a significant loss of tariff revenues, with possible negative indirect social impacts if expenditure on health, education and social support programmes is reduced.
- Women tend to be among the most vulnerable to adverse impacts, although opportunities also arise for higher skilled jobs and improved working conditions.

Environmental issues

- Global environmental impacts are expected to be negative as the volume of international trade increases.
- The impacts on climate change and global biodiversity are adverse overall, arising primarily through increased transport and pressures for increased agricultural production in biologically sensitive areas.
- Local effects in either direction occur for water, air and soil quality, water quantity, soil erosion and biodiversity. Adverse effects are particularly significant in areas of high existing stress.
- The adverse environmental effects can in principle be countered by technology or regulatory measures. However, in many developing countries, environmental regulation tends to be insufficiently strong to counter adverse effects. Similar limitations apply to international agreements on the containment of global environmental impacts.

Mitigating measures

- Areas for support include strengthening domestic capacity in environmental and economic regulation, and adjustment assistance to avoid adverse impacts on social groups that lose from trade-induced changes
- The various aid for trade initiatives that have been proposed need to be integrated in a coherent programme of support which uses trade opportunities as an engine for growth.
- Similar action at the global level is needed to counter adverse impacts on climate change and biodiversity.

Source: IARC, 2006b

entailed reducing the extent of trade liberalization under negotiation to be considerably less ambitious than originally proposed. This outcome is consistent with the study's findings, which indicate that in the absence of effective mitigation and enhancement measures the original proposals offer only small gains with potentially large adverse effects.

The modest extent of the expected economic benefits identified in the SIA contrasts with conventional economic expectations of trade liberalization, resulting from recent developments in economic modelling techiniques (Piermartini and Teh, 2005; Scrieciu, 2007). Before the advent of computable general equilibrium (CGE) models the beneficial effect of trade liberalization on static equilibrium economic efficiency and welfare was well understood, but little quantitative information was available. Early models gave relatively large numbers for multilateral liberalization, although even these were smaller than expected in comparison with the welfare gains occurring at normal rates of economic growth (Weisbrot et al, 2004). The magnitude of the predicted gains has subsequently fallen, primarily because recent modelling studies use assumptions and data that are more realistic than previous ones, and partly because the ambitions for the Doha Round have been scaled down.

The other principal findings indicate that, even when allowing for the potentially larger economic benefits that may result from dynamic development effects, significant intervention is needed through parallel policies in order to deliver those benefits to the countries and social groups in greatest need, and to avoid significant adverse social and environmental impacts occurring as economies adjust to the changes in production levels induced by the reduction of trade barriers. The final overview SIA presented a set of recommendations for the mitigation and enhancement measures that would be needed.

The SIA of the Euro-Mediterranean Free Trade Area

The creation of the EMFTA is a key component of the Euro–Mediterranean Partnership (EMP) between the European Union and ten Mediterranean Partner Countries (MPCs) in the southern and eastern Mediterranean (Figure 3.1). The partnership covers political and safety partnership, economic and financial partnership (including the EMFTA), and social, cultural and humanitarian partnership. Sustainable development has been adopted as one of the EMP's guiding objectives.

As with the other studies at regional or bilateral level, the SIA differed from those conducted for the WTO Doha agenda in needing to cover far fewer countries in addition to Europe (10 instead of 150). As well as allowing a sharper focus in the assessment of impacts this also enabled closer consultation with civil society groups throughout the region.

Figure 3.1 *The Euro-Mediterranean Free Trade Area*

The Mediterranean has a long trading history that has given it a strong regional identity. It has economic, cultural and political ties that predate the origins of European civilization in the cities on its northern shore, trading with, warring with and making peace with the older civilizations to the east and their own trading outposts on the southern and western shores. Many active networks of civil society organizations have been established covering economic, social and environmental issues. Several of these bring together all three parts of the region (North Africa, the Eastern Mediterranean and Southern Europe). Active coordination mechanisms have also been established by Mediterranean parliamentary groups, including members of the European Parliament and of national parliaments in the EU and partner countries.

The consortium formed to carry out the SIA included partner organizations in both North Africa and the Eastern Mediterranean.[2] The Eastern Mediterranean partner based in Beirut (the United Nations Economic and Social Commission for West Asia) made use of its extensive experience of working with regional groups in developing and managing the consultation programme for the consortium as a whole.

The SIA-EMFTA programme (IARC, 2007) consisted of the following elements, each with a report published for public consultation before proceeding to the next stage:

- methodology proposals;
- baseline study;
- development of scenarios;
- regional overview SIA;
- mitigation and enhancement for key issues and sectors;
- sub-regional case studies;
- proposals for a regional monitoring mechanism;
- final SIA report.

The study assessed four components of a trade liberalization scenario for the region. The first three covered removing trade barriers between the EU and partner countries for industrial products, agriculture and services, and the fourth examined their removal between MPCs (South–South trade liberalization).

Many economic modelling studies of trade liberalization in the Mediterranean region were available in the literature, and no additional modelling was needed specifically for the SIA. A comparative analysis of these studies provided quantitative information on the static equilibrium effects similar to that obtained for the WTO studies. Assessment of the longer term dynamic effects was based primarily on qualitative analysis.

The key impacts identified by the study are summarized in Box 3.4.

Box 3.4 Key potential impacts of the EMFTA

Impacts in the European Union

- A small net gain in economic welfare for industrial products. For agriculture, services and south–south liberalization the additional impact on welfare for the EU is close to zero.
- Potentially larger economic gains in the longer term for services, and to some extent for industrial products. These are dependent on individual investment decisions and other aspects of economic and development policy in both the EU and MPCs.
- Potentially adverse social effects arising from agricultural liberalization, restricted to local areas of EU Mediterranean countries (Spain, Greece, Italy, Portugal and southern France, and probably also Cyprus and Malta).
- In some areas the affected workers will include temporary migrants from MPCs, with a knock-on effect on social issues in MPCs.
- The social impacts will be associated with local environmental impacts, which are expected to be beneficial for water consumption and biodiversity, and potentially adverse for amenity value.

Impacts in Mediterranean Partner Countries

- A small beneficial impact on economic welfare in most countries, although a short term negative effect is possible in some countries.
- Greater increases in welfare may occur in the long term, but these are strongly dependent on domestic reforms and investment decisions. There are large potential economic benefits from fuller regional integration, but to achieve them, other policy measures are needed in addition to South–South trade liberalization.
- Some beneficial social and environmental impacts occur in both the short term and the long term, accompanied by others that may be significantly adverse unless effective mitigating action is taken.

The potentially adverse impacts of greatest concern are:

- a significant rise in unemployment, particularly for liberalization of EU–MPC trade in industrial products and agriculture, and to a lesser extent for services and South–South liberalization;
- a fall in wage rates associated with increased unemployment;
- a significant loss in government revenues in some countries, with consequent social impacts through reduced expenditure on health, education and social support programmes;
- higher environmental and social stress in cities, resulting from declining rural employment and accelerated rural-urban migration;
- greater vulnerability of poor households to fluctuations in world market prices for basic foods;
- adverse effects on the status, living standards and health of rural women, associated with accelerated conversion from traditional to commercial agriculture;
- significant adverse local impacts on water resources, soil fertility and biodiversity in areas of high existing stress;
- higher air pollution and coastal water pollution from greater international transport;
- higher waste generation from greater use of packaging materials.

Many of these potential impacts occur primarily in the short or medium term, which may be as long as ten to fifteen years over the full period of adjustment. Unless effective action is taken in the short term, some impacts may continue into the long term.

Global environmental impacts

- An overall adverse impact on climate change, arising primarily through increased transport and greenhouse gas emissions.
- An overall adverse impact on global biodiversity, through pressures for increased agricultural production in biologically sensitive areas in MPCs.

Both of these scale effects can in principle be countered by technology or regulatory effects. In itself, the EMFTA does not include measures which will strengthen these positive effects sufficiently to counter the adverse ones.

The study indicates an overall economic gain for the EU and MPCs combined, part of which could be directed towards parallel actions to mitigate the expected impacts.

Source: IARC, 2007

Many of the potential impacts listed in Box 3.4 were published as preliminary findings during preparations for the Ministerial Conference of the Euro–Mediterranean Partnership in 2005. Several civil society organizations and parliamentary groups referred to these preliminary SIA findings in their pre-conference representations to the EC and MPC governments.[3] No evidence has been identified to indicate whether or not these representations or the SIA itself influenced the outcomes of the conference directly, but the action plan that it agreed reflected several of the preliminary SIA recommendations (IARC, 2006a).

The overall conclusions presented in the final report of the study are summarized in Box 3.5.

Box 3.5 Overall conclusions of the SIA-EMFTA

- In parallel with other strategic measures at the national and regional level the EMFTA is capable of making a major contribution to achieving the objectives of the Euro-Mediterranean Partnership and hence to the sustainable development of the region.
- Implementation of the EMFTA on its own will make only a small contribution to the economic objectives of the EMP, and needs to be accompanied by appropriate parallel measures if significant adverse social and environmental impacts are to be avoided at the local, regional and global level.
- The parallel measures that are necessary to enhance the beneficial effects of the EMFTA and to avoid significant adverse impacts include actions both at the regional level and nationally in each of the partner countries.
- In order for the EMFTA to make its full potential contribution to the sustainable development of the region, the Euro-Mediterranean Partnership itself needs to be re-invigorated and re-directed towards clearly defined economic, social and environmental goals for each of the partner countries and for the region as a whole.
- Any such re-invigoration of the Euro-Mediterranean Partnership should be based on a strategic review of its objectives and of the interactions between the EMFTA and the other components of the Partnership in contributing to those objectives.

Source: IARC, 2007

The conclusions summarized in Box 3.5 suggest a lack of integration between trade policy and other regional initiatives, which limits the potential gains available from the EMP and risks significant adverse social and environmental impacts occurring from its trade liberalization component.

The EMP has the goal of fully implementing the EMFTA by 2010. For liberalization of trade in industrial products, bilateral agreements between the EU and most of the partner countries were concluded prior to the SIA study, along with the development of trade agreements between MPCs. For this component of the liberalization scenario the prime aim of the study was to identify mitigation and enhancement measures that could be applied in parallel with implementation of the agreements. Negotiations for agriculture and services were launched subsequently and are still in progress.

Impact assessment and the formulation of trade policy

The EC has undertaken to publish positioning papers giving its response to each of the SIA studies after full interdepartmental discussion of the recommendations. Papers have been published to date for the SIA of the EU-GCC (Gulf Cooperation Council) negotiations and for several of the sectoral studies for the WTO Doha agenda.[4] Responses are not yet available for the final overview SIA of the WTO negotiations or for the SIA-EMFTA.

Typical responses for the WTO sectoral studies fall into one of five main categories:

- New action is proposed.
- Possible new action is under consideration.
- More detailed analysis is needed before decisions on action can be taken.
- Sufficient action is already being taken.
- The Commission disagrees with the SIA findings.

Proposed actions in the first group tend to be non-specific, such as raising the awareness of EC delegations. This suggests that the SIA studies have yet to have a major direct influence on the EC's negotiating positions.

The EC has stated in a recent communication that it aims to 'build a more comprehensive, integrated and forward-looking external trade policy that makes a stronger contribution to Europe's competitiveness' (European Commission, 2006a). The communication states that those aspects of the WTO Doha agenda that were rejected by developing countries at the Cancun Conference in 2003 (investment, public procurement, competition policy and more stringent rules on intellectual property rights) will be pursued through bilateral and regional trade agreements. The EC will 'continue to factor other issues and the wider role of trade policy in EU external relations' into these agreements, 'but in order for trade policy to help create jobs and drive growth, economic factors must play a primary role'.

The EU's approach to SIA of trade policy is conducted publicly, assesses impacts in all affected countries and is intended to be impartial. This creates potential conflicts with a negotiating process that is necessarily confidential and gives priority to the EU's economic interests. The EC does not expect its negotiating positions to be completely different from the results of an SIA, but it accepts that there will be inconsistencies (European Commission, 2002a). Under the mechanism it has established for resolving such inconsistencies the Commission modifies its negotiating position if it considers the result to be robust, but otherwise it may not. In view of the high levels of uncertainty inherent in strategic impact assessments at the policy level (Partidario, 2000) there is considerable scope for rejecting the findings of SIA studies on these grounds.

At the regional level of the EMFTA there are indications that the SIA findings may have had some influence on the negotiations, via representations from civil society groups and from parliamentarians in the EU and MPCs rather than through any observable change in Europe's negotiating position. At the multilateral level of the WTO Doha agenda negotiating positions have moved towards less ambitious proposals, because of limited progress in the negotiations rather than in response to the SIA findings.

The two examples examined above are fairly typical of all the SIA studies in showing that appropriately designed trade reforms have the potential to make a significant contribution to the development of developing countries, and, with appropriate parallel measures, can do so in an environmentally sustainable manner. It has proved difficult to realize these goals through a negotiating process in which the prime aim of each party is to maximize its own economic competitiveness in relation to the others. If international trade is to be steered more closely towards sustainable development goals the negotiating process needs to be constrained by stronger policy in non-trade areas.

Possible future directions for impact assessment of trade policy

Trade negotiators are not responsible for halting climate change, preventing global biodiversity loss or reducing world poverty. They operate under the assumption that increasing international trade improves economic performance and increases the resources that can be devoted to these issues, but responsibility for addressing them lies elsewhere. Trade agreements can readily comply with international environmental agreements or labour standards, but do not define them, and may interpret any lack of precision in a way that is favourable to trade. In negotiating a trade agreement negotiators aim for an outcome that is favourable for their own country, and often for particular economic interests in that country. The SIA process as currently established contributes to the public dialogue, but it does not necessarily contribute to the negotiations or their outcomes. The mandate for Europe's trade negotiators is based on separate impact assessments, the findings of which are confidential.

The two forms of impact assessment used by the EC to assess its trade policy are not incompatible with each other. The IA process contributes to the development of a negotiating mandate, while the SIA process contributes to a public dialogue that may influence the application of that mandate. The SIA studies also provide information that non-trade policy makers may use in developing measures to counter any adverse impacts of trade policy in Europe and elsewhere, or measures that combine with trade policy to enhance the potential benefits. Integrating the two IA processes could in principle provide a better environment for policy learning in both trade and non-trade areas (Ruddy and Hilty, 2008). It would, however, necessitate developing means by which the combined process would retain sufficient confidentiality to protect Europe's negotiating positions, while remaining sufficiently transparent to make a meaningful contribution to the public dialogue.

The principal difficulties of steering trade policy towards sustainable development goals lie in the lack of international agreements in non-trade areas that are sufficiently strong to restrain trade policy from having adverse impacts in those areas. Until such time as parallel mechanisms of global and regional governance have been strengthened IAs can play only a limited a role (George, 2007). That role may, however, be extended by wider use of the techniques that the EC has pioneered.

The findings of the EU multi-country studies have tended to be insufficiently specific to influence policy in developing countries, and are not necessarily trusted by policy makers in those countries. They have, however, highlighted areas of concern that may be studied in more depth using similar methods by each country individually in the preparation of its own negotiating position. The United Nations Environment Programme (UNEP) has led a programme to help build capacity in developing countries for undertaking integrated IAs of this nature, with the support of the EC (UNEP, 2006). An expansion of such assistance may be particularly beneficial for smaller developing countries and least developed countries, which do not currently have the capacity to support their negotiators with detailed assessments of the impacts of other countries' proposals, or even of their own proposals.

This would assist developing country negotiators in some respects, but it would not remove an inherent problem in the development of trade policy. In developing countries as well as in developed ones, negotiating positions tend to be strongly influenced by the interests of key economic actors. Social and environmental issues at the local, regional and global level often receive little attention even when reliable information is available.

Multi-country SIA studies similar to those undertaken for the EC might make a larger contribution to addressing this problem if undertaken on behalf of the wider international community, rather than being commissioned by one of the main negotiating parties. Such studies might for example be commissioned jointly by a group of international bodies such as UNEP, United Nations Development Programme (UNDP), International Labor Organization (ILO), World Health Organization (WHO), United Nations Industrial

Development Organization (UNIDO) and United Nations Conference on Trade and Development (UNCTAD), with a joint steering committee to supervise the process, and the WTO and other relevant international bodies invited to participate as observers. The findings of such studies would have no mandate to influence the WTO negotiations directly. However, they may carry sufficient weight and credibility to reinforce the pressures that are brought to bear by concerned parliamentarians and global civil society as a whole. This in turn may contribute to wider understanding of the relationships between trade, development and environment, and to the evolution of global mechanisms through which their interactions can be managed more effectively.

Stronger initiatives may be taken at the regional level. In the Mediterranean region the EU and its partner countries cooperate through the EMP. This pursues a wide range of development objectives, of which the creation of a free trade area is just one component. In parallel the EU and partner countries have developed a Mediterranean Strategy for Sustainable Development (UNEP/MAP, 2005). Further refinement of the sustainable development strategy, and its adoption as the defining strategy of the EMP, would allow trade policy to be made subordinate to sustainable development and steered more strongly towards sustainable development goals. A similar approach might be taken for other regional agreements, such as between the EU and ACP countries or between other OECD countries and developing countries.

Conclusions

Many of the studies undertaken in the EU's SIA programme have shown that the economic benefits that have traditionally been expected from the efficiency gains of trade liberalization are small, and that significant adverse impacts can occur in the absence of effective parallel policies at both national and international level. These findings have not had a major influence on trade negotiations, in which each country's prime aim is to maximize its own economic competitiveness. The principal difficulty of steering trade policy towards sustainable development goals lies in the relative weakness of international governance in non-trade areas. The chapter has identified steps through which the IA techniques pioneered by the EC may make a stronger contribution to addressing this shortcoming at both global and regional levels.

Notes

1 The reports can be accessed via the DG Trade website and the SIA website maintained by Manchester University Impact Assessment Research Centre (www.europa.eu.int/comm/trade, www.sia-trade.org).

2 The SIA-EMFTA consortium comprised IARC (University of Manchester, lead partner), ESCWA (Beirut), CITET (Tunis), ODI (London), Bocconi University (Milan), Deloitte-Touche (Copenhagen), CIHEAM (Montpellier).

3 The Euro-Mediterranean Parliamentary Assembly Resolution on Economic and Financial Issues, Social Affairs and Education (21 November 2005) was

formulated 'having regard to the Executive Summary of Phase 2 of the Sustainability Impact Assessment Study of the Euro-Mediterranean Free Trade Area'.

4 The EC's positioning papers are available at: http://ec.europa.eu/trade/issues/global/sia/studies_wto.htm.

References

CEC (1999) 'Final analytical framework for assessing the effects of the North American Free Trade Agreement (NAFTA)', Commission for Environmental Cooperation, Montreal

CRBM, FOEE, Greenpeace and WIDE (2006) 'Learning lessons from sustainability impact assessments', Statement by Campaign to Reform the World Bank, Friends of the Earth Europe, Greenpeace International and Women in Development Europe for the Trade SIA Stocktaking Conference, Brussels, 21–22 March 2006

EC (European Commission) (2002a) 'Communication from the Commission on impact assessment', COM(2002)276, European Commission, Brussels

EC (2002b) 'Sustainability impact assessment', Directorate General for Trade, European Commission, Brussels, www.europa.eu.int/comm/trade/issues/global/sia/index_en.htm, accessed 10 July 2008

EC (2005) 'Impact assessment guidelines', SEC(2005)791, European Commission, Brussels

EC (2006a) 'Impact assessment in practice', European Commission, Brussels, http://ec.europa.eu/governance/impact/practice.htm, accessed 10 July 2008

EC (2006b) 'Global Europe: Competing in the world. A contribution to the EU's growth and jobs strategy', Communication from the Commission to the Council, the European Parliament, and the Committee of the Regions, European Commission, Brussels

George, C. (2007) 'Sustainable development and global governance', *Journal of Environment and Development*, March, vol 16, no 1, pp102–125

George, C. and Goldsmith, B. (2006) 'Impact assessment of trade-related policies and agreements: Experience and challenges', *Impact Assessment and Project Appraisal*, vol 24, no 4, pp254–258

Government of Canada (1992) NAFTA 'Canadian Environmental Review', Ottawa

IARC (2006a) 'Final global overview trade SIA of the Doha Development Agenda', Impact Assessment Research Centre, University of Manchester

IARC (2006b) 'Sustainability impacts of the Euro-Mediterranean Free Trade Area: Final report on Phase 2 of the SIA-EMFTA project', Impact Assessment Research Centre, University of Manchester

IARC (2007) 'Sustainability impact assessment of the Euro-Mediterranean Free Trade Area: Final report of the SIA-EMFTA project', Impact Assessment Research Centre, University of Manchester

Kirkpatrick, C. and George, C. (2006) 'Methodological issues in the impact assessment of trade policy: Experience from the European Commission's SIA programme', *Impact Assessment and Project Appraisal*, vol 24, no 4, pp325–334

Kirkpatrick, C. and Lee, N. (1999) 'WTO New Round: Sustainability impact assessment study (Phase Two report)', Institute for Development Policy and Management (IDPM), University of Manchester

Kirkpatrick, C. and Lee, N. (2002) 'Further development of the methodology for a sustainability impact assessment of proposed WTO negotiations (final report)', IDPM, University of Manchester

Kirkpatrick, C., Lee, N. and Morrissey, O. (1999) 'WTO New Round: Sustainability impact assessment study (Phase One report)', IDPM, University of Manchester

Krugman, P. (1997) 'What should trade negotiators negotiate about?', *Journal of Economic Literature*, vol 35, pp113–120

Lamy, P. (2003) 'Proceedings of EC seminar on SIA of trade agreements: Making trade sustainable?', Brussels, 6–7 February 2003, http://ec.europa.eu/comm/trade/issues/global/sia/seminar.htm, accessed 10 July 2008

Odell, J. S. (2006) (ed) *Negotiating Trade: Developing Countries in the WTO and NAFTA*, Cambridge University Press, Cambridge

OECD (1994) 'Methodologies for environmental and trade reviews', Organisation for Economic Co-operation and Development, Paris

Partidario, M. (2000) 'Elements of an SEA framework: Improving the added value of SEA', *Environmental Impact Assessment Review*, vol 20, pp647–663

Piermartini, R. and Teh, R. (2005) 'Demystifying modelling methods for trade policy', WTO Discussion Paper No 10, World Trade Organization, Geneva

Rodrik, D. (2004) 'Growth strategies', Harvard University John F. Kennedy School of Government, http://ksghome.harvard.edu/~drodrik/growthstrat10.pdf, accessed 10 July 2008

RSPB and Birdlife International (2003) *Trade and Environment: Sustainable Development and Sustainability Impact Assessments*, Royal Society for the Protection of Birds (RSPB), The Lodge, Sandy, and Birdlife International, Cambridge

Ruddy, T. F. and Hilty, L. M. (2008) 'Impact assessment and policy learning in the European Commission', *Environmental Impact Assesessment Review*, vol 28, pp90–105

Scrieciu, S. (2007) 'How useful are computable general equilibrium models for sustainability impact assessment?', in C. George and C. Kirkpatrick (eds) *Impact Assessment and Sustainable Development: European Perspectives and Experience*, Edward Elgar Publishers, Cheltenham

Solidar (2005) 'Trade for decent work – decent life: Assessment before agreement', Statement for the 6th Ministerial Conference of the WTO, Hong Kong

SUSTRA (2003) 'Sustainability impact assessment', Policy Briefing Paper, Trade, Societies and Sustainable Development Network

UNEP (2006) *Economics and Trade Branch Bulletin*, issue no 20, Geneva, www.unep.ch/etb/ebulletin/ebulletin_issues/ebulletin20_EN.pdf, accessed 10 July 2008

UNEP/MAP (2005) 'Mediterranean strategy for sustainable development', UNEP(DEC)/MED WG. 277/4, United Nations Environment Programme Mediterranean Action Plan, Athens

USTR (1993) 'The NAFTA: Report on environmental issues', Office of the US Trade Representative, Washington DC

Wade, R. H. (2003) 'What strategies are viable for developing countries today? The World Trade Organization and the shrinking of "development space"', *Review of International Political Economy*, vol 10, no 4, pp621–644

Weisbrot, M., Rosnick, D. and Baker, D. (2004) *Poor Numbers: The Impact of Trade Liberalization on World Poverty*, Center for Economic Policy and Research, Washington DC

WIDE (2004) 'Joint NGO statement on sustainability impact assessments of EU trade policy', Network Women in Development Europe (WIDE), Brussels

WTO (2007) 'Regional Trade Agreements: Goods rules: The basic rules for goods', www.wto.org/english/tratop_e/region_e/regatt_e.htm, accessed 10 July 2008

WWF (2002) 'Changing the balance of trade', Proceedings, Seminar on Sustainability Assessment of EU Trade Policy, Brussels, 9–10 July 2002, http://assets.panda.org/downloads/july2002balancedtradeproceedings_mt0n.doc, accessed 10 July 2008

Part 2
The New Challenges of Trade Liberalization: Beyond SIA

4
Trade SIAs and the New Challenges of Trade Liberalization

Tancrède Voituriez, Paul Ekins, Hernan Blanco, Ingmar Von Homeyer and Dirk Scheer

Introduction

In spite of the substantial developments made in Trade SIA methodology since its inception in 1999, as noted in Chapter 3, Trade SIAs have not made the contribution to the European Union's trade negotiation position that might have been expected. Indeed, the EU position in trade negotiations remains objected to for its conservative and protectionist stance, particularly in the agricultural sector, and for its aggressive bargaining on market access in bilateral negotiations such as those undertaken under the controversial framework of Economic Partnership Agreements – all such positions being taken in a way *against* the conclusions of Trade SIAs. It looks as if Trade SIAs did little to ease the negotiation process, and the negotiators did not ask much of Trade SIAs. We argue in this chapter that these two failures are linked and, in particular, that Trade SIAs do little to benefit trade negotiations because they fail to address a number of important factors that cause negotiators to resist free trade today.

The main contribution of this chapter lies in streamlining the different motives against free trade from a sustainable development perspective. The underlying intuition is that not all motives to resist trade liberalization are equally valid, and that assessing the validity of negotiating positions from a sustainable development perspective, prior to assessing the impacts of trade agreements per se, is a prerequisite to improving the sustainable development component of trade agreements as called for by the European Council Decision and by the Preamble of the Agreement establishing the World Trade

Organization (WTO). Our proposition also seeks to respond to the criticism of current Trade SIAs according to which 'in order for the SIAs to have any policy relevance, the current [handbook] must be amended to recommend that SIAs are to be integrated *before* and *during* the negotiations ... but certainly not *after*, since this would prove politically irrelevant'.[1]

We start in the next section by describing the implicit assumptions made in Trade SIAs regarding governments' decisions, then we compare them to what mainstream political economy suggests, and finally argue for bridging the gap between these two. The following section outlines what such a bridge would look like, providing a tentative framework wherein the different motives to depart from free trade are listed. Identifying among them what would be the genuine sustainable development motives is the difficult task that the third section comments on and argues for. The fourth section summarizes a number of methodological implications for the Trade SIA approach. The final section concludes with suggestions for further research and development of Trade SIAs.

Trade SIAs and political choice

Governments face a complex range of arbitrations, not only between different kinds of impacts within each group of actors, but also between groups of actors (producers, taxpayers, consumers, etc.), facing changing types of impacts. National benefits and damages arising from trade liberalization are not uniformly distributed among the population. If a liberalization scenario brings net positive impacts but if these impacts are unequally distributed, it is likely that the scenario will face decisive political opposition. Matching the likely impacts of trade liberalization with the preferences of each group of actors, and reconciling these with broader commitments to achieve sustainable development is the challenge facing trade negotiators under the auspices of the WTO.[2]

The implications of a rule-based approach of trade liberalization for welfare, rights, choices, can be socially desired or not. Ideally the government should not only know the future impacts of trade liberalization in 'economic', 'social' and 'environmental' terms, but it should also be able to map the gains and losses across different economic groups. A relevant type of information Trade SIA should provide in this respect is a mapping of the relationships between different types of liberalization options (tariff reduction, domestic support decoupling, sanitary regulation, etc.) and the distributional effects among different economic agents, including non-monetary effects. For instance, the perception of 'losses' induced by environmental pollution, and consequently, the implicit demand for policy intervention, can vary across different levels of income groups, whose relative share in national income is likely to be affected by trade liberalization. To account for this circular relationship, the impact of trade liberalization on income distribution and on the environment should not be conducted separately. The three sustainable development pillars should be integrated within one single evaluation process.

The question Trade SIAs have addressed so far seems, however, to be the following: if one liberalizes an economic sector, what are the consequences going to be on the environment, on social and economic indicators or proxies? The implicit assumption is that governments make arbitrage between these three sets of variables, considering one after the other. By assessing impacts on the three pillars of sustainable development (economic, social, environmental) separately, Trade SIAs seem to define governments' decision process in terms of balancing, say, 'good' environmental impacts with 'bad' social impacts, a thankless task because of the reciprocal relationships between these two. As Olivier Godard (2008) notes,

> *sustainable development is presented as founded on three pillars: economic development, environmental protection, social equity, hence the famous 'triple bottom line' concept adopted by business. Although this metaphor is well diffused and allows a first approach, it leads to misconceptions to two regards: it looks as if the three pillars have the same conceptual status regarding the goal of sustainable development and it shows each pillar as independent of the others and self-supporting.*

Mapping the relationships between the distributive impacts of trade and changes in sustainable development concerns or 'preferences' among economic groups is a still open empirical field of research. On the one hand, the political economy of trade liberalization seldom includes the environment among the preferences of pressure groups, and focuses instead on economic objectives: 'Industry associations, labour unions, consumer lobbies and government agencies all interact in determining the policy outcome' underline Hoekman and Kostecki in their reference book on the political economy of the WTO (Hoekman and Kostecki, 2001, p29). Strikingly, no mention is made of environmental lobbyists, and implicitly of environmental concerns, in their list of pressure groups. 'The WTO is somewhat analogous to a mast to which governments can tie themselves to escape the siren-like calls of various pressure groups' (Hoekman and Kostecki, 2001, p29). Basically, environment is a by-product of trade and of production processes, which should be addressed as a 'first best' through targeted, domestic policies. Environment is not a trade issue as such; it only becomes so in a second-best world. Economic objectives come first.

On the other hand, environmental economics awkwardly considers distributive issues. In fact, Godard argues, the core issue of sustainable development is about finding social and technical ways to harmonize environmental protection and economic development. To this regard, he insists, social equity, in the distributive or procedural meaning, belongs to the category of means to achieve the goal: conceptually, 'there was no need to introduce the concept of sustainable development to put distributive issues and concern for equity at the forefront of development'. Godard concludes:

> *If we try to get a deeper understanding of the conceptual renewal associated with the goal of sustainable development, we shortly discover that the true stake we should explore is the one for which the consideration of the environmental pillar is reframing the way we understand the logic and landmarks of the other two: what are the new stakes and the new directions in thinking about social equity when we introduce environmental issues in the landscape? What are the new stakes and the new directions in thinking about economic development when we introduce environmental issues in the landscape? And on top, what about re-thinking development when the two previous questions are taken together? This is what sustainable development is about.* (Godard, 2008)

Environment comes first.

Between the political economy approach of trade policies that focuses on economic gains and losses, and the too-limiting assumptions of Trade SIAs over the variables of political choice scattered throughout 'economic', 'environmental' and 'social' effects, a bridge is to be built. Bridging these two strands of expertise and literature would lead to integrate more political economy into Trade SIAs, meaning focusing more on gainers and losers, and conversely to open our understanding of the political economy of trade negotiations through the integration of non-market impact variables, which would allow for a more comprehensive accounting for what gainers and losers feel as gains and losses in environmental terms.

To help do so, we proceed in two steps. We investigate first the main motives for governments to resist free trade in a second-best world. Then we turn to the issue of establishing whether such motives are valid from a sustainable development perspective, that is, do they contribute or not to fulfil the overarching sustainable development objective assigned to trade liberalization within the WTO multilateral framework?[3]

Identifying motives to depart from free trade

Motives to depart from free trade have been a puzzling feature for decades not to say centuries now – at least for trade economists. One can recall the famous words from Krugman (1997, p113), 'If economists ruled the world, there would be no need for a World Trade Organization: ... global free trade would emerge spontaneously from the unrestricted pursuit of national interest'. To isolate motives to depart from free trade, one has to separate explanations about certain countries' reluctance to engage in liberalization, from explanations about the inability of a trade agreement or an organization such as the WTO to commit its contracting parties and/or members to go further down the free trade road.

The former set of explanations is centred on states' implicit preferences against further liberalization. It almost ignores other states' preferences and tries to explain why 'the compelling economic case for unilateral free trade carries hardly any weight among people who really matter' (Krugman, 1997, p113). There, the economic case for liberal trade is essentially unilateral: a country serves its own interests by pursuing free trade regardless of what other countries may do. Trade treaties are odd and paradoxical features of international relations. Anyone who has tried to make sense of international trade negotiations, Krugman adds,

> *eventually realizes that they can only be understood by realizing that they are a game scored according to mercantilist rules, in which an increase in exports – no matter how expensive to produce in terms of other opportunities foregone – is a victory and an increase in imports – no matter how many resources it releases for other uses – is defeat. The implicit mercantilist theory that underlies trade negotiations does not make sense on any level, indeed it is inconsistent with simple adding-up constraints but it nonetheless governs actual policy.* (p114)

In practice, Krugman concludes, 'this particular set of bad ideas has led to pretty good results'.

The second set of explanations focuses on multilateral trade institutions, agreements and rules. It seldom digs into one particular state's preferences for or against further liberalization and rather contemplates the external effects of trade policies. Contrary to the unilateral case, the case for liberalization is explicitly multilateral, because countries can be made potentially worse off if they liberalize while other countries do not do so. Multilateral trade agreements are the necessary devices that help countries move from a Nash equilibrium, prisoner dilemma position, to a cooperative, welfare enhancing freer trade situation. Though this case was acknowledged by trade economists after the seminal contribution of Johnson in the 1950s on the basis of optimal tariff arguments made by Torrens in the large country case one century before, it only appears in footnotes or in the introductions of papers by world-class economists such as Bhagwati or Krugman for whom the rationale for trade liberalization remains unilateral.[4] The most powerful and convincing exposition of the economic case for multilateral negotiation is rather recent and is due to Bagwell and Staiger (1999), as discussed in some detail in Chapter 2. The question raised by this literature, and the answers found as to why countries fail to embrace free trade, are obviously different from what is provided by the first set of explanations. The question there is no longer how to enable countries to withstand their lobbies and reform their inefficient policies, but what kind of rules and compensatory arrangements can help countries decrease the adverse effects of their policies on other countries and decrease other countries' adverse effects on their own economy.

The issues addressed in these two broad sets of literature define what might be called the 'contextual realities' of trade negotiations. Countries enter into such negotiations because they desire to increase their access to the markets of others, and recognize that, to achieve this, they will need to open up their markets in return. However, they also recognize that trade liberalization may have other consequences for their social welfare, which may or may not be made explicit during the negotiations. From these considerations it is possible to derive four possible explanations, motives or arguments to depart from free trade:

1 The classic desire to protect domestic industries.
2 The adjustment costs arising from trade liberalization.
3 Market failures, especially negative environmental externalities, which may be exacerbated by trade liberalization.
4 Collective (non-market) social preferences, which may be violated by trade liberalization.

These four arguments are now explored in more detail in turn.[5]

The political economy argument

Studying the interactions between national leaders who are concerned with both providing a high standard of living to the general electorate and collecting campaign contributions from special interest groups, the Grossman–Helpman (1994) 'Protection for Sale' model, concerning the political economy of trade protection, yields compelling predictions for the cross-sectional structure of import barriers.[6] The rationale for trade agreements is then mostly to allow governments to overcome their national interest-groups in a way that increases the welfare of the general electorate. In this perspective, trade agreements serve as exogenous constraints for economic reforms that governments would not dare to, or simply could not, pass against the interest of some specific groups:

> *Trade negotiations may be based on a false theory, but by setting exporters as counterweights to producers facing import competition they nonetheless are politically crucial to maintaining more or less free trade. That is, the true purpose of international negotiations is arguably not to protect us from unfair foreign competition, but to protect us from ourselves.* (Krugman, 1997, p118)

Hoekman and Kostecki (2001) explicitly reckon that 'a rationale for the [WTO] organization is that political constraints prevent government from adopting more efficient trade policies, and that through the reciprocal exchange of liberalization commitments these political constraints can be overcome'. In the presence of overwhelming special interest group pressure for protectionism, the WTO (2007) *World Trade Report* notes, a trade agreement acts as an additional constitutional constraint, a logical extension of the national constitution to safeguard the latter, an international peg or anchor against government misdemeanour and lobby influence.

The adjustment cost argument

Should a transition period be required for the economy to adjust to liberalized trade and reap efficiency gains, arbitrage between short-term social cost mitigation and long-term efficiency gain maximization is likely to be made in favour of short-term social cost mitigation provided that losers are 'vocal' (the 'loud losers'). This cost minimization attitude would be consistent with the mercantilist approach of trade liberalization wherein imports are minimized and exports maximized.[7] The political unattractiveness of implementing deep structural changes for a modest short-term aggregate welfare gain, if any, plausibly explains the limited appeal of the free trade doctrine. For example, estimates by the United States Department of Agriculture (USDA) soon after the Doha Round was launched (Burfisher, 2001) show that the one time (i.e. static) welfare gains of world agricultural trade liberalization would be about $31 billions, equivalent to 0.1 per cent of world aggregate gross domestic product (GDP) and 1 per cent of consumer expenditures on agricultural and agricultural-related goods. In developed countries, gains would amount to 0.16 per cent of GDP and 2 per cent of consumer expenditures on agricultural goods. Ratios drop to 0.05 per cent of GDP and 0.2 per cent of consumer expenditures on agricultural goods in developing countries. Aggregate gains even turn into losses for those countries whose imports come from Organisation of Economic Co-operation and Development (OECD) countries. This means that in such a case, countries face a static comparative disadvantage when opening up to trade. At stake for them is to build comparative advantages, an argument close to the infant-industry protection case made in the 1960s after the Principles of Political Economy of John Stuart Mill.[8]

The picture is different in the long run where all countries are expected to gain in most of trade models – though no clear normative assumption allows generalizing such a happy end (see Chapter 1).[9] In any case, one clear issue then relates to the identification of short-term losers among the population and of the best and most acceptable way to compensate them for the adjustment cost they are expected to bear. The budgetary cost of such a compensation is an overwhelming constraint, because short-term losers are to be compensated by long-term – meaning virtual – gains. To overcome such a constraint, Panagariya (2005) suggests that

> *the global community would do well by accepting [that] free trade in both developed and developing countries increases efficiency, and [that] increased aid from developed to the developing countries, especially the least developed countries (LDCs), can be used among other things to offer adjustment to those free trade would temporarily displace.*

Still, the way to fix adjustment costs may not be that simple (see Chapters 10 and 11).

The externalities argument

The environment, society and culture provide many important non-market goods and services (for example, in the environmental field, climate stability, clean air and water, biodiversity and landscapes) that contribute to human welfare. It is abundantly clear (see Chapter 3) that economic activity, and the trade liberalization that expands it, can degrade or destroy these non-market goods and services, the classic negative externality effect. Stern (2007, pxviii) argues that 'climate change is the greatest market failure the world has ever seen', and on the estimates that he gives for the damages it might cause, it is clearly important for any contribution from trade liberalization to climate change (through increases in output) to be properly taken into account in assessments as to whether such liberalization is desirable.

Once these issues are taken into account, it is quite possible that some countries may be close to their efficiency frontier, meaning that only modest, not to say nil, gain can be expected from further liberalizing certain sectors. It is then possible that the production (or refraining from production) of a particular product in a particular way, inefficient in market terms, turns out to be efficient once positive (and negative) externalities and public-good like services joined to the production of this good have been taken into account. This is particularly the case with economies of scope between the production of a market output and the production of a non-market output, meaning that it is less costly to produce both products within the same production process than to produce them separately. In such situations protection can be more efficient than free trade (Le Cotty, 2007; Le Cotty and Mahé, 2007). The multilateral issue in such a case is to compare non-market gains in the country diverting from free trade with market-share losses in trade partner countries for the sector or product at stake. Difficulties with making the comparison include finding an appropriate metric and deriving a feasible compensation scheme (see Chapter 13).

The collective preferences argument

This classic externality case has been broadened and extended over the last five years toward what has been called the 'collective preferences argument'. The collective preferences argument was exposed by Pascal Lamy (2004) when he was EC DG Trade commissioner. The argument (lengthily exposed in Chapter 8) presumes that the expansion of trade and trade discipline jeopardizes the 'social fabric' of sovereign states by restricting legitimate choices a government may wish to embrace so as to satisfy its citizens' preferences on societal issues. Essential services provision, precautionary environmental and health regulations, protection against the products of child or forced labour, appeared during the different presentations of the argument by Pascal Lamy as possible illustrations. Because there is no science-based definition nor universality in what is an 'essential service' and what is not, different 'preferences' regarding sectors to be open to free competition and sectors that should not cannot be generalized across countries. Collective preferences over societal choices might hence conflict through the expansion of international trade. Thus the need, Pascal Lamy (2004) concluded, to design special safeguard and flexibility mechanisms allowing countries to escape their commitment to further liberalize trade on effective collective preferences grounds, while compensating their trade partners for the losses induced by incomplete market access.

Notwithstanding the lack of any science-based definition of universality of collective preferences, some collective preferences are, or can become, so widely shared that they may be called universal preferences. There are some examples in the 'exemptions' clause of GATT, Article XX, where it is accepted that countries may depart from GATT disciplines to pursue objectives of public health and the conservation of natural resources, and that the use of prison labour does not constitute a valid source of comparative advantage. Other universal preferences may be expressed through UN organizations, such as the 1998 Declaration on Fundamental Principles and Rights at Work of the International Labour Organization, or its resolution on child labour, or numerous multilateral treaties on particular environmental issues, or even the UN's own Universal Declaration of Human Rights.

There is currently a lack of clarity as to how these non-trade universal preferences relate to the trade rules of the WTO, which is an obvious source of tension both inside trade negotiations, where countries may be seeking to express these preferences, and outside, where pressure groups may seek to bring pressure on negotiators to take these preferences into account. To the extent that they do so, it would seem hard to argue that observation of these universal preferences should trigger compensation payments, in the same way that might be held reasonable for observing only nationally held collective preferences.

Implications for trade sustainability impact assessments

Going beyond the protectionist bias

Existing Trade SIAs tend to assess the overall impact of trade liberalization on each of the three sustainable development pillars. We argue that an 'overall impact' assessment needs to include collective preferences, which depend both on economic (viz. national income, resources endowment) and non-economic (culture, history) factors. We further argue that the challenge for SIA is not only to show a particular state that the reform scenarios of its trade policies are sustainable or not, but also to help it understand that other states have different views on sustainability, whose translation in trade bargaining can eventually focus on escaping reciprocal market access. To us, both views can be compatible with sustainability, depending on the relative priorities a society gives to each pillar of sustainable development and on the way it adds them up. This implies first that the contribution of SIAs to trade negotiations – which is very limited at the moment – should be extended in order to increase reflexivity, meaning that each negotiating side should be provided a better understanding of the collective preferences of the other. A second and interrelated implication is that disentangling the motives of pressure groups to depart from free trade from the genuine sustainable development – or 'collective preferences' – motives is a challenge to be urgently addressed by SIAs. It is essential that SIAs seek to distinguish between the motive of protectionism – seeking to protect sectoral economic interests at the cost of wider social welfare – and the promotion of widely held and democratically expressed collective preferences, which actually contribute to wider social welfare, which might be reduced by trade liberalization if such preferences are negated. We propose in Chapter 13 a way of disclosing a country's effective collective preferences over trade-related issues through an international compensation mechanism.

Reducing uncertainty on who gains and who loses

Evidence reviews show that trade liberalization has in the past caused winners and losers in the labour market, and that workers' skill appears to be most important in determining whether they are among the winners or among the losers. In terms of future research priorities, as Anderson and Cali note in Chapter 11, one area would be more time-series, household-survey based analyses of trends in the returns to education and skill in low-income countries, since most current studies relate to middle- and high-income countries. Similarly, research on the impact of trade reforms across geographical areas within countries is a further important area of investigation. This could usefully be accompanied by more research on the duration of job search and/or unemployment spells associated with trade liberalization, the size of the wage gains or wage losses associated with job mobility following liberalization, and how this varies across workers with different levels of skill. For the time being, current practices in Trade SIAs seem to over-rely on aggregated computable general equilibrium (CGE) modelling. A recommendation argued for by Anderson in Chapter 10 is to increase the use of quantitative approaches other than CGE modelling. To take his example, consider how households are likely to be affected by a trade agreement as consumers. Such effects are recognized in the Trade SIA of an EU-Mercosur agreement, but could be investigated in more detail using the basic micro-simulation approach.

Last, as far as policies are concerned, the existing consensus is that direct compensation for the losers from trade reform should not generally be sought, and that instead policy makers should concentrate on providing broad-based social protection and/or insurance. This is challenged by Anderson and Cali (Chapter 11), on the grounds that the appropriate policy response when people are adversely affected by shocks (viz. unavoidable events) is not necessarily the appropriate policy response when people are adversely affected by reforms – viz. by collective social decisions. The arguments for and against compensation should be assessed on a case-by-case basis; there is no real basis for automatically ruling compensation out a priori.

Improving knowledge on dynamic effects

Most trade liberalization simulation models, like CGE, do not account for welfare changes between two market equilibria. Their approach is basically comparative and static, even if some ad hoc assumptions on productivity growth instill some dynamics in CGEs and some refinement in the welfare value attached to long-term market equilibrium. In all cases the same rationale prevails, which is to compare two possible states of the world, without clear understanding of the successive states over which the world economy has to pass in between. CGEs are therefore a source of misunderstanding. Trade SIAs tend to list environmental and social impacts of trade liberalization within the broad, macro picture given by CGEs. According to trade economists, these impacts can be addressed by appropriate policies; they occur and can be observed indeed only because governments have not implemented the appropriate environmental policies to correct externalities (funded by liberalization welfare gains) and to assist displaced workers in their attempts to change job and/or region. These are the so-called adjustment costs of trade liberalization. For most trade economists, these costs are transitory and for this reason, often neglected, being regarded as a negligible share of an ever-growing pie. For governments, dealing with such costs lies at the core of their mandate. Reconciling the politics and the economics of trade liberalization requires a huge amount of innovation on the modelling of expectations and of disequilibrium in imperfect and dynamic markets, something closer to computable disequilibrium models (CDM) than old fashioned CGEs. Chapter 1 provides some further arguments for the need for disequilibrium modelling of trade impacts.

Assessing impacts along the value chain

Product chain assessment is an emerging methodology for a better understanding of the dynamics of global economic transformation processes. Instead of focusing on countries and their level of economic development as the ultimate units of account, product chain assessment takes economic actors, markets, products and substance flows as a starting point. In this manner product chain assessment offers the prospect of reflecting more accurately the dynamics of markets subject to liberalization and the relationship between producers and consumers. The methodological basis for product chain assessment is, however, still rudimentary. A significant effort to develop this methodology appears particularly promising from the perspective of analysing the sustainability impacts of globalized and fragmented product chains – in particular, in the light of ongoing liberalization policies.

In our view, Trade SIAs should deliver comparable results between and within sectors and branches. SIA in the field of international trade should hence bear two general perspectives in mind: the inter-sector perspective and the intra-sector perspective. The comparability of sustainability performances between sectors (inter-sector perspective) is straightforward for policy makers when negotiating on trade policies, since assessment results give hints on which sectors, with appropriate flanking measures, to favour so as to improve *sectoral* sustainability. But because trade occurs within as well as across sectors, intra-sectoral sustainability benchmarking should be used in a complementary way to assess existing differences of sustainability impacts within a branch, considering geographically dispersed product-life-cycle analysis. Issues relating to value chain analysis are explored in more detail in Chapter 12, and, in respect of commodities, Chapters 7 and 14.

Targeting participation

Public participation in policy making is increasingly recognized not only as an extension of democratic ideals, but also as a means to improve policy performance. Approaches to participation in impact assessment have co-evolved with impact assessment methodology and benefited from both knowledge gained from inclusion of participation in broader policy and management and growing recognition of its utility. But inclusion of public participation in Trade SIAs of EU trade agreements is particularly challenging because of many factors: among others, the privacy of the negotiation process, multinational participants and the general complexity of the consequences of trade agreements. Previous experience in SIAs of trade agreements as well as the wider body of participation literature and expert consultation, suggest improvements to the methodology and integration of public participation in SIAs. In particular, it seems that a programme for participation in SIAs should be based on a set of realistic, clearly stated objectives and be regionally tailored based on likely regional impacts, public stakes and local capacity. Further, transparent incorporation of participant input and two-way communications among contractors and negotiators are two areas that need attention to improve the legitimacy and political relevance of the SIA. In addition, public participation may strengthen the link between SIAs and trade negotiations if it is systematically incorporated in the analysis of issues that tend to block progress in the negotiations. This point, which is developed in Chapter 9, applies in particular to issues associated with cultural or normative concerns that are difficult to quantify and monetize and would likely require an increased use of deliberative methods.

Conclusion

The difficulties in achieving mutually beneficial multilateral trade agreements form the backbone of this chapter. Drawing from the academic literature and our experience of trade negotiations, we propose a set of three motives explaining why countries choose to depart from free trade. Such arguments pave the way of the successes and failures of past negotiations, from the 1947 Havana Charter to the Doha Development Round. The persistence of such motives is challenging for the trade community taken in a broad sense, for it basically underlines serious gaps between the expected consequences of trade and its real impacts, as well as between our understanding of the possible mismatch between collective preferences and actual political choices.

Although widely shared by research institutions, with significant improvements over recent years, Sustainability Impact Assessment (Trade SIA) of trade liberalization remains a challenging exercise for it has to take into account the distribution of impacts among population groups and, over time, jointly with some potential changes in the social value attached by each of income groups to the environmental impacts occurring along the liberalization process. Addressing these challenges will not be easy and will require stubborn research. However, if Trade SIAs are to fulfil their potential and make an effective contribution to trade deals, it seems to us that they will have to explore the directions outlined in this chapter, and this seems a prize worth considerable effort and innovation in terms of how Trade SIAs are carried out.

Notes

1 NGO Statement on the Draft Handbook for Sustainability Impact Assessment, April 2005, available at www.foeeurope.org
2 This rather idealistic statement rests upon a literal reading of the WTO Charter, which speaks of 'raising standards of living ... and expanding the production of and trade in goods and services, while allowing for the optimal use of the world's resources in accordance with the objective sustainable development...'
3 In answers below, reference is made to free trade even if trade negotiations aim at liberalizing trade, making it less 'unfree', rather than freeing trade completely, simply because free trade provides the benchmark against which gains and losses a country may face are valued in the overwhelming majority of economic studies.
4 See for example footnote 1 in Krugman (1997, p113): 'Students of international trade theory know that there is actually a theoretical caveat to this [economic case for unilateral free trade] statement: large countries have an incentive to limit imports – and exports – to improve their terms of trade, even if it is in their collective interest to refrain from doing so. This "optimal tariff" argument, however, plays almost no role in real-world disputes over trade policy.' See also Bhagwati (1988).
5 The reader interested in a mirror exercise underlying the reasons for a country to cooperate and commit toward freer trade will find in the excellent 2007 WTO *World Trade Report* some very useful material.
6 An empirical investigation can be found in Goldberg and Maggi (1999).
7 To quote Krugman (1991): 'To make sense of international trade negotiations, one needs to remember three simple rules about the objectives of the negotiating countries: 1. Exports are good. 2. Imports are bad. 3. Other things equal, an equal increase in imports and exports is good. In other words, Gatt-think is enlightened mercantilism.'
8 For a renewed formulation of the argument, turned into 'infant economy protection', see Greenwald and Stiglitz (2006).
9 See also the budding literature on transition and/or adjustment costs analysis and measurement, and in particular Furusawa and Lai (1999), Bacchetta and Jansen (2003) and De Cordoba et al (2005).

References

Bacchetta, M. and Jansen, M. (2003) 'Adjusting to trade liberalization: The role of policy', Institutions and WTO Disciplines, WTO Special Studies 7, Geneva, April

Bagwell, K. and Staiger, R. W. (1999) 'An economic theory of GATT', *American Economic Review*, vol 89, no 1, pp215–248

Bhagwati, J. (1988) *Protectionism*, MIT Press, Cambridge, MA

Burfisher, M. E. (ed) (2001) 'Agricultural policy reform in the WTO: The road ahead', Agricultural Economics Report AER 802, Economic Research Service, US Department of Agriculture

De Cordoba, S., Laird, S. and Serena, J. (2005) 'Trade liberalization and adjustment costs', Trade Analysis Branch, UNCTAD, Geneva

Furusawa, T. and Lai, E. L. C. (1999) 'Adjustment cost and gradual trade liberalization', *Journal of International Economics*, vol 49, pp333–361

Godard, O. (2008), 'Rethinking globalisation in the light of sustainable development', Mimeo, Chaire du Développement durable, Sciences-Po, Paris

Goldberg, P. K. and Maggi, G. (1999) 'Protection for sale: An empirical investigation', *American Economic Review*, vol 89, no 5, pp1135–1155

Greenwald, B. and Stiglitz, J. (2006) 'Helping infant economy grow: Foundations of trade policies for developing countries', *American Economic Review*, vol 96, no 2, pp141–146

Grossman, G. and Helpman, E. (1994) 'Protection for sale', *American Economic Review*, vol 84, no 4, pp833–850

Hoekman, B. M. and Kostecki, M. M. (2001) *The Political Economy of the World Trading System*, 2nd Edition, Oxford University Press, New York

Krugman, P. R. (1991) 'The move toward free trade zones', Paper presented at Policy Implications of Trade and Currency Zones symposium, Federal Reserve Bank of Kansas City, Jackson Hole, WY

Krugman, P. R. (1997) 'What should trade negotiators negotiate about?', *Journal of Economic Literature*, vol 35, March, pp113–120

Lamy, P. (2004) 'The emergence of collective preferences in international trade: Implications for regulating globalisation', DG Trade, European Commission, Brussels

Le Cotty, T. (2007) 'La coordination multilatérale des politiques agricoles en présence de biens non marchands', PhD Thesis, Montpellier University

Le Cotty, T. and Mahé, L. P. (2007) 'Multifunctionality and international coordination: Can the WTO be content with decoupling?', *European Review of Agricultural Economics*, Revised Paper submitted

Panagariya, A. (2005) 'Agricultural liberalisation and the least developed countries: Six fallacies', *The World Economy*, vol 28, no 9, pp1277–1299

Stern, N. (2007) *The Economics of Climate Change: The Stern Review*, Cambridge University Press, Cambridge

WTO (2007) *World Trade Report*, Geneva

5
Investment: The Context Matters

Daniel Blobel, Benjamin Görlach and Wesley Ingwersen

Introduction

Investment has proven to be a highly controversial issue in the context of international trade negotiations. At the core of the controversy are concerns that the texts of investment agreements have failed to strike the balance between investor rights and obligations, and unduly limited countries' capacities to regulate. Developing countries in particular have voiced concerns about investment agreements interfering with or even working against their development agendas. Ultimately, investment agreements have latently been perceived as a threat to national sovereignty.

Despite investment being a much-debated issue, there have been few approaches to develop environmental and sustainability assessment methodologies specific to investment agreements. Notably, while the European Commission (EC) has been running a programme for Sustainability Impact Assessments (SIAs) of trade agreements since 1999, investment issues have taken a relatively minor role in the assessments. This is partly due to the suspension of investment negotiations at the World Trade Organization (WTO) level, which prevented investment issues from being analysed in depth in the SIAs of WTO negotiations. However, it also seems likely that there has not been enough explicit recognition of the differences between trade and investment, with the consequence that the present SIA methodology is particularly adapted to trade in goods but becomes difficult to apply in other areas. The challenges encountered with service sector SIAs point in this direction.

Adapting assessment methodologies for trade agreements to investment raises a number of issues. While trade-flows in principle follow price differences reflecting comparative advantages, investment flows depend on individual investors' decisions, which in turn are influenced by a number of factors. Negotiations on investment agreements are not so much about removing barriers (such as tariffs, in the case of trade negotiations), but about creating rights and obligations between investors and their host countries. The uncertain relationship between investment agreements and ensuing investment, as well as between investment and potential benefits for the host country, has important consequences for the assessment methodology to be applied to investment agreements.

Typically, the debates on investment agreements have centred on the regulatory changes they induce. This direction of analysis, which could be called top–down, would have to be complemented by a bottom–up perspective that starts from the knowledge of the sustainability impacts of individual foreign investment projects available from case studies and literature reviews.

This chapter summarizes findings from research within a project aimed at further developing the EC's SIA methodology, and therefore focuses on the European context. Nevertheless, it also considers assessment methodologies applied by entities outside Europe. After providing a brief historical background, the chapter analyses the key features of investment and investment agreements. It then reviews the assessment methodologies applied to investment agreements to date, and the different categories of investments and its impacts that may be applied in a sustainable development context. As a synthesis of findings, recommendations on assessment methodologies for investment agreements are developed.

Characteristics of investment and investment agreements

Historical background of investment agreements

Negotiations for the creation of an international investment regime date back to the period immediately following the Second World War, when a charter for an International Trade Organization (ITO) was drafted. A chapter on investment was a part of this charter, but no consensus could be achieved, and the full ITO never came into existence. The General Agreement on Tariffs and Trade (GATT), which did emerge from the negotiations, contained no provisions for foreign investment (Kurtz, 2002).

Under the WTO, which was created from GATT in 1995, no comprehensive multilateral investment agreement was achieved either. However, several WTO agreements relate to investment issues, notably the Trade Related Investment Measures (TRIMS) agreement and the General Agreement on Trade in Services (GATS). TRIMS deals most explicitly with investment, but is limited to the prohibition of certain performance requirements on foreign investors that are supposed to negatively affect trade in goods. GATS, in distinguishing among several modes of cross-border service supply, addresses investment mainly through the mode of a commercial presence of a service supplier in a foreign country.

In the past one and a half decades, the controversy on investment agreements was mainly fuelled by the experiences with the investment chapter of the North American Free Trade Agreement (NAFTA), concluded in 1994. NAFTA's investment provisions gave investors more freedom and protection than most pre-existing investment agreements (Mann and Araya, 2001). The criticism of this approach grew strong enough to precipitate the failure of the negotiations on a Multilateral Agreement on Investment (MAI) within the Organisation for Economic Co-operation and Development (OECD) in 1998, as well as the indefinite suspension of the negotiations about an investment agreement within the WTO.

In the absence of a multilateral investment agreement, nations began in the late 1960s to turn to the use of bilateral investment treaties (BITs). BITs have since proliferated, with around 2400 BITs having been concluded by 2004.[1]

Differences between trade and investment

As Konrad von Moltke (von Moltke, 2000) states, past attempts to establish an international investment regime have not sufficiently taken into account the different characteristics of trade and investment and have therefore unsuccessfully tried to use the existing GATT/WTO trade regime as a model. The following paragraphs outline some distinctions between typical trade and investment activities and their consequences for related agreements, with particular reference to the aforementioned source.

Time frame

Trade in goods occurs within a limited time frame. Trade in services may extend over longer time and often involves a more complex buyer–seller relationship. The time horizon of investments is typically long term, as far as foreign direct investment (FDI) is concerned, while portfolio investments tend to be very short-term activities.

Static vs. dynamic

Investments can change their nature, or character, over time, whereas trade typically relates to the exchange of goods or services with clearly defined properties.

Higher complexity, lower predictability

Another important aspect is that investment flows depend on a more complex bundle of factors than trade flows, which essentially follow price differences reflecting comparative advantages and are thus more predictable. Importantly, there is no certainty that investment agreements really lead to an increase in foreign investment activity. Empirical studies lead to the conclusion that the existence of bilateral investment agreements is at best a supplementary condition for attracting FDI. They found that other criteria are more important, including openness, market size and economic stability (Cosbey, 2005).

Moving barriers vs. creating rights

The focus, when it comes to investment agreements, moves away from the goods or services offered, to the producer or service provider as an actor and their status as a legal entity. From removing barriers to the free flow of goods (such as tariffs), the focus shifts to creating certain rights. In this context, von Moltke speaks of the 'economic citizenship' of a foreign investor (von Moltke, 2000, p49).

Important elements of investment agreements

This section briefly reviews some major elements typically contained in investment agreements, along with the problems that may be associated with them.

The **definition of investment** applied in agreements varies considerably. A major issue is the question of whether to include portfolio investment, which is often seen as less desirable than direct investment because of its higher volatility, which may aggravate financial crises.

Determining the **scope** of investment liberalization also includes the decision on which **sectors** to open to foreign investment. This is determined in one of two primary styles – positive and negative list approaches. Where a positive list approach is applied, as in the GATS agreement, sectors are not opened unless specifically included. On the other hand, the negative list approach, which has been adopted by NAFTA, includes all sectors unless a sector is granted an exception.

Most investment agreements grant rights only to investors once the investment has been made (**post-establishment rights**). However, NAFTA and certain other agreements grant investors certain rights, such as **national treatment,** even before the investment has been made (**pre-establishment rights**), which implies granting them the right of entry into a foreign market (**right of establishment**). Creating such a right significantly impairs the host government's ability to screen investments to ensure favourable conditions for development (Cosbey et al, 2004, p9), especially where it is combined with a negative list approach to the opening of sectors.

The prohibition of **expropriation** in NAFTA Chapter 11 covers direct as well as indirect expropriation or nationalization, as well as measures 'tantamount to nationalization or expropriation'. The main concern with expropriation provisions in investment agreements relates to the question of what exactly constitutes indirect expropriation, and what is 'tantamount'[2] to it. In NAFTA, there is a lack of guidance as to whether 'indirect expropriation' extends to normal regulatory changes that negatively affect the value of an investment (Kurtz, 2002, p16). More recent agreement texts, including the 2004 US Model BIT, have aimed at providing more clarity on this point, which nevertheless is still an issue of contention.[3]

The full relevance of such expropriation provisions only becomes clear in combination with **investor–state dispute settlement procedures**. The broad interpretation of investor rights by tribunals in NAFTA-related cases, where investors have brought claims for compensation, has provoked concern for states' sovereign right to regulate (Mann and Araya, 2001). Furthermore, investor–state dispute settlement provisions provide foreign investors direct access to international forums, circumventing domestic courts: a possibility that is not at the disposal of domestic firms.

Performance requirements are an instrument by which host countries can, at least theoretically, influence foreign investors' actions in such a way as to harness them for their development objectives. Both NAFTA, and to an even greater extent the MAI draft, contain a long list of prohibitions of performance requirements such as technology transfer, domestic content requirements and export-related requirements. To a lesser extent, these prohibitions also apply to performance incentives (e.g. tax breaks), which are non-binding advantages offered to investors for complying with performance measures. Although the imposition of performance requirements by host countries has not always proven effective (Cosbey, 2005), their general prohibition in investment agreements has provoked criticism.

Sustainability assessments of investment agreements: State of the art

This section reviews sustainability and environmental assessments of trade and investment agreements that have been carried out for governmental bodies, with respect to the methodological lessons that can be drawn for the assessment of investment agreements. We will at first examine EU SIAs and then turn to the Environmental Reviews (ERs) performed by the US Trade Representative and Environmental Assessments (EAs) undertaken by the Canadian government. Finally, the Analytic Framework for Assessing the Environmental Effects of the North American Free Trade Agreement (NAFTA) will be discussed. This overview reflects the state of the art as of 2006.

EU SIAs

Most of the EU's Trade SIAs performed so far have not addressed investment issues in detail. Investment liberalization is directly discussed in the overview studies of the WTO agenda, notably in the preliminary assessment of the pre-Seattle WTO agenda (Kirkpatrick and Lee, 1999) and the preliminary overview study on the Doha agenda (George and Kirkpatrick, 2003). However, these studies do not treat investment at a level of detail such that they could be used as a model for related assessment methodologies. Relevant methodological references for investment agreements, however, may not only be found in assessments of agreements explicitly addressing investment, but also where services liberalization is involved: the liberalization of what is called 'trade in services' usually encompasses direct investment in the form of firms establishing a commercial presence abroad. Therefore the sectoral studies within the SIA of WTO negotiations that address the liberalization of services also need to be taken into account, namely the 2003 SIA of environmental services (Bisset et al, 2003) and the 2005 SIA of distribution services (Arkell and Johnson, 2005).

In addition, EU SIAs have also been performed for a number of regional trade and cooperation agreements. While these regional agreements usually include investment provisions, mostly in the context of services liberalization, not all related SIAs have discussed investment issues in detail. The SIA of the EU–Chile Association Agreement (Planistat, 2002) contains a fairly elaborated methodological discussion on assessing the impacts of investment and services liberalization. Investment, as related to services liberalization, has also been addressed in the SIA of the Euro-Mediterranean Free Trade Area (EMFTA) (Kirkpatrick et al, 2006a).

General characteristics of the EU methodology

The EU methodology for Trade SIAs addresses impacts on all 'pillars' of sustainable development (economic, social, environmental), within the EU as well as for its trade partners. Its core element is a 'causal chain analysis' that aims at tracing impacts from a specific trade measure, or a package of measures, on a set of economic, social and environmental indicators. Often, sector studies have been carried out in order to analyse more in-depth the impacts that an agreement is likely to have on selected key sectors. Among the methods applied are economic modelling, literature reviews and expert consultations.

Problems of quantification

From the SIAs carried out so far for services, problems of quantification become visible that can be expected to be at least of the same order when assessing investment. These problems relate to a lack of available data, as well as the inherent difficulty to quantify non-tariff barriers. Related to the latter aspect is the complexity of surrounding (especially host country) factors that may have a greater influence than the liberalization measure itself. The EC's *Handbook for Trade Sustainability Impact Assessment* states that modelling results 'shed light only on a part of the negotiations (mainly tariff related) on a static basis, dynamic effects being more difficult to assess. Modelling ignores a huge part of the trade agenda, such as trade in services, trade rules and investment' (EC, 2006, p36).

The two services sector studies within the SIA of Proposed WTO Negotiations are both largely qualitative and do not involve economic modelling. The distribution services study report explains this methodological choice, stating that no isolated sector data on international trade and financial flows could be obtained from official statistics. While this fundamental lack of data is specific to the distribution sector, the report also mentions that data 'for the services sectors as a whole remain poor', and that aggregate figures for FDI flows in general 'may be very unsatisfactory particularly in the case of developing countries' (Arkell and Johnson, 2005, p11).

The SIA of the EU–Chile Association Agreement is mostly based on findings of computable general equilibrium (CGE) modelling. However, the report mentions that the CGE analysis needed to be complemented by other methods, and especially highlights the lack of data in the cases of services and FDI. In addition, the report points out that characteristically,

> *FDI does not flow steadily as it is the outcome of discrete investment decisions by individual enterprises with no set frequencies. These changes in company-level business strategies cannot readily be predicted from aggregate data... The path of aggregate FDI, even over the medium term, is therefore 'lumpy' and unpredictable: at best only general trends can be projected.* (Planistat, 2002, p151)

Modelling studies of services liberalization have introduced tariff, or tax, equivalents to allow for a quantitative estimation of non-tariff market barriers. However, these methods need to be further refined and it is controversial to what extent they may result in reliable predictions. Kirkpatrick et al (2006b) cite results of recent CGE modelling studies on welfare gains from services liberalization, undertaken, inter alia, by the World Bank. They note the wide range of estimations and quote one of the studies saying that these estimations are 'highly speculative'. In the EMFTA SIA, Kirkpatrick et al (2006a) point to similar methodological problems when citing a range of studies modelling the regional impacts of services liberalization. Nevertheless, they acknowledge that the modelling results 'do however indicate the possible magnitude of effects'.

Cause–effect pathways

Aside from the obstacles to quantifying the development of investment, the question arises to what extent results of economic modelling can inform the assessment of impacts on other dimensions of sustainability. In a methodological reflection, the EU–Chile SIA report acknowledges that 'information on sustainability issues is generally not fully available and consistent, with the possible partial exception of economic data' (Planistat, 2002, p41). Therefore a two-stage methodology was used, which commences with a macro-economic analysis and continues with detailed studies of social and/or environmental issues in specific sectors or areas of study. 'Because of this switch of disciplines, the information and indeed the concepts used will normally be different between the first and second stages' (p41). While predictions of changes in economic indicators constitute potentially valuable information when assessing social and environmental parameters, in SIA practice a lack of established cause–effect relationships often leads to a discussion of social and environmental effects that is separated from the discussion of quantitative estimations of economic effects. The EU–Chile SIA itself is symptomatic in this respect: regarding the potential social and environmental consequences of the increases of economic activity in services, the analysis is confined to a retrospective reference to the screening and scoping stage of the assessment study. In a comment on the study, the heavy reliance on CGE modelling was furthermore criticized by putting into question the basic assumption made in the report, that 'effects on sustainability only exist in so far as associated economic impacts occur previously' (Planistat, 2002, p238[4]).

Another problem becomes visible in the WTO environmental services sector study and reappears in the final overview SIA of the Doha Agenda (Kirkpatrick et al, 2006b). The environmental services study bases the predicted sustainability impacts on developing countries on many conditionalities and ends up with a scoring table that contains questions marks for a number of environmental and social indicators. The study particularly highlights the role of domestic regulation: 'If regulation of the water sector is absent, or ineffective, the potential economic, social and environmental gains from services liberalization will be significantly reduced, and even reversed' (Bisset et al, 2003, p57). While this estimation appears realistic, it puts into question the value of the methodology applied, which essentially aims at predicting impacts of a monolithic 'additional liberalization' scenario and therefore cannot provide meaningful results where other factors of impact are more influential than the liberalization induced by an agreement.

Impact on regulation

As has been pointed out, the impact on governments' regulatory capacity is a central issue in the context of investment agreements. A potential weakness of the EU SIA methodology therefore is that it does not provide for a systematic analysis of related impacts, focusing instead on an indicator framework that essentially aims at tracing the impacts of changes in economic activity that are supposed to follow from an agreement. As an example, the SIA of environmental services liberalization does not analyse the impact of GATS rules on domestic regulation options, despite the impacts of GATS on domestic regulation being highly controversial (in particular in connection with essential services). The distribution services study, in contrast, includes various references to the potential impact of GATS on national regulation and on how existing legislation could be modified in order to comply with the GATS commitments.

US Environmental Reviews

In the US, ERs are prescribed for Free Trade Agreements (FTAs), but not for BITs. However, as FTAs negotiated by the US usually contain investment provisions, existing ERs also provide a reference for the investment context. One serious limitation in the scope of US ERs is that they focus strongly on the domestic consequences of trade agreements. The consequences for trade partners are examined to a much lesser extent, although they may be more important in many instances.

In the ERs of FTAs carried out in recent years, the FTAs' investment provisions are mainly addressed in the context of regulatory environmental impacts. While the ERs of the US–Chile FTA (USTR, 2001; USTR, 2003a) and the FTA with Central American States and the Dominican Republic (CAFTA-DR) (USTR, 2003b; USTR, 2005) also undertook some screening of sectors where increases in investment flows can be expected as a consequence of the agreement, they do not provide quantitative estimations, and the assessment of environmental implications remains vague.

The respective ERs' sections on regulatory environmental impacts of investment provisions provide some insight into the concerns that have been raised in this context, and the improvements made in recent agreement texts in comparison with NAFTA. However, it may be seen as a weakness in the assessment methodology that the responsibility of the ER lies with government authorities, not with an independent consultant or committee. As a result, the ER texts often read as a justification for the content of the agreement, rather than an analysis exploring its possible consequences in a systematic way.

Canadian Environmental Assessments

Unlike in the US, the obligation to carry out EAs in Canada is not limited to trade agreements, but extends to bilateral investment treaties, which in Canada are named FIPAs (Foreign Investment Protection and Promotion Agreements). Similarly to US ERs, the scope of assessment is severely limited by the fact that the assessment is only required to account for impacts within Canada, not for those that might occur in the partner country of the agreement. Both FIPA assessments carried out so far[5] found that no significant consequences are expected because the resulting increase of inward FDI into Canada will be negligible. This conclusion led to the decision not to carry out a full EA.

NAFTA methodology

The 'Analytic framework for assessing the environmental effects of the North American Free Trade Agreement' (CEC, 1999) differs from the methodological approaches of EU SIAs and US ERs in that it is primarily designed for ex-post monitoring, not for ex-ante assessments. Like the US ERs and in contrast to EU SIAs, it concentrates on the environmental dimension of impacts. Despite these limitations, the 'analytic framework' may be helpful as a reference for sustainability assessments of investment agreements in several respects. Unlike the methodologies discussed above, it contains clearly separated checklists for trade and investment effects. Moreover, it dedicates specific attention to the following aspects, which have been less clearly addressed in other frameworks: the effects of relocation and geographical concentration of production; the effects of corporate concentration and the driving forces of companies' environmental behaviour; impacts of trade and investment on infrastructure; and the influence of changing trade and investment patterns on local cultures and civil society organization.

Tracing the sustainable development impacts of investment

While there are limited examples of impact assessments for investment agreements, numerous case studies and literature reviews are available regarding the sustainable development effects of foreign investment as such. Rather than elaborating on the substantive findings of empirical studies on investment impacts, this sections aims at reviewing the different categories along which the various types of investment, as well as their effects, may be classified.

Categorizations of investment

The following basic categories of foreign investment are considered useful when assessing sustainable development impacts.

Direct investment vs. portfolio investment

Portfolio investment is often regarded as less desirable, or more risky, than direct investment. It is not always included in the investment definitions of investment agreements. However, it can be difficult to draw the line between both types of investment, and direct investment is often accompanied by portfolio investments.

Mode of entry

Regarding an investment's mode of entry, two forms are commonly distinguished: greenfield investment (the establishment of a completely new facility), on the one hand, and mergers and acquisitions (M&As) on the other hand.

The motivation of an investor

Dunning (1993) uses the motivation of the investor to distinguish between four different types of investment:

- resource-seeking investment, undertaken to gain access to resources in other countries;
- market-seeking investment, intended to gain direct access to local markets;
- efficiency-seeking investment, undertaken to rationalize the structure of a company's activity (this may also include taking advantage of cheap labour, administrative or environmental cost abroad);
- strategic asset-seeking investment, undertaken to protect or augment the existing ownership-specific advantages of the investing firms or to reduce those of their rivals.

Sectors of investment

The environmental and sustainability effects of foreign investment activities may differ greatly depending on which sector they take place in. For instance, investments in the resource extraction sectors tend to cause significant environmental damages while typically generating weak employment and spillover effects. Investments in essential services sectors also warrant particular attention because of their potentially significant impacts on society.

Linkages to the environment

Starting from work carried out at the OECD,[6] a range of categories of effects of trade liberalization on the environment have been established that have been taken up by various other authors and entities.[7] With some variations, the main categories are: product effects, technology effects, scale effects, structural effects and regulatory effects. While these categories were developed in the context of trade, they also apply to investment. However, their application in this context might require some adjustment.

Regulatory effects pertain to an agreement itself, while the other effects may be observed as a consequence of individual (or aggregate) investment undertakings following an agreement. Therefore they need to be analytically separated from the other categories.

Product effects are environmental effects associated with the properties of traded products. They will be of relevance mainly in the case of market-seeking investment and, more specifically, where this investment is targeted at expanding the market for a given product rather than substituting imports.

Technology effects are associated with changes in production technologies. The shift of focus from trade to investment may require an expansion in the scope of this category. Foreign investment activities not only influence the use of technologies, but also the development of human skills; they are relevant to education, labour skills, entrepreneurial culture and so on, including environmental awareness. This dimension may be referred to as '**qualification effects**'.

Scale effects are associated with changes in the scale of economic activity. They may occur either as direct effects resulting from an increase in production capacities or as indirect effects associated with economic growth.

Structural effects are associated with changes in the patterns of production and consumption. In the investment context, this category will specifically relate to shifts in the sectoral structure of the economy triggered by foreign investment activities. Certain sectors may gain importance, or new sectors may emerge, thanks to the foreign investment. Furthermore, backward linkages with suppliers may lead to structural shifts in supply industries.

In addition, George and Kirkpatrick (2003)[8] introduce the category of '**location effects**', which is particularly relevant in the investment context – the environmental effects associated with the transfer of production from one country to another.

There may be further effects of FDI that are not explicitly included in any one of the aforementioned categories. Arguably, this is the case with an investor's impact on local infrastructure. This includes the creation of infrastructure for an investor's needs, as well as the potentially excessive use an investor makes of the existing infrastructure.

Existing literature reviews on the investment–environment relationship suggest an analytical framework expanding beyond the categories cited above, which relate to the effects of increased FDI on environmental quality. Araya (2005) identifies two additional 'clusters' around which analytical and empirical work concerning the FDI–environment relationship can be arranged: **impacts from policy-based competition for FDI, and drivers and leverage points for cross-border environmental performance**. The former analytical category includes what has been referred to as 'regulatory effects' above and can be further subdivided into three main aspects:

- The impact of environmental standards on location decisions of individual enterprises; this relates to the 'pollution haven' hypothesis (the concentration of production in areas where environmental legislation or its enforcement is weak).
- The impacts of international competition for FDI on environmental regulation; this relates to the concerns over a 'race to the bottom' (lowering of environmental standards) or standards being 'stuck in the mud'[9] (i.e. governments refrain from raising them).
- The impacts of investment protection rules on environmental regulation.

The latter 'cluster' – the drivers for company-level environmental behaviour – has attracted increased research interest in recent years. It relates to the concept of 'pollution halos' – cases where foreign investors perform better than domestic ones in environmental terms, and spread good practice. Building on Hansen (1999), Araya (2005) identifies a range of influencing factors, including firm and sector characteristics as well as pressures from regulation, consumers and various stakeholder groups.

Suggestions for an assessment methodology for investment agreements

This section suggests a methodological framework for sustainability assessments of investment agreements. While it builds on the EU methodology for SIAs of trade agreements, it aims to include the particular properties of investment activities and investment agreements, as well as the experiences gathered from assessment methodologies applied in other countries or regions, as specified above.

Figure 5.1 aims at providing an overall picture of the relationships to be examined by the investment SIA.

Overall assessment structure

The basic structure of the EU SIA methodology includes four steps:

1 screening and scoping;
2 main analysis;
3 flanking measures;
4 ex-post monitoring.

We would follow this structure, while proposing the following key elements for the main analysis (i.e. step 2) of an investment agreement:

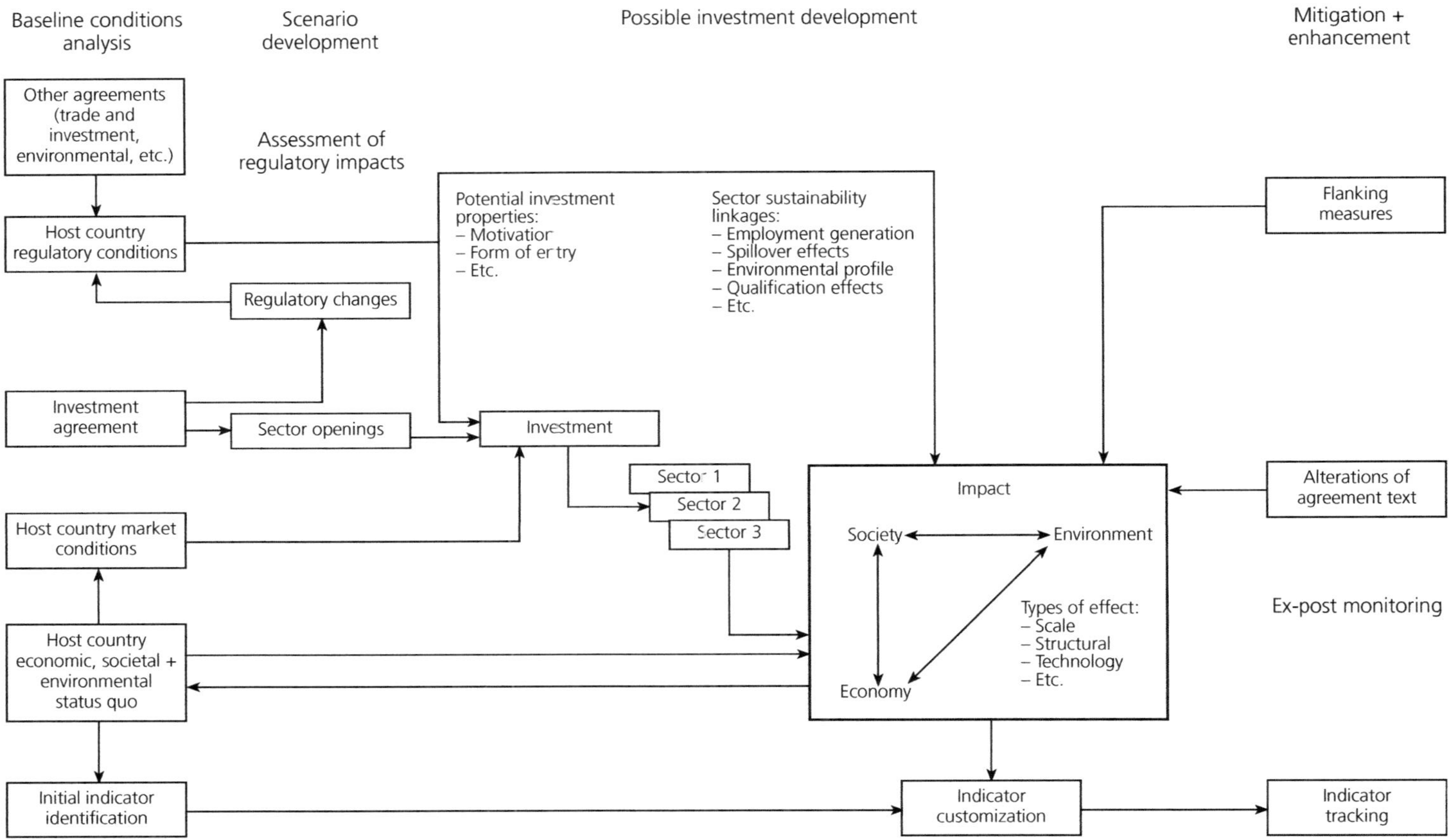

Figure 5.1 *Possible pathways of analysis in an investment SIA*

- **Assessment of the status quo.** This will include the regulatory and institutional situation in the potential host country/host countries of foreign investment, as well as the status of the economy. The aim will be to examine the prospects of the host country economy to attract foreign investment, identify major institutional risks and needs for institutional capacity building. This part of the analysis should also consider existing FDI in the host country and the sustainability effects it has had so far.
- **Possible investment development after the agreement.** This should first tackle the question of how likely an increase of foreign investment is at all as a consequence of the agreement, and then in what sector new investment is likely to take place, and what would be the benefits and risks in terms of sustainable development.
- **Overall impact on regulation.** This refers to the question of how the existence of the agreement will change the regulatory context, and will have to take into account both domestic regulation and existing agreements (trade and investment agreements, environmental and other agreements). It should also take into account the effects that the current competition for investors has on regulation, and assess in which way the agreement would affect this.
- **Assessment of individual elements of the agreement.** 'Elements' means provisions such as the definition of investment, right of establishment, treatment standards, prohibitions of performance requirements, expropriation provisions and dispute settlement procedures. In addition to analysing the impact on national regulation, the possible influence of individual provisions in the agreement on actually occurring investment should also be taken into account. This part of the assessment would be an appropriate place to make suggestions for 'fine-tuning' the agreement text.

Framework of sustainability themes and indicators

A set of indicators should start to be defined when assessing the status quo (in particular where information on the sustainability effects of existing investment is available), and applied and refined when assessing the possible development of investment after an agreement. We understand indicators as measures of sustainability effects that are, at least in principle, quantifiable. Importantly, however, the quantification of sustainability indicators is confronted with difficulties not only because of data constraints, but also raises more fundamental questions in the context of ex-ante assessments. Meaningful quantification of most indicators will be possible only in an ex-post monitoring.[10]

Another argument for not limiting the assessment framework to quantifiable indicators is that a too narrow approach in this sense would risk missing important dimensions of impacts, notably those related to broader and possibly fundamental societal implications. This includes a range of political and/or societal 'motives to depart from free trade' (Voituriez et al, 2006), which constitute potential obstacles to the success of negotiations.

Box 5.1 Investment themes and indicators: The economic dimension

- Total investment and share of FDI. (This indicates the overall success of an FDI-led development strategy, and in particular whether FDI crowds out or stimulates domestic investment)
- Employment (if possible, determining the role of foreign companies)
- Tax revenue (in particular, from foreign companies)
- Balance of payments
- Degree of economic concentration (number and size of enterprises operating in a given sector)
- Degree of economic diversification (number and balance of economic sectors)

Box 5.2 Investment themes and indicators: The social dimension

- Equity (in particular, income distribution and gender equity)
- Labour conditions (in particular, analysing the differences between foreign and domestic employers)
- Supply with essential goods and services (arguably, this is even more important than financial income levels of the population, and may have a direct relationship with FDI where the provision of such services is assigned to foreign investors)
- Impact on indigenous communities and ethnic minorities
- Migration effects
- Human rights record
- Qualitative changes in production/consumption patterns and lifestyles and possible resulting conflicts with ethical rules, belief systems etc.

We therefore propose to complement quantifiable indicators for the classic 'dimensions' of sustainability (economic, social, environmental) with variables that are more likely to be treated in a descriptive way, and which aim at reflecting the full range of impacts. Furthermore, we propose to introduce a fourth category of indicators that we would call 'qualification indicators', encompassing human skills (i.e. education levels) as well as technology transfer and development. Such indicators could provide essential information on how foreign investment contributes to building a society's capacities to pursue sustainable development.[11] Boxes 5.1 to 5.5 propose some themes and indicators that appear of particular relevance with respect to the sustainable development implications of investment.

Box 5.3 Investment themes and indicators: The environmental dimension

- Resource use (including the use of particular resources as well as the aggregate environmental contribution to per capita production and/or consumption)
- Environmental quality (absolute and per-unit emission levels of key polluting agents)
- Biodiversity (impacts related to land-use pressure from additional economic activity, as well as altered production and distribution methods)

Box 5.4 Investment themes and indicators: The qualification dimension

- Workforce qualification (in particular, differences between domestic and foreign employers, as well as possible contribution of FDI to overall trends)
- Technology transfer and diffusion
- Research and development expenditure (overall and at firm level)
- Entrepreneurial culture (e.g. introduction of environmental management systems)

Box 5.5 Investment themes and indicators: Other (non-quantifiable) aspects

- Informal regulatory forces (relating to the balance of power between foreign investors on one side and government/local authorities and communities on the other side)
- National sovereignty and security (referring in particular to opening up certain sensitive sectors to foreign investment)

Assessment of possible investment development after the agreement

Due to numerous uncertainties, it will be very difficult to establish any quantitative relationship between the conclusion of an agreement and the additional investment it will induce. It will be yet more difficult to establish quantitative relationships between the agreement and the sustainability effects of investment activities in individual sectors. Therefore the analysis should not rely too much on the quantitative prediction of effects; arguably, more important is in which direction (with regard to sustainability) development will move with any marginal increase in investment, and by which means a) investment can be increased; and b) its positive effects can be enhanced, and negative effects reduced.

With respect to the status of the host country economy, a range of factors should be explored to estimate not only the likelihood of attracting foreign investment in general, but also the motivation (e.g. resource-seeking, market-seeking) that is likely to drive FDI in that country. Among the most significant factors will be: macroeconomic stability, market size, the structure of the labour market, a country's natural resource endowment, levels of research and development and the structure of capital markets.

As the sustainability impacts of FDI vary greatly depending on the sector in which FDI takes place, **sector studies** will occupy an important role in the assessment. Along with an overall quantitative estimation of aggregate FDI levels, the assessment will therefore have to identify those sectors for which the most important development of FDI can be expected, and/or which appear most sensitive with regard to sustainability impacts.

Steps of sectoral analysis

For each sector, in addition to assessing the direct effects of investment activities, care should be taken to identify 'forward' and 'backward' linkages to other sectors and the sustainability implications these may have in turn. This 'linkages' analysis should also include possible implications related to the creation and use of infrastructure.

In order to assess the environmental impact of FDI in a given sector, the analysis should take two basic steps. In a first step, the environmental profile of a sector needs to be identified, which indicates whether the sector generally has a low or high environmental impact, and what environmental parameters it affects. In a second step, it needs to be analysed whether FDI is more likely to exacerbate or to mitigate these environmental effects. In more detail, the following factors should be taken into account:

The environmental profile of the sector. This includes resource and infrastructure requirements, pollution intensity, and the environmental implications of the use and disposal of products.

Scale effects. Is FDI likely to increase overall economic activity in this sector, or is it likely to replace domestic-owned production capacities?

Technology effects. Is FDI likely to reduce per-unit environmental impacts as compared to domestic-owned production? Or, on the contrary, is there a risk of FDI introducing more disruptive, less environmentally adapted production methods?

Product effects. These may mainly occur where a foreign investor sells products or services on the host country's market. New products or services may lead to a change in consumption patterns with environmental impacts such as increases in energy use and waste generation.

Location effects. An assessment of the net environmental impact of FDI needs to take into account the overall development of economic activity within a sector, including in the source country of investment: will the investment increase overall activity in this sector, as it would with an expansion of foreign markets, or will activity mainly be shifted from one country to another, as is likely for efficiency-seeking investment? This analysis would take into account the likely international differences in the environmental performance of companies (the per-unit environmental impact) within this sector, depending on the differences in environmental regulation and other factors.

Time horizons and distribution of impacts

It is essential to differentiate impacts along **time horizons** (short-term and long-term impacts) and according to their **geographical and social distribution**. This differentiation allows identification of local or temporal concentrations of impacts that require attention and mitigation, but tend to become invisible in a more aggregated presentation. The timescale analysis would also indicate whether long-term benefits outweigh short-term adjustment costs, or, on the contrary, short-term economic gains will be accompanied by long-term environmental degradation. **Irreversible impacts** should specifically be accounted for.

Conclusions

It is highly context-dependent to which extent the conclusion of an investment agreement actually leads to an increase in FDI, and whether such investment translates into sustainable development benefits. In particular, the following contextual factors appear relevant:

- A country's 'investment climate', as determined by its domestic institutional and regulatory framework as well as the characteristics and state of its economy, overall appears more determinative of the investment that will happen than the mere existence of an investment agreement.
- Likewise, the host country's regulatory framework will be determinative of the usefulness of foreign investment in terms of sustainable development.
- The circumstances of an individual investment, such as including sectoral characteristics and the motivation of an investor, are determinative of its sustainable development potential.

Experience with past assessments shows that FDI development is difficult to quantify, due to a lack of statistical data as well as the complex network of influencing factors. Even where forecasts can be generated from economic models, assessments have mostly failed to connect this data to social and environmental indicators. Due to the dependency on contextual factors, in some cases it has been impossible to predict not only the extent, but even the direction of change. Rather than predicting a specific outcome of investment liberalization, a sustainability assessment should focus on what conditions need to be met in order to ensure additional investment will occur and render sustainable development benefits. Rather than exploring one overall 'with agreement' scenario, it may be appropriate to develop more differentiated partial 'with measures' scenarios.

In addition, it should be ensured that sustainability assessments take duly into account those aspects that have proven to be the most contentious ones in past and ongoing debates on investment agreements. This refers to the issues of national sovereignty and maintaining regulatory capacity, and the adequate balance of investor rights and responsibilities.

Notes

1 Source: UNCTAD investment treaty database, accessed 13 December 2006.
2 Other agreement texts have used the term 'equivalent', which has been seen as somewhat less problematic. Cf. CIEL (2004), p60.
3 Cf. CIEL (2004).
4 Comment made by the Chilean organization RIDES (Research and Resources for Sustainable Development).
5 The EAs of the FIPAs with Peru (DFAIT, 2005, 2006a) and India (DFAIT, 2006b).
6 See, for instance, OECD (1994).
7 For example, Kirkpatrick et al (2004), UNEP/IISD (2005).
8 See also Kirkpatrick et al (2004).
9 Cf. Zarsky (1999).
10 It is worth noting that the 'core' and 'second tier' indicators of the EU SIA methodology are at a more general level than what are considered indicators in the indicator system of the United Nations Commission on Sustainable Development; rather, they correspond to 'themes' and 'sub-themes' in that system.
11 The current EU SIA methodology uses the category of 'process' or 'institutional' indicators instead, which goes in a similar direction but includes aspects that are likely to be better reflected within the description of the institutional background, the analysis of impacts on regulation and the recommendations on flanking measures.

References

Araya, M. (2005) 'FDI and the environment: What empirical evidence does – and does not – tell us', in Lyuba Zarsky (ed) *International Investment for Sustainable Development*, Earthscan, London and Sterling, VA, pp46–73

Arkell, J. and Johnson, M. D. C. (2005) 'Sustainability impact assessment of proposed WTO negotiations', Final Report for the Distribution Services Study, International Trade and Services Policy (ITSP) in association with Impact Assessment Centre, Institute for Development Policy and Management, University of Manchester, commissioned by the European Commission, www.sia-trade.org/wto/Phase3B/Reports/DistributionFR14June05.pdf, accessed 21 February 2006

Bisset, R., Flint, D., Kirkpatrick, C., Mitlin, D. and Westlake, K. (2003) 'Sustainability impact assessment of proposed WTO negotiations: Environmental services with particular reference to water and waste management', Institute for Development Policy and Management, University of Manchester, commissioned by the European Commission, www.sia-trade.org/wto/Phase3A/EnvironFinal.pdf, accessed 10 June 2003

CEC (1999) 'Analytic framework for assessing the effects of the North American Free Trade Agreement (NAFTA)', Commission for Environmental Cooperation, www.cec.org/files/pdf/ECONOMY/Frmwrk-e_EN.pdf, accessed 1 May 2003

CIEL (2004) 'Separate comments of TEPAC members on the U.S.-Central American Free Trade Agreement (CAFTA)', The Center for International Environmental Law, in TEPAC (ed) *The U.S.-Central American Free Trade Agreement. Report of the Trade and Environment Policy Advisory Committee*, pp55–63 www.ustr.gov/assets/Trade_Agreements/Regional/CAFTA/CAFTA_Reports/asset_upload_file789_5933.pdf, accessed 8 May 2006

Cosbey, A. (2005) 'International investment agreements and sustainable development: Achieving the Millennium Development Goals', International Institute for

Sustainable Development (IISD), commissioned by the International Development Research Centre, www.iisd.org/pdf/2005/investment_iias.pdf, accessed 20 March 2006

Cosbey, A., Mann, H., Peterson, L. E. and Moltke, K. (2004) 'Investment and sustainable development: A guide to the use and potential of international investment agreements', International Institute for Sustainable Development (IISD), Winnipeg, Manitoba, www.iisd.org/pdf/2004/investment_invest_and_sd.pdf, accessed 20 March 2006

DFAIT (2005) 'Initial environmental assessment (EA) of the Canada–Peru Foreign Investment Protection and Promotion Agreement (FIPA)', Department of Foreign Affairs and International Trade, www.dfait-maeci.gc.ca/tna-nac/documents/FIPA2005-en.pdf, accessed 27 February 2006

DFAIT (2006a) 'Final environmental assessment of the Canada–Peru Foreign Investment Protection Agreement (FIPA)', Department of Foreign Affairs and International Trade, www.dfait-maeci.gc.ca/tna-nac/env/pdf/Canada-Peru_FIPA_FINAL_EA_August_2006_EN_.pdf, accessed 17 November 2006

DFAIT (2006b) 'Initial environmental assessment (EA) of the Canada–India Foreign Investment Protection and Promotion Agreement (FIPA)', Department of Foreign Affairs and International Trade, www.dfait-maeci.gc.ca/tna-nac/env/pdf/Canada-India_FIPA_Initial_EA_September2006.pdf, accessed 17 November 2006

Dunning, J. H. (1993) *Multinational Enterprises and the Global Economy*, Addison-Wesley, Wokingham, UK and Reading, MA

EC (2006) *Handbook for Trade Sustainability Impact Assessment*, European Commission, External Trade, http://trade.ec.europa.eu/doclib/docs/2006/march/tradoc_127974.pdf, accessed 1 June 2008

George, C. and Kirkpatrick, C. (2003) 'Sustainability impact assessment of proposed WTO negotiations. Preliminary overview of potential impacts of the Doha Agenda: Assessment of individual trade measures', Institute for Development Policy and Management, University of Manchester, commissioned by the European Commission, www.sia-trade.org/wto/Phase3A/OverviewFinal2.pdf, accessed 10 June 2003

Hansen, M. W. (1999) 'Cross border environmental management in transnational corporations: An analytical framework', Copenhagen Business School (CBS), www.unctad-10.org/pdfs/preux_fdipaper5.en.pdf, accessed 28 August 2006

Kirkpatrick, C. and Lee, N. (1999) 'WTO new round. Sustainability Impact Assessment study: Phase two, main report', Institute for Development Policy and Management and Environmental Impact Assessment Centre, University of Manchester, commissioned by the European Commission, http://idpm.man.ac.uk/sia-trade/Phase2/frontpage2.htm, accessed 31 January 2003

Kirkpatrick, C., George, C. and Scrieciu, S. S. (2004) 'The implications of trade and investment liberalisation for sustainable development: Review of literature', Impact Assessment Research Centre, Institute for Development Policy and Management, University of Manchester, commissioned by the Department for Environment, Food and Rural Affairs, http://idpm.man.ac.uk/iarc/Reports/IARCWP4.pdf, accessed 19 July 2005

Kirkpatrick, C., George, C., Ahmad, B., Alessandrini, S., Cherfane, C. C., Colley, R., Nafti, R., Richardson, L. and te Velde, D. W. et al (2006a) 'Sustainability impacts of the Euro–Mediterranean Free Trade Area: Final report on Phase 2 of the SIA-EMFTA Project', Impact Assessment Research Centre (IARC), Institute for Development Policy and Management, University of Manchester, commissioned by the European Commission, www.sia-trade.org/emfta/en/Reports/Phase2 FinalreportMar06.pdf, accessed 5 December 2006

Kirkpatrick, C., George, C. and Scrieciu, S. (2006b) 'Sustainability impact assessment of proposed WTO negotiations: Final global overview Trade SIA of the Doha Development Agenda. Final report', Impact Assessment Research Centre (IARC), Institute for Development Policy and Management, University of Manchester, commissioned by the European Commission, www.sia-trade.org/wto/FinalPhase/FINAL_OVERVIEWJul2006.pdf, accessed 5 December 2006

Kurtz, J. (2002) 'A general investment agreement in the WTO? Lessons from Chapter 11 of NAFTA and the OECD Multilateral Agreement on Investment', *University of Pennsylvania Journal of International Economic Law*, vol 23, no 4, pp713–789, http://papers.ssrn.com/sol3/papers.cfm?abstract_id=384260, accessed 26 May 2008

Mann, H. and Araya, M. (2001) 'An investment regime for the Americas: Challenges and opportunities for sustainability', Yale Center for Environmental Law and Policy, www.isdlaw.com/pdfs/Mann%20Araya%20Final.pdf, accessed 1 June 2008

OECD (1994) 'Methodologies for environmental and trade reviews', OCDE/GE/(94)103, Organisation for Economic Co-Operation and Development, Paris, www.oecd.org/dataoecd/54/1/36767000.pdf, accessed 1 June 2008

Planistat (2002) 'Sustainable impact assessment (SIA) of the trade aspects of negotiations for an Association Agreement between the European Communities and Chile (Specific agreement No 1)', Planistat-Luxembourg, CESO-CI, http://trade.ec.europa.eu/doclib/docs/2005/february/tradoc_112362.pdf, accessed 1 June 2006

UNEP/IISD (2005) *Environment and Trade: A Handbook*, United Nations Environment Programme (UNEP), Division of Technology, Industry and Economics (Economics and Trade Branch), Geneva, and International Institute for Sustainable Development (IISD), Winnipeg, www.iisd.org/pdf/2005/envirotrade_handbook_2005.pdf, accessed 21 April 2004

USTR (2001) 'Draft environmental review of the proposed U.S.–Chile Free Trade Agreement', Office of the US Trade Representative, http://portalces.org/index2.php?option=com_sobi2&sobi2Task=dd_download&fid=564&no_html=1, accessed 26 May 2008

USTR (2003a) 'Final environmental review of the U.S.–Chile Free Trade Agreement', Office of the US Trade Representative, www.ustr.gov/assets/Trade_Agreements/Bilateral/Chile_FTA/asset_upload_file411_5109.pdf, accessed 26 May 2008

USTR (2003b) 'Interim environmental review U.S.–Central America Free Trade Agreement', Office of the US Trade Representative, www.ustr.gov/assets/Trade_Agreements/Regional/CAFTA/asset_upload_file946_3356.pdf, accessed 26 May 2008

USTR (2005) 'Final environmental review of the Dominican Republic–Central America–United States Free Trade Agreement', Office of the US Trade Representative, www.ustr.gov/assets/Trade_Agreements/Bilateral/CAFTA/asset_upload_file953_7901.pdf, accessed 26 May 2008

Voituriez, T., Ekins, P., Blanco, H., Homeyer, I. and Scheer, D. (2006) 'Making trade sustainable impact assessment more relevant to trade negotiations', *Impact Assessment and Project Appraisal*, vol 24, no 4, pp335–342

von Moltke, K. (2000) 'An international investment regime? Issues of sustainability', International Institute for Sustainable Development (IISD), Winnipeg, Manitoba, http://ces.iisc.ernet.in/hpg/envis/sdev/investment.pdf, accessed 26 May 2008

Zarsky, L. (1999) 'Havens, halos and spaghetti: Untangling the evidence about foreign direct investment and the environment', Conference on Foreign Direct Investment and the Environment, The Hague, The Netherlands, 28–29 January 1999, Organisation for Economic Co-operation and Development, www.olis.oecd.org/olis/1998doc.nsf/LinkTo/NT00002C96/$FILE/01E91439.PDF, accessed 26 May 2008

6
Sustainability Impacts of Liberalizing Trade in Services: Assessment Methodologies and Policy Responses

Jesko Hirschfeld, Clemens König and Ana Bachurova

The challenge posed by traded services

Services include 'any service in any sector except for services supplied in the exercise of governmental authority'. The latter are services supplied 'neither on a commercial basis, nor in competition with one or more service suppliers' (GATS Article 1). The General Agreement on Trade in Services (GATS) was adopted in the course of the Uruguay negotiation Round and entered into force in 1995. As laid down in the preamble, it is intended to contribute to trade expansion 'under the conditions of transparency and progressive liberalization'. It provides a legally binding framework of rules and principles for trade in services. It applies to all 'measures affecting trade in services'(Article 1). *Measures* mean any action relevant to trade taken by central, regional or local governments and authorities or non-governmental bodies in the exercise of delegated powers (Article 1). Measures affecting trade in services can potentially be found in almost any domain of domestic regulation.

Emerging relevance of trade in services

In 2005 exports of commercial services amounted to a value of 2415 billion US$, which represents nearly a fifth of total world exports. In the period 2000 to 2005, the value of world trade in services grew by 10 per cent annually – at the same rate as trade in merchandise goods – with Europe showing an impres-

Table 6.1 *Leading exporters and importers in world trade in commercial services, 2005*

Rank	*Exporters*	*Value (billion US$)*	*Shares (%)*	*Rank*	*Importers*	*Value (billion US$)*	*Shares (%)*
1	United States	354.0	14.7	1	United States	281.2	12.0
2	United Kingdom	188.7	7.8	2	Germany	201.4	8.6
3	Germany	148.5	6.2	3	United Kingdom	154.1	6.6
4	France	115.0	4.8	4	Japan	132.6	5.6
5	Japan	107.9	4.5	5	France	104.9	4.5
6	Italy	93.5	3.9	6	Italy	92.4	3.9
7	Spain	92.7	3.8	7	China	83.2	3.5
8	Netherlands	76.7	3.2	8	Netherlands	70.9	3.0
9	China	73.9	3.1	9	Ireland	66.1	2.8
10	Hong Kong, China	62.2	2.6	10	Spain	65.2	2.8

Source: WTO (2006), p19

sive performance in annual export growth: +12 per cent. The exports and imports of European services now account for more than half of the global trade in services (WTO, 2006, pp3–13). The leading export nations are the US (14.7 per cent of world exports in commercial services), UK (7.8 per cent) and Germany (6.2 per cent). The same nations lead also the import side – in a slightly permutated ranking: US 12.0 per cent, Germany 8.6 per cent and UK 6.6 per cent. Table 6.1 summarizes the volumes and shares of trade in services for the ten leading exporters and importers in 2005.

The SIAMETHOD sub-project on services concentrated on three specific service sectors, carrying out case studies on environmental services, tourism and related travel services, and transport services. Two of these sector studies (transport, environmental services) are presented below. Far more details on all the case studies are available in Hirschfeld et al (2006).

Trade in services differs from trade in goods in that no tangible items are moved. Often, the transaction requires direct contact between the producer and the consumer of the service. The GATS defines 'trade in services' by four *modes of supply* (GATS Article 1):

- **Mode 1: Cross-border trade:** for example, cross-border legal advice by electronic means, online banking or telemedicine.
- **Mode 2: Consumption abroad:** for example, international tourism.
- **Mode 3: Commercial presence:** for example, services supplied by a subsidiary, agency or branch office.
- **Mode 4: Presence of natural persons:** for example, services supplied by an information technology professional working abroad.

The GATS aims to promote trade liberalization through implementing three core principles:

1 **The Most-Favoured-Nation (MFN) Treatment** principle prohibits discrimination. With respect to its domestic regulation, each member must accord 'to services and service suppliers of any other member treatment no less favourable than that it accords to like services and service suppliers of any other country' (Article 2). The MFN requirement is a basic obligation under the GATS. Exceptions are, however, possible, if they have been listed in a specific schedule.
2 **Market Access** is concerned with the removal of barriers to trade listed in Article 16: national legislation limiting the 1) number of service suppliers, 2) value of allowed transactions, 3) number of service transactions or quantity of service output and 4) number of employees in a sector, or imposing 5) restrictions on the legal form of the foreign service supplier or 6) percentage limitations on the participation of foreign capital. Note that, except for the latter two cases, such provisions are not necessarily discriminatory in nature.
3 **National Treatment** requires a country to accord to services of any other member 'treatment no less favourable than that it accords to its own like services and service suppliers', that is, not to discriminate against foreign suppliers (Article 17). Treatment is considered to be less favourable 'if it modifies the conditions of competition in favour of services or service suppliers of the Member compared to like service or service suppliers of any other Member' (Article 17). Contrary to the MFN requirement, there is no automatic obligation for a member to grant either market access or national treatment. This is only the case if a member has explicitly undertaken a specific commitment with respect to a given sector and mode of supply in the country's schedule of commitments, which forms an integral part of the GATS. This is usually referred to as the GATS' bottom–up approach to liberalization.

The specific commitments undertaken by WTO members are in many regards a mere reflection of the status quo in 1995 – that is, the commitments of the Uruguay Round did not represent a substantive move towards liberalization. At the same time, Article 19 provides for 'successive rounds of negotiations, beginning no later than five years from the date of entry into force ... with a view to achieving a progressively higher level of liberalization'. Accordingly, a new series of negotiations – called GATS 2000 – was initiated in 2000. The Doha Ministerial Declaration of 2001 reaffirmed the goal of achieving a higher level of liberalization of trade in services. The negotiations follow a 'request and offer' approach: countries offer market access and national treatment in exchange for commitments they request their trading partners to undertake. However, the negotiations have made no more progress than the rest of the Doha Round.

Although the GATS' bottom–up approach apparently leaves the decision to liberalize at the discretion of members, many argue that GATS has kindled a global rush towards liberalization and privatization that especially developing countries may find hard to resist. Critics point to possible adverse social and environmental consequences of liberalization promoted by the GATS. Clearly, the fear of a loss of national regulatory sovereignty and of negative environmental and social impacts is at the heart of most criticism.

Restrictions on market access may be an important instrument of environmental protection strategies. For example, restricting the total number of operators in an area can prevent the overuse of natural resources or limit emissions. Joint-venture requirements could be a means to ensure the economic participation of local communities. Limitations on national treatment, including de facto discriminations, may serve to pursue policy objectives such as promoting the use of certain energy sources (e.g. solar power) or restraining the marketing of services that have been produced in an unsustainable way. Since the GATS definition of like services does not allow for environmental or social considerations, discriminating against unsustainable production methods abroad would be incompatible with WTO standards. Even if there is no automatic obligation for countries to liberalize, once unconditional commitments have been undertaken, the country may find its ability to pursue an independent social and environmental policy substantially reduced. Since the precise meaning and scope of GATS rules and disciplines are still far from being clear, a thorough assessment of the 'regulatory impact' of further commitments under the GATS would be worthwhile.

Case studies

Transport services

Transport services under the GATS comprise land, air and maritime transport of freight and passengers. Land transport is further divided into road and rail transport. The coverage of air services is limited to services complementary to flying operations, such as aircraft repair and maintenance, computer reservation services and marketing. The core flying operations are excluded to preserve the current regulatory regime governing international air transport. This involves an elaborate structure of over 3500 bilateral agreements and the independent jurisdiction of the International Civil Aviation Organization (ICAO). A review of air services began in 2001, but little progress has been made (Findlay, 2004).

Public provision of transport services has been common historically through public monopolies or regulation of private activities, as these services often show public good characteristics or a tendency towards natural monopoly. This especially holds for the service infrastructure (ports, roads, rails, etc.). In many cases, public service suppliers were vertically integrated – that is, responsible both for the provision and maintenance of the infrastructure and the service operation itself. Since the early 1980s, however, both infrastructure and service operations have increasingly become subject to privatization and liberalization. While privatization means a shift of ownership from public to private, liberalization includes market opening and deregulation in order to increase competitive pressures that are presumed to benefit consumers and public budgets. Privatization and liberalization were typically accompanied by the separation of formerly vertically integrated enterprises into independent entities owning the infrastructure, maintaining it, and supplying the service, respectively.

Privatization and liberalization have been motivated by the prospect of higher private investment, better responsiveness to consumers' needs and reduced costs, benefiting users as well as relieving public budgets. Such confidence in the benefits of privatization has been criticized by pointing to its detrimental effects. With regard to railway services, WEED (2005) identified the following negative impacts: domination of markets by a few private operators (former public monopolist or other); job losses and decline in training levels of employees; shortcomings in infrastructure maintenance; safety risks due to poor coordination between operating companies; price rises without improvement of quality; higher need for subsidies in order to encourage private sector participation; loss of public control over private operators. In many cases, this seems to be quite the contrary of what proponents of privatization expect it to yield.

GATS is not directly about privatization. It does not apply to services 'provided in the exercise of governmental authority' (Article 1), and does not prohibit the establishment or maintenance of government monopolies. Moreover, it is compatible with various regulatory arrangements. Its bottom–up approach allows WTO members to manage their obligations and commitments and tailor them to the desired level of government involvement.

If, however, a country chooses fully to commit a sector, it must be aware of a number of incompatibilities between trade liberalization and certain forms of public sector involvement. Preferential treatment accorded to a public service provider – for example, a public bus company in municipal transport or a public terminal operator – conflicts with national treatment, because public ownership of a supplier does not preclude 'likeness' under the GATS. Maintaining a public monopoly would obviously be irreconcilable with market access (Krajewski, 2003a).

Moreover, in a WTO negotiation context, pressure to liberalize trade may include pressure to privatize, or to undertake commitments that can only be fulfilled if fuller privatization is embarked upon. Nonetheless, for the purpose of assessing the impact of services trade liberalization, one must take care not to confuse the effects of privatization and trade liberalization. As EUKOM (2005a) puts it: 'The Commission has always maintained that trade liberalization is about introducing competition, not about the process of privatization. Of course, the two processes are frequently part of the same domestic reform process, but for the purpose of a robust causal analysis the distinction is crucial.'

Europe is both the main exporter and importer of transport services, followed by Asia and North America, with about 50 per cent of world exports originating in Europe (WTO, 2006). The share of transport services in total services trade lies between 20 and 30 per cent depending on the region. Differentiating by transport modes, maritime and air transport services are the most relevant traded transport services, with each sub-sector representing about one third of G7 countries' transport services exports and two fifths of imports.

As pointed out above, the provision of transport services is characterized by far-reaching government involvement that is only gradually being reduced via privatization and liberalization. Accordingly, commitments under the GATS with respect to transport services have been limited so far, with a high rate of qualifications or limitations in all modes. This may also be one of the reasons why trade liberalization in transport services has not received much attention in the public debate surrounding the GATS so far.

Recent negotiations on trade liberalization in the transport sector

The European Commission (EC) summarized its revised requests to its trading partners, published in January 2005, as follows:

> *The EC focuses its requests on maritime transport, air transport and auxiliary transport services (freight forwarding and agency activities) for almost all WTO-members. For the advanced economies it also addresses road transport and elements of rail. At the same time the EU has introduced significant flexibility in its request to developing economies: to allow an approach with tailor-made, simple and suitable commitments.* (EUKOM, 2005b, p8)

As for the EU's 'revised initial offer' in the Doha service negotiations, the 25 member states subscribed to the principle of unlimited access to international maritime transport and offered non-discriminatory use of their ports. Regarding mode 3, the offer provided for foreign services suppliers being able to establish a commercial presence in the EU territory a wide spectrum of services ranging from cargo handling to maritime agency services on the same footing as EU suppliers. In the air transport sector, market access was offered for ground handling and airport management. For other transport services, the regime resulting from the Uruguay Round was maintained.

In February 2006, under the new negotiation modalities for services agreed upon at the Hong Kong Ministerial Conference in December 2005, the EU Commission submitted 'plurilateral requests' in the maritime and air transport sector, pointing out that 'the objective of the EU is an internationally competitive maritime industry which observes international standards of safety and environmental protection' and urging the commitment of WTO members to 'guarantee non discriminatory conditions' for international maritime transport on cargo and passengers and on a number of auxiliary services (EC, 2006).

Environmental services

Characterizing 'environmental services', the current study mainly refers to the Organisation for Economic Co-operation and Development (OECD) definition: '...activities which produce goods and services to measure, prevent, limit, minimize or correct environmental damage to water, air, and soil, as well as problems related to waste, noise and ecosystems'. For a more detailed discussion of classification issues see Hirschfeld et al (2007).

The global environmental industry (goods and services) was estimated to have reached a trade volume of 522 billion US$ in 2000, which is about the size of the global pharmaceuticals and information technology markets (Vikhlyaev, 2002), with markets in the developed countries contributing over 90 per cent (sales). Services including water utilities represented two thirds of the market in 1998. Markets in developed countries are mature – that is, highly competitive and with a sophisticated customer base. Changes in environmental regulation are the most important factors driving demand. Markets in developing countries, in contrast, have urgent environmental and resource management needs, with the following sequence of priorities: water delivery, wastewater treatment, air pollution control, solid waste disposal, hazardous waste management, remediation (OECD, 2001).

It has been widely recognized that eliminating barriers to trade in environmental goods and services may be a crucial means to improve environmental protection and reach the sustainability goals. Paragraph 31(iii) of the Doha Ministerial Declaration (2001) calls for negotiations on 'the reduction or, as appropriate, elimination of tariff and non-tariff barriers to environmental goods and services'. Maintaining a public monopoly amounts to a denial of market access to foreign suppliers and must be scheduled under the GATS (if the sector has been 'listed' in the first place). Increased private sector participation in the provision of environmental infrastructure services has thus become a major force driving trade (by increasing the 'tradability' of these services). Other important factors are overcapacities in developed countries, consolidation among providers and the adoption of worldwide environmental standards creating demand (OECD, 2001, p16).

Many environmental services are part of integrated 'solution' packages also involving the supply of environmental goods and application of environmental technology. Due to the heterogeneity of the sector, only few generalizations referring to the industry as a whole are possible. At the subsector level, the following trends can be observed (OECD, 2001):

- The water treatment sector tends to be dominated by large multinational companies mainly of European origin, many of which are formerly public water utilities. Important players are: Ondeo/Suez, Veolia/Vivendi, Thames/RWE, SAUR/Bouygues, International Water/Bechtel.
- The waste management sector is more fragmented among small and medium-sized companies. Some important players are: Onyx/Vivendi, Sita/Suez, RWE Umwelt.

- Pollution remediation and prevention activities tend to involve the integrated provision of equipment, technology and services, with project managers calling in the required specialists on a contract basis.
- Environmentally related engineering, consulting and project management services tend to be provided by environmental divisions of big engineering firms, entering contract and partnership arrangements with smaller firms.

As regards environmental infrastructure services (water treatment, waste disposal services, etc.) in particular, the role of the private sector has been limited historically. In addition to their importance to human health and social concerns, public provision was encouraged by the fact that many of these services tend to be natural monopolies due to high fixed costs. Without appropriate regulation, private provision of these services would lead to inefficient duplication of networks or exploitation of consumers by a private monopolist (Krajewski, 2003a). Some environmental infrastructure services also exhibit characteristics of a public good, with private actors having no incentive to supply it, creating a need for public provision of these services (OECD, 2001).

Accordingly, until recently, responsibility for providing infrastructure services was claimed by governments through public monopolies or granting of exclusive supplier rights in most countries. Moreover, for social policy reasons, infrastructure services used to be subsidized in many countries.

In recent years, things have changed gradually. Private participation in the supply of environmental infrastructure services has become widespread (especially in France, the UK and Latin America). In general terms, private provision is expected to yield the following benefits (OECD, 2001):

- Inflow of technical and managerial expertise.
- Improvement of operating efficiency.
- Large-scale injection of capital.
- Reduction of the need for subsidies.
- Increased responsiveness to consumer needs and preferences.
- In developing countries: improved ability to address societal problems such as rapid population growth, migration, air pollution and so on, under budgetary constraints.

However, increased participation of the private sector needs to be accompanied by effective regulation. If ownership of water utilities is transferred to private companies, the natural monopoly situation will nevertheless subsist, requiring a close monitoring to prevent abusive practices. Moreover, imposing price limits and universal service delivery requirements may interfere with shareholder interests, but may be essential from a social and political perspective.

The potential benefits of services liberalization are often deduced under idealized market conditions. In real world imperfect market conditions, 'win–win' outcomes are not guaranteed, and both gainers and losers should be expected. Past experiences in trade liberalization in environmental services have not always proved encouraging. An OECD study on the environmental, economic and developmental benefits has identified potential 'losers' from the trade liberalization in the environmental services sector (OECD, 2005).

Consumers may face newly introduced or considerably raised prices for environmental infrastructure services. Private operators charge for the services provided not only to cover investment and operating costs, but also to generate profits. Fees are usually a key part of the negotiations in the course of privatization of formerly public services. Loss of employment within existing service providers can easily occur – due to new management approaches of the private company now in charge.

Some of the key findings in the literature study of George and Kirkpatrick reveal that aggregate economic welfare gains are not necessarily shared by all countries and all socio-economic groups within these countries (George and Kirkpatrick, 2004). Moreover, the study identified many cases where the environmental and social impacts are negative, mainly due to ineffective domestic environmental and distributional policies. And also the WTO itself recognizes potential social costs resulting from trade liberalization policies: labour displacement, depreciation of skills, need for professional retraining, regional relocation (WTO, 1998).

Services and the 'contextual realities' of trade negotiations

Chapter 4 (pp91–92) proposes a number of 'contextual realities' of trade negotiations to explain why a trade agreement may not be reached, even when significant economic gains are to be expected. These are here explored with respect to services.

The protectionist bias argument

Lobbyist activities are prominent not only in the commodities sector, but also in the services sector. Due to the comparably 'voluntary' character of integrating specific service sectors into the GATS commitments most countries have only committed services the liberalization of which is not fiercely disputed domestically. Mainly the infrastructure-related services are often exempted from trade liberalization processes: water supply and discharge, energy, transport, and such. Many of these services are still supplied by state-owned or closely state-related enterprises and their outputs are regarded as containing considerable proportions of public goods. In these cases, protectionist lobbying activities are not easily distinguishable from the adjustment cost and collective preferences arguments that are discussed below.

The adjustment cost argument

Adjustment costs of the liberalization of trade in services can occur in various cases. Especially if domestic service sectors are still underdeveloped, liberalization can allow foreign competitors to dominate domestic markets very soon after the opening. Since this process can be sequenced by committing only certain *modes of supply*, negative employment effects can be prevented more easily than in the case of the liberalization of commodity sectors (see Chapter 7). Despite the employment effects, the 'siphoning off' of profits is one of the problems causing conflicts, for example in the tourism sector as well as in the infrastructure-related services.

The externality argument

Liberalization of trade in services can cause negative external effects. Possible examples are increased passenger transport, water use and wastewater emission resulting from a liberalization of trade in tourism services. An opening of the markets for infrastructure-related services (concerning energy, transport, water supply and discharge) can show ambiguous effects – some positive as well as negative external effects. A fear of negative externalities can cause considerable political conflict and pose an obstacle to the progress of trade negotiations. If a country does not have the regulatory capabilities to prevent or to internalize these negative externalities, trade liberalization could harm the environment and might reduce domestic welfare, depending on the ranking of environmental concerns in domestic preferences.

The collective preferences argument

In some cases, the liberalization of trade in services can interfere with the realization of collective preferences. Some societies might prefer to leave infrastructure-related services within public ownership or management. A domestic ownership of certain service sectors (such as banking, electricity, health care, transport and tourism) might be appreciated. One way to deal with these reservations is already integrated within the GATS framework: the possibility to commit only certain *modes of supply*. This enables a country to liberalize only as far as it is tolerated by domestic collective preferences. GATS Article VI demands that national laws and regulations should be 'administrated in a reasonable, objective and impartial manner' – which might be specified by the WTO dispute resolution system. This clause might interfere with the right of domestic authorities to regulate the service sectors. Attempts to challenge domestic regulations in the course of a WTO dispute settlement process might collide with domestic collective preferences if widely appreciated domestic regulations differ significantly from those in potential export countries.

Among the services, especially the liberalization and opening of supply of fresh water is highly disputed. In many countries people understand the supply of fresh water as a human right (although still not guaranteed in many countries). A liberalization of the water sector, which might lead to a foreign ownership of important infrastructure institutions, is often seen as a loss of national sovereignty, endangering the secure supply of a basic need to everybody – while others argue that privatization of formerly public services will lead to efficiency gains, and possible negative effects could be prevented by setting up a comprehensive legal framework regulating the management practice (e.g. non-exclusion from fresh water supply).

Existing methodologies

Compared to economic assessments and environmental impact assessments (EIAs) there are still only few available Sustainability Impact Assessments (SIAs) of the effects of trade liberalization – especially of trade in services. And among these Trade SIAs there are only very few that take into account all the 'contextual realities' identified in Chapter 4 as critical to the progress of trade negotiations. Table 6.2 summarizes a number of SIA approaches and rates their coverage of the four 'contextual realities'.

Table 6.2 *Assessment matrix of existing Sustainability Impact Assessment methods towards 'contextual realities' of the liberalization of trade in services*

	Conventional EIAs	*EU Trade SIA handbook 2006*	*RIDES tourism SIA 2006*	*IDPM environmental services SIA 2003*	*ITSP/IDPM distribution services SIA 2005*	*RIDES/ Adelphi transport SIA 2003*
1 Protectionist bias	.	.	+	.	.	+
2 Adjustment cost	.	++	++	+	++	+
3 Externality	++	++	++	++	++	++
4 Collective preferences	.	.	+	.	.	.

++ method takes contextual reality directly into account
\+ method takes contextual reality indirectly into account
. method does not take contextual reality into account

Causal chain analysis

According to Kirkpatrick and Lee (2002), 'the fundamental purpose of causal chain analysis (CCA) is to identify the significant cause effect links between a proposed change in an existing trade agreement (or proposed new agreement, or New Round) and its eventual economic, environmental and social impacts (i.e. its impacts on sustainable development)' (p31). As the approach is only supposed to be illustrated here, we shall concentrate on one example (maritime auxiliary services) and one dimension of sustainable development (economic impacts).

Availability of 'door-to-door' logistics services integrating different modes of transport (multimodality) and including the extensive use of information and communication technology have become vital to competitiveness in world goods markets. If developing countries lack the infrastructure and operational capacities to meet these requirements, their export prospects are in jeopardy (Devlin and Yee, 2005). What is more, as a result of declining tariffs on goods, the relative importance of transport costs in the determination of trade patterns continues to grow. Fink et al (2002) investigate the determinants of the cost of shipping in US imports. Their empirical analysis examines the following factors potentially explaining the variation in shipping costs across originating countries and US ports ('liner transport prices for US imports'): a regional variable (namely, the custom district in the US) to capture differences in the quality of maritime auxiliary and port services in the US; a product variable to capture differences in the physical properties of shipped goods; the share of containerization for a given line and product; shipping distance; economies-of-scale effects; and three policy variables reflecting institutional features of the US trading partner – existence of a cargo reservation policy, barriers to foreign supply of cargo handling services and the number of port services mandatory for incoming ships – as indicators of the general openness of the trading partner's port regime. Moreover, the authors investigate the influence of private anti-competitive practices.

Fink et al (2002) find distance, containerization and, as already mentioned, the existence of private price-fixing agreements as statistically significant with the expected sign of coefficient. The evidence on restrictive policies is mixed. The existence of a cargo reservation policy is not statistically significant in any of the regressions – underlining its limited importance in practice. Mandatory use of port services, on the other hand, turns out to be more relevant than barriers to trade in cargo-handling services, which are not significant in any of the regressions. Fink et al (2002, p101) concede that their analysis 'has focused solely on the maritime leg of the transport journey and has not examined distortions on the inland section. Evidence suggests that the ocean leg accounts for a little more than a third of total door-to-door shipping charges.'

Tongzon and Heng (2005) find that handling charges are positively affected (i.e. reduced) by private sector participation in port operations. World Bank (2001) describes two examples of successful attempts at port reform in Argentina and Colombia, which both entailed significantly lower handling costs. In Colombia, average vessel waiting time was reduced from ten days to several hours and the throughput of containers per vessel per hour went up from 16 to 25. In Argentina, work productivity increased from 800 to 3000 tons per worker per year and the cost for container imports decreased from 450 to 120 US$ per ton.

Regulatory capability

Nevertheless, quantitative approaches to CCA have a number of methodological limitations: first, absence of data or at least severe data limitations are ubiquitous, especially when it comes to social and environmental impacts. Moreover, unlike tariffs, non-tariff barriers to trade in services are hard to quantify. In the econometric studies just discussed, several policy variables were included to capture the main features of a country's regulatory regime and assess their effect on an impact variable (here, shipping cost). However, trade liberalization may also give rise to novel forms of regulation or at least radically transform current regimes. Unfortunately, no reliable data regarding the effects of such policy changes are available.

We therefore argue that when it comes to assessing the impact of services trade liberalization, CCA's quantitative emphasis is not always sufficient to characterize the entire range of sustainability effects. For this reason, we propose a complementary approach, which concentrates on how trade liberalization affects governments' ability to regulate. This aspect is not altogether absent in IDPM (Institute for Development Policy and Management) methodology. Under the heading 'Descriptive (case study) methods', mention is made of 'a number of regulatory-based impact studies using somewhat different forms of juridical and organisational analysis, which have contributed to the impact assessment of rule changes within international trade agreements' (Kirkpatrick and Lee, 2002, p37), but not much attention is devoted to it in actual assessments. Regulatory capability is mainly mentioned in relation to 'mitigation and enhancement' measures, that is, proposals for measures governments could take in order to mitigate the adverse effects, and enhance the positive effects, of trade liberalization (see, for example, the SIA of distribution services carried out by Arkell and Johnson, 2005).

Countries generally differ in their capability (and willingness) to design policy frameworks to shape the process of economic growth and development in a sustainable way. This feature of a country's governance structure can be described as its ex-ante regulatory capability.

Furthermore a country's regulatory capabilities determine the chances to shape the process of growth and development in a sustainable way. Trade liberalization may under specific circumstances support the emergence of more sustainable governance structures, but there exist numerous examples of governments being overstrained by the task of setting up regulatory frameworks to limit detrimental sustainability effects.

If a country chooses to fully liberalize a given service sector under the GATS, its ability to pursue sustainable policies in that area will *ceteris paribus* be reduced. Hence, a country's ex-post regulatory capability for a given sector will generally be lower than its ex-ante capability.

Why does trade liberalization reduce a country's ability to pursue sustainable policies? The magnitude of the effect will obviously differ across service sectors and countries. Yet, full liberalization always entails that countries are no longer permitted to pursue policies that a) discriminate between suppliers from different trading partners; b) discriminate between foreign and domestic suppliers; and c) restrict market access. It is generally assumed that at least some sustainable policies rely on precisely such measures.

Much public debate has concentrated on the GATS effects on national 'regulatory autonomy' (Sinclair and Grieshaber-Otto, 2002). Moreover, several scholarly publications address the issue (Krajewski, 2003b; Lang, 2004; Pauwelyn, 2005; Holmes, 2006). Lang, for example, gives various examples of 'socially motivated' regulations of the water industry that, given what is known about GATS today, appear to be incompatible with full liberalization commitments (for being discriminatory). For a long time, such assertions were bound to be speculative, as little case law was available, but worries as to GATS's deep impact on national regulatory capability have been fuelled by a recent WTO decision.

In the 'US Gambling' case, Antigua accused the US of violating its commitments in 'recreational services' by banning all online gambling, including that supplied by foreigners (see Pauwelyn, 2005 and Holmes, 2006 for summaries and Chapter 8 for further discussion). Both the Panel Report and the Appellate Body found that the ban did not amount to a mere 'regulation' of the sector, the right to which is explicitly recognized by the GATS and which is only subject to the weak disciplines of Article VI (transparency and objectivity of measures, etc.), but a violation of a market access commitment. However, the Appellate Body eventually acknowledged that the ban was a legitimate restriction on market access because it served to protect public morals, a ground for restrictions allowed by Article XIV.

Pauwelyn (2005) observes that the distinction between domestic regulation and market access is considerably blurred by the WTO decision. The consequence, he warns, might be that national legislation could become subject to challenges under GATS to a much broader extent than previously thought. Pauwelyn criticizes the WTO bodies for effectively ignoring the crucial difference between market access and domestic regulation. While market access commitments are concerned with ruling out such protectionist devices as formal numerical quotas, it is, he argues, a severe mistake to regard any regulatory measure that happens to have the effect of reducing or limiting the number of foreign suppliers in the market as violating market access. This overlooks the fact that regulation may serve a legitimate, non-protectionist purpose. Pauwelyn argues that '[t]he mere fact that domestic regulation has the effect of restricting the number of imports does not make it a market access restriction' (2005, p159).

If the WTO dispute settlement bodies continue to interpret market access as extensively as in the 'US Gambling' case, the successive steps of commitments according to GATS disciplines may severely reduce national regulatory capabilities – with detrimental consequences for the implementation of sustainability oriented regulatory regimes.

Existing responses

Among the numerous attempts to tackle the 'contextual realities' of the process of liberalization of the trade in services, six examples of existing responses are briefly presented and rated concerning their coverage of the four 'contextual realities' (see Table 6.3).

As mentioned above, one possibility to deal with these 'contextual realities' is already incorporated within the GATS framework: theoretically, countries are committing sector by sector and only as far as they want. The four 'modes' (cross-border trade, consumption abroad, commercial presence, presence of natural persons) allow for a sequencing of the liberalization process. Nevertheless developing countries are subject to a not-insignificant degree of 'liberalization pressure' since GATS commitments are often seen as parts of negotiation packages that integrate liberalization offers concerning trade in goods, services and intellectual property rights. If a developing country desires the industrialized countries to further liberalize agricultural trade, negotiators from the North might try to force it to liberalize its service sectors attractive to foreign investors in return.

Public referenda were used in a number of cases to assess the public preferences – mainly by municipal communities with respect to the liberalization of water and energy supply. In some cases privatization was rejected by the public, in others it was accepted. Referenda might be a means to come to broadly accepted political decisions concerning a potential opening of markets touching sensitive services sectors.

In the recommendations of the 'Practical Plan to Achieve the Millennium Development Goals' the UN Millennium Project asks the high-income countries to open their markets to developing country exports, to help least developed countries raise their export competitiveness through investments in critical trade-related infrastructure (including electricity, roads and ports) and human capital (health, education, training). Concerning the liberalization of trade in services, the UN Millennium Project's Task Force on Trade sees a need for regulation to address complex issues of market structure, market failures and non-economic objectives to ensure that the liberalization process results in competition and increases access to services by the poor. This requires increased research and assistance as well as 'appropriate care to the nature, pace and sequencing of reform'.

Initiatives like 'Water & Sanitation for the Urban Poor' (WSUP) bring together non-governmental organizations (NGOs), multinational water companies, international organizations and academic institutions. WSUP is designed as a partnership network for giving advice, building regulatory capacities and supporting projects designed to help the urban poor to improve their water and sanitation supply situation.

In the field of tourism services there exists a number of initiatives to cope with the sustainability effects of global tourism development – influenced also by further steps in the liberalization of trade in services. In 1998 the Code of Conduct for the Protection of Children from Sexual Exploitation in Travel and Tourism was initiated by End Child Prostitution, Child Pornography and the Trafficking of Children for Sexual Purposes (ECPAT) Sweden in cooperation with Scandinavian tour operators and the World Tourism Organization. A considerable number of international tour operating companies signed this Code or put up individual Codes of Conduct comprising several dimensions of sustainability impacts. The Tour Operators Initiative (TOI), launched in 2000, is designed to promote a 'sustainable tourism development'. In September 2006 the Secretary-General of the United Nations World Tourism Organization made a strong commitment to the UN Millennium Development Goals. Especially towards the reduction of poverty, tourism enterprises are asked to promote more tourism flows towards the developing world, to increase the proportion of local products in the hotels' supply chain, to provide better paid job opportunities to local people in tourism destinations of developing countries and generally to raise the awareness of development problems.

Table 6.3 *Potential of existing initiatives to tackle the 'contextual realities' of the process of liberalization of the trade in services*

	GATS	*Public referenda*	*UN Millennium Project*	*Water & Sanitation for the Urban Poor*	*Code of Conduct (Tourism) 1998*	*Tour Operators Initiative 2000*
1 Protectionist bias	+/-	.	.	.	.	.
2 Adjustment cost	+/-	+	++	++	.	++
3 Externality	+/-	+	++	++	.	++
4 Collective preferences	+/-	++	.	+	(+)	+

++ initiative directly tackles contextual reality to some extent
\+ initiative only indirectly tackles contextual reality
. initiative does not tackle contextual reality
\- initiative has the potential to deepen the contextual reality barrier to agreement

[shaded] initiative potentially provides a compensation mechanism

Conclusions

- The effects of further liberalizing trade in services have rarely been investigated with EIAs and extremely rarely with SIAs so far.
- This overlooks the importance of the booming trade in services, its relevance to world trade volumes and to domestic impacts of an ongoing liberalization of trade in services.
- The effects of trade liberalization are often supplemented or multiplied by domestic privatization and deregulation policies that in many cases were in turn initiated by international organizations like the World Bank or the International Monetary Fund (IMF).
- The process of liberalizing the trade in services often touches sensitive issues like national infrastructure, supply of basic needs and national security.
- The case studies show that the extent to which trade in services liberalization can boost or hamper the development process (in the direction of the UN Millennium Goals) strongly depends on domestic regulatory capacities.
- Without good governance and a well-sequenced process, 'weak' countries might easily find themselves worse off and liberalization of the trade in services may aggravate domestic economic, environmental and social problems.
- Developing countries will not be satisfied with a mere reference to potential global gains from liberalization of the trade in services and its subsequent growth. Explicit support and transfer mechanisms must be developed and implemented before and alongside the liberalization process – and not only promised – if negotiators are to believe that such liberalization really will contribute to achieving their sustainable development goals.

References

Arkell, J. and Johnson, M. D. (2005) 'Sustainability impact of proposed WTO negotiations: Final report for the Distribution Services Study', Report prepared for the European Commission, Brussels

Devlin, J. and Yee, P. (2005) 'Trade logistics in developing countries: The case of the Middle East and North Africa', *World Economy*, vol 28, no 3, pp435–456

EC (European Commission) (2006) 'EU and others launch "plurilateral" process to boost Doha services negotiations', DG Trade, European Commission, Brussels, 28 February 2006, http://trade.ec.europa.eu/doclib/docs/2006/february/tradoc_127631.pdf

EUKOM (2005a) 'Sustainability impact assessment of DDA negotiations: Sectoral study on Environmental Services, European Commission Position', http://europa.eu.int/comm/trade/index_en.htm, accessed 30 February 2007

EUKOM (2005b) 'Summary of the EU's revised services offer in the Doha negotiations', DG Trade Press Release, 2 June 2005, Brussels

Findlay, C. (2004) 'Transport Services training module', The World Bank, Washington DC

Fink, C., Mattoo, A. and Neagu, I. (2002) 'Trade in international maritime services: How much does policy matter?', *The World Bank Economic Review*, vol 16, no 1, pp81–108

George, C. and Kirkpatrick, C. (2004) 'Trade and development: Assessing the impact of trade liberalisation on sustainable development', *Journal of World Trade*, vol 38, no 3, pp441–469

Hirschfeld, J., König, C., Haum, R., Bachurova, A. and Tröger, J. (2006) 'Sustainability impact assessement methodologies for specific service sectors', Working Paper prepared for the EU-financed research project SIAMETHOD, www.iddri.org/iddri/html/projet/sia_method/index2.htm

Hirschfeld, J., König, C., Haum, R., Bachurova, A. and Tröger, J. (2007) 'Sustainability impact assessement methodologies for specific service sectors', Final Report of the SIAMETHOD sub-project on services, Paris, Berlin

Holmes, P. (2006) 'Trade and "domestic" policies: The European mix', *Journal of European Public Policy*, vol 13, no 6, September, pp815–831

Kirkpatrick, C. and Lee, N. (2002) 'Further development of the methodology for a sustainability impact assessment of proposed WTO negotiations', Final Report to the European Commission, Manchester

Krajewski, M. (2003a) 'Public services and trade liberalization: Mapping the legal framework', *Journal of International Economic Law*, vol 6, no 2, pp341–367

Krajewski (2003b) *National Regulation and Trade Liberalization in Services: The Legal Impact of the General Agreement on Trade in Services (GATS) on National Regulatory Autonomy*, Kluwer Law International, The Hague, London, New York

Lang, A. (2004) 'The GATS and regulatory autonomy: A case study of social regulation of the water sector', *Journal of International Economic Law*, vol 7, no 4, pp801–838

OECD (2001) *Environmental Goods and Services: The Benefits of Further Global Trade Liberalisation*, OECD, Paris

OECD (2005) 'Opening markets for environmental goods and services', OECD Policy Brief, September

Pauwelyn, J. (2005) 'Rien ne va plus? Distinguishing domestic regulation from market access in GATT and GATS', *World Trade Review*, vol 4, no 2, pp131–170

Sinclair, S. and Grieshaber-Otto, J. (2002) *Facing the Facts: A Guide to the GATS Debate*, Canadian Center for Policy Alternatives, Ottawa

Tongzon, J and Heng, W. (2005) 'Port privatization, efficiency and competitiveness: Some empirical evidence from container ports (terminals), Transportation Research Part A', *Policy and Practice*, vol 39, pp405–424

Vikhlyaev, A. (2002) 'Environmental goods and services: Defining negotiations or negotiating definitions?', UNCTAD *Newsletter*, pp33–60

WEED (2005) Öffentliche Dienstleistungen unter Privatisierungsdruck', Working Paper, World Economy, Ecology and Development, Berlin

World Bank (2001) 'World Bank port reform tool kit', http://siteresources.worldbank.org/INTPRAL/Resources/338897-1164990391106/00_TOOLKIT_FM_Vol1.pdf, accessed 30 June 2008

WTO (1998) 'Environmental services', Background Note by the Secretariat, S/C/W/46, 6 July, World Trade Organization, Geneva

WTO (2006) *International Trade Statistics 2006*, World Trade Organization, Geneva

7
The Impacts of Liberalizing Trade in Commodities

Robin Vanner and Paul Ekins

Introduction

Commodities can be defined as: '*a raw material or primary agricultural product that can be bought and sold*'. The term therefore refers to goods that have not undergone extensive processing. How commodities, especially agricultural commodities, are produced and sold has absolutely fundamental implications for sustainable development. This explains why the proposals put forward in the Doha trade negotiations to liberalize trade in agricultural commodities have been so contentious and why, ultimately, it has not been possible to come to an agreement on them.

Commodities can be classified and subdivided depending on the issue under consideration. The most common classification divides agriculturally produced commodities from commodities such as metals and minerals, which are extracted from stocks in the earth, and are therefore non-renewable. An alternative classification for commodities relates to how the trade flow tends to be treated within national governments' trade policies. A key determinant of this will be whether developing countries are in competition with a developed country's production, and therefore whether the developed countries will be prone to protect their domestic production in the face of lower-cost imports.

More and more, commodities are upstream of an increasingly complex web of product chains that go to produce modern consumer products. Most of the value of the product is normally associated with the processing of the commodity, rather than with the basic commodity itself, and the desire to capture this value is an important element in trade negotiations about commodities.

This chapter is in two parts. Part I provides an overview of sustainable development impacts from commodity production, as well as a discussion of current barriers to more sustainable commodity production and trade patterns. Part II explores how Sustainability Impact Assessments (SIAs) have been applied to proposals to liberalize trade in commodities. It also discusses how important commodities are in the underlying arguments opposing trade liberalization that have been discussed in Chapter 4. The conclusions of the chapter point forward to Chapter 14 on how the sustainability impacts associated with the production of traded commodities can be enhanced or mitigated in order for trade to contribute towards sustainable development.

Part I: An overview of sustainable development impacts from commodity production

Trade in commodities and the environment

Kox (1993) categorizes environmental impacts from commodity production in terms of pollution and resource depletion. In relation to resource depletion, he then divides natural stocks into three: renewable, semi-renewable and unrenewable (or non-renewable). This categorization of stocks leads to the categorization of commodities into mining and other commodities (agricultural, fisheries and forestry) where the former represents a depletion of a non-renewable stock and the rest can at least in principle represent renewable processes. Figure 7.1 summarizes the types of environmental impacts often associated with the production of commodities.

Impacts from the mining of commodities

Export mining has negative impacts in both the extraction and the processing stages. Kox (1993, p2) describes the most common problems at the excavation and ore removal phases as being: the destruction of plant and animal habitats; land subsidence; erosion, silting of lakes and streams; dust pollution; trace metal pollution; giant waste heaps; acid drainage (sulphur in overburden); and metal contamination of lakes, streams and groundwater. In addition to this, he reports that open cast mining (for example copper, tin, zinc and bauxite) often contributes heavily to soil erosion by demolition of vegetation and soil structure. In the ore concentration phase of production the most common problems are: waste generation (tailings); organic chemical contamination (residues of chemicals used in concentrators) as well as acid drainage.

Impacts from growing agricultural commodities

As far as agricultural commodities are concerned, the key environmental differentiator is whether the commodity is a tree or a field crop. Field grown crops (like cotton, soya or tapioca) cause much more erosion problems and require greater inputs of chemical fertilizers (Kox, 1993, p2). The production of so called cash crops for export (like soya, cotton, tobacco, bananas, cocoa, coffee, rubber and sugar cane) has been linked with abundant use of agrochemicals,

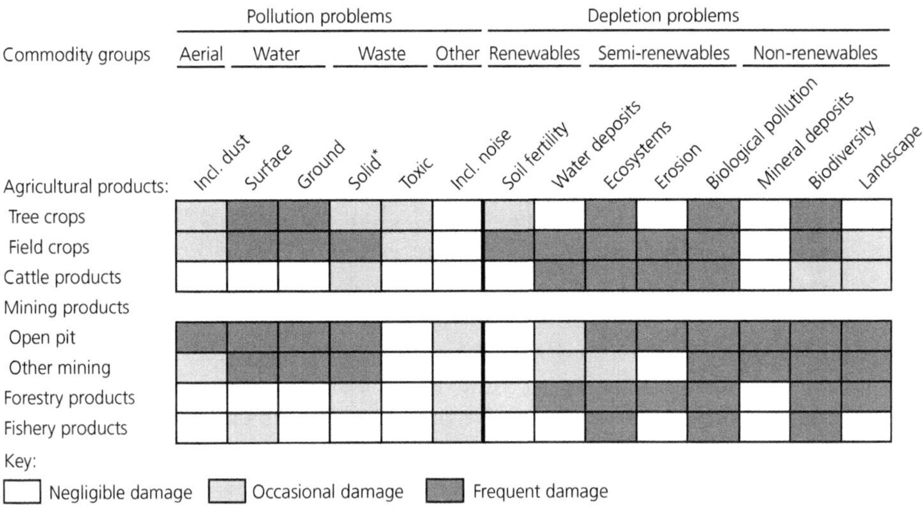

Note: * including salinization.
Source: Adapted from Kox (1993, p3)

Figure 7.1 *Environmental impacts associated with commodity production*

especially when production units are large. The excessive use of agrochemicals has the potential to cause cumulative long-term effects in the form of pesticide residues in animal and food chains (Kox, 1993, p2). Beyond this, the particular environmental impacts tend to be crop and location specific.

Kox reported massive deforestation in the Amazon, Southeast Asia and certain parts of Africa and identified export production of tropical hardwood as a major cause (Kox, 1993, p4). Whilst this may have been the case in the early 1990s, this link is less evident in the present day. Deforestation brought on by forest clearance is still very much occurring and in some cases can be linked back to export commodity production such as cattle ranching. CIFOR (2004) reports that much of the recent loss of Brazil's Amazonian forests is due to the high international demand for Brazilian beef. In addition they report that between 1990 and 2001 the percentage of Europe's processed meat imports that came from Brazil rose from 40 to 74 per cent (CIFOR, 2004).

Impacts from fishing

Fisheries are often open and common resources and are therefore prone to excessive fishing. Overfishing of coastal and deep-sea areas negatively affects the regeneration capacity of fish populations. In addition, Kox (1993, p4) reports that some fishing practices contribute to devastation of coral reefs and the sea bottom. UNEP (1999, pxi) reports a tremendous growth in Uganda fish exports that led to the industry becoming Uganda's main foreign exchange earner outside of traditional agricultural exports, but also to a variety of concerns over the long-term sustainability of the industry. These concerns are reported to include:

- overfishing and resource depletion;
- the loss of biodiversity associated with introductions of exotic species and unsustainable fishing methods;
- effluent pollution from fish processing and other industries;
- the degradation of coastal ecosystems and environmental health conditions associated with rapid development of the industry;
- resource mismanagement due to the lack of harmonized national environmental standards among those countries with riparian rights over Lake Victoria (Uganda, Kenya and Tanzania).

Trade in commodities and development

Much of the debate relating to trade, and particularly trade in commodities, centres on issues of development. Advocates of trade liberalization believe that an open and fair international trading system can provide benefits for people in developing countries, and increasing resources for managing environmental harm that might be generated by greater economic output (see for example Bhagwati, 2004).

Trade theory suggests that trade liberalization should provide net economic benefits for all participating countries. This theory is reinforced by the various SIAs undertaken during negotiations involving the European Union (EU) (see Chapter 3). There is also some retrospective evidence of economic benefits for developing countries' participation in international trade. Brander (2005, p3) reports a general perception that trade has contributed to the economic development of between 20 and 25 low- and middle-income countries, largely in South and East Asia and Latin America. He also reported that the least developed countries, particularly in sub-Saharan Africa, that are at best marginal participants in the trading system have, as yet, been unable to take similar advantage of the market openings that are available. This leaves outstanding the question as to whether this model of export-led development can (or should) be promoted in least developed countries (LDCs). If such a path is followed, what can trade negotiators do to ensure that any benefits are distributed in a way that reduces poverty whilst avoiding significant environmental impacts during development transitions?

The interaction between economic development and the environment is a greatly researched topic, in part through the hypothesized existence of Environmental Kuznets Curve (EKC) relationships. The EKC theory proposes that in the early stages of economic growth, degradation and pollution increase. However, beyond some level of income per capita (which will vary for different environmental impacts) the trend reverses, so that at high income levels economic growth leads to environmental improvement[1] (Stern, 2004). This can, to some extent, be confirmed by the development patterns already experienced by developed countries. Grossman and Krueger (1995) found that 'economic growth brings an initial phase of deterioration followed by a subsequent phase of improvement', and that the turning points for the different pollutants vary, but in most cases they come before a country reaches a per capita income of US$8000. This finding does not, however, show that economic growth causes this relationship and therefore does not guarantee that the same will be the case for presently developing countries.

Analysis undertaken by Cole (2004) explores the downturn shape of the EKC in developed countries and finds that it was the result of three drivers: increased demand for environmental regulations, trade openness and a shift towards greater imports of manufactured goods from other countries that may become pollution havens (Cole 2004, p79). If the latter of these three drivers was to be the dominant cause for the decline, such a decline in pollution might not be achieved as easily by the LDCs. The evidence for pollution havens is by no means certain. Von Moltke (2003, p4) reports that 'there is no evidence for the systematic development of pollution havens'. He does, however, accept that the 'steady shift of commodity production, in particular of minerals, from Europe and the population centres of North America towards rural areas and developing countries may be promoted not only by the rising cost of land but also by increased environmental rules'. Under such a scenario, developing countries may well desire a cleaner environment as they develop, but there will be few countries willing to accept the dirtier production. An alternative solution may well lie in the transfer of cleaner technologies, but this would represent a quite different development path to that experienced by developed countries.

Structural barriers to export led development

It is believed that 'a country has to have a certain level of infrastructure before it can draw benefits from more trade openness' (EC, 2006, Preface by the then EU Trade Commissioner Peter Mandelson). When this is not the case for a particular country, policies to promote greater equity are required in order to alleviate poverty and achieve development (Brander, 2005, p3). Although such measures may be proposed within an SIA, there is no guarantee of uptake by national governments and trade partners have limited influence over their implementation. Therefore, the question of equitable development and poverty alleviation may well be dependent on the governance structure in developing countries.

Therefore, if it is accepted in principle that trade liberalization has the potential to promote development in the LDCs, in reality there are a number of barriers to such trade-led development.

Barriers to a more sustainable commodity system

The characteristics of commodity production and the markets served have led to the long-term trends of increasing capacity and production, fluctuating but in general declining prices relative to manufactured goods, overproduction and resource depletion, environmental pollution and in many cases community decline. In addition to these characteristics, a combination of subsidies and global political circumstances have led to a declining share in commodity production from the LDCs, and an increasing share for the most developed countries. These issues are now explored in turn.

The 'commodity trap'

In an ideal market, a decline in price would result in a proportionate response by producers to reduce output. This is not always the case with commodity production. A report by the Sustainability Institute (2003) describes a tendency for some commodity producers to both reinvest profits in increased capacity when prices are high, and increase production efficiency to maintain revenues when prices are low. This latter trend is due to the lack of alternative sources of income available to producers, as well as the very real financial plight they face when prices fall. Production can therefore expand irrespective of price. In response markets will naturally expand to absorb the increased production, which in turn can often lead to price fluctuations. These drivers are often referred to as the 'commodity trap' and explain why resource-rich countries are often outperformed economically by countries with scarce resources (see Brander, 2005, p4).

Depletion of stocks

Levels of production are limited by the extent of the resource. Ideally, for sustainability of renewable resources, the level of production would be less than or equal to their regeneration rate, but this does not occur in the production of the vast majority of renewable commodities. If the resource is open to all to access there will be no incentive for individuals to forgo production. Irrespective of access arrangements, signs of scarcity are often only felt long after the regeneration rate has been exceeded. Even when producers receive notable signals of scarcity, capacity will only decrease once the declining rates of return for a given harvest effort lead to unit short-term production costs being greater than consumers' willingness to pay. In the event that consumers have been enjoying large consumer surpluses, or they value highly the rarity of the commodity, or technical change reduces production costs, the resource may well be exploited to the point of collapse. This is becoming the case for many of the world's fisheries.

Terms of trade and price fluctuations

Fluctuating and declining commodity prices and the highly competitive nature of commodity markets leads to limited margins for investing in infrastructure or cleaner technologies, and may contribute to the 'commodity trap' (see above). The rent within product chains is often captured by large vertically integrated transnational companies who utilize the trading structures established under colonial rule (see Girvan, 1987).

Price fluctuation associated with traded commodities is an important barrier to sustainable development in many developing countries. The removal of international and domestic commodity price stabilization schemes means that commodity producers in developing countries are no longer protected against price volatility. Declines in commodity prices have been occurring over a long period of time. Figure 7.2 provides an example of a price trend for cotton in recent decades (1970 to 2001) and shows that the price paid for cotton has both fluctuated and declined over recent decades.

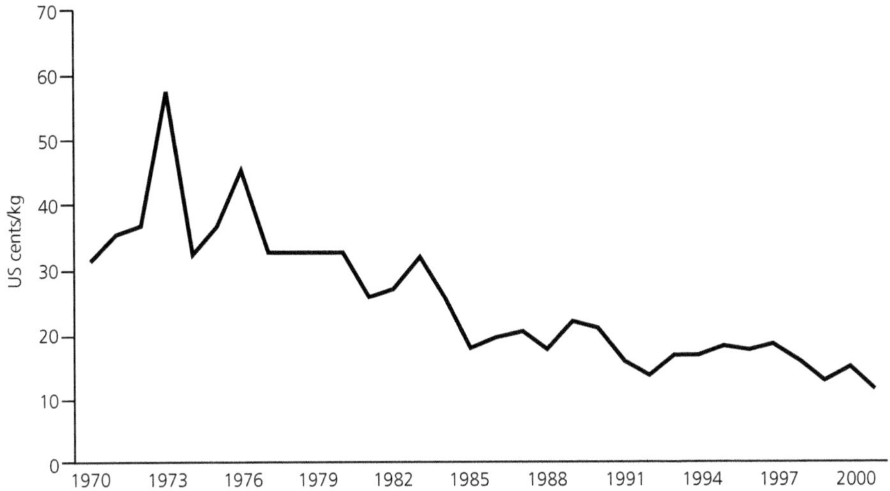

Source: FAO (2003, p30)

Figure 7.2 *Deflated prices for cotton*

In 2002 the price index of agricultural commodities, deflated by the price index of manufactured exports of industrial economies in US dollars, was one half of the same index in 1980 (UNCTAD, 2004, p82). This is consistent with what was proposed in the Prebisch–Singer thesis in 1950. The Prebisch–Singer thesis suggested that, in the long term, prices for primary commodity exports will fall in relation to prices of manufactured imports (reported in UNCTAD, 2004, p82). In economic terms the hypothesis explains this by a divergence between the income elasticity of demand for primary products and the income elasticity of demand for manufactured products. In material terms, the global economy is dematerializing, meaning that less material is required to perform the same function, and so the value within the product chain is increasingly being captured in the manufacturing process. Overall, in the period under consideration, the terms of trade for commodity-producing countries have declined.

Political and governance barriers

In recent decades, developed countries' share of the world market for commodities has increased, mainly at the expense of the formerly socialist countries of Eastern Europe, but also at developing countries' expense. In fact there has been a long-term decline in the LDCs' share of commodity trade as shown in Figure 7.3. UNCTAD (2004, p80) reported that, although total volumes of traded commodities increased at an annual average rate of 7.2 per cent from 1966 to 2000, LDCs' share of this growth was only 2.2 per cent and their overall share actually declined by 5 per cent during this period.

The lack of governance and political stability in some developing countries prevents national policies that might mitigate the threats and distribute the benefits of trade liberalization equitably. In addition, lack of political stability

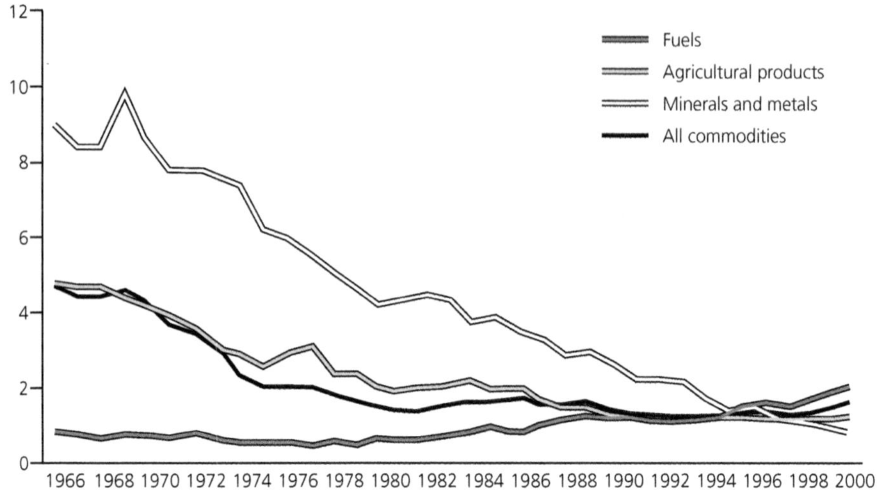

Source: UNCTAD (2004, p79)

Figure 7.3 *Share of least developed countries in commodity exports (%)*

can lead to reduced foreign investment and therefore reduced incomes available to developing countries.

The agricultural policies of developed countries often limit developing countries' access to commodity markets where they have a comparative advantage. Where developed countries are not in competition, tariff escalation often prevents developing country producers from achieving the greater profits that would be available if they processed their own commodities before export.

Whilst the decline in LDCs' share of agricultural commodities can be in part explained by developed countries' subsidy measures, metal products can enter developed-country markets at very low tariffs. However, sub-Saharan Africa's share in traded metal commodities declined by 3.1 per cent from 1996 to 2000. The decline was greater still at 5.1 per cent if South Africa is excluded (UNCTAD, 2004, p79). This decline was reported to be due to a lack of investor confidence and therefore a preference for 'safe havens' in developed countries. In contrast, Latin American countries continued being able to attract foreign investment in mining, and Asian countries were able to experience a 2 per cent increase in share during this period, in part due to rapidly growing domestic demand, which provided a secure base for expanding exports of processed metal products.

The LDCs are often provided with trade preferences in order to avoid tariff barriers. In the case of the EU, this is administered through the 'Everything But Arms' (EBA) arrangements. Since 2000, LDCs have free access to the EU market under the EBA arrangement, with temporary exceptions for rice, sugar and bananas (UNCTAD, 2004, p80). However, it has been reported that the EU already had pre-existing preferences for most of the goods in question and that the EBA arrangements are having little impact. Yu and Vig Jensen (2003, p1) found that the negative impact on the EU and third countries seems to be quite small and that the total welfare impacts of the EBA are less than US$300 million for all the LDCs.

For all these reasons, many non-governmental organizations (NGOs) presently engaged in debates about trade and sustainable environment are often highly critical of the impact trade has on the poorest people in the world (see for example FOEI, 2003), as well as on their environments. However, whilst it may be far from certain that current trading structures will lead to appropriate development for these people, it may also be the case that low incomes and poor environmental practices would have occurred irrespective of trade. Many of the barriers to development as identified above are essentially failures of governance (that is, failure of the international community to provide equitable trading arrangements and the failure on the part of developing country governments to provide stable investment environments and manage the impacts of production or invest in higher value alternatives to primary commodity production). It is therefore argued by some that the governance structures that affect the trade in commodities need to be improved in order to achieve appropriate development in LDCs, rather than halting the move towards the liberalization of trade.

For example, Ekins (1994, p14) explores the possibility that commodity production for export might lead to the expropriation of land previously used for poor subsistence farmers and indigenous peoples, arguing that this could lead to these people being forced to use more marginal and environmentally sensitive lands, leading to greater environmental degradation and therefore acting as a further driver for poverty. However, it is the lack of governance at the national level, leading to the interests of the least well off being unprotected, rather than the international trading system, that is the root cause of this outcome. At the same time it is clear that the impacts of such failings in governance can be amplified when the lending policies of international institutions lead to substantial pressure on LDCs to pay back debt with foreign exchange. The need for trade liberalization to be combined with appropriate governance structures is therefore a central issue in the trade, development and environment debate.

Part II: The Sustainability Impact Assessment of commodity trade liberalization

General SIA framework

SIAs aim to identify and describe the cause, the magnitude and the nature of each sustainability impact in a way that can be easily understood and compared with other sustainability impacts. Each sustainability impact identified needs to be causally linked to the trade measure or measures that are considered to be its origins. There are four stages to the SIA as proposed within the EU–Chile SIA (Planistat, 2002, p17):

1 **Description** of the scenarios or possible outcomes of the trade negotiations.
2 **Identification** of the effects to be studied and the methods of analysis. This task includes the screening of the expected outcomes of the trade agreement for possible impacts, and the 'scoping' or definition of the methods to be used to examine the areas of interest in more depth.
3 **Assessment** and comparison of the main sustainability impacts and analysis of the quality of the information available.
4 **Development** of mitigation and enhancement responses to the sustainability impacts as identified (often called flanking measures).

For the EU–Chile SIA, preliminary screening and evaluation of the initial economic effects of the trade agreement (stage two) is made through a Computable General Equilibrium (CGE) framework, namely the General Trade Analysis Project (GTAP) model:

> *This is a tool for analyzing market transactions based on utility maximization and profit maximization by economic entities such as households and businesses, as well as inter-market transactions. The model is able to quantitatively assess the impacts of economic policy changes on the industrial structure, resource allocation, income allocation, and other items through changes in relative prices and the changes in the behaviour of economic entities in response to relative price changes.* (Planistat, 2002, p45)

Stage three of SIAs uses methods to identify specific potential sustainability impacts due to the results from the model. Both quantitative and qualitative methods are used; and information and analysis is collected and discussed with national and international sector experts with differing viewpoints. The final assessment summarizes and compares the full impact of the trade agreement. This is done through causal chain analysis (CCA), which aims at identifying the significant cause–effect links between a proposed trade measure and its consequent economic, social and environmental impacts. Mitigating and enhancement (otherwise known as 'flanking') measures are discussed and proposed in stage four. These are activities that could be undertaken to counteract or mitigate a negative sustainability impact or to enhance a positive sustainability impact. The mitigation of potentially negative impacts often relates to the implementation of domestic policy.

SIAs and commodities

The process of assessment (i.e. stages three and four) of the impacts of commodity production within the SIA framework largely follows the same process as the analysis of other sectors. There is a very wide range of methods of assessment used for each sector when considered in detail. However, there is a generic identifiable process for all sectors. This is shown here with reference to the processes required for the assessment of grains, other agriculture and forestry within the EU–Chile SIA (Planistat, 2002, pp81–100):

1 **Agreement scenario:** The CGE model is used as a projection of future changes if agreement is reached.
2 **Base case:** Historical trends within the sector are used as the basis for a base case scenario.
3 **Sector analysis:** Present issues and pressures within the sector are identified and the impact of changes in output assessed (for example, as to whether the impacts are scaled with output, or whether technological improvements will reduce this scale effect).
4 **Sustainability assessment:** A range of methods are used to further assess the secondary impacts (environmental, social and economic) of the projected changes relative to the base case scenario.
5 **Drawing up of flanking measures:** The knowledge gained during the sector analysis and sustainability assessments is used to propose mitigation or so called flanking measures.

Secondary impacts

Blobel et al (2005, p7) discuss five types of trade-related effects: product effects (effects on trade flows in certain products); scale effects (effects on the level of economic activity); structural effects (effects on the structure of economic activity); regulatory effects (effects on environmental and social regulations); and technology effects (effects on technology transfer and production processes). The CGE model does not just consider direct changes in the scale of trade due to changes in tariff regimes, but also estimates corresponding changes in demand for industrial inputs within a country. Retaining the EU–Chile as an example, Chile is already a major producer and exporter of copper to the EU. The reduction in tariffs on copper imported from Chile might only cause a small increase in demand for the commodity. However, reductions in tariffs on manufactured goods might lead to a much larger shift in production of goods made in part with domestically mined material. Therefore, such equilibrium models can begin to predict structural changes.

Assessment methods

For processes 3, 4 and 5 as identified above in the EU–Chile SIA, 'Both quantitative and qualitative methods are used; and information and analysis is collected and discussed with national and international sector experts with differing viewpoints' (Planistat, 2002, p18). It is difficult to generalize the types of assessment methodologies applied for commodity production. However, due to its extensive requirement for land and use of environmental services, SIAs of commodity production often adapt approaches used within Environmental Impact Assessments (EIAs). Another characteristic of commodity production, particularly agricultural production, is its extensive use of unskilled labour. To understand the vulnerability of these workers to change, in-depth analysis of the sector and its labour force is required as well as analysis of the prospects of commodity price fluctuation.

The Institute for Development Policy and Management (IDPM) methodology (see Chapter 3) applies the general approach of CCA to assess the social and environmental outcomes associated with a particular market response predicted by the General Trade Analysis Project (GTAP) model (Blobel et al, 2005, p8). The use of economic models as the basis of predicting social and environmental outcomes has its pitfalls, particularly when modelling the behaviour of commodity producers. As will be discussed in the next section, the behaviour of producers and the lack of governance capacity mean that commodity markets do not always conform to assumptions of profit maximization models, particularly in relation to developing countries. CCA is therefore a useful way to distinguish the consequences of trade liberalization from pre-existing structural issues. To achieve this, a sound country-specific sectoral analysis is crucial. If this line of argument is accepted, global and country level SIAs that set out to predict the likely impacts of multilateral reforms to agricultural subsidy need to be treated with great caution. They cannot generate in-depth understanding of the particular market responses and governance failures of the main commodity producing countries and how these might interact.

An often used alternative is to use descriptive in-depth case study approaches to provide on-the-ground, empirical insights that cannot be generated with modelling approaches. A drawback of such approaches is that their methodologies are insufficiently developed or explained and they are often unable to separate their findings from other factors of change. Such case studies risk merely identifying associations between traded commodity production and sustainability impacts and are therefore not in a position to provide valid predictions for future trade liberalization. Another disadvantage is that there is a very limited possibility to generalize from case studies (see Blobel et al, 2005).

In their analysis of uncertainty, Blobel et al (2005, p10) propose that uncertainty is not always the result of a lack of data or adequate methodological tools but may also result from differing conceptions of reality, priorities and systems of value of different actors. They go on to report on an entirely different approach to the assessment of cause–effect relationships. The approach examines the factors that make a socio-ecological system vulnerable or resilient to changes, and makes an assessment of the ability of such systems to respond to changes.

Outputs from SIAs

There are two main outputs for each sector: a summary table showing the sustainability impacts of the proposed agreement, and a list of flanking measures to mitigate and enhance any significant potential impacts. As an example, the summary table for the grains and other agriculture sectors within the EU–Chile SIA is shown in Figure 7.4.

SIA processes applied	Impact of Agreement 1 and 3	Base case 2 and 3	Equity 3 and 4	Reversibility 2–4	Capacity to change 2–5
1 Economic					
Real income	△	?	▽		
Net fixed capital formation	△	△	▽		
Employment	?▽	▽	▽		
Consumer effects	▽	△			
2 Social					
Poverty	▽	▽			△
Health and education	▽	▽			△
3 Environmental					
Environmental quality	▽	▽			△
Biological diversity					
Other natural resource stocks	▽	▽			△

Key:

○ Non-significant impact compared with the base situation.
△ Positive lesser significant impact (marginally significant, by itself, to the negotiation decision).
▽ Negative lesser significant impact (marginally significant, by itself, to the negotiation decision but a potential candidate for mitigation).
▲ Positive greater significant impact (likely to be significant, by itself, to the negotiation decision).
▼ Negative greater significant impact (likely to be significant, by itself, to the negotiation decision. Requires serious consideration for mitigation).
◊ Positive and negative impacts likely to be experienced according to context.
? Net effect is uncertain.

Note: The impact of the agreement is always filled in but the other columns are completed as required to describe the sustainability impact.
Source: Adapted from Planistar (2002, p88)

Figure 7.4 *Example summary of sustainability impacts (for the grains and other agriculture sectors in the EU–Chile negotiations)*

In addition to the sustainability impacts which might be expected under the agreement, sector level summary tables also consider:

- **existing conditions** – extent of existing economic, social and environmental stress in affected areas;
- **equity** – equity of change and how it affects different sectors of the population;
- **irreversibility** – the potential for irreversibility of the change;
- **capacity to change** – the regulatory and institutional capacity to implement mitigation or flanking measures.

Flanking measures

An important part of the SIA process will be the prevention, mitigation and enhancement measures (so called 'flanking measures') that are proposed to tackle the identified sustainable development impacts. These will commonly propose phased liberalization to allow for market actors to adjust, policies to improve governance structures and market competitiveness and, failing this,

Box 7.1 Example of prevention, mitigation and enhancement (flanking) measures (WTO fisheries)

To prevent, mitigate and/or enhance the identified impacts, the following recommendations are proposed:

Economic and trade related measures

- Gradual (rather than precipitate) reduction of tariffs to allow fisheries and processing industries to adapt to changes.
- In relation to non-tariff measures, capacity building of standards boards.
- Investments for the provision of infrastructure, support systems and modern efficient technology to make developing country suppliers more competitive.
- Marketing initiatives such as development of new domestic, regional or overseas markets, and targeting of 'higher-end' quality markets.
- Development of aquaculture into a medium to large-scale commercial industry (e.g. Africa).
- Development assistance or other support from the international community to help cover losses from preference erosion.

Social measures

- Design and implementation of alternative livelihoods and employment programmes.
- Retraining and skill development measures in particular for women.
- Existing social subsidies should be continued and strengthened to help the poor in the fisheries sector using more holistic indicators of poverty (e.g. India).
- Support for the shrimp sector around the Gulf of Mexico and specific programmes geared to native communities in North America.
- Special and Differential Treatment of small-scale and artisanal fisheries.

Environmental measures

- Application of an ecosystem approach in response to environmental concerns related to aquaculture production as well as capture fisheries.
- Development of fishmeal substitutes.
- Private sector initiatives and public/private partnerships.
- Eco-labelling should be considered as a tool to achieve both fisheries management and marketing objectives.
- Stopping of illegal, unreported and unregulated (IUU) fishing.
- Reduction or redeployment of fishing capacity.

Source: Kleih et al, 2006, pp12–13

social and environmental protection initiatives to prevent the impacts. Some proposed flanking measures will be aimed at tackling very particular issues as identified in the particular SIA. However, many will appear in most SIAs. A good example of a relatively generic set of proposed flanking measures is shown by the SIA on fisheries and the World Trade Organization (WTO) (Kleih et al, 2006) as shown in Box 7.1.

SIAs and the agricultural sector

Vanner and Ekins (2006) give a detailed analysis of the approach of SIAs to the minerals, forestry and fisheries sectors, as well as to agriculture, but for reasons of space only the analysis of agriculture is summarized here.

The agricultural sector is a very large and diverse sector that produces significant volumes of commodities that are traded between many countries. In addition, agricultural commodities have undergone only limited liberalization and tend to be the subject of numerous trade disputes. It would not therefore be feasible to cover all of the issues for the whole sector in a satisfactory level of detail. This section therefore considers the sector through a SIA study (Maltais et al, 2002) that assesses the prospects of global-level trade liberalization in two food crops (wheat and edible oil crops) with reference to eight country case studies. It is often these basic food stuffs that are the subject of the most contentious trade disputes and barriers.

The countries considered are reported in three groups:

1 Net food-importing developing countries (Egypt and Senegal).
2 Net food-exporting developing countries (Indonesia, Argentina and India).
3 Net food exporting developed countries (Australia, the US and the EU).

The following liberalization scenarios were used for the analysis:

- **The baseline scenario** only assumes that the Uruguay Round Agreement on Agriculture is fully implemented.
- **The intermediate scenario** comprises a gradual approach to liberalization in the sector that incorporates the EU negotiation objectives. The objectives include:
  - retention of 'blue' and 'green' boxes,[2] possibly with some updating;
  - an ongoing process of reducing trade barriers, support for exports and domestic agriculture whilst retaining these boxes;
  - support for various non-trade concerns including the multifunctional role of agriculture, food safety and quality, protection of the environment and animal welfare;
  - support for special and differential treatment of agriculture in developing countries, including increased (duty-free) market access for the least developed countries.
- **The liberalization scenario** assumes 'general acceptance, within all country groups, of comprehensive trade liberalization in agricultural products and the removal of discriminatory market practices in domestic markets. This would require elimination of all forms of export subsidies, domestic support measures and import duties' and 'that very limited, future changes are made to mitigate adverse environmental and social impacts'.

The following sustainable development impacts were reported in Maltais et al (2002):

Net food-importing developing countries (Egypt and Senegal)

- **Economic and social impacts:** Negative economic and social impacts due to increasing wheat import bills. Food security problems for vulnerable groups, such as rural women in the agricultural sector. Small-scale farmers are potentially impacted by increased competition from international markets, and inability to adequately improve productivity in an increasingly competitive domestic market, and commodity price/food security impacts.
- **Environmental impacts:** Senegal would see some negative environmental impacts due to increases of production in the groundnut sector, as there is no indication that currently unsustainable farming practices will be significantly affected by liberalization (negative environmental impacts are not causally linked in the Egyptian case).

Net food-exporting developing countries (Indonesia, Argentina and India)

- **Economic impacts:** In Indonesia and Argentina, positive economic impacts can be expected for both liberalization scenarios. The economic impacts are not conclusive for India but depend on India's ability to meet domestic wheat demand.
- **Social impacts:** In all cases it is also suggested that vulnerable groups, especially small-scale farmers and the rural poor, may be negatively affected by liberalization. These groups may be more severely affected by the liberalization scenario due to problems in adjusting to more significant economic changes. In Indonesia, some social groups would gain while others, particularly forest dwelling indigenous groups, would incur negative impacts. Specific causal links were more difficult to establish in the Argentina and Indian cases. India in particular demonstrates a great deal of diversity between regions, although the potential for negative gender impacts is clear.
- **Environmental impacts:** There is a wide diversity in the results for these three countries.
  - Indonesia demonstrates clear negative impacts for its forests, especially in the liberalization scenario, where a direct causal link is found in the assessment.
  - Argentina shows no significant negative environmental impacts in the short term and only potential impacts in the longer term due to increases of input use and dependence on domestic policy developments.
  - In the Indian case the environmental impacts are poorly causally linked, resulting in more ambiguous results.

Net food-exporting developed countries (Australia, the US and the EU)

There are positive economic impacts for all of these countries in both liberalization scenarios.

- **In Australia** positive impacts entail both positive overall *economic* welfare impacts and positive impacts on producers. Short-term social impacts are anticipated due to positive economic impacts in the sub-sectors. However, over the long term there are risks of potential negative social impacts associated with the adjustments needed to manage land degradation problems, particularly associated with dry-land salinity issues. As a result, social impacts in the long run are more dependent on emerging circumstances. Negative *environmental* impacts are associated with production increases and problems with dry-land salinity, and tend to also be more significant over the long run.
- **In the US,** large farm households are expected to gain while intermediate farm households may face some adjustment problems in an increasingly competitive market. As a result *social* impacts are shown to be positive in the intermediate scenario and more ambiguous in the liberalization scenario. The intermediate scenario entails more opportunities to use domestic support measures to mitigate negative impacts on intermediate farmers and to deal with *environmental* impacts of the sector.
- **In the EU** we see positive *economic* impacts from liberalization in terms of general welfare and budgetary expenses, but clear negative impacts on producers, particularly in the liberalization scenario. This results in more context-specific economic impacts. *Social* impacts are expected to be more positive in the intermediate scenario as there is some indication that the EU has a better-established agenda to address social and environmental impacts in the agricultural sector. Ambiguous environmental impacts are shown in the liberalization scenario due to predictions of production decreases. More regionally specific analysis is required to establish the environmental effects of these production decreases.

Opposition to liberalization of trade in agricultural commodities

The discussion above (and in Vanner and Ekins (2006), for other sectors) shows that SIAs have proved effective in identifying the impacts (positive and negative) of commodity trade liberalization. They have also proposed flanking measures to mitigate the negative impacts. However, these proposals have had a limited impact on the Doha trade negotiations and, in respect of agriculture, have not proved adequate to enable a successful conclusion to be reached. This section identifies why trade negotiations in the current global economic context are so difficult to conclude. To be effective, SIA analysis and proposals will have to reveal and take explicit account of all the motives and arguments to resist trade liberalization that were identified in Chapter 4:

- **Protectionist bias argument:** Protectionist lobbies act to protect vested interests.
- **Adjustment cost argument:** The social costs during the process of economic adjustment might represent a barrier to liberalization even though the prospective long-term efficiency gains might be greater.
- **Externality argument:** Some countries may be worse off due to the social and environmental impacts of liberalization.
- **Collective preferences argument:** The social fabric might be endangered by a proposed trade liberalization. The preferences may be particular to a country or region or have a more universal expression, for example in a multilateral agreement.

It is worth exploring how the impacts predicted by existing SIAs for commodity sectors would map onto these arguments. To do this, it is useful to try to further generalize and characterize the results of the SIAs discussed in the previous section. Although this represents a highly simplified characterization of a complex situation, it does begin to demonstrate how these arguments against commodity trade liberalization can begin to be addressed. In terms of the impacts from liberalization in these sectors, there appear to be three distinct groups of countries experiencing characteristic sustainable development pressures as a result of trade liberalization:

- **Developed countries** mostly face overall reductions in outputs due to the removal of their trade barriers with corresponding consumer and revenue benefits. Whilst some sectors will respond by further intensifying leading to environmental pressures, many others will decline leading to social adjustment costs and long-term changes to communities and rural environments.
- **Low-cost developing countries** (such as Brazil, China and India) are likely to increase their levels of production in response to liberalization. The economic benefits may often be captured by larger rather than small companies, although the benefits will in many cases trickle down in the form of increased employment. Environmental pressures are likely unless technological transfer occurs and governance structures respond. More vulnerable producers and consumers might face social impacts as a result of the loss of direct and indirect subsidies.
- **Vulnerable developing countries** such as African, Caribbean and Pacific (ACP) and LDCs will often struggle to compete due to increased competition and the loss of trade preferences. Consumer prices may also rise as a result of the removal of developed countries' subsidies. These changes will cause several social and environmental pressures as some producers respond to intensify production to maintain revenues. The degree of social and environmental impacts, and the ability of the populations to adjust, is dependent on the governance capacity available within these countries to implement mitigating policies.

The protectionist bias argument and commodities

Agricultural lobbies in Organisation for Economic Co-operation and Development (OECD) countries clearly have a motive to promote the protection of agricultural markets against cheaper imports from developing countries. Whilst the arguments put forward by such lobbyists will tend to be expressed in terms of wider social interests, their prime motive is to maintain their sector's interest against competition. For example, within the fisheries sector, there are pressures to maintain quota and subsidy levels even when there is evidence of declining fish stocks. This is motivated both by concerns about the social costs to communities and by the more narrow interests of boat owners. It would appear that the protectionist lobbies of the minerals and forestry sectors have been somewhat less effective in shaping trade policy, in developed countries at least. To understand the degree to which protectionist lobbies have been successful in influencing agricultural and fisheries trade policies, it is necessary first to make a judgement on the influence that the other three motives for resisting trade liberalization have had, in the light of what is considered to be justifiable by the evidence in the SIAs.

The adjustment cost argument and commodities

At least some of the sustainable development impacts anticipated for developed countries as a result of liberalization might be considered to be temporary adjustment costs and, although costly for the people involved, do not outweigh the long-term benefits of liberalization. The level of these costs would depend on the speed that trade barriers are removed and the level of adjustment support available within the country. The kind of phased-in decoupled support provision being proposed within the WTO negotiating rounds, combined with the high level of governance capabilities available in developed countries, means that these impacts would be limited. This perhaps explains why at least some developed countries are prepared to enter into serious negotiations over the liberalization of these sectors, albeit with some reservations and conditions.

Low-cost developing countries face a number of economic and social changes as a result of liberalization. A range of economic structural changes might occur as a result of economic development. Also, more vulnerable producers and consumers would need to adjust to the loss of subsidies and governments might have to respond to the environmental pressures brought on by increased production and act to protect some environments and communities. However, in the context of overall economic growth, these adjustments have generally been considered (by their governments at least) to be a tolerable part of these countries' ongoing development.

This leaves out areas of impacts that may not be considered to be adjustment costs. These include:

- **adjustment costs** that, due to a lack of governance in some more vulnerable countries, actually represent a permanent cost that may outweigh the benefits of liberalization;

- **permanent impacts** that in aggregate outweigh any long term economic benefit to an individual country;
- **changes that are not acceptable** to either some or all negotiating parties because they pose a threat to the fabric of society concerned.

The externality argument and commodities

Avoidable external costs

Voituriez et al (2006), and Chapter 4, suggested that for some countries, the sustainable development impacts posed by further liberalization are so great that it may not be in their interest to proceed in the absence of mitigation or compensation arrangements within trade agreements. Indeed the externalities resulting from existing liberalization may have already exceeded the economic benefits for developing countries. This may have gone unacknowledged, as the trade models used within SIAs anticipated net economic gains. Many SIAs have recommended that exporting governments should regulate and mitigate the impacts of trade liberalization. However, many LDCs do not have the capacity (or the political will) to implement such measures, and the communities involved often have insufficient power and representation to demand it. A positive outcome from further trade-liberalization measures may require targeted assistance from trade partners in order that all parties can gain from the potential economic benefits of trade liberalization without imposing excessive sustainable development impacts on vulnerable communities.

Unavoidable external costs

It is also possible that a proposed trade liberalization poses unavoidable sustainable development impacts that are considered to exceed the benefits of liberalization. Such a situation might occur for example when the impacts are set to scale up with production and exceed environmental carrying capacities. This is by no means a straightforward judgement for trade negotiators to make as sustainable development impacts cannot readily be put into monetary terms and compared with economic benefits. Nevertheless, this is the judgement that is required and if any one negotiating party considers that the overall costs outweigh the benefits, they will be unlikely to wish to proceed. The potential to achieve overall benefits may still remain via compensation arrangements, so that this problem may still be open to resolution if compensation payments are made, perhaps in the form of targeted transfers of clean production technologies.

The collective preferences argument and commodities

With regard to agricultural commodities, the changes and decline in agricultural production in developed countries predicted by SIAs might be considered to threaten the fabric of rural communities, and the environmental maintenance of the countryside, as well as the food security of the countries involved. Voituriez et al (2006) and Chapter 4 proposed that countries be allowed to escape from trade liberalization whilst compensating loser countries. Based on the evidence in the SIAs presented earlier, some kind of compensation would be due to the lower-cost developing countries that stand to gain the most from a more open agricultural trading system. The more vulnerable LDCs may also be due compensation as a result of developed countries' collective preferences on agriculture. However, as present trade preferences mean that trade barriers faced by these countries' exports are often very low, compensation might be limited to compensating for the impacts due to export subsidies and the instability caused to international commodity markets by overproduction.

This is not to say that collective preferences need to rule out trade liberalization, but they do need to be taken explicitly into account. And, of course, preferences are not static. Lamy (2004) proposes that collective preferences might converge and harmonize as a part of the wider process of globalization. However, Lamy (2004) also believes that little should be done to steer this process and that any attempt to do so would probably be counterproductive. By providing an open and participatory forum for the discussion and understanding of collective preferences (see Chapter 9), a revised SIA approach, perhaps introducing more explicitly the possibility of international compensation, might provide the potential to move the process of trade negotiation from a situation of impasse.

In the event that a trade partner proposes that a social preference is universal, and this is disputed within a trade negotiation, this could perhaps be resolved with reference to existing practices, norms, conventions and treaties, either within the WTO regime (which generally favours trade liberalization, subject to considerations of sustainable development, with exceptions articulated in Article XX of the General Agreement on Tariffs and Trade (GATT)), or when expressed through other multilateral agreements.

Conclusion

The analysis in this chapter has shown that the production and trade of commodities has serious implications, potential and actual, for sustainable development across its economic, social and environmental dimensions. These implications have been the subject of a number of SIAs in the context of proposals for trade liberalization, and the SIAs have proved themselves able to give important and useful insights into many of the potential sustainable development impacts of the liberalization of trade in commodities. However, perhaps because there is as yet no robust methodology for the systematic quantitative comparison of economic, social and environmental impacts, the recommendations from the SIAs do not seem to have had a significant impact on the negotiations for the liberalization in (especially agricultural) commodity trade.

The Doha negotiations themselves have been stalled largely by a failure to agree on agricultural trade liberalization. The perceived economic benefits of liberalization generated by SIAs have proved unable to overcome deep-rooted arguments against further liberalization. This leaves a situation in which new initiatives seem required to address the current sustainable development impacts (and especially the environmental impacts) of commodity production and trade.

This theme is taken up again in Chapter 14, which looks at what kinds of new initiatives might be undertaken in accordance with the legal framework defined by GATT/WTO, and then surveys other initiatives of a voluntary nature that are seeking to address the negative environmental and social impacts of much commodity production as revealed in the SIAs.

Notes

1 This implies that the environmental impact indicator is an inverted U-shaped function of income per capita.

2 Generally the WTO classifies subsidies into boxes depending on the level of trade distortion that they cause. In the case of agricultural subsidies the blue and green boxes are less distortive than amber box subsidies, which should be reduced.

References

Bhagwati, J. (2004) *In Defence of Globalization*, Oxford University Press, Oxford

Blobel, D., Knigge, M., Gorlach, B. and Gehring, M. (2005) 'Report on sustainability impact assessment of trade agreements', Concerted Action on Trade and Environment (CAT&E) state of the art report, July, www.cat-e.org/

Brander, L. (2005) 'Report on trade and development', CAT&E state of the art report, October, www.cat-e.org/

CIFOR (Centre for International Forestry Research) (2004) 'Beef exports fuel loss of Amazonian forest', CIFOR 1993–2004, website update Monday, 27 September 2004, www.cifor.cgiar.org/docs/_pf/1/_ref/publications/newsonline/36/beef_exports.htm

Cole, M. A. (2004) 'Trade, the pollution haven hypothesis and the Environmental Kuznets Curve: Examining the linkages', *Ecological Economics*, vol 48, no 1, pp71–81

EC (2006) *Handbook for Trade Sustainability Impact Assessment* (with a preface by P. Mandelson, European Commissioner for Trade), European Commission, External Trade, March, http://europa.eu.int/comm/trade/issues/global/sia/seminar0306_en.htm

Ekins, P. (1994) 'International trade at a crossroads', presented to the conference on Trade and Environment, Harvard University, 29–30 April, www.ap.harvard.edu/mainsite/papers/tne/ekins/ekins.pdf

FAO (Food and Agricultural Organization of the United Nations) (2003) 'Agricultural commodities: Profiles and relevant WTO negotiating issues', prepared by the Commodities and Trade Division as a background document for the Consultation on Agricultural Commodity Price Problems, 25–26 March 2002, Rome, www.fao.org/Regional/LAmerica/prior/comagric/negocia/documentos/profiles.pdf#search='Major per cent20flows%20in%20traded%20commodities'

FOEI (2003) 'Business rules: Who pays the price? How corporate influence in the WTO impacts people and the environment', Friends of the Earth International, August 2003, Issue 103

Girvan, N. (1987) 'Transnational Corporations and non-fuel primary commodities in developing countries', *World Development*, vol 5, no 5, pp713–740

Grossman, G. and Krueger, A. (1995) 'Economic growth and the environment', *Quarterly Journal of Economics*, vol 110, no 2, pp353–377

Kleih, U., Greenhalgh, P., Marter, A. and Peacock, N. (2006) 'Sustainability impact assessment of proposed WTO negotiations: Final report of the Fisheries sector study', prepared by Natural Resources Institute, University of Greenwich, UK, and NAP Fisheries UK in association with Impact Assessment Research Centre, Institute for Development Policy and Management, University of Manchester, Consultation Draft: 10 May 2006, www.sia-trade.org/wto/FinalPhase/FISHERIESFINAL_May2006.pdf

Kox, H. (1993) 'International agreements to deal with environmental externalities of primary commodity exports: With emphasis on international commodity-related environmental agreements', Paper presented to the International Conference 'Striking a Green Deal: Europe's Role in Environment and South–North Trade relations', The European Parliament, Brussels, 7–9 November 1993, published in L. Isaksson and C. Moorcraft (eds) (1993) *Striking a Green Deal*, Environment and Development Resource Centre (EDRC), Brussels, pp39–50

Lamy P. (2004) 'The emergence of collective preferences in international trade: Implications for regulating globalisation', speech by EU Trade Commissioner Pascal Lamy at the Conference 'Collective Preferences and Global Governance: What Future for the Multilateral Trading System?', 15 September, Brussels, www.trade-info.cec.eu.int/doclib/docs/2004/september/tradoc_118929.pdf

Maltais, A., Nilsson, M. and Persson, A. (2002) 'Sustainability impact assessment of WTO negotiations in the major food crops sector', Final Report, May, http://ec.europa.eu/comm/trade/issues/global/sia/studies_wto.htm#foodcrop

Planistat (2002) 'Sustainable impact assessment (SIA) of the trade aspects of negotiations for an association agreement between the European Communities and Chile' (Specific agreement No 11), Final Report, October, http://trade.ec.europa.eu/doclib/docs/2006/september/tradoc_112388.pdf

Stern, D. (2004) 'The rise and fall of the Environmental Kuznets Curve', *World Development*, vol 32, no 8, pp1419–1439

Sustainability Institute (2003) 'Commodity systems challenges: Moving sustainability into the mainstream of natural resource economies', Sustainability Institute Report, April, http://sustainer.org/pubs/SustainableCommoditySys.2.1.pdf

UNCTAD (2004) 'Development and globalization: Facts and figures', United Nations Conference on Trade and Development, New York and Geneva, www.unctad.org/Templates/webflyer.asp?docid=4848&intItemID=2364&lang=1&mode=downloads

UNEP (1999) 'Environmental impacts of trade liberalization and policies for the sustainable management of natural resources: A case study on Uganda's Fisheries sector', United Nations (UNEP/99/6), New York and Geneva, www.unep.ch/etu/etp/acts/capbld/rdone/ugda.htm

Vanner, R. and Ekins, P. (2006) 'SIAs and negotiating "contextual realities" (SIAMETHOD): New SIA approaches for traded commodities', Working Paper from SIAMETHOD, December, Policy Studies Institute, London

Voituriez, T., Ekins, P., Blanco, H., Von Homeyer, I. and Scheer, D. (2006) 'Making trade sustainable impact assessment more relevant to trade negotiations', *Impact Assessment and Project Appraisal*, vol 24, no 4, December, pp335–342

Von Moltke, K. (2003) 'Report on trade in commodities', CAT&E state of the art report, IVM / IDDRI, September, www.cat-e.org/

Yu, W. and Vig Jensen, T. (2003) 'Tariff preferences, WTO negotiations and the LDCs: The case of the "Everything But Arms" initiative', Working Paper 04/03, Danish Research Institute of Food Economics, Frederiksberg, www.ictsd.org/issarea/atsd/Resources/docs/Tariffpref.pdf

8
The Potential Role for Collective Preferences in Determining the Rules of the International Trading System

Tristan Le Cotty and Tancrède Voituriez

Introduction

In September 2004, the then European Trade Commissioner Pascal Lamy organized a conference on 'Collective preferences and global governance: What future for the multilateral trading system?'. In his keynote address, Pascal Lamy stressed that whatever its benefits, international market opening also had a destabilizing impact on the economic and social fabric, and potentially on societal choices. He argued secondly that while efforts had been made to develop accompanying measures to deal with the effects of market opening on industry and employment, the threat to societal choices had so far not received proper attention. The challenge, in his view, was to design an open trading system that everyone accepts and that safeguards legitimate social choices.

Europe's collective preferences were identified as including values like multilateralism, environmental protection, food safety, cultural diversity, the public provision of education and health care, precautions in the field of biotechnology and welfare rights. Eroding such values while further liberalizing trade would appear as a loss for the European Union (EU), according to Pascal Lamy. Mr Lamy proposed a new temporary safeguard clause to be added to the World Trade Organization (WTO) Agreements, potentially accompanied by a compensation mechanism aimed at those who would suffer from these safeguards.

Even though Pascal Lamy's diagnosis of the fear and the threat roused by globalization has been strikingly confirmed by the backlash against globalization we face today, his proposition stirred up controversy among EU trade partners and stakeholders, and criticism among a few academics. Still, his nomination at the WTO as Director General, and the considerable difficulties finalizing the Doha Round of trade negotiations, somehow left the debate on collective preferences unfinished. In the perspective of the inescapable reform of the WTO, the objective of this chapter is to re-examine the case of the potential role of collective preferences in determining the rules of the international trading system. The question we focus on is whether seeking to take explicit account of collective preferences can help to provide the multilateral system with better responses to societies' expectations and fears concerning globalization, notably within the EU.

Trade can be a means for emerging countries to raise per capita income, which would in turn tend to raise social demand for non-traded goods such as education, health, environment and better social conditions. Thus, trade is not necessarily an obstacle to the fulfilment of the non-trade aspects of collective preferences. Nevertheless, it seems that the rigour of international rules relating to trade, compared to the non-trade multilateral rules and agreements, favours preferences for tradable goods and services over non-tradable values and considerations. Therefore, one may wonder whether the global legal system is able to ensure the fulfilment of collective preferences for non-tradable goods as well as the provision of tradable goods.

We start by evaluating the current state of the debate on collective preferences. We then provide a definition of collective preferences based on the economic definition of preferences and social choice. As a next step we explore the relevant WTO agreements and dispute cases to draw their main implications in terms of collective preferences. The next part suggests possible methodological elements to assess European preferences in a selected number of issues. Key policy implications are outlined before the conclusion.

The state of the debate on collective preferences

The core of the debate: Common goals and heterogeneous collective preferences

The WTO expanded the General Agreement on Tariffs and Trade (GATT) mandate by covering new sectors such as services and intellectual property rights, and including domestic policies like farm policies. Such an expansion towards 'reserved domains' of sovereignty obviously generated friction and dissension among populations, non-governmental organizations (NGOs) and politicians. The NGO campaign against the General Agreement on Trade in Services (GATS), on the grounds that it could disrupt the social contract on particular aspects of public services provision, united resistance to the WTO in the mid-1990s.

As long as trade negotiations were only concerned with tariffs, the increase in trade occurred at the expense of specific existing activities, but only political preferences[1] for these sectors were challenged. Citizens outside these sectors would not have been affected by the trade increase as long as governments were allowed to mitigate economic changes with unconstrained domestic policies. Now that negotiations deal with domestic policies, public choices regarding domestic issues are being made under the potential constraint of international trade rules. The fact that efficient public policy can be implemented in a non-trade distortive way whatever the policy goal (hence whatever the collective preferences) is a key issue for trade negotiations in all sectors. But this overall requirement that public choices should not alter trade may be at the root of a growing feeling among citizens that they are losing control over their political destiny.

This feeling is not equally perceived throughout the world. In some countries, citizens do not necessarily have the feeling that governments are mandated to serve their collective preferences, or that governments actually serve these preferences in a reliable and efficient way. In such contexts, the perception of the WTO threat to public choice is limited because public choice itself does not necessarily guarantee the fulfilment of collective preferences. Furthermore, countries with low environmental or social standards face trading partners with higher standards and, all else being equal, higher production costs. For them, the trade increase would not threaten these non-trade aspects of their collective preferences. Finally countries from the old world with long-standing traditions and cultural heritage may adopt the view that their identities and values have contributed to the sustainability of their society, and are reluctant to let them be challenged by the global trading system.

Nevertheless, many countries are facing potential contradictions between their willingness to cooperate through multilateral coordination and their will to defend their citizens' collective preferences. For instance emerging countries often have lower preferences for environmental concerns than Organisation for Economic Co-operation and Development (OECD) countries and see the perspective of CO_2 limitations as a 'threat' to their priorities. This threat will probably not be expressed in trade negotiations, but in multilateral environmental agreements. Conceptually, the need for emerging countries to comply with environmental cooperation in spite of the low weight of environmental concerns in their collective preferences is comparable to the need for OECD countries to comply with trade rules in spite of relatively lower importance given to the increased availability of merchandise in their collective preferences.

Therefore, heterogeneity in collective preferences in a context of global cooperation is a global concern.

Is there a European specificity on collective preferences?

Even though his conception of collective preferences is rather universal – 'collective preferences are the end result of choices made by human communities that apply to the community as a whole' – Lamy's diagnosis mainly rests on European examples.

The EU perception of the issue indeed shows some specificity. Environmental and social standards and policies in Europe are higher than in most other countries, reflecting the average income and subjective values of Europeans. In comparison with most countries, expectations concerning global environmental and social goals in Europe are probably higher than those concerning an increase in the availability of commodities. This may explain why trade rules may be seen in Europe as a potential source of constraints on their collective preferences, whereas non-trade negotiations are mostly viewed as an opportunity (to meet their preferences for non-trade goals).

The role given by European citizens to their public institutions in mitigating the social effects of job losses is also important in the European perception of international trade. Recent debates on globalization confirm that the perception of a threat in several European countries is real and that policy makers are somewhat shorter of political support for globalization than one might have guessed when the WTO Round was launched. Hence, in a survey on 'Trade victims', *The Economist* contends that 'Rather than affecting entire industries, or whole factories, global competition will affect individual jobs – skilled as much as unskilled. Such a shift helps explain the popular nervousness about globalization. Many more workers are worried that their jobs will be at risk' (*The Economist*, 20–26 January 2007, p31). The fear of lining up with the next WTO Round's losers pervades the population.

Trade measures are sometimes considered as the last resort protection for those sectors that could not compete in a global economy. The budget expenditures required to compensate losers could increase in the short term if trade liberalization were to be imposed.

'In advanced countries with social welfare programs in place, it should be primarily spending on social security and welfare that is correlated with exposure to external risk...' (Rodrik, 1998, p1019). But increased public expenditure is not an auspicious development in a global economy either. Since increased public expenditures can have a negative effect on potential investments and productivity, trade liberalization is considered by many as the end of the welfare states in Europe (Box 8.1).

This is probably part of the reason why welfare states in Europe perceive the expansion of the WTO rules as a threat to the policy space of its different member states. Assuming that the champions of globalization are equally sensitive to the losers, expanding Trade Adjustment Assistance (TAA), as US Democrats did in winter 2006, is politically easier than hastening the process of reforming the welfare states. It may justify the EU's need to postpone reforms under the umbrella of trade protection. The need for temporary safeguards is understandable in this respect.

Box 8.1 The political economy of globalization and job insurance

Following Garrett (1998, 2001), we can distinguish two basic positions on the relationship between the dynamics of public expenditure and globalization. The 'efficiency' hypothesis highlights competitiveness pressures and exit threats by mobile asset holders. The 'compensation' hypothesis, in contrast, emphasizes the domestic dislocations generated by globalization and the incentives for government intervention in the economy that these generate.

The efficiency hypothesis

The fundamental tenet of the efficiency hypothesis is that government spending beyond minimal market-friendly measures, such as defence, securing property rights and other fundamental public goods, reduces the competitiveness of national producers in international goods and services markets. Income transfer programmes and social services distort labour markets and bias investment decisions. Moreover, government spending must be funded either by borrowing or by increasing taxes. Income and consumption taxes reduce the profitability of work and investment in the country. Borrowing results in higher real interest rates, depressing investment. If this also leads to an appreciation in the real exchange rate, the competitiveness of national producers is reduced. Therefore, the efficiency hypothesis supports the idea that globalization creates incentives for governments to reduce public expenses.

The compensation hypothesis

Short-term expansion of the scope of markets is likely to increase citizen support for government spending to compensate for increased inequality and economic insecurity. These are two strong political incentives to increase public expenses in response to globalization that may offset the competitiveness pressures generated by market integration.

Source: Garrett (1998, 2001)

A summary of potential and actual controversies raised by collective preferences

The political debate on the potential value of referring to collective preferences in trade negotiations is still at an early stage, and the scientific contribution to this debate as such is also limited.

Nevertheless, the question raised relates to existing debate on the role of the WTO in global governance. United Nations Conference on Trade and Development (UNCTAD) uses the concept of 'policy space' to designate the decision-margin countries should maintain in order to pursue social or economic goals, and highlights the risk of the erosion of this policy space by international trade. For UNCTAD, the concept of policy space is particularly relevant for Southern countries, whose development may require specific protection. UNCTAD highlights the potential constraints of trade rules and conditionality linked to loans or aid in particular. In this sense, the question of whether or not specific needs justify trade-affecting measures relates to that of whether or not specific collective preferences justify trade-affecting measures. The United Nations Environment Programme (UNEP) has also indirectly provided useful contributions to the debate, notably through its analysis of the relationships between multilateral environmental agreements (MEAs) and trade rules. UNEP calls for better cooperation between the WTO and the secretariats of multilateral environmental agreements to improve coherence between multilateral institutions and to strengthen the enforcement of MEAs. To some extent, UNEP's work can also be interpreted as an effort to better integrate collective preferences in multilateral institutions. In the same sense, the International Labour Organization (ILO) aims at ensuring the fulfilment of globally accepted minimal labour rights in a context of increased competition. The ILO's work also sustains the debate on the need for balancing the collective preferences for social needs and economic growth.

This chapter uses the approaches taken by these organizations to address the question of whether collective preferences can be useful for the trading system, keeping as close as possible to the orientation given by Pascal Lamy. This orientation is a new one because it is general in outlook, rather than being concerned with specific issues, and because its purpose is to improve trade rules. According to Pascal Lamy's intuition, fears that social choices might be called into question by an all-powerful WTO were behind the rejection of globalization. His main message to trade negotiators and policy makers was that whether or not these fears were justified, they should be met with a credible response (Lamy, 2004, p1). Even if the debate on collective preferences has not yet spread very far, this orientation seems promising in the long run. The aim of improving trade rules and the general orientation of trade negotiations is likely to attract the interest of negotiators because each country has collective preferences to fulfil. The same does not hold for discussions on specific issues.

Pascal Lamy initiated the debate on collective preferences and the global governance of the world trading system as he approached the end of his term as European Commissioner for Trade. A 'non-paper' on the same issue was drafted in November 2003 and first released by the Commission on 18 February 2004. The non-paper's first objective was to 'justify different/higher and restrictive standards vis-à-vis trade partners' (EC, 2004, p1). Its second aim was to react to information leakage after the *Financial Times* published an article on 6 February indicating that DG Trade had prepared a document on the issue. The official birth of the project was hence controversial in itself. Its original content proved controversial too.[2] When this paper was completed and presented in Brussels on 15 September 2004, it did not receive the imprimatur of the Commission. Some of the most important possible reasons include the uncertainty on the precise meaning and implications of the concept, as well as fears of misinterpretation by trading countries. Since then, DG Trade has not continued explicit work on collective preferences, partly because of these uncertainties and partly because of the priorities of the WTO agenda.

A follow-up to the conference took place within the framework of the DG Trade Civil Society Dialogue in Brussels in October 2004. Two months later in Paris, the French think tank 'En Temps Réel' convened a meeting on Pascal Lamy's proposition. A publication of Pascal Lamy's paper, as well as

Charnovitz and Wyplosz's comments made during the December meeting in Paris, were published in 2005 (En Temps Réel, 2005). A synthesis of the reactions formulated during these three events highlights the following three main objections:

Objection 1: Are collective preferences really an issue in the world trading system? Which issues could be better addressed through the concept of collective preferences than through the existing concepts of externalities, social choices and public goods? The novelty of the concept in the WTO framework and the specific problems addressed remained unclear.

Very few academics endorsed Pascal Lamy's diagnosis, and when they did, they took their distance from Lamy's proposals. The most notable example is Steve Charnovitz (2005), who stated that

> *The problem Lamy addresses is real. Countries will often adopt different public policies, and, as Lamy says, trade becomes a 'natural point of intersection for different systems of collective preferences'. Clashing or distinctive collective preferences between governments have led to trade disputes (e.g. hormones), and will assuredly do so in the future. When WTO rules inhibit domestic autonomy, that can undermine public support for the trading system.* (Charnovitz, 2005, p452)

Charnovitz mentioned that concerns similar to those raised by Lamy had been formulated before Lamy wrote his essay. Ironically, some earlier proposals were even made by some critics of Lamy's initiative, including Bronckers (1999) and Bhagwati (2004). Others dated back to a few years before, such as Rodrik (1996) and Perdikis et al (2001), without Lamy's mentioning them. According to Charnovitz's analysis, Pascal Lamy's thoughtful diagnosis seems apposite, at least in academic terms.

To clarify this, it seems worthwhile going back to the economic meaning of collective preferences to understand its potential relevance in a multilateral trading context.

Objection 2: The concept and practical implications of collective preferences are unclear, including the compensation mechanism. What is the current legal status of collective preferences under WTO rules? What status changes seem to be needed?

We investigate both questions, examining current rules, and possible future changes to these rules.

Objection 3: Taking into account collective preferences could reinforce asymmetry in the world trading system (in favour of rich countries) and trigger further protectionist policies. Collective preferences that would simply protect domestic producers from international competition would not be recognized as a sustainable policy at the WTO. The problem is that only governments know their own motives for implementing a policy, which may arise from both protectionist reasons and public interest.

We investigate this debate by analysing actual policies in different countries in order to obtain some objective indicators of preferences.

Definitions and aggregation issues

Individual preferences are the implicit hierarchies established by each citizen for different possible states of the world. Economically, these states of the world are characterized in particular by the combinations of each private good purchased by this person and the degree to which each public good affects his welfare.[3]

In simple terms, preferences reflect people's priorities regarding the way they allocate their resources across different uses, including the quality of private goods, their social expectations, and more generally the combination of public goods they expect, including the environment, public infrastructure and transportation, health care, education, military safety, civil safety and local environmental characteristics. All these expectations and purchases are subject to individual budget constraints that limit their private and social demands for these goods and services, and to subjective factors such as culture, information, living conditions and tastes.

An extended understanding may include political preferences, in other words the political support they agree to bring to each activity sector or social group.

Another extended understanding includes people's expectations regarding the characteristics of the world as a whole, in particular social and environmental conditions in other countries. These are referred to as outwardly directed preferences (Charnovitz, 2005).

Collective preferences take the idea of individual preferences to the community level. Thus, collective preferences are the relative hierarchy that the majority of a community establishes between all possible states of the world. In the context of the world trading system, collective preferences are the scheme of priorities between different possible uses of resources that societies of different scales reflect in their public choices in order to improve their living conditions.

For non-market goods and values, public intervention is generally needed to fulfil social expectations. The challenge for the government before delivering on public goods and protecting social values is to establish its own perception of the preferences of the society as a whole – the collective preferences of the community to which it is accountable. Democratic governments adjust to what they think are collective preferences in a given period through a complex decision-making process (negotiations, surveys, elections, parliamentary initiatives etc.).

Three implications must be underlined. First, the central government decision-making process can be interpreted as a means of arbitrating between individual preferences. This means that the current provision of public goods (through public policies) and the satisfaction of social values in a given society do not directly account for the collective preferences of the country, but merely reflect a particular choice in a given political context, which will be submitted to citizens' evaluation (through voting, polling, trade union initiatives etc.). Collective preferences are not necessarily impaired by policy reforms, and they cannot justify all current policies in a given country.

Secondly, multilateral trade negotiations do enter the above-mentioned political process of democratic governments, helping willing governments to account for national collective preferences during the preparatory process of trade negotiations, or in their wake. For instance, collective preferences at the world level for fair access to generic medicines would not have been revealed without the TRIPS (Trade-Related Aspects of Intellectual Property Rights) negotiations and backlash.

Thirdly, trade negotiations may improve some aspects of people's preferences, especially the availability of commodities, and neglect other aspects such as resource conservation and equity. Therefore, trade influence on domestic policies does not mean that collective preferences are always threatened by trade (since trade may contribute to them); it means that the various elements of their preferences are not equally taken into account at the world level. At the national level, trade negotiations lead to unequal pressure on policy reforms in favour of trade improvement over improvements in non-trade concerns.

The WTO legal framework and collective preferences

The dilemma of the multilateral governance system is to achieve common goals, which requires constraints and new directions for national policies, without limiting the possibility for national collective specificities. The goals of global governance themselves are supposed to improve the fulfilment of certain aspects of collective preferences that nations share at the world level. These include, for example, the freer-trade of commodities (WTO), the protection of biodiversity (Convention on Biological Diversity) and the prevention of climate change (Kyoto Protocol).

The fact that multilateral disciplines impose changes in domestic policies does not necessarily imply that collective preferences are threatened, provided that trade negotiators have a sufficiently broad perception of their country's collective preferences. Nevertheless, the different aspects of collective preferences are unevenly represented in each negotiation because of the negotiation path itself, and this can create imbalance's among the different elements of collective preferences for some countries.

The relevant WTO agreements to deal with collective preference issues

The WTO provides rules whereby non-trade elements of national collective preferences can be preserved through non-trade concerns, or 'legitimate domestic measures'. Following Charnovitz, we identify four distinct mechanisms for this: national treatment; existing safeguards; general exceptions; and the Dispute Settlement Body ruling.

National treatment

National treatment requires that countries offer foreign providers equivalent conditions to those offered to national providers. Theoretically, this leaves room for countries to set domestic policies to promote their collective preferences, as long as these apply without discrimination against like products.

For instance, in the Sanitary and Phytosanitary measures (SPS) agreement, national treatment enables the protection of preferences for high sanitary standards,[4] provided it can be proved that the measure is justified on internationally recognized grounds. As shown in the beef hormone case, this does not allow countries to differentiate products if the necessity of this differentiation is not established on internationally recognized bases. In this case, states cannot regulate trade to reach their public objectives. For instance, individual citizens must reflect their private preferences for production methods – assuming their information enables them to do so – through their purchases. Economic theory can support this approach as long as the consumer is the only person involved in the purchase, but not when public aspects are involved in this consumption. For instance, the risk of viruses spreading after importation must be established according to generally accepted scientific criteria, which may not reflect uncertainty or a national desire for precaution (itself perhaps a collective preference), before it can be addressed through trade regulation, which may be an obstacle to policy efficiency.

Furthermore, national treatment opposes upstream trade regulation for attributes such as

- preferences for higher labour standards in trading partner countries;
- political preferences (to support and protect social groups that could be threatened by lower-cost imports);
- animal welfare (if not visible in the product's final characteristics).

Whether or not linkages between trade and such concerns are legitimate is a highly controversial issue that cannot be solved in a straightforward way. At this stage, it must be recalled that the spirit of the WTO national treatment principle is to prevent such linkages, in other words to prevent countries from using trade regulation in the name of these concerns.

But it is important to note that many sectors are not covered, or not fully covered, by the national treatment principle. Public services are not covered by this principle since they are partly or fully provided through the national public budget. Existing tariffs are a way to ensure the protection of political preferences in favour of national providers. Agricultural policies still ensure advantages for national farmers, for example.

Existing safeguards

In principle, temporary safeguards are not meant to promote collective preferences, but only to respond to a short-term necessity to cope with exceptional world trade circumstances. These safeguards consist in temporarily restricting imports (theoretically for four years at the most, exceptionally for eight years), if a domestic industry is threatened by a surge in imports. In theory, safeguard measures cannot be targeted at imports from a particular country. When a country restricts imports in order to safeguard its domestic producers, the exporting countries can seek compensation through consultations.

Such safeguards are often considered ambiguous because they potentially contain a protectionist effect in favour of targeted sectors.

For all these reasons, existing provisions for safeguards should perhaps not be considered as a tool adapted to collective preferences.

General exceptions

The general exceptions allow trade regulation for a limited set of motives, under the conditions of non-discrimination and non-protectionism. In principle, as noted above, temporary safeguards are not meant to promote collective preferences, but only to respond to a short-term necessity to cope with exceptional world trade circumstances.

GATT Article XX lists a number of non-trade concerns for which trade measures are allowed, provided the trade distortion they generate is minimal. Analysis of a number of conflicts shows how these provisions can be used effectively in defence of collective preferences for non-trade concerns, along with their limitations.

As long as the need for trade measures to meet non-trade objectives can be assessed, and as long as this assessment is validated by international criteria, there is potential for countries to use this article. However, in many cases, the appreciation of the legitimacy of trade measures is critical. A typical case for subjective non-trade concerns is provisions motivated by public morals. The perception of policies that are necessary for moral reasons is of course very subjective, and difficult to assess in a multilaterally accepted manner. Even the provision on human, animal and plant health is no guarantee for countries with high standards. The appreciation of health risks themselves is very different in rich and poor countries for an equivalent level of physiological impact.

GATT Article IV on cinematograph films provides another example of a possibility for countries to use quantitative import restrictions to implement their cultural preferences.

The GATS agreement is another example of the WTO leaving room for the expression of collective preferences, partly because this is a new and complex issue to agree upon, and partly because many governments are very sensitive to their country's conception of public services (see Chapter 6). Thanks to the positive list approach, countries are allowed to choose the sectors they agree to open to foreign competition, with all other services sectors being exempt from multilateral liberalization. For now, the collective preference for the public provision of any service can be preserved. In due course, however, the negotiation incentives might lead countries to put these services on the table. If societies cannot choose the economic role they wish their government to play in services provision, the sense of a loss of sovereignty might be much stronger than it is now for commodity trade.

The Dispute Settlement Body ruling

The Dispute Settlement Body (DSB) has the power to evaluate whether domestic policies are necessary to implement collective preferences (non-trade concerns). 'Whether WTO rules actually do infringe legitimate domestic measures will depend on how they are adjudicated by WTO panels and the Appellate Body.'

Possible infringements lie in the many ways WTO rules can potentially prevent non-protectionist domestic measures designed to achieve national preferences. Charnovitz gives a list of policies that could be challenged by the corresponding WTO agreements.

The GATT laws themselves give few indications as to the legitimate non-trade concerns that could justify specific measures. Precedents on these concerns and appropriate policies are very recent and in the decades to come will reveal the boundaries between legitimate and illegitimate policies for non-trade concerns.

Examining DSB cases

The US–EU beef hormone dispute

The EU–US beef hormone dispute can be interpreted as an example where the EU ban on US beef was considered an unnecessary policy to defend EU collective preferences according to the first ruling.[5] Since the EU assessment of the policy rationale based on the sanitary risk was considered unconvincing, it means that the alleged EU preference for hormone-free beef was not considered a good reason for trade restriction. The trade retaliation imposed by the US can be interpreted as the 'price to pay' (for the loss of market share in the US) by the EU to maintain its policy for alleged European preferences. This indicates that countries can still defend their collective preferences in the absence of proven risk, but must suffer retaliation.

After the entering into force of EU new Directive (2003/74/EC) regarding the prohibition on the use in stockfarming of certain hormones, the EU stated that there was no legal basis for the continued imposition of retaliatory measures by Canada and the US. According to the EU, the US should have ended its retaliation, which it did not. This indicates that the assessment of the need for the trade restricting policy may be more flexible than one might think.

The main insight we draw out of this case is that the substantial content of the alleged collective preferences counts less than the efforts to use internationally recognized methods to justify the policy in favour of these preferences.

Furthermore, we can infer from this dispute that no trade regulation of production methods would be allowed if it were not justified by risks, but rather by tastes or beliefs.

The shrimp/turtle dispute

In very simple terms, we can interpret this case as a conflict between the US and a group of shrimp-exporting Asian countries, the US having relatively higher preferences for the conservation of endangered turtles than Asian countries.

After an improvement of the US assessment of the need to maintain its ban on shrimp imports from a number of Asian countries, its alleged preferences were recognized as legitimate by the Appellate Body. The Appellate Body's report explicitly refers to CITES (Convention on International Trade in Endangered Species) as an argument to legitimate the import ban under GATT Article XX on general exceptions to trade rules. Below is an abstract of the Appellate Body's report:

> *All species of sea turtles have been included in Appendix I of the Convention on International Trade in Endangered Species of Wild Flora and Fauna (the 'CITES') since 1975... In paragraph 7.58 of the Panel Report, the Panel noted: 'The endangered nature of the species of sea turtles mentioned in [CITES] Annex I as well as the need to protect them are consequently not contested by the parties to the dispute'.*

This means that international conventions can also potentially be used as an argument for trade measures to protect collective preferences. It must be noted that although the WTO could have compelled the US to remove its ban in the case of a ruling in favour of the Asian countries, it cannot compel these countries to modify their fishing techniques in such a way as to meet conservation objectives. Interestingly, it also illustrates that in the absence of explicit linkages between trade and non-trade agreements, disputes tend to be adjudicated in the WTO framework, which is likely to give more weight to trade liberalization (the explicit objective of the WTO) than to other values or concerns.

Finally, as in the previous case, the purpose of the policy is not so much at the core of the ruling as the assessment method used to establish the necessity of the policy.

Antigua and Barbuda–US gambling dispute

After Antigua and Barbuda challenged the US ban on cross-border Internet gambling and betting on moral grounds, the US argument of the defence of public morals was acknowledged as a legitimate objective of the US measures at stake. The conflict was not solved by resorting to a reference as to what the appropriate 'moral level' should be. But the US failed to demonstrate that its prohibitions applied to both foreign and domestic service suppliers in a manner that did not constitute 'arbitrary and unjustifiable discrimination', as required by the chapeau of Article XIV on public moral defence exceptions. It would otherwise have won its case and made its own preferences for moral defences override Antigua's preferences for increased market access.

Again, even though the WTO does not challenge the content of collective preferences, the possibility of showing the necessity of a trade measure – which depends on this content – is the key element of the ruling.

Some insights from the cases examined

A generic conclusion we can draw from these precedents is that panels do not judge the substance of collective preferences, but the way in which countries assess their need for a specific measure. The improvement of the assessment method has even resulted in the panel making changes to its decisions (as with the shrimp and hormone cases). In both cases, this improved assessment has turned in favour of non-trade concerns.

Still, the condition that a measure must be necessary if it is to be allowed raises questions. According to basic principles of public policy, a policy does not need to be necessary to be fruitful. Decision makers' intuitions or beliefs are probably the most common way of implementing policies in favour of a community. Existing policies are hardly ever 'necessary' to achieve a given purpose. Alternative ways to achieve this goal always exist. It may be argued, for instance, that better labelling is more trade-friendly than import regulation, and still makes it possible for each consumer to choose whether they prefer higher quality purchases (with fewer health risks) or whether they prefer cheaper purchases. In this sense, trade restrictions are not necessary to achieve a level of safety corresponding to each person's income and risk perception. But as long as the information is never complete and as long as the health effects may not be limited to the consumer, trade regulation, while not strictly necessary, may be more efficient than trade-friendly policies to achieve the same objective of ensuring a satisfactory level of protection against health risks. WTO precedents therefore tend to increase the cost of legitimating social choices in favour of public goods.

Nevertheless, these types of trade-related assessments of collective preferences provide very interesting input for the implementation of non-trade conventions. The US assessment of endangered turtles and the EU assessment of the hormone case can both contribute to improving explicit links between trade and non-trade conventions, and can feed the discussion in alternative forums.

Trade law and non-trade law relationships

According to our analysis, collective preferences encompass non-trade values and trade values, the relative weight of each differing across countries. The WTO rules in general are likely to increase demand for private goods, which are important elements of collective preferences, and this should not be neglected. Trade in this respect contributes to ensuring lower prices and increasing export earnings. These two aspects can improve people's living conditions and also increase the income share available for public goods. Health care, education and labour standards remain closely correlated with national income.

Still, as we have seen, trade dispute settlements enforce trade rules, and trade rules alone (with few exceptions). This progressively leads national short-term decision making, constrained by trade rules, to favour trade-friendly policies at the expense perhaps of socially or environmentally friendly policies. The Kyoto Protocol is an example of a non-trade convention that is not widely implemented because of a weak application mechanism in relation to its ambitions. Thus, national decision making between the willingness to regulate polluting industries – and meet Kyoto objectives – and the willingness to export, typically turns in favour of the latter. The same is true of the Convention on Biological Diversity (CBD). Therefore, in simple terms, private elements of collective preferences tend to be more easily provided than public elements. The whole governance system seems unbalanced and countries with higher collective preferences for public goods and non-trade concerns are probably more threatened than others by this unbalanced governance.

Towards an assessment of 'European collective preferences'

Policies and preferences are not synonymous because policies are often inherited from a world in which interaction between countries was not as widespread and rule-based as today, and where governments tended to satisfy people's expectations from the national perspective alone. Thus, policies probably ignore some of the potential value of coordination in terms of improving the fulfilment of collective preferences. Furthermore, policies arise from a complex interplay of lobbies and one can imagine that the welfare of silent groups (including marginal populations and future generations) is probably underestimated in existing policies.

Nevertheless, because of selective democratic pressure on proposed policies, we still consider that existing policies are a reasonable starting point from which to draw elements of collective preferences.

Our aim is of course not to describe the complete collective preferences scheme, which would be impossible. Preferences being comparisons between observed and non-observed states of the world, one can at the most analyse the prevailing arbitration between different allocations of resources in the existing state of the world in the country under consideration.[6] These arbitrations are supposed to account for the social demand for each non-market good in question (the other parameters of the state of the world being taken as given).

This illustrates the relative value attributed by the society to different non-market goods in comparison with the value attributed by other societies to these non-market goods given the existing level of these non-market goods actually observed in these countries, and given all other factors that may influence public choices. However, where possible, we do take account of the revenue effect on choices in order to avoid attributing to preferences what is actually due to income.

Labour rights

Legislation on labour rights can be used to reflect the arbitration between people's demand for higher income and their demand for non-consumption attributes like leisure. Among these labour rights, the legislation on working time could be compared between countries, provided parameters like legal holidays are considered. To avoid such a complex comparison, we compare the effective yearly working time – instead of the legislation – which gives another indicator of the preferred arbitration between leisure and income. Linear regression suggests that the EU has a relatively higher preference for leisure over income or consumption goods than most other countries. This preference for leisure over income is negatively correlated with the income level, but we can also identify regional effects. In particular the average yearly working time is very homogenous among European countries of different income levels, meaning that the regional influence overcomes the average income influence in Europe. The regional effect can also be highlighted by the comparison between the EU and Asian countries where the preference for leisure is lower than would be expected for non-Asian countries of the same income level.

All other things being equal, this implies that, on average, increased consumption is not valued as highly in Europe as it is elsewhere, which provides another non-mercantilist explanation for the EU's prudent attitude towards the potential consumption-based gains obtained from further liberalization.

Food quality

National legislation on food quality gives indications of countries' preferences for quality attributes expressed in terms of income. Several indicators show that European preferences for food quality attributes are higher than in many countries, but they are also specific.

European legislation on geographical indications provides specific protection for product origin and production methods. Trademarks are not given the same protection. In comparison, US legislation provides similar protection for trademarks and geographical indications. The dispute between the EU and the US over EU legislation on geographical indications seems to confirm the cliché whereby the European vision of quality is linked to the product origin and the conservation of traditional production methods, and so on, whereas the American vision is based on innovation, science and the composition of products.

The recognition of origin as a quality attribute in the absence of any measurable difference in the product, challenges the non-discrimination principle based on the like product criteria. Again, this can also explain the EU's position at the WTO, which recognizes science-based preferences more readily than tradition-based preferences.

Public expenditures

Public expenses are a major source of information on countries' collective preferences for different types of public goods and services. Apart from agriculture and regional development, most public expenses are left to national sovereignty. Efforts to harmonize agricultural expenses have shown how difficult it is to aggregate preferences at the regional level as soon as public good funding is involved, in spite of relatively similar development levels. Nevertheless, European national public expenses (as a share of GDP) indicate similarities between European countries, even in non-agricultural sectors.

We consider the relative income share given by each country to any public expense. This income share accounts for average collective preferences for a public good estimated for a given level of all other public goods and income levels.

European countries' preferences for public services are relatively high, especially for university education and public health care, which may confirm Lamy's statement.

This could imply that for European citizens, public contributions to individual needs play a part in social welfare.

Policy implications

The risk of collective preferences being understood as a new ad hoc tool for protectionism in rich countries should not be ignored. Whereas we can broadly define protectionism as the defence of economic interest groups whose contribution to public goods (rather than market outcomes) is not widely recognized or supported by citizens, policies for collective preferences are aimed at fulfilling citizens' expectations, including public good provision. Among these policies, some can potentially have impacts on trade. Therefore, the risk of misinterpretation is real and must be addressed. The following proposals are designed to minimize the risk of such an interpretation, and still sustain the debate on the long-term architecture of global institutions.

In principle, existing trade rules and dispute settlements do not remove the possibility for countries to design policies in favour of their collective preferences for public goods and non-market aspects of their own living conditions. One should not ignore the ability of the DSB to take account of the variability of these non-market concerns among societies, provided they can be assessed. Precedents on environment, health, food safety and moral issues show that panels and the Appellate Body already arbitrate between conflicting preferences by assessing the 'legitimacy' of collective preferences that have an impact on trade. To do so, they assess whether external references (international treaties, science-based knowledge or other government practices) support the 'importance' of the 'common interests or values' protected by the policy measure at stake.

Nevertheless, the WTO judgement of these policies imposes a series of conditions that question the sustainability of non-measurable elements of preferences – like moral values – and that increase their cost. Some lawyers convincingly argue that dispute precedents, such as gambling, are overly restrictive of WTO member states' sovereignty because of the reference to external 'common interest or values' and the unclear process of 'weighing and balancing'.[7] They indeed demonstrate that current uncertainty in WTO rulings on these two aspects may thwart domestic policies in ways that are unpredictable.[8] They further recall that panels and the Appellate Body may not always be infallible, so that a collective preference mechanism may offer the defendant government a way out of its compliance obligation while giving the dispute system the opportunity to refine and correct the case law.[9] These objections are motivated by the possible infringement of social choices by WTO rules. Even though they do not all refer to collective preferences, they do provide support to the concept and to the argument that it should be reflected in WTO jurisprudence.

Despite the current biases against their recognition, a safeguard for collective preferences in general would perhaps not serve the purpose of ensuring the usefulness of collective preferences in the trade context, if these preferences only concern national living conditions. We instead suggest the development of assessment rules in such a way as to account for heterogeneous preferences when the assessment of the necessity of the policy cannot be established on an international basis. A more flexible way of assessing the need for the policy would be to compare the level of public good achieved by this policy with the level achieved by other existing policies in comparable sectors in this country. For instance, in countries where public expenses for public health care are high, trade measures preventing imports with low sanitary standards should probably not be looked upon as protectionist measures.

When policy goals concern not only domestic living conditions, but also global public goods or foreign living conditions, the case for safeguards is potentially different. As long as the consistency between trade rules and multilateral non-trade rules is not established, collective preferences for non-trade concerns are potentially unfulfilled, and this bias is likely to become increasingly important in trade negotiations. It is true that trade rules can call upon international conventions to rule on a dispute, but since the international non-trade rules are still barely enforced, the bias in favour of trade purposes remains. Therefore, we suggest that a new type of safeguard should be negotiated for policies based on international conventions, in spite of the potential trade effect of these policies. Processes and production methods, including environmental and social criteria, may be part of import choices as long as they serve multilateral cooperation purposes. While trade bans are probably not the best way of enforcing UN conventions, trade policy removal can also act as an obstacle to such conventions – such as the climate change protocol – in the absence of the effective implementation of these conventions.

In practical terms, a safeguard for policies in favour of multilateral conventions seems legitimate, and could potentially accelerate the search for better coherence between international laws. As long as countries using such safeguards expect third countries to meet production standards that have been agreed upon in international conventions, these safeguards do not require compensation. If the expected standards exceed the level agreed upon in these conventions, compensation seems legitimate to help third countries to improve production standards. This potentially includes the case for minimal labour rights, biodiversity protection, resources conservation and climate change prevention. The implementation of such a safeguard implies increasing the availability of shared information on countries' production methods and standards. It is indeed hardly conceivable that a country would agree to finance compensation without a reasonable level of confidence in the actual fulfilment of its expectations regarding the trading countries' standards.

Such improved coherence is of course a long-term challenge at the multilateral level. In contrast, regional agreements are promising fields for countries to learn from each other's preferences when multi-sector arbitration is necessary. More ambitious conditionality to trade preferential agreements can be agreed upon at the regional level because a broader range of issues can be negotiated. Furthermore, regional and bilateral agreements seem the appropriate level at which to test the above compensation.

Conclusion

European collective preferences appear to be in favour of balanced development where environmental values and social values play a large part in social welfare. Europe's attention to its own environmental and social conditions is high, and its attention to other countries' environmental and social conditions is also increasing. The need for more consumption is not perceived in Europe as an essential priority for social welfare, as it is in many countries, partly because the essential basic needs of most people are satisfied, and partly for historical and cultural reasons.

Existing trade rules allow some degree of protection of national collective preferences for several societal concerns that could be threatened by unregulated trade.

Since the creation of the WTO, countries must be accountable for their collective preferences and the policies designed to implement them. Societies' fears of losing sovereignty over their social choices stem partly from this new international accountability requirement. Trade rules and case law on non-trade concerns and exceptions show that provided this effort for accountability is made, the DSB tends to acknowledge and leave room for the heterogeneity of collective preferences, as far as sanitary and environmental standards are concerned.

Very often, public environmental or sanitary policies are implemented because governments feel they will be socially accepted and even desired, without any kind of assessment apart from continuous democratic regulation. Among countries' perceptions of the need for regulations, beliefs, habits and tastes play a major role in shaping adequate policies, and the scientific need is only one determinant. The DSB ruling might introduce a long-term bias selection in favour of preferences for measurable risks at the expense of subjective elements of preferences. In particular, existing trade rules do not readily allow the defence of preferences for moral values through trade measures (like trade bans for unacceptable working or environmental conditions in third countries).

Furthermore, the advance of the enforcement of trade rules over that of non-trade rules at the multilateral level creates another bias: the multilateral incentives for national legislation to be reformed in such a way as to increase the availability of material goods, and the multilateral incentives for them to evolve in such a way as to integrate global non-trade objectives are unbalanced.

Therefore, the idea of a new safeguard for collective preferences has to be considered even if there is a risk of this insightful concept being immediately associated with rich countries' new rhetoric for protectionism. Using trade to promote environmental and social goals in third countries has never met with widespread support, either from economists or from Southern countries.

Nevertheless, assuming that collective preferences (hence willingness to pay) exist in Europe for raising these standards abroad, and as long as the lack of consistency between trade laws and non-trade laws on labour and environmental standards remains so striking, the claim for a temporary safeguard for policies in favour of outward-directed preferences seems interesting. The respect of basic human rights in foreign countries, or heavy local pollution due to production methods in foreign countries, are examples of this kind. If the living conditions in third countries expected by the importing countries are superior to the minimal standards agreed upon in international treaties, a safeguard would not be legitimate unless compensation is paid by the trade-restricting country. Consequently, international assessments of national standards should be registered and enforced by an independent body to alleviate the bilateral dispute procedures.

More importantly, as far as preferences for global public goods are concerned (climate change prevention, ocean pollution, the depletion of global resources, etc.), such a temporary safeguard should prevail according to the same rules. Temporary import restrictions on countries that do not respect international agreements on global public goods should be allowed and not compensated, as long as the link between the product and the non-respect of the global good provision rules is established. They would be associated with compensation if the standards expected by the trade-restricting country were higher than those agreed upon in international treaties. Compensation would then be used to improve these standards.

As far as collective preferences for local public goods are concerned (a society's collective preferences for its own living conditions), it seems that safeguards are not appropriate. The improvement of international recognition of different assessment methods for non-measurable aspects of preferences (like beliefs, customs, etc.) is probably more promising. An international organization to provide consumers with reliable information about production methods would also be of great help.

For sectors like services, for which the negotiation process is still at an early stage, the effect of trade laws on collective preferences will potentially be considerable because today's heterogeneity in collective preferences is reflected by a huge heterogeneity in national legalization. The services sector embodies societies' collective preferences for public services over private services and the legal duties of the latter. European citizens are probably not ready to allow access to heath, education, energy, water, military security, information and transportation to be provided by the international market, even when these services are offered by private operators. Negotiations on countries' rights to ensure a certain degree of access to these services in a liberalized future are perhaps a prerequisite to the GATS negotiation on private services liberalization.

For services, as for all subjective dimensions of collective preference, increased flexibility in WTO requirements regarding the evaluation of defendant countries' assessments seems necessary in order to integrate multilateral non-trade objectives in a more systematic way, along with non-scientifically assessable aspects of socially desired policies.

Notes

1 Political economics defines collective preferences as the differentiated weights that a government attributes to social groups when maximizing a social utility function.
2 Guy de Jonquieres (2004) 'Lamy studies radical idea for imports veto', *Financial Times*, 6 February 2004, p9; Editorial, 'Lamy's big idea', *Financial Times*, 10 February 2004, p14; 'EU "collective preferences" concept rings alarm bells in Washington', *Food Chemical News*, 12 April 2004, p25; 'UNICE slams Lamy over "collective preferences"', *European Report*, 1 May 2004.
3 Welfare is an ordinal measurement of satisfaction (or utility), depending on these goods and services.
4 Higher than internationally recognized standards, like those registered at the Codex Alimentarius.
5 It is of course questionable whether the EU communities effectively have higher preferences for hormone-free beef than the US, or if the EU simply needs new protectionist devices. However, our aim is not to judge countries' real motivations, but the effects of the WTO practices if countries indeed have collective preferences for such concerns as hormones in beef.
6 Describing all European preferences would imply being able to answer questions such as: what would be the average European willingness to pay to increase national education services by one unit (say one teacher), if average GDP per capita were 300 euros per year, 400 euros per year, etc. and if the existing level of education were 1 teacher for 1 million people, 2 teachers for one million people, etc., and if the average consumption of beef were 100g per year, 200g per year, etc. All this would give the European collective preferences scheme that could be compared to other countries' preferences schemes.
7 See Marwell (2006).
8 Charnovitz (2005).
9 Charnovitz (2005).

References

Bhagwati, J. (2004) *In Defense of Globalization*, Oxford University Press, New York

Bronckers, M. C. E. J. (1999) 'Better rules for a new millenium: A warning against undemocratic developments in the WTO', *Journal of International Economic Law*, vol 2, no 4, pp547–566

Charnovitz, S. (2005) 'An analysis of Pascal Lamy's proposal on collective preference', *Journal of International and Economic Law*, vol 8, no 2, pp449–472

En Temps Réel (2005) 'Mondialisation et préférences collectives: La réconciliation?', Cahier 22–23, www.entempsreel.org

European Commission (2004) 'The emergence of collective preferences in international trade', DG Trade Non-Paper, draft version

Garrett, G. (1998) *Partisan Politics in the Global Economy*, Cambridge University Press, New York

Garrett, G. (2001) 'Globalization and government spending around the world', *Studies in Comparative International Development*, vol 35, no 4, pp3–29

Lamy P. (2004) 'The emergence of collective preferences in international trade: Implications for regulating globalisation', Mimeo

Marwell, J. C. (2006) 'Trade and morality: The WTO public morals exception after gambling', *New York University Law Review*, vol 81, pp802–842

Perdikis, N., Kerr, W. A. and Hobbs, J. E. (2001) 'Reforming the WTO to defuse potential trade conflicts in genetically modified goods', *The World Economy*, vol 24, no 3, pp379–398

Rodrik, D. (1996) 'Labour standards in international trade: Do they matter and what do we do about them?', in R. Z. Lawrence, D. Rodrik and J. Whalley (eds) *Emerging Agenda for Global Trade: High Stakes for Developing Countries*, Overseas Development Council, Washington DC

Rodrik D. (1998) 'Why do more open economies have bigger governments?', *The Journal of Political Economy*, vol 106, no 5, pp997–1032

Part 3
Breaking the Impasse: The National Policy Framework

9
Improving Public Participation in Sustainability Impact Assessments of Trade Agreements

Ingmar von Homeyer, Matthew Collins and Wesley Ingwersen

Introduction[1]

The value of the public voice in policy making is embedded in the policy of the European Union (EU), explicitly recognized in the Rio Declaration adopted at the 1992 Earth Summit (UN, 1992),[2] and reflective of age-old democratic principles on which most modern systems of government are based. But the reasons for including public participation in the policy-making process extend beyond the principle of inclusion and into strategy, as the European Commission (EC) has stated, 'improved participation is likely to create more confidence in the end result and in the institutions which deliver policies' (EC, 2001). In the wake of international trade agreements, where there is a potential for cascading effects that can indirectly influence a significant portion of the populations of consenting nations, public participation is especially important both in principle and to assure a more effective and acceptable outcome.

This chapter first posits key qualities that participation can contribute to the policy-making process, basic prerequisites to participation, and the forms of participation, which we use to guide our evaluation and suggestions. Then we attempt to describe challenges to participation specific to the context of international trade and investment, in order to bring to light the special circumstances for participation in Sustainability Impact Assessments (SIAs). We next turn to existing participation techniques that have been employed in the EU SIAs carried out to date. An evaluation of participation in existing assessments, in consideration of both participation objectives and the challenges of the context, reveals room for improvement. We then build on this analysis and the advice of those who have experience with participation in previous assessments of trade agreements to suggest improvements in participation techniques, timing and integration with negotiations that will both consolidate the role of participation in SIAs and increase its utility to trade negotiators, governments and the general public.

Public participation in policy making: Goals, prerequisites and forms

Goals of public participation

The following section outlines five principal goals of public participation in policy making: credibility, legitimacy, trust, ownership and improved policy performance. These goals have emerged from a range of authors and contexts and are moreover generally applicable to participation in a wide range of areas.

The **credibility** of a given policy is understood primarily through the perceived technical and scientific validity of its information base and assumptions. When the sources of information, the policy process and the conclusions drawn are recognized as trustworthy, the policy is generally understood as credible (Cash et al, 2002). A central determinant of a policy's achieving or failing to achieve credibility is whether or not it holds up to critique from civil society, politicians, the scientific community and/or the general public. In this respect, it is often the technical adequacy of a policy that is in question (Eckley, 2001). Introducing experts in relevant policy, scientific and/or academic fields to the process can help to ensure that the policy meets technical concerns. Similarly, credibility can be enhanced through the inclusion of specific 'local' knowledge that may be 'hidden' from the policy community.

Broadly, **legitimacy** can be viewed as 'a generalised perception or assumption that the actions of an entity are desirable, proper, or appropriate within some socially constructed system of norms, values, beliefs, and definitions' (Suchman, 1995, p574). In other words, when the policy and the process are understood as 'desirable, proper and appropriate' and reflect the values of society, they can be regarded as legitimate. Not only can public participation infuse the policy process with empirical, technical or specific localized inputs, but it can also incorporate individual and collective values and perspectives. By including such values and preferences in the policy process, the public is more likely to view the policy as legitimate and fair and have greater confidence in decision makers (UNEP et al, 2003).

An additional objective of public participation is to create public **trust** in the policy and more generally in the policy-making process. By establishing credibility and legitimacy, a sense of trust in policy and policy making can be facilitated. In addition, including citizens in decision making signals a commitment from the government to listen and adhere to public concern. Creating trust has numerous benefits to both the governing and the governed. Trust can facilitate potentially long-lasting collaborative relationships (Mayer, 2001), build public support for government policies (UNEP et al, 2003), provide greater legitimacy for the government in general (Mayer, 2001) and strengthen government–citizen relations (Bastidas, 2004). Ultimately, trust in the government and its policies should be seen as much harder to gain than lose and public participation is an effective means to achieving such trust.

Ownership of a policy process, in the context of public participation, generally implies a sense of citizen or stakeholder involvement in, and shared responsibility for, the policy process. By facilitating citizen ownership of a policy, policy makers can hope to gain improved government–citizen relations (OECD, 2001) and ease the implementation of the policy and provide for more lasting solutions (UNEP, 2001). Additionally, 'ownership' of a policy gives the public added incentives to participate, cultivate and care for political processes in the future (OECD, 2001).

If citizens are informed and engaged throughout the process of policy formation, they are more likely to accept the final outcome, as their concerns and expectations have been fed into the process (OECD, 2001). In turn, this leads to **improved policy performance**. As a by-product of the four aforementioned objectives, the greater trust and acceptance of policy facilitated by public participation more generally can help with implementation. Additionally, if public participation is successful in conflict resolution and consensus building, social conflict between groups is likely to be eased (Rydin and Pennington, 2000). Through addressing the concerns of citizens, the subsequent durability of a policy can additionally be fostered (OECD, 2005).

Prerequisites for public participation

In order for relevant participation to take place, the affected citizenry must be targeted and appropriately contacted; in order to generate meaningful participation, the participants must be both informed and capable. This hinges on a policy-making process that is transparent. As noted by Blanco and Connors, 'the first task in any public participation program is to obtain a systematic, comprehensive and yet strategic **understanding of the citizens** in the regions and countries affected by the trade agreement. Without this social data base for the citizens of the regions and/or countries, it is impossible to select appropriate participation techniques or sequence and schedule them effectively' (Blanco and Connors, 2005).

Transparency implies access for citizens and stakeholders to government information, processes and policies. Access to information can be split into two subcategories: active access, in which citizens have the right to transmit and incorporate information and demands into the policy process; and passive access, in which citizens are able to obtain information from the government on policy processes (Héritier, 2003). Moreover, transparency is both a *prerequisite* for effective public participation, insofar as citizens must be informed to participate meaningfully, as well as a *facilitator* of participation, in that well-informed citizens are more likely to take interest in a given policy

(Environmental Law Institute, 1997; OECD, 2001). Transparency has the added benefits of improving implementation, avoiding potential conflict throughout the policy process (Environmental Law Institute, 1997), tempering corruption and rent-seeking (UNEP, 2001) and facilitating overall trust in the government (UNEP, 2001).

Just as transparency is necessary to ensure an informed citizenry, **capacity building** is often necessary in order to ensure quality participation. This does not apply equally in all situations and among all participants, and ensuring transparency and/or general participation may sometimes be enough to meet capacity building needs. As such, participation can be seen as a means of capacity building. Nevertheless, in order for participation to be effective it is important, especially when dealing with policies that have not historically been open to the broader public, to consider capacity building efforts. Capacity building often takes the form of training and/or education, but can take a number of forms such as, for example, the payment of or compensation for travel and labour costs.

Capacity building has the benefit of allowing marginalized groups and their knowledge to enter the policy process (UNEP, 2001). Additionally, it can open complex and technical policies to public participation (Donelly et al, 1998). At the international level, capacity building may be necessary to enable organizations from capacity-poor developing countries to take part in participation (SUSTRA, 2003).

Participants and forms of participation

To incorporate participation into an assessment, three broad categories of participants need to be engaged, both independently and in some cases simultaneously: stakeholders, experts and officials. **Stakeholders** are individuals or groups that have a 'stake' in the policy. This often includes public and private interest and business groups. Stakeholders are essential target groups that may provide enhanced legitimacy, trust and policy performance. **Experts** are persons recognized for their training or experience in a particular subject area and are essential to assuring credibility. **Officials** are part of the government or bureaucracy. They may be elected or appointed. Whether or not their participation in assessment furthers or hinders the aforementioned objectives partly depends on how their involvement is perceived by stakeholders. Just as members of society have multiple roles, participants often in reality fit into multiple categories (e.g. elected officials are often stakeholders and may be experts).

Generally speaking, these techniques can be situated between two poles: **non-deliberative** and **deliberative techniques**. Non-deliberative techniques can be considered forms of 'passive' or indirect participation, and are based on the dissemination and solicitation of information. Deliberative techniques, on the other hand, are more 'active' and are generally aimed at either consensus building or dispute resolution among the public. Among these techniques are **citizen forums, dialogue processes** and **working groups** (OECD, 2001). In practice, the techniques employed often incorporate both deliberative and non-deliberative characteristics, and only rarely are they 'purely' deliberative or non-deliberative in nature. The selection of participants and successful application of participation techniques is context-dependent and should be implemented based on an understanding of political, social and cultural factors that define the participants' region.

Challenges to, and contributions of, public participation in SIAs

The organization of public participation in Trade SIAs needs to take account of the specific characteristics of trade negotiations, including substantive complexity, national variation, better linkage of SIAs and trade negotiations and of addressing the 'contextual realities' of trade liberalization.

Substantive complexity

First, the relationship between trade agreements and the variety of potential changes to economies, livelihoods and the environment that may ensue as a result of them are very complex. Substantive complexity of agreements may be attributed to various factors, including the multi-dimensionality of the impacts (economic, social, environmental), their wide geographical coverage and the many intricate chains of causality that link trade and foreign investment with people and their environment. On one hand identifying these causal relationships may be assisted by the participation of experts and civil society, who may possess a better knowledge of local context. On the other hand it is as challenging to predict all the potential changes as it is to convey them in an objective manner to a diverse audience. These conditions only serve to increase the importance of stakeholder participation (Gibson et al, 2005).

National variation

Secondly, especially for agreements occurring between developed and developing countries, there may be significant differences in the types of effects felt, the capacity to monitor and regulate impacts, the knowledge of social structures and preferences of affected stakeholders and, especially relevant here, the capacity for public participation.

Expectations for stakeholder participation within different countries and across various segments of society should be based in part on the strength of civic institutions and the legacy of the public role in decision-making processes. Reviews of the role of participation in impact assessment in Turkey, Bulgaria and China reveal some positive experiences but less success than may be expected in Western countries with a longer history of public participation (Almer and Koontz, 2004; Günes and Coflkun, 2005; Tang et al, 2005).

Linking SIAs and negotiations

The weak link between SIAs and trade negotiations presents a third challenge to meaningful public participation in trade policy. Trade negotiations typically take place behind closed doors among government-designated negotiators. The relative insulation of the negotiating process from outside influences means that, if anything, Trade SIAs are more likely to influence the negotiating mandate than the final agreement that is reached in the negotiations. This is reinforced by the lack of any compelling obligation to incorporate findings of the SIA into the final agreement. Poor transparency due to the confidentiality of some negotiating points further limits the dissemination of relevant information to SIA contractors as well as to outside experts and stakeholders. Finally, as SIAs are typically unilateral products, mandated and conducted by one party, other parties may call their legitimacy and or credibility into question. However, public participation in Trade SIAs also offers significant opportunities to increase the transparency of the issues at stake in the negotiation process and the credibility of SIAs. On the one hand, public participation may increase transparency if stakeholders disclose information gained outside the negotiation process and which one side at the negotiation table has tried to shield from the other. On the other hand, provided that stakeholders are sufficiently independent from the government and do not have incentives to conceal their true position or withhold relevant information, they may increase the credibility of SIAs if they support the assessment's findings.

'Contextual realities' of trade liberalization

Since the public protest at the WTO ministerial in Seattle in 1999, free trade policies have met with increased resistance on a number of grounds. Traditional barriers to free trade remain sticking points in negotiations, including pressure from economic interests to protect non-competitive sectors (protectionism), and social costs caused by loss of sector-specific changes in competition (adjustment costs). However, in addition other concerns have come to the forefront, including externalities and 'collective preferences' which if widely held across countries may be considered, and 'universal exceptions'. Frequently, these factors are difficult to identify and evaluate because they result from indirect effects of trade liberalization that occur outside the strictly economic sphere. More specifically, externalities as a result of trade liberalization are usually associated with environmental and social costs that are not sufficiently reflected in prices and, therefore, remain unaccounted for in a market environment. Trade liberalization may undermine important cultural and normative social practices and traditions as reflected by 'collective preferences' that may extend beyond products to include preferences for specific production processes. Finally, 'universal exceptions' from trade liberalization may be called for in areas where free trade threatens ownership and production structures in areas that provide fundamental, universally recognizable public welfare benefits, such as access to clean water. These 'contextual realities' of trade liberalization are likely to resurface in future negotiations of trade agreements. Once again public participation may often be an important tool that can help to increase transparency, thereby helping to identify and address these issues in a credible manner in the context of SIAs. For example, claims by one negotiating party that certain production processes constitute important and highly valued cultural practices are more credible if they are supported by civil society organizations.

The state of public participation in SIAs

In light of the vast reach of trade agreements and complex changes that potentially ensue in economies, societies and the environment in their wake (UNEP and International Institute for Sustainable Development, 2000), adoption of participation techniques that evolved in project-based environmental impact assessment (EIA), or those designed for other more regionally restricted activities may not always be best-suited for SIAs. Yet as SIAs largely evolved from EIA (Montgomery, 2000), vestiges of participation methods from these assessment appear in modern assessments, especially in government-mandated assessments of trade agreements by the US and Canada. Some of these same methods surface in EU SIAs, but their sustainability-oriented objectives and continued evolution has resulted in a broader and more intensive participation methodology.

Opportunities for participation have generally increased over the course of the development of EU SIAs. The first EU SIA was begun in 1999 for the proposed WTO negotiations in step with the development of the methodology, at which time public participation was very limited. Since then other SIAs have also been conducted or initiated, including for the Euro-Mediterranean Free Trade Area (EMFTA), the EU–ACP (African, Caribbean and Pacific) negotiations, EU–Gulf Cooperation Council (GCC) negotiations and the EU–Chile trade agreement. The most recent SIA of EMFTA is still ongoing and utilizes the most extensive public consultation process of any SIA thus far.[3]

As stated by the EC, the general goals of the EU SIA public participation process include '...ensur[ing] a greater understanding and awareness among stakeholders of the SIA methodology but also to increase transparency and accountability' (EC, 2005). Implicitly, at least, these goals can be linked to the five identified overarching themes (credibility, legitimacy, trust, ownership and improved policy performance). While the goals of the individual EU SIAs are not always explicitly stated, they can generally be interpreted as aligning with some, most or all five of the principal goals.

Stakeholder involvement. In SIAs proactive steps have been taken to disseminate information to and gather input from a wide variety of stakeholders. Steps taken include formation of stakeholder networks through existing multinational government organizations, NGOs, civil society organizations (CSOs); creation of lists of pertinent stakeholder groups; centralized dissemination of information; and staging of regional meetings and workshops.

Identification of participants in public participation has been pursued mainly through use of larger umbrella organizations that have a capacity to facilitate information exchange between contractors and CSOs and NGOs representing stakeholders in agreement countries. The EMFTA SIA consultants for instance identified three such organizations, including the Mediterranean Commission on Sustainable Development (MCSD), the Regional Mediterranean Programme for the Environment (SMAP) Steering Committee and the General Union of Arab Chambers of Commerce, Industry and Agriculture (Institute for Development Policy and Management, 2004).

Tracking lists of stakeholder holder groups were also used in the EMFTA SIA. The use of these lists was meant to ensure that information provision and solicitation was balanced among various stakeholder groups.

The most common means of information dissemination is through a main project website. Project announcements, reports and regular newsletters have been published through these websites, which are maintained by SIA consultants. Information distributed by the SIA consultants themselves is typically restricted to European languages – predominantly English – and distributed electronically.

Consultative meetings with stakeholders have taken place in the form of regional workshops in negotiating partner countries for the EU–ACP and EMFTA SIAs. Virtual online discussion groups were deployed for multinational stakeholder discussion in the EU–ACP SIA (PriceWaterhouseCoopers, 2005). Goals of these workshops include explaining the SIA process, sharing preliminary findings and collecting feedback, as well as using the meetings to establish contact with more regional groups for further consultation opportunities.

Expert consultation. The EMFTA SIA was the first to use an international advisory committee to assist in identification of stakeholders and important regional issues. This EMFTA SIA advisory board consists of representatives from Friends of the Earth, MedNet, Blue Plan, the Economic Research Forum for the Arab Countries and Turkey (ERF), and the UNEP Economics and Trade Branch. These organizations were chosen for their expertise with trade, development and environment issues in the region. One-on-one expert interviews have also been conducted for solicitation of expert opinion. Sources for these interviews may come from the informal SIA Expert Network that was created for the SIA of WTO negotiations (Impact Assessment Research Centre, 2005).

Official consultation. SIA consultants are advised by an inter-directorate steering committee, consisting of representatives from various EC Directorate Generals, who comment and revise SIA reports as well as provide recommendations for improvement of SIAs and identify fields of further analysis.

In the EMFTA study, limited consultations were arranged with government officials from the European Parliament and the European Council. However, past SIAs have been criticized for their inadequate consultation with government officials.

The use of umbrella organizations has been useful for consultation with officials of foreign governments. For example, the EMFTA consultants met with the respective Mediterranean country ministers of the environment through the League of Arab States (Institute for Development Policy and Management, 2004).

Summary

Among impact assessments of trade agreements, participation in the most recent SIAs (e.g. EMFTA) represents a growing attempt to inform stakeholders and to engage them not only passively but in a more deliberative manner. The use of multinational networks for collecting stakeholder opinion has been especially indispensable toward this end. However, though no formal system exists to measure the quality or sufficiency of participation in trade agreement impact assessments, shortcomings are apparent. Unclear participation objectives in SIAs, inadequate forms of provision and solicitation of information, a weak link to negotiations and other obstacles to participation play a role in hindering the achievement of credibility, legitimacy, trust, ownership and improved policy performance. Many of these failures can at least partly be attributed to the aforementioned challenges to participation.

Improving the process of public participation in SIAs

Clarifying the objectives

In the earliest stages of an SIA it is important to develop objectives for participation to guide the design of measures to facilitate participation, to clarify the role and limits that public participation will have in the assessment, and to organize the incorporation of input from stakeholders, experts and government officials into the assessment. To date many of the SIAs have named awareness raising, input for SIA direction and increased SIA process transparency as important objectives (Institute for Development Policy and Management, 2004; PriceWaterhouseCoopers, 2004, 2005). Objectives have set forth modest but vague expectations for participation, not defining the extent of public integration. This could be in part due to the logistical challenges and financial limitations of the studies, as well as the limited precedent for more proactive participant involvement in the SIA process. Although they would likely increase public understanding and confidence of their role, more concrete participation objectives would be misleading unless followed with appropriate opportunities for participation. On the other hand, vague objectives could lead to an interpretation that may also lead to unrealistic expectations among participants. Unfulfilled expectations for participation could have a negative impact on the motivation of stakeholders to participate constructively (Creighton, n.d.). More concrete objectives would be beneficial, but should only be incorporated if contractors can follow through with an appropriate participation programme.

Forming networks to reach participants

Although the technology exists, via the Internet, to enable direct contact between SIA contractors and stakeholders of all rungs of society, possession of the technology is not universal and even when the technology is available, many other social, political and educational, as well as logistical gaps may exist between contractors and stakeholders. In assessments of smaller-scale development projects and programmes in developed world countries – for which methods of participation in EIAs were originally designed – these gaps may not be as large or as impossible to close. However, reaching out to the very diverse and broad audiences potentially affected by international trade agreements is best facilitated indirectly through networks for a number of reasons. Among others, contractors have limited time and resources to solicit opinions from all groups directly; they lack a pre-established rapport with stakeholder groups that would increase their legitimacy; and barriers of language and cultural norms often hinder direct communication. These issues have likely contributed to disappointing quantities and qualities of participation in recent SIAs.

The emerging method of overcoming the obstacles to successful participation in SIAs is through the use of networks of government organizations, NGOs and CSOs with more specific knowledge of relevant national and subnational issues and with existing connections to stakeholder groups, experts and government officials. Cooperation with pre-existing networks would be valuable in investigating and defining the potential opportunities to further improve multinational stakeholder involvement and thus SIA credibility from the beginning of the process.

Identification/selection of participants

Although trade agreements can potentially have ripple effects that may affect many sections of society in one way or another – such as consumption-related effects or potential economy-wide benefits resulting from a reduction of price levels in one sector – it would be unrealistic to try to engage all relevant actors at once. More prudent is an issue-oriented approach that could use network organizations and the 'social database' to identify representatives of affected stakeholders and relevant experts specific to an expected impact. A potential negative consequence of reliance on existing networks to map and access stakeholders is that groups that are particularly well represented within these networks are positioned to play a disproportionate role in the SIA, and non-connected or non-represented stakeholders may be left out. To overcome this potential downside there has to be an emphasis on balanced, representative participation and capacity building.

Capacity building

Capacity building has the benefit of allowing marginalized groups and their knowledge to enter the policy process (UNEP, 2001). The identification and pairing of relevant stakeholders and experts in relation to particular trade-related impacts as described above should therefore be followed by the formulation of a plan for enabling stakeholders to participate adequately and effectively.

Capacity building may then be supported by various measures, the simplest being ensuring the transparency of the SIA exercise, adequate information provision (see below), timely invitations to meetings, and so on. In other cases more interactive forms of information provision and solicitation, such as regional workshops, may be required. It may be necessary to compensate groups for travel expenses and in some cases even for the preparation of input into the consultation process.

Information provision

Providing information on the trade agreement being negotiated and its potential impacts as well as the SIA process serves an important capacity-building function that can raise awareness, encourage stakeholders to engage in the SIA process, improve the relevance of stakeholder contributions and maintain stakeholder interest and trust in the SIA. It has become apparent from previous SIAs that adequate provision of information involves a choice of appropriate media and language for delivery, targeted delivery of information and appropriate timing of delivery.

The vehicle that is used to provide information (i.e. dedicated website, e-mail newsletter, traditional newsletter, etc.) will impact which stakeholders are involved in the participation process. Whereas some stakeholders can be contacted and communicated with via a website or email, other stakeholders may not have access to the Internet. The fact that while the EU–GCC SIA website generated approximately 12,000 hits, only approximately 2600 'successful' hits were generated, and moreover that only around 500 of these successful hits were from outside Europe and North America (Vanderstricht, 2005), illustrates that stakeholders in different regions may have different capacities or practices with regard to the use of the Internet. While some stakeholders will benefit from comprehensive information and long documents, many stakeholders would be better served by specifically targeted information. Some stakeholders may desire summaries or information targeted at their particular industry or geographical area, but have no interest in comprehensive or highly technical documents. Sarah Richardson, lead author of the EU–ACP SIA, suggested that more targeted information may be more useful even if it is more limited (Richardson, 2005).

Information solicitation

Methods used to solicit written information from stakeholders in past SIAs also had media-related flaws. The quantity and quality of input received from stakeholders through websites have often not met the expectations of SIA contractors. Electronic submissions for the EU–ACP meetings were not as substantial as desired (Richardson, 2005). In the case of discussion boards implemented on the EU–GCC SIA website, the quality of discussion was not as high as hoped (Vanderstricht, 2005).

Submission of written comments is not limited to the Internet, as hand-written or printed comments are typically welcomed. However, there are other questions of the appropriateness of written media extending to all forms, which arise from other cultural and political circumstances that may be present in participating nations. For instance, in the EU–GCC SIA, some stakeholder groups did not wish to be constrained by a written position (Vanderstricht, 2005).

Verbal information solicitation has its own drawbacks. For example, purely verbal comments are likely to be less technical and detailed than written comments. If participants do not speak the same language, there is a need for interpretation, which tends to be more costly than translation of written documents. In addition, interpretation is time-consuming and may to some extent act as a break on the communication flow. While verbal communication may be more open and flexible than written comments, it may often be confronted with similar difficulties, such as capacity constraints or unwillingness to be bound by a particular position (Vanderstricht, 2005). These difficulties provide further evidence of the challenge of direct communication between contractors and stakeholders or experts, and gives further support to the subcontracting of these tasks out to members of a network with whom participants may have greater trust or comfort. At least one precedent for this exists: the EU–ACP SIA, for instance, contracted a small portion of work out to a network of Caribbean NGOs (Richardson, 2005).

Meetings with stakeholders

SIA contractors face the significant challenge of gathering input from large, diverse and widely spread pools of stakeholders. To reach many of these audiences and increase understanding of the issues at stake, to solicit quality input, and to improve legitimacy, trust and ownership, physical meetings with stakeholder representatives may be the most effective option. Furthermore, depending on their format, meetings may offer the opportunity for **deliberative** participation, which can be valuable for improved understanding of the issues and exchange of viewpoints. They may also potentially provide avenues for reaching compromises between different stakeholder groups or between stakeholders and officials, though this is unprecendented in SIAs and would require a stronger position of participation in the SIA and a stronger role of SIA in the negotiations than yet realized.

In some EU regional meetings or workshops related to SIAs, a forum for stakeholder meetings has been organized. The challenges of staging these meetings are manifold and the resulting output may not have been of commensurate value. From the experience from the EU–ACP SIA, large meetings were extremely time and resource intensive to plan, and less valuable than smaller meetings for getting substantive input (Richardson, 2005). Aside from being costly and time-intensive to set up (for the organizers) and attend (for the stakeholders), it may be difficult to schedule such a meeting so as to best fit into the time frame of the studies. Given that SIAs and negotiations are undertaken in parallel, it may also be the case that by the time a large meeting is organized, some of the potential topics of discussion will already have been addressed in the negotiations. Smaller meetings staged by regional network organizations may be a good alternative for overcoming budgetary and logistical constraints.

The use of deliberative meetings focused on dialogue between and among stakeholders or representatives should contribute to stronger interaction between different stakeholder groups, compared with information exchange between DG Trade of the EC and single actors/groups. The sum of single opinions is normally less than the result of an interactive discussion that has all stakeholders involved.

Meetings are an important form of face-to-face communication that one SIA contractor has found to be indispensable in the SIA process (Vanderstricht, 2005). Furthermore, dialogue may have intrinsic positive externalities, as the process of participation creates ownership, which may perhaps even exceed the value of the outcome of participation (Abaza, 2005).

Selecting stakeholder input

Successful participation requires that civil society and stakeholders not only be provided relevant information and given the chance to voice their concerns, but also that their input is incorporated into the SIA. It is important that this process is transparent with respect to both the selection of contributions that are incorporated into the SIA and the way in which they are incorporated. For example, if participation is to contribute to increasing the legitimacy of the SIA process, it will not be sufficient to show that a representative sample of actors has been involved in the participation exercise. In addition, it will be necessary to show that all actors and contributions have been given due attention and to explain why and how certain contributions had a stronger impact on the SIA than others. If public participation is to enhance the credibility of SIA findings, similar requirements are necessary. If, for instance, an SIA partly bases a claim that certain trade measures will have negative implications for collective preferences on comments received in the context of public participation, it will be necessary to explain in more detail how these conclusions were derived from the participation exercise.

By instigating participation programmes indirectly through a network, rather than mediating participation programmes directly, the need for establishing methods to transparently convey, organize, select and process participant input increases. This aspect of SIAs, currently characterized by lack of a systematic process and a lack of transparency, needs significant improvement.

Expert participation

The multi-sector, multi-nation and potentially highly complex impacts of trade agreements make it especially important to open the study to broader scrutiny by experts with a wide range of backgrounds. This includes experts from different disciplines, but also those with different national, regional and institutional affiliations, including with academia and those with stakeholder-specific expertise. In particular with respect to impacts in non-EU countries, consulting non-EU experts can provide a necessary 'reality check' (Richardson, 2005) and give the study more credibility and legitimacy. Relevant experts are often available in developing countries, but there may be a need to prove the relevance and provide the motivation to participate (Abaza, 2005).

Expert participation should be linked to stakeholder input, and vice versa. Representatives of stakeholder groups, such as NGOs, may have a role to play in expert selection and accountability, as they may be more familiar with the experience and biases of selected experts than SIA contractors. Stakeholder groups may also be able to offer a 'reality check' for conclusions of experts. At the same time, experts themselves may be helpful in identifying under-represented stakeholder groups, or in putting local stakeholder perspectives in a regional and global context.

Government consultation

A transparent outlet for official participation in SIAs could have strong benefits for both negotiator and public perception of the SIA. The existing inter-directorate steering committee for SIAs provides a link to the EC. This link may facilitate the input of additional expertise and provide insight into the motivations and goals of the trade negotiators, which could be valuable for prioritizing information collection and scheduling relevant participation.

Success in engaging officials may run into similar challenges as engaging the public and experts, namely, that the officials may need to understand the purpose of the SIA and its potential benefits before agreeing to participate. Consultation with the European Parliament and Commission was undertaken in the EMFTA SIA, and based on the experience contractors found it difficult to arrange consultation if officials felt it was insignificant (Kirkpatrick, 2005). Using networks of governments officials (e.g. the Arab League consulted in EMFTA study) is likely a good option for contact with foreign officials.

Integrating SIAs and trade negotiations

A common critique of the SIA process is that it suffers from a lack of policy relevance due to a number of factors, such as timing and funding, lack of integration into the negotiation process and lack of negotiating partner buy-in. Although SIAs may be completed in coordination with the negotiations, there is nevertheless the perception that SIAs have little genuine impact on the course of negotiations and that they may not always address all the relevant issues. This in turn negatively impacts the motivation of stakeholders to actively contribute to the SIA process.

SIAs and trade negotiations can be better integrated in a number of ways:

- Organizing participation around key issues particularly important to the success of negotiations, in particular those issues that may be difficult to address using traditional tit-for-tat bargaining. These include questions with strong cultural or normative dimensions, such as concerns related to collective preferences and universal exceptions, but also externalities and adjustment costs, which often cannot easily be quantified and monetized. Public participation can help to verify the relevance of these concerns – for instance impacts on food culture or on certain religious or moral convictions – in particular when it proceeds via a deliberative dialogue with relevant groups rooted in civil society. Given the subjectivity of these issues, this would often be difficult to do in the abstract – that is, without involvement of relevant groups.

- Linking SIA practitioners and negotiators (Vanderstricht, 2005). Negotiators need to provide 'real-time' information to contractors to improve the relevance of investigations and scheduling of participation, and contractors need to provide regular updates on estimation of sustainability impacts so that negotiators will be aware of these issues and take interim results into account in the negotiations.
- Fostering a sense of multilateral ownership is needed in order for negotiators of non-EU parties to be willing to consider SIA results (Vanderstricht, 2005) and to attract the interest and input of stakeholders in non-EU countries.

The incorporation of public input, especially on issues of concern in the negotiations, will likely make the SIA more pertinent to trade negotiators (Institute for Development Policy and Management, 2004, p37), which should increase public ownership of the process and in turn encourage greater participation.

An example participation scheme

Figure 9.1 presents an example of a scheme for conducting an issue-specific participation plan. The scheme provides a timeline by which participation shadows trade agreement negotiations on a particular issue, such that participation can remain relevant to negotiations and output can potentially be incorporated into policy.

The process begins with the SIA contractor statement of participation objectives, and continues by establishing an advisory network to assist with identifying key issues. Based on the negotiation framework, a pending issue serves as the basis for building a staged participation programme involving experts, stakeholders and government officials. Participants help SIA contractors determine a sufficient scope from which the study proceeds, and both general and targeted information is continually provided to build participant capacity. Communication between SIA contractors and negotiators informs negotiators on the issues at stake and also relates developments in negotiations to contractors to keep the SIA relevant. More deliberative techniques are utilized to seek mutual understanding and compromise solutions among participants, which are eventually synthesized into a report delivered in time to contribute to decision making on the issue at stake.

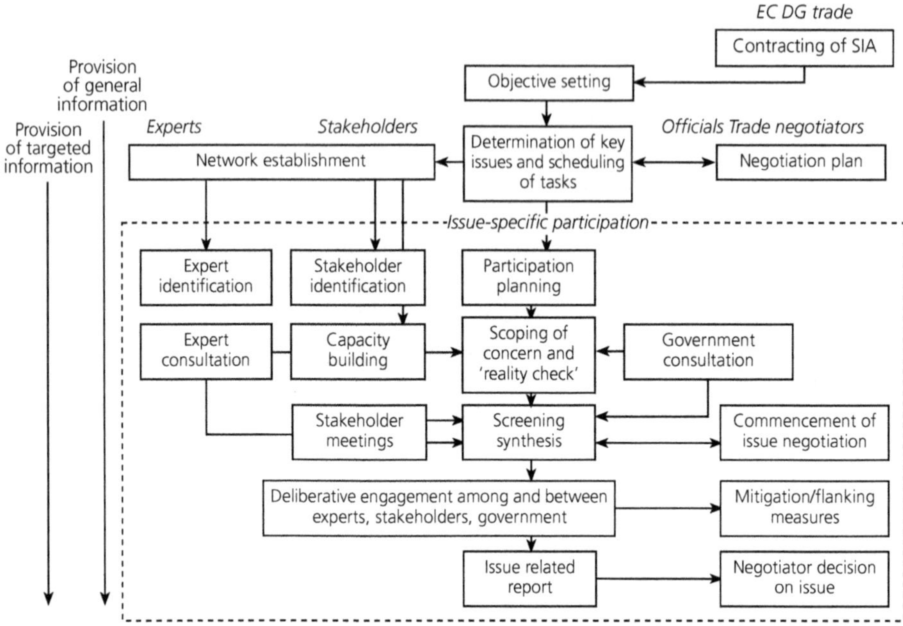

Figure 9.1 *An example of an issue-specific participation scheme*

Conclusion

A programme for participation in SIAs should be based on a set of realistic, clearly stated objectives and be regionally tailored based on likely regional impacts, public stakes and local capacity. In general it seems helpful to form networks of government organizations, NGOs and CSOs to develop a 'social database' of stakeholders. This is likely to be effective in helping to identify relevant stakeholder groups but also to build participant capacity and to design regionally appropriate participation techniques. A suggested process of issue-specific participation was recommended to be timed with negotiations, though this process can only serve as one example as participation planning remains dependent on a number of factors, including transparency of the negotiation agenda, logistical and budgetary constraints of the contractors, stakeholder interest and capacity for participation, and issue-specific appropriateness for engaging stakeholders, experts and government officials. Transparent incorporation of participant input and two-way communications among contractors and negotiators are two areas that need attention to improve the legitimacy and political relevance of the SIA. In addition, public participation may strengthen the link between SIAs and trade negotiations if it is systematically incorporated in the analysis of issues that tend to block progress in the negotiations. This applies in particular to issues associated with cultural or normative concerns that are difficult to quantify and monetize and would likely require an increased use of deliberative methods of public participation. The potential of public participation to increase transparency and the credibility of independent civil society organizations is key to this. Future experience in SIAs will provide further learning experiences that, if they are built on increased participation, are likely to increase stakeholder engagement, improve the quality of SIAs, strengthen the role of SIAs in the negotiations, and improve policy performance.

Notes

1 This article draws heavily on two contributions to SIAMETHOD, a research project supported by the European Union's 6th Research Framework Programme: Von Homeyer et al, 2006a, 2006b.
2 See Rio Declaration, Principle 10 (UN, 1992).
3 As of December 2006 two of three phases of the EMFTA SIA are complete. See www.sia-trade.org/emfta/en/

References

Abaza, H. (2005) Telephone interview about participation in UNEP trade impact assessment studies, Ecologic, Berlin

Almer, H. L. and Koontz, T. M. (2004) 'Public hearings for EIAs in post-communist Bulgaria: Do they work?', *Environmental Impact Assessment Review*, vol 24, no 5, pp473–493

Bastidas, S. (2004) 'The role of public participation in the impact assessment of trade policies', Paper presented at the Impact Assessment for Industrial Development Annual Conference, IAIA'04, Vancouver

Blanco, H. and Connors, D. (2005) Electronic communication, Ecologic, Berlin

Cash, D., Clark, W., Alcock, F., Frank, N., Eckley, N. and Jäger, J. (2002) 'Salience, credibility, legitimacy, and boundaries: Linking research, assessment and decision-making', Research Working Paper, John F. Kennedy School of Government, Harvard University, Boston

Creighton, J. (n.d.) 'How to design a public participation program', Office of Intergovernmental and Public Accountability, U.S. Department of Energy, Washington DC, http://web.em.doe.gov/ftplink/public/doeguide.pdf

Donelly, A., Dalal-Clayton, B. and Hughes, R. (1998) *A Directory of Impact Assessment Guidelines*, 2nd Edition, International Institute for Environment and Development, London

EC (European Commission) (2001) *European Governance: A White Paper* (COM: 428/2001/final), European Commission, Brussels

EC (2005) *Impact Assessment Guidelines* (COM: SEC/791/2005), European Commission, Brussels

Eckley, N. (2001) 'Designing effective assessments: The role of participation, science and governance, and focus', Report of a workshop co-organized by the European Environment Agency and the Global Environmental Assessment Project, Copenhagen, Denmark

Environmental Law Institute (1997), 'Transparency and responsiveness: Building a participatory process for activities implemented jointly under the Climate Change Convention', Research Report, Environmental Law Institute, Washington DC

Gibson, R., Hassan, S., Holtz, S., Tansey, J. and Whitelaw, G. (2005) *Sustainability Assessment: Criteria, Processes and Applications*, Earthscan, London

Günes, Y. and Coflkun, A. (2005) 'Legal structure of public participation in environmental issues in Turkey', *Journal of Environmental Assessment Policy and Management*, vol 7, no 3, pp543–568

Héritier, A. (2003) 'Composite democracy in Europe: The role of transparency and access to information', *Journal of European Public Policy*, vol 10, no 5, pp814–833

Impact Assessment Research Centre (2005) *SIA Trade Newsletter*, no 2 (January), University of Manchester, Manchester

Institute for Development Policy and Management (2004) 'Sustainability impact assessment study of the Euro–Mediterranean free trade area: Final Report on Phase 1 of the SIA–EMFTA project, University of Manchester, Manchester

Kirkpatrick, C. (2005) Telephone interview concerning participation in EU–GCC SIA, Ecologic, Berlin

Mayer, S. (2001) *Stakeholder Identification and Involvement: Expert Teamwork in Preparing a National Strategy for Waste Prevention and Processing in Austria*, Austrian Federal Environmental Agency, Vienna

Montgomery, J. (2000) 'Lessons from past environmental reviews in the United States', in *Assessing the Environmental Effects of Trade Liberalisation Agreements: Methodologies*, OECD, Paris

OECD (2001) *Citizens as Partners: Information, Consultation and Public Participation in Policy-making*, OECD, Paris

OECD (2005) Programme of Dialogue and Cooperation with China, Center for Cooperation with Non-Members, www.oecd.org/dataoecd/60/37/34617750.pdf

PriceWaterhouseCoopers (2004) 'Sustainability impact assessment (SIA) of the negotiations of the trade agreement between the European Community and the countries of the Cooperation Council for the Arab States of the Gulf (GCC): Final Report', prepared for the European Commission, Brussels

PriceWaterhouseCoopers (2005) 'Sustainability impact assessment (SIA) of the EU–ACP Economic Partnership Agreements: Phase Two: Final Report (revised)', prepared for the European Commission, Brussels

Richardson, S. (2005) Telephone interview concerning participation in EU–ACP SIA, Ecologic, Berlin

Rydin, Y. and Pennington, M. (2000) 'Public participation and local environmental planning: The collective action problem and the potential of social capital', *Local Environment*, vol 5, no 2, pp153–169

Suchman, M.C. (1995) 'Managing legitimacy: Strategic and institutional approaches', *Academy of Management Review*, vol 20, no 3, pp571–610

SUSTRA Trade, Societies and Sustainable Development Network (2003) 'Sustainability impact assessment', Policy Brief Paper, based on conclusions of SUSTRA seminar, 26–27 March 2003, Center for Philosophy of Law (CPDR), Université catholique de Louvain, Louvain-la-Neuve, Belgium, www.agro-montpellier.fr/sustra/publications/policy_briefs/policy-brief-sia-eng.pdf

Tang, S. Y., Tang, C. P. and Lo, C. W. H. (2005) 'Public participation and environmental impact assessment in mainland China and Taiwan: Political foundations of environmental management', *Journal of Development Studies*, vol 41, no 1, pp1–32

UN (1992) Rio Declaration on Environment and Development, Rio De Janeiro

UNEP (2001) *Reference Manual for the Integrated Assessment of Trade Related Policies*, UNEP, Geneva

UNEP and International Institute for Sustainable Development (2000) *Environment and Trade: A Handbook*, IISD, Winnipeg

UNEP, UNDP, World Bank and WRI (2003) *Participation and Accountability. World Resources 2002–2004: Decisions for the Earth: Balance, Voice, and Power*, UNEP, Geneva, http://governance.wri.org/pubs_content_text.cfm?ContentID=1696

Vanderstricht, C. (2005) Telephone interview concerning participation in EU–GCC SIA, Ecologic, Berlin

Von Homeyer, I., Knigge, M., Görlach, B., Collins, M. and Ingwersen, W. (2006a) 'Report on methods for public participation in SIAs of trade agreements', Ecologic, Institute for International and European Environmental Policy, Berlin

Von Homeyer, I., Ingwersen, W., Knigge, M. and Görlach, B. (2006b) 'Public participation in SIAs and contextual realities', Ecologic, Institute for International and European Environmental Policy, Berlin

10
Identifying Trade Victims

Edward Anderson

Introduction

It is generally accepted, among economists, that increases in a country's openness to trade and investment have distributional implications. In other words, some groups of people gain more than others, while some may lose out, at least in the short run. This chapter discusses ways of identifying, in advance of a particular trade reform or trade agreement, those groups that are likely to gain more than others, and those groups that may lose out.

Analysing the distributional implications of a proposed trade agreement is clearly an important part of a Trade Sustainability Impact Assessment (SIA). It clearly falls under one of the main stated objectives of such an SIA, which is 'to provide an in-depth assessment of the likely changes caused by the trade agreement on economies, social development and the environment' (EC, 2006, p11). It is also clearly important in terms of meeting another objective of a Trade SIA, which is to 'provide guidelines for the design of possible accompanying policy measures ... intended to maximise the positive impacts of the trade negotiations in question, and to reduce any negative impacts' (EC, 2006, p7).

Unfortunately, it is very difficult to make ex-ante predictions about the likely distributional effects of a trade reform or agreement. To illustrate, consider the labour market. Here, one can identify at least five characteristics that will affect the extent to which an individual worker will gain from a reform or agreement: the sector in which they are based, prior to the reform or agreement; their ability to move between sectors, following the reform or agreement; their education, skills and experience; their preferences (as consumers) for different goods and services; and their subjective discount rate.

Many of these characteristics are hard to measure, representing the first problem. A further problem is that the relationship between these characteristics and the overall outcome for a particular worker can be complicated, depending on a whole set of further considerations. For example, workers of a particular skill level may gain from lower import tariffs in one country or time period, but lose out in another country or time period. These problems are no less when we consider distributional effects arising in other areas of an economy, beyond the labour market.

Despite the difficulties, methods and tools do exist for making predictions about the distributional effects of trade reforms and agreements. Each suffers from certain drawbacks, which should not be underestimated, but each also offers insights and predictions that assist the policy maker in certain important ways. Existing Trade SIAs draw on and apply some of these methods, but there appears to be scope for increasing their use further.

The chapter is organized as follows. The first section discusses existing quantitative approaches used by economists for making ex-ante assessments of the distributional effects of trade reforms and agreements. This includes a short review of the use of these approaches in the recent Trade SIA of the proposed EU–Mercosur trade agreement. The second section takes a step back, and discusses insights derived from traditional trade theory relevant to the distributional effects of a trade reform or agreement, focusing in particular on how increased openness affects the returns to different factors of production. This theory is relatively well-known, so the discussion is relatively brief. The third section then uses the insights derived from this discussion to propose a new approach for making ex-ante assessments. This approach is designed specifically for assessing the direction and magnitude of increased openness on different groups within a country, via its effects on the returns to different factors of production. The concluding section provides some recommendations for the analysis of distributional effects in future Trade SIAs.

Existing approaches

This section describes four main approaches used by economists to make quantitative, ex-ante predictions about the distributional effects of trade reforms. These are referred to as 'micro-simulation', 'extended micro-simulation', 'CGE modelling' and the 'micro-macro synthesis'. Each is an example of a method used in the Poverty and Social Impact Assessment (PSIA) approach, defined by the World Bank (2003, p1) as the 'analysis of the distributional impact of policy reforms on the well-being or welfare of different stakeholder groups, with particular emphasis on the poor and vulnerable'. However, while methods in PSIA are designed for assessing all types of policy reforms, and include methods for ex-ante and ex-post analysis, the approaches discussed here are particularly suited to the ex-ante analysis of trade reforms.

A basic framework

Before setting out the four approaches themselves, it is helpful to begin by setting out the different sorts of effects that may arise following a trade reform or agreement. This is done in Figure 10.1. The starting point is a proposed change in a country's trade policy, such as a reduction in import tariffs. This causes a change in the domestic prices of at least some internationally traded, final goods and services (box 1 in the figure). These changes in domestic prices then have a series of effects throughout the domestic economy (boxes 2–8), which can be distinguished in terms of the rough time horizon over which they would normally be expected to occur.

Beginning with the short term, there are immediate effects on households' purchasing power (box 2) and firms' profits (box 3). These effects are immediate in the sense that no offsetting changes in households' or firms' behaviour are taken into account.

Turning to the medium term, four sets of effects can be distinguished. First, there are effects on households' consumption patterns induced by changes in domestic prices (box 4). Generally, we would expect households to increase consumption of goods that have fallen in price and reduce consumption of goods that have risen in price.

Secondly, there are effects on firms' demand for factors of production within each sector of production (box 5). In a sector experiencing falling prices, we would expect demand for factors of production to fall, as firms seek to reduce output or exit the sector altogether. By contrast, in a sector experiencing rising prices, we would expect demand for factors of production to rise, as existing firms seek to increase output and new firms seek to enter the sector. These changes in demand will normally be associated with changes in either the returns to, or the employment of, factors of production in each sector.

Thirdly, there are effects on the allocation of factors of production between sectors caused by differences in the returns and/or employment opportunities across sectors (box 6). The outcome of this reallocation process will normally cause the economy-wide level of demand for some factors of production to rise, and for some other factors to fall. These changes in economy-wide levels of demand will have corresponding effects on either the returns to, or the employment of, each factor of production.

Fourthly, there are effects on the domestic prices of goods and services that are not traded internationally (box 7). These may be caused either by changes in households' consumption patterns, or by changes in levels of output of the different sectors. They will have additional effects on households' purchasing power.

Finally, considering the longer term, there are effects on the supply of factors of production, levels of technology and perhaps also levels of efficiency in production stemming from economies of scale (box 8).

Micro-simulation

The first approach used by economists to make quantitative, ex-ante predictions about the distributional effects of trade reforms is commonly referred to as 'micro-simulation'.[1] This approach can be used to estimate the immediate effects of the initial changes in the domestic prices of internationally traded

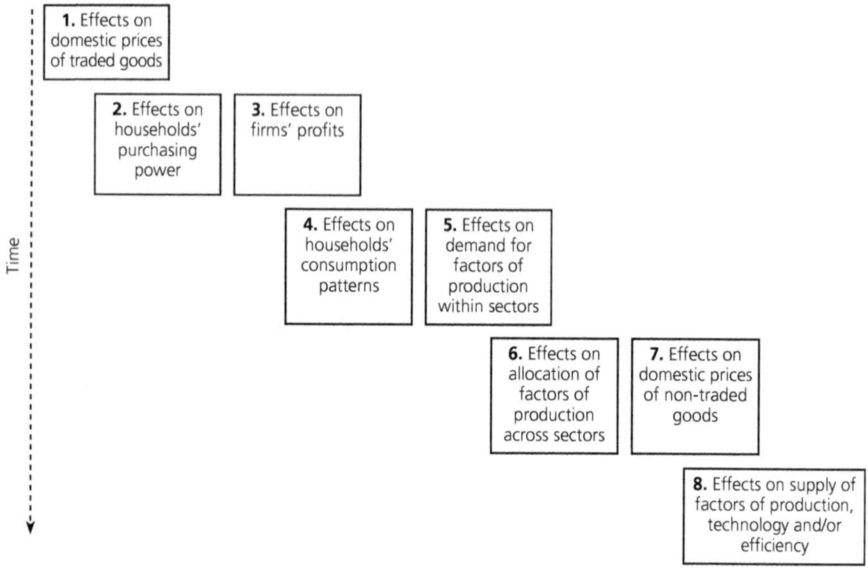

Source: Author

Figure 10.1 *Distributional effects of trade reforms: A basic framework*

goods caused by a trade reform (boxes 2 and 3), for different groups of households in the population. It is an example of 'direct impact analysis' in the wider PSIA approach (World Bank, 2003, p21), defined as 'a simple assessment of who is directly affected by a policy change, and how much they are affected. It assumes no behavioural response from affected households or groups.'

Consider first the effect on households' purchasing power. If we assume that households' consumption patterns, and levels of nominal income remain constant, the effect of the price changes is given by:

$$\Delta m_h = -\sum_i q_{ih} \cdot \Delta p_i \qquad (1)$$

where Δm_h is the effective change in the level of income for household h, q_{ih} is the quantity of each internationally-traded good i consumed by the household, and Δp_i is the change in the domestic price of each of those goods.

Consider now the effect on firms' profits. If we assume that firms' output levels and use of inputs remain constant, the effect of the price changes on a firm's profits is given by:

$$\Delta \pi_k = \sum_i y_{ik} \cdot \Delta p_i \qquad (2)$$

where $\Delta\pi_k$ is the change in profits for firm k, and y_{ik} is the level of output of each internationally traded good i produced by the firm.

A special case arises when households are both consumers and producers of the internationally traded goods that have changed in price. This is common in many developing countries, as for example when households in rural areas both consume and produce an agricultural export commodity. In this case, the effect on the household, assuming no changes in consumption patterns, or output or input levels, is given by:

$$\Delta m_h = \sum_i (y_{ih} - q_{ih}) \cdot \Delta p_i \qquad (3)$$

In this case therefore, the effect of a change in the price of a particular commodity depends on whether a household is initially a net seller or a net buyer of the commodity.

The main advantages of the micro-simulation approach are its relatively low data requirements, and the fact that the analysis can be done at a highly disaggregated level. However, the approach also suffers from clear drawbacks. In particular, it only captures the immediate effects on households and firms (boxes 2 and 3), and ignores all the other potential effects illustrated in Figure 10.1 (boxes 4–8).

Extended micro-simulation

The second approach can be called an 'extended micro-simulation' approach. This goes one step further than the basic approach outlined above, by allowing for the effects of changes in the domestic prices of internationally traded goods on either a) the returns to at least some factors of production (boxes 5 and/or 6); and/or b) the domestic prices of at least some goods that are not internationally traded (box 7).

An early example of this approach was provided by Ravallion (1990), who allowed for increases in the domestic price of rice in Bangladesh to have a positive effect on the rural wage rate, via increased demand for labour. The elasticity of the wage rate with respect to the price of rice was estimated econometrically, using annual time-series data on rice prices and rural wages in the country during 1950–1980.

A more recent example of the approach is Porto (2003), who allowed for the changes in the domestic prices of traded goods in Argentina stemming from Mercosur to affect the returns to three factors of production (unskilled, semi-skilled and skilled labour), and the domestic prices of four types of non-traded goods (housing, transport and communication, health and education, and leisure). As in the Ravallion (1990) study, the elasticities of the returns to each factor of production, and the price of each type of non-traded good, with respect to the domestic prices of traded goods were estimated econometrically, using time-series data.

In this extended micro-simulation approach, the overall effect of the changes in the domestic prices of internationally traded goods on a household can be calculated as:

$$\Delta m_h^{\times} = \sum_i \left[(y_{ih} - q_{ih}) + \sum_l x_{ih} \cdot \varepsilon_{il} + \sum_j (y_{jh} - q_{jh}) \cdot \varepsilon_{ij} \right] \cdot \Delta p_i \quad (4)$$

where x_{ih} is the net supply of factor of production l by household h, ε_{il} is the elasticity of the return to that factor with respect to the price of traded good i, y_{jh} and q_{jh} are the levels of output and consumption of non-traded good j by household h, and ε_{ij} is the elasticity of the price of non-traded good j with respect to traded good i.

The advantage of this extended micro-simulation approach is that it takes into account some of the other potential effects of trade reforms: in particular, the effects on factor returns (boxes 5 and/or 6) and the effects on the prices of non-traded goods (box 7). In this way it addresses, at least in part, the main drawback of the basic micro-simulation approach. The main drawback with the extended approach is that its data requirements are much greater. In particular, estimating the elasticities of factor returns and non-traded goods prices with respect to the prices of traded goods requires comparable time-series data over a significant period of time. This may be lacking in many countries.

CGE modelling

The third approach is to use a computable general equilibrium (CGE) model. This involves specifying a fully developed model of the economy, including the different sectors of production that make up the economy, the different factors of production used in each sector (e.g. land, capital, skilled labour, unskilled labour), the quantitative relationships between the use of factors of production and output in each sector, the different groups of households in the population, distinguished by the factors of production they own, and the quantitative relationship between prices, incomes and welfare (or utility) for each group of households.

Once set up in this way, a CGE model can be used to simulate the impact of changes in the domestic prices of internationally traded goods, caused by changes in trade policy, on different groups of households. The overall effects on each group of households are typically expressed using the concept of 'compensating variation': the change in income that would leave a household as well off following the changes in prices and factor returns as it was before those changes.

The main advantage of a CGE model is that it can take into account the various different effects of a trade reform, including effects on households' consumption patterns (box 4), the allocation of factors of production across sectors (box 6), and on the price of non-traded goods (box 7). In addition, and in contrast to the extended micro-simulation approach, it does this without requiring large amounts of time-series data on factor returns and/or goods prices.

On the other hand, one clear disadvantage is that CGE models can be difficult to develop, and have large data requirements of their own. Another is that, as a way of managing the complexity and data requirements, the numbers of production sectors, factors of production and number of household types included in a CGE model are kept fairly low. This means that the analysis can only be done at a quite aggregated level, thereby limiting the amount of information provided about distributional impacts.

Another drawback is that a CGE model does not provide much information about the short-term effects of trade reforms. For example, any 'adjustment effects' associated with declining demand for factors of production within sectors (box 5) are generally not captured by a CGE model, which typically assume perfect mobility of factors of production across sectors. Similarly, any short-term effects on firms' profits (box 3) are generally not captured, since CGE models generally assume free entry and exit of firms in each sector, which in turn implies that any positive or negative profits in a sector are quickly dissipated. This is a problem in that the short-term, adjustment effects of trade reforms are often of key interest to policy makers.

The macro–micro synthesis

A fourth and final approach is referred to as the 'macro–micro synthesis'.[2] This approach consists of two stages. The first involves using a CGE model to estimate the effects of changes in the prices of internationally traded goods, caused by a trade reform, on the returns to each factor of production and on the domestic prices of non-traded goods. This is done at a fairly high level of aggregation. The second stage involves using household-survey data to estimate, at a much more disaggregated level, the overall effect of the changes in domestic prices, and the changes in the returns to each factor of production, on different groups of households in the population. This overall effect is given by:

$$\boldsymbol{\Delta} m_h = \sum_i (y_{ih} - q_{ih}) \times \boldsymbol{\Delta} p_i + \sum_l x_{ih} \times \boldsymbol{\Delta} w_l + \sum_j (y_{jh} - q_{jh}) \times \boldsymbol{\Delta} p_j \qquad (5)$$

where Δp_i are the changes in the domestic prices of internationally traded goods, Δw_l are the changes in the returns to factors of production, and Δp_j are the changes in the domestic prices of non-traded goods.

A good example of this approach is the study by Chen and Ravallion (2003) on the likely distributional implications of China's accession in 2001 to the WTO. The estimated effects of the accession on factor returns and domestic prices are derived from an earlier CGE analysis. The remaining terms are obtained from official household surveys for the year 1999. Another good example is the study by Ianchovichina et al (2002) on trade reform and poverty in Mexico.

The advantage of the macro–micro synthesis is that the analysis of distributional effects can be done at a much higher level of disaggregation than with a standard CGE model. The disadvantage is a slight loss in the theoretical consistency of the approach. In particular, while the CGE analysis takes into account changes in firms' and households' behaviour following greater openness, the estimated impacts on the welfare of each household do not.

Approaches used in Trade SIAs

At this stage it is worth discussing approaches used in Trade SIAs to assess distributional effects of a trade agreement. Rather than review all Trade SIAs carried out, this section uses the study of the EU–Mercosur free trade agreement as a case study. This is a good example to focus on, since it is the most recent Trade SIA to be carried out, and the methodology used in the study is arguably the most advanced used to date.[3]

The main quantitative tool used in the EU–Mercosur Trade SIA is a CGE model. The model allows the authors to estimate the effects of an EU–Mercosur trade agreement in each of the four Mercosur countries (Argentina, Brazil, Paraguay and Uruguay), and in the EU. The model is mainly used for predicting the aggregate, 'economic' impacts in each country. As the authors point out, however, the model also sheds some light on the distributional, 'social' impacts. First, it predicts the effects of a trade agreement on the returns to capital, skilled labour and unskilled labour in each country. The reasoning here is that the greater the effect on the returns to unskilled labour, in absolute terms and relative to other factors, the more likely it is that poverty and inequality will decline as a result of an agreement. Secondly, the CGE model predicts the changes in levels of output in each sector of the economy. Here, the reasoning is that individuals employed in those sectors experiencing reductions in output are more likely to experience negative adjustment costs, such as unemployment, as a result of a trade agreement.

The use of a CGE model in the EU–Mercosur Trade SIA in fact illustrates quite well the main drawbacks of the approach. First of all, the level of aggregation in the model is quite high. There are, for example, only five factors of production (two categories of labour, capital, land and natural resources) and just one representative household. This may reflect data constraints, but it means that the amount of information provided about distributional effects is not large. In particular, there is no sense of potential winners or losers within these broad categories of factors, and no sense of how households with different consumption patterns may be affected differently. This limitation is recognized by the authors, for example:

> *CGE models are by design not particularly well suited for poverty analysis due to their lack of disaggregated information at the household level and their inability to distinguish between poor and non-poor households.* (IDPM, 2007, p96)

Secondly, the predictions of the CGE model relate to the distributional effects of the trade agreement after a period of adjustment has taken place. Thus although the model is used to indicate where adverse adjustment costs may arise (i.e. in sectors predicted to decline in size), these adjustment costs are not incorporated into the model itself.[4] Thus the CGE model provides no indication as to the possible magnitude of those costs. This is again recognized by the report's authors:

> *The model follows the standard computable general equilibrium modelling approach and assumes that total employment is fixed at the national or regional level. Workers from a declining sector are able to immediately find work in an expanding sector, hence, the model allows only for the evaluation of inter-industry shifts in employment. Transitional and persistent unemployment effects are not generally evaluated within a CGE modelling framework.* (IDPM, 2007, p95)

The CGE model in the study is designed only to provide a first insight into the distributional consequences of an EU–Mercosur trade agreement. These first insights are to be followed up with further analysis. For this analysis, mainly qualitative assessments appear to have been used. In other words, there is no (apparent) use of any of the other quantitative approaches discussed in this section – that is, micro-simulation, extended micro-simulation or the macro–micro synthesis. There is nothing wrong with qualitative assessments. However, there are areas of the analysis that could arguably be strengthened by including more quantitative assessments. This is discussed further below.

Summary and discussion

Clearly, there currently exist a range of approaches for making ex-ante predictions about the distributional implications of trade reforms. Each has certain advantages, but each also suffers from certain drawbacks. No one method appears unambiguously better than another, which suggests that their use in combination would be the best approach.

Arguably the biggest challenge lies in going beyond partial equilibrium thinking, especially on the supply side. In particular, there is a need to look beyond the immediate impacts of price changes on firms' profits (box 3 in Figure 10.1), or on the demand for factors of production within production sectors (box 5), and to consider the effects of induced changes in the allocation of factors of production across sectors on the economy-wide returns to, and/or employment opportunities for, the different factors of production (box 6).

Currently, there are two main ways of doing this. The first, used in the 'extended micro-simulation' approach, uses time-series econometrics to estimate the elasticity of factor returns with respect to the prices of internationally traded goods, using historical time-series data. The second, used in CGE modelling and the macro–micro synthesis, involves predicting the changes in factor returns, given a set of price changes and specified production relationships in each sector. However, each of these approaches has been shown to suffer from certain drawbacks: in particular, both have high data requirements. The next section discusses whether it is possible to make predictions about the effects of openness on factor returns on the basis of more general theory, without having to develop a fully specified CGE model or estimate a potentially complex series of time-series regressions.

Insights derived from theory

Any approach to making ex-ante predictions about the effects of trade reforms on factor returns must be grounded in theory. In this context, arguably the best starting point is the well-known Stolper–Samuelson theorem. The 'essential version' of this theorem (Deardorff, 1994) predicts that, in a country that produces two goods, using two factors of production:

> *a rise in the relative price of one good raises the real return to the factor of production used intensively in producing that good, and lowers the real return to the other factor.*[5]

The intuition underlying this theorem is also well-known, but is worth repeating. As domestic prices rise in one sector relative to the other, factors of production are drawn into that sector, which therefore expands. The expanding sector tends, however, to demand relatively more of one factor – its 'intensive factor' – than is available in the other, declining sector. As a result, the overall level of demand for the intensive factor in the expanding sector is bid up, raising its relative return, while the overall level of demand for the other factor is bid down. Under the assumptions made by Stolper and Samuelson, this effect is such as to raise the real wage of the intensive factor in the expanding sector, and reduce the real wage of the other factor.

Insights based on the Stolper–Samuelson theorem inform a large amount of discussion regarding the distributional effects of trade. For example, in the conclusion to their study on the distributional effects of trade liberalization in Morocco, which uses the basic micro-simulation approach, Ravallion and Lokshin (2004, p22) state that:

> *...we can speculate on the likely impacts of allowing real wages to adjust ... it can be argued that the export-oriented cash crops that will replace cereals will tend to be more labour-intensive than cereals. Thus we would expect higher aggregate demand for the relatively unskilled labour used in agriculture, and hence higher real wages for relatively poorer groups.*

Similarly, in their review of the effects of trade liberalization on poverty, McCulloch et al (2001, p77) declare that:

> *The basic insight of the S–S theorem applies very broadly... Generally speaking (but not inevitably), if the prices of goods intensive in the use of unskilled labour increase, we would expect unskilled wages to increase.*

Insights from the Stolper–Samuelson theorem have also been used to provide the underlying intuition for results generated from CGE models. Consider, for example, the following statement from the study by Warr (2001, p913) of export taxes on rice in Thailand:

> *As the price of rice is forced down through an export tax, the return to factors used intensively in rice production fall. Rice production is intensive in the use of unskilled labour and the export tax thus operates to reduce the return to unskilled labour and raise the returns to other mobile factors, including skilled labour and mobile forms of capital... This general equilibrium effect is analogous to the famous Stolper–Samuelson mechanism of international trade theory.*

At first sight therefore, the Stolper–Samuelson theorem appears to offer a good basis for making predictions about the distributional implications of trade reforms. Unfortunately, things are not that simple. The reason is that the predictions of the 'essential' version of the Stolper–Samuelson theorem apply to a country with just two sectors of production and two factors of production, and do not automatically translate to more realistic cases in which there are many sectors and many factors of production (some of which may be specific to certain sectors). In the words of McCulloch et al (2001, p77), 'for all its elegance, Stolper–Samuelson is not sufficient to answer questions of trade and poverty in the real world'.

There are in fact two versions of the Stolper–Samuelson theorem which apply in a more general context. The first is the 'friends and enemies' version (Deardorff, 1994), which has also been termed the 'winners and losers corollary' (Leamer and Levinsohn, 1995). This predicts that:

> *when the domestic price of a traded good changes, the real returns to at least one factor of production rise, while the real returns to at least one factor fall.*

This prediction applies whatever the number of production sectors or factors of production in an economy, although it does still rely on certain other assumptions, such as non-joint production (Deardorff, 1994, p17; Feenstra, 2003, p69). The more serious drawback with this version of the theorem is that it is very limited as a piece of ex-ante policy advice. In particular, it says nothing about which factors of production gain and which lose: '...it does not attempt to define intensively and non-intensively used factors or to use such definitions to specify which factors will gain and lose from a price change' (Deardorff, 1994, p17).

The second version of the Stolper–Samuelson (1941) theorem that applies in the more general context is the 'correlations' version, according to which:

for any vector of goods price changes, the accompanying vector of factor price changes will be positively correlated with the factor-intensity-weighted averages of the goods price changes.

Two points are worth noting about this prediction. First, the prediction is only for a correlation, not a definitive relationship. In other words, while we would *expect on average* that factors with higher factor-intensity-weighted average price changes will gain more than factors with lower such price changes, this is not a guaranteed outcome for any particular pair of factors. Secondly, the prediction says nothing about changes in the absolute returns to different factors of production; it only predicts which factors will gain more, or lose less, relative to others. Third, the prediction also says nothing about changes in the real returns, absolute or relative, to different factors of production, it only relates to the nominal returns.[6]

Despite these qualifications, this 'correlation' version of the Stolper–Samuelson theorem captures the spirit of the 'essential' version, namely that it is the intensities with which factors are used in different sectors that determines how they are affected by trade. In other words, 'the general pattern of gains and losses [following changes in the domestic prices of traded goods] is related to the intensities with which factors are used in the production of the goods' (Deardorff, 1994, p17).[7]

A potential new approach

This section outlines a potential new approach for making ex-ante assessments about the distributional effects of trade, which draws on the 'correlation' version of the Stolper–Samuelson theorem described above. The approach is illustrated using a simple hypothetical example.

Consider a model in which there are three sectors of production, and six factors of production, three of which are specific to a sector and three of which are perfectly mobile across the three sectors. The first step of the approach is to write down the proportional changes in the domestic price of each sector occurring as a result of the proposed trade reform or agreement. These are denoted $\hat{p}_i$ and are shown in the second column of Table 10.1.

The second step is to write down the intensities with which each factor is used in each sector. There are in fact several different ways of defining and

Table 10.1 *Calculating factor-intensity-weighted average price changes: A hypothetical example*

	$\hat{p}_i$	θ_{i1}	θ_{i2}	θ_{i3}	θ_{i4}	θ_{i5}	θ_{i6}
Sector 1	20%	0.2	0.0	0.0	0.4	0.2	0.2
Sector 2	10%	0.0	0.2	0.0	0.2	0.4	0.2
Sector 3	–10%	0.0	0.0	0.2	0.2	0.2	0.4
λ_j	–	20%	10%	–10%	10%	7.5%	2.5%

Source: Author

measuring intensity. In this context, however, the intensity with which a factor is used refers to its cost share: the share of the total cost in a given sector i, which is made up of payments to a particular factor of production j. This is denoted θ_{ij} and given by:

$$\theta_{ij} = \frac{w_j \cdot X_{ij}}{C_i} \tag{6}$$

where C_i is total costs in sector i, X_{ij} is the amount of factor j employed in sector i, and w_j is the return to factor j. The values of θ_{ij} for each sector and factor are shown in columns 3–8 and rows 2–4 of Table 10.1. Note that for the specific factors of production, the terms θ_{ij} are zero for all sectors except one. Note also that the cost shares sum to unity for each sector.

The third step is to calculate the 'factor-intensity-weighted averages' of the price changes. These are denoted λ_j and are given by:

$$\lambda_j = \frac{\sum_i \theta_{ij} \cdot \hat{p}_i}{\sum_i \theta_{ij}} \tag{7}$$

The values of these weighted average price changes are shown in the fifth row of Table 10.1. For the specific factors of production, these are simply equal to the price change in the sector to which the factor is specific, but for the mobile factors they are weighted averages of the price changes in all three sectors. The key point is that the higher the factor-intensity-weighted average price changes, the better it is for any particular factor. It indicates that, on average, prices are tending to rise by more, or fall by less, in those sectors in which the factor is used more intensively.

The prediction of the correlation version of the Stolper–Samuelson theorem is that the factor-intensity-weighted averages λ_j will be positively correlated with the proportional changes in factor prices, denoted $\hat{w}_j$. Of course, when doing ex-ante analysis, this correlation cannot be observed, since the changes in factor prices are unknown. However, we can calculate the implications of a particular expected pattern of changes in factor returns for any particular group of households. To do this, we first write the nominal income of a group of households as:

$$y_h = \sum_j w_j \cdot k_{jh} \tag{8}$$

where k_{jh} is the amount of factor j owned by households h.[8] If we assume that the ownership of factors of production by each household does not change, then the proportional change in household income following a change in factor returns is given by:

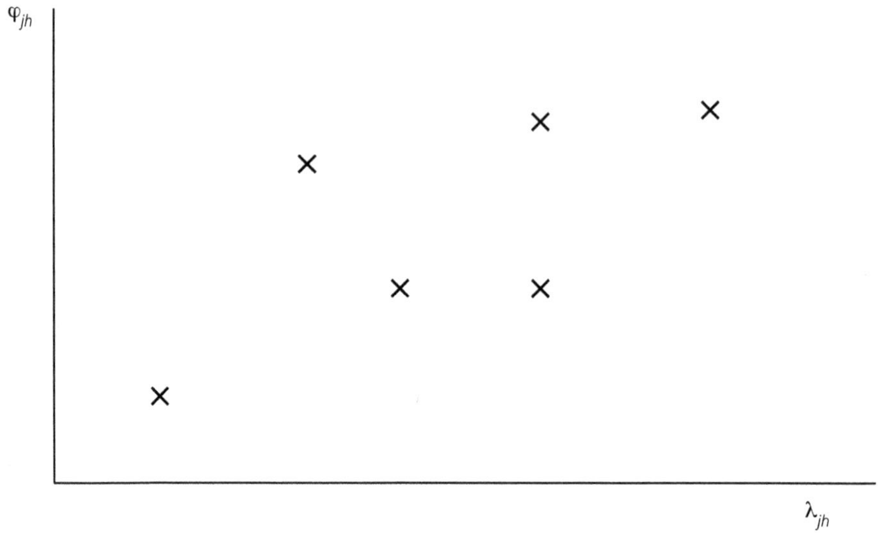

Source: Author

Figure 10.2 *Relationship between factor-income sources and factor-intensity-weighted average price changes: A hypothetical example*

$$\hat{y}_h = \sum_j \varphi_{jh} \cdot \hat{w}_j \tag{9}$$

where φ_{jh} is the share of income of households h accounted for by factor j.

We now consider the correlation between the factor-intensity-weighted averages λ_j and the factor ownership shares φ_{jh}, for a particular group of households. This can be plotted and would look something like Figure 10.2. This correlation gives an idea as to how favourable are the price changes for the households being considered, via their likely effect on factor returns. The greater the positive correlation, the more favourable the price changes are; the greater the negative correlation, the less favourable they are. An absence of correlation would indicate a set of price changes with relatively 'neutral' implications for households, via their effects on factor returns. If the correlation is calculated for different groups of households in the population (e.g. each income decile or geographical area), one can get a sense of which groups are likely to gain, or lose out, relative to others, as a result of the likely changes in factor returns.

For this approach to be feasible, both λ_j and φ_{jh} must be measured at reasonable levels of disaggregation. In principle this can be done, although in practice there are likely to be significant challenges in doing so. One problem is that the level of disaggregation of factors of production in readily available industry-level data may not be very high. For example, levels of employment and wage payments may not be broken down by level of skill (or a proxy, such as occupation), and even if they are, the breakdown may only be quite limited (e.g. production and non-production workers).

Another problem is that even if we have detailed data on use of different factors of production by different sectors (e.g. from detailed firm or farm surveys), we may well not have data on the price of each factor. For example, production of an agricultural export commodity may make use of certain factors (e.g. irrigation equipment, animal power, family labour) for which a formal rental market, with an associated price or rate of return, does not exist. For these reasons, the feasibility of the approach outlined in this section will tend to vary across countries, depending on context and data availability.

It is also worth stressing other limitations of this approach. In particular, the results give an indication only of expected changes in the nominal incomes of different household groups. It does not provide indications of expected changes in real incomes, any assessment of which would need to take changes in the prices of consumer goods into account, and households' preferences in consumption. For this reason, the approach should be seen as additional or complementary to, rather than a substitute for, approaches to measuring effects on price changes induced by trade reforms on households' purchasing power, such as the basic 'micro-simulation' approach described above and/or extensions to it.

Despite these limitations, the approach outlined here still provides a way of strengthening ex-ante assessments regarding the distributional effects of trade reforms, across households or groups. It is based on a well-established theorem already used in making qualitative assessments about the potential effects of trade reforms on household incomes, which occur as a result of changes in factor returns induced by changes in the structure of the economy (box 5 in Figure 10.1). It simply extends these assessments in a more quantitative direction, by linking to observed factor intensities across sectors and sources of income across household groups. Perhaps most importantly, the approach reflects general-equilibrium considerations, but does this without requiring a fully specified CGE model or econometric analysis of long time-series data.

Summary and recommendations

Making ex-ante assessments of the likely distributional effects of a trade reform or agreement is a difficult exercise. This chapter has discussed four existing approaches for making such assessments: micro-simulation, extended micro-simulation, CGE modelling and the macro–micro synthesis. It has also discussed the use of these methods in the recent Trade SIA of the proposed EU–Mercosur trade agreement. Finally, it has used insights from traditional trade theory to propose a new approach, designed specifically for assessing impacts of a trade reform or agreement on different groups of households, via its effects on the returns to different factors of production.

The chapter ends with two main recommendations for the analysis of distributional effects in future Trade SIAs. The first is to increase the use of quantitative approaches other than CGE modelling. To give one example, consider how households are likely to be affected by a trade agreement as consumers. Such effects are recognized in the Trade SIA of an EU–Mercosur agreement (see, for example, IDPM, 2007, p96), but could be investigated in more detail using the basic micro-simulation approach. In particular, given the prevailing pattern of trade between the EU and Mercosur, it is likely that a trade agreement would raise the domestic price of agricultural commodities in Mercosur countries, and lower the domestic price of manufactured goods. Given this, there is a need to collect information on the shares of expenditure on agricultural commodities and manufactured goods for different groups of households. One could then judge the overall effect of the likely price changes arising from an EU–Mercosur agreement on the purchasing power of different groups of households using equation (1) on p212. One could also take into account the fact that many households in rural areas may be both producers and consumers of the agricultural commodities that have changed in price (i.e. using equation (3) on p213).

Another example concerns the impact of a trade agreement on rural labour markets. For example, it is recognized in the EU–Mercosur Trade SIA that an expansion of the agricultural sector in Mercosur countries may raise the demand for labour in rural areas, with potentially positive impacts on rural wages and/or employment opportunities (see, for example, IDPM, 2007, p79). This issue could be investigated in more detail by looking at any existing estimates of, or perhaps seeking to provide new or updated estimates of, the elasticity of rural wage rates in Mercosur countries with respect to agricultural prices, as under the extended micro-simulation approach. A similar analysis could also usefully be done for the elasticity of rural land rents with respect to agricultural prices, since higher rental prices often drive the displacement of poor tenant farmers, with potential adverse effects on rural poverty.

Of course, carrying out these sorts of approaches would require additional time and resources, and there are overall time and resource constraints when doing a Trade SIA. The required information may also not always be available, especially in terms of estimating the factor price elasticities. However, given the importance of assessing distributional effects in meeting the overall objectives of a Trade SIA, it would appear warranted to at least explore these possibilities.

The second recommendation is for Trade SIAs to report, at the outset, which sectors in an economy are likely to experience rising prices as a result of a trade agreement, and which are likely to experience falling prices. This would make it easier to incorporate some of the other quantitative approaches for assessing distributional effects into Trade SIAs. Information on likely price changes is a first step, for example, in assessing the short-run effects of a trade agreement on households' purchasing power and firms' profits. It is also a first step in assessing the more medium-run effects on households' incomes, via changes in returns to the factors of production.

Of course, figuring out the likely effects of a trade agreement on domestic prices is itself a difficult exercise, even focusing on internationally traded goods. Nevertheless, it does appear to be a question of such importance for analysing distributional implications that it would be worth treating, in Trade SIAs, explicitly and at the outset.

A final issue relates to the conceptual distinction, made in the underlying Trade SIA methodology, between 'economic' and 'social' impacts. This distinction is rather blurred, and the danger is that distributional issues get sidelined in the process. For example, one can analyse both 'economic' impacts (e.g. on real income, employment) and 'social' impacts (e.g. on health and education) at an aggregate level. The key issue, of course, is to go beyond aggregate level analysis and consider how impacts differ across households: but this is true for both the economic impacts and the social impacts. Currently, the analysis of social impacts in Trade SIAs covers both the aggregate social impacts and the disaggregated economic impacts. A better and more instructive approach would be to distinguish between 'aggregate' and 'distributional' impacts within each of the categories of 'economic' and 'social'.

Notes

1 The underlying approach is set out in Deaton (1997, pp183–187). It is also referred to as the 'cost of living' or 'partial equilibrium' approach (Hertel and Reimer, 2004, p9).

2 This term is taken from Hertel and Reimer (2004).

3 The study has been carried out by a team led by the Institute for Development Policy and Management at the University of Manchester. The final report of phase 1 of this study was published in November 2007, while the inception report for Phase 2 of the study was published in June 2008 (see www.sia-trade.org/mercosur/index.shtml). In the words of the authors, the methodology used for the study includes 'significant extensions to the methodology used in previous SIAs' (IDPM, 2008, piv).

4 The CGE model used in the study assumes perfect mobility of factors of production across sectors of the economy, except land, which is limited to the agriculture sector.

5 This version of the Stolper–Samuelson theorem is simply a statement about the links between domestic prices and factor returns in an economy under certain assumptions (e.g. constant returns to scale). Only under its 'general' and 'restrictive' versions is the Stolper–Samuelson theorem combined with the Heckscher–Ohlin theory of the determinants of trading patterns between countries, to generate statements regarding the effects of greater openness to trade on the real returns to scarce and abundant factors of production (Deardorff, 1994).

6 If we assume that the owners of different factors of production have equal preferences in consumption, then we can say that the changes in the relative real returns to each factor are equal to the changes in the relative nominal returns. In general, however, we cannot make this assumption: for example, if unskilled wages are low relative to skilled wages and/or the returns to land, then basic necessities such as food are likely to account for a much larger share of consumption for unskilled workers.

7 It may be that the 'correlation' version of the theorem is what McCulloch et al (2001, p77) have in mind when they use the phrase, 'Generally speaking (but not inevitably)' in describing Stolper–Samuelson-type effects.

8 Writing household income in this way is based on the assumption that there are zero profits (e.g. because of entry and exit of firms in each sector). This is a common assumption to make in general equilibrium modelling.

References

Chen, S. and Ravallion, M. (2003) 'Household welfare impacts of China's accession to the World Trade Organisation', Policy Research Working Paper 3040, The World Bank, Washington DC

Deardorff, A. (1994) 'Overview of the Stolper-Samuelson Theorem', Chapter 2 in A. Deardorff and R. Stern (eds) *The Stolper-Samuelson Theorem: A Golden Jubilee*, University of Michigan Press, Ann Arbor, MI

Deaton, A. (1997) *The Analysis of Household Surveys: A Microeconometric Approach to Development Policy*, John Hopkins University Press, Baltimore, MD

EC (2006) *Handbook for Trade Sustainability Impact Assessment*, External Trade Department, European Commission, Brussels

Feenstra, R. (2003) *Advanced International Trade*, Princeton University Press, Princeton, NJ

Hertel, T. and Reimer, J. (2004) 'Predicting the poverty impacts of trade reform', Policy Research Working Paper 3444, The World Bank, Washington DC

Ianchovichina, E., Nicita, A. and Soloaga, I. (2002) 'Trade reform and poverty: The case of Mexico', *World Economy*, vol 25, pp945–972

IDPM and partners (2007) 'Trade sustainability impact assessment (SIA) of the association agreement under negotiation between the European Community and Mecosur. Overall Preliminary Trade SIA EU–Mercosur', Final Report (revised), November 2007, Institute for Development Policy and Management, University of Manchester

IDPM and partners (2008) 'Trade Sustainability Impact Assessment (SIA) of the Association Agreement under negotiation between the European Community and Mecosur', Final Overview and Sector Studies Inception Report, June 2008, Institute for Development Policy and Management, University of Manchester

Leamer, L. and Levinsohn, J. (1995) 'International trade theory: The evidence', Chapter 26 in G. Grossman and K. Rogoff (eds) *Handbook of International Economics*, vol III, Elsevier Science, Amsterdam

McCulloch, N., Winters, A. and Cirera, X. (2001) *Trade Liberalisation and Poverty: A Handbook*, Centre for Economic Policy Research, London

Porto, G. (2003) 'Using survey data to assess the distributional effects of trade policy', Development Research Group, The World Bank, Washington DC

Ravallion, M. (1990) 'Rural welfare effects of food price changes under induced wage responses: Theory and evidence for Bangladesh', *Oxford Economic Papers*, vol 42, no 3, pp574–585

Ravallion, M. and Loshkin, M. (2004) 'Gainers and losers from trade reform in Morocco', Policy Research Working Paper 3368, The World Bank, Washington DC

Warr, P. (2001) 'Welfare and distributional effects of an export tax: Thailand's rice premium', *American Journal of Agricultural Economics*, vol 83, no 4, pp903–920

World Bank (2003) *A User's Guide to Poverty and Social Impact Analysis*, The World Bank, Washington DC

11
Trade-induced Changes in Labour Market Inequalities: Current Findings and Policy Implications*

Edward Anderson and Massimiliano Calì

Introduction

Even the best designed trade reform creates winners and losers.[1]

Increased exposure to international trade, arising from trade reforms or improvements in transport and communications infrastructure, has in the past tended to cause winners and losers. Many have gained from increased exposure, but others have lost out, either in absolute or relative terms, at least in the short run. There are also widespread fears that current reforms at the multilateral level, such as the phasing out of the Multi-Fibre Agreement, will cause hardship for workers displaced by imports from lower-cost suppliers. This paper discusses some of the dimensions along which trade creates winners and losers in the labour market, and the implications this has for government policy.

Trade liberalization creates winners and losers in the labour market along various lines. This paper focuses on winners and losers defined along sector, skill and geographical lines. In each case, the beneficial impacts for winners

* An earlier version of this paper was presented at the Annual World Bank Conference on Development Economics (ABCDE), Tokyo, 29–30 May 2006, Parallel Session I: Trade-induced changes in economic inequalities: adjustment issues and policy implications for developing countries, organized by IDDRI, Paris. The authors are grateful to Tancrède Voituriez for suggestions and encouragement.

come in the form of higher earnings and/or more secure employment, while the adverse impacts for losers come in the form of lower earnings and/or displacement and unemployment. The next section of the paper reviews the most recent theory and evidence on which sectors and/or skill groups have gained in this sense from trade reforms, and which have lost out.

The policy issue is whether governments should intervene to transfer to the losers some of the benefits of trade enjoyed by the winners, and, if so, how much and through what channels. There are various arguments for and against such action, which can be classified under three headings: political, equity-based and efficiency-based. These are discussed in the third section of the paper.

The fourth section considers the more specific policy options available to a government wishing to transfer in some way some of the benefits enjoyed by the winners to the losers. Here there are difficult issues regarding: a) who should be eligible for assistance; b) how, and in what form, assistance should be provided; and c) how assistance can be provided in such a way that does not discourage the labour force adjustments that can greatly increase the benefits of trade. However, lessons can be drawn from Organisation for Economic Co-operation and Development (OECD) country examples, including the Trade Adjustment Assistance Programme in the US and the experience of 'active' labour market programmes in the US and Western Europe.

Two caveats need to be mentioned at the outset. First, increased trade has varied and multiple effects, of which effects on the labour market are only one. Often the most important effects of trade reforms are on consumers and producers, through their effects on final goods prices.[2] We do not claim that the effects of trade reforms on the labour market are the most important effects of those reforms, but they are relevant and sufficiently complex to merit separate treatment.

Secondly, trade reforms at the multilateral level can create winners and losers across countries, as well as within countries. There is, for example, quite a lot of debate about whether countries likely to lose out from the current round of WTO trade negotiations (mainly by losing preferential access to previously protected developed country markets) should be offered compensation for this loss, in the form of a temporary increase in aid for example.[3] The issues are closely linked, but this paper focuses on winners and losers within countries only.

Winners and losers from trade: Theory and evidence

Winners and losers by sector

One dimension by which winners and losers from trade are defined in the labour marker is the sector in which workers are initially based. Basic theory suggests that, in the immediate aftermath of trade reform, workers in industries or sectors that lack a comparative advantage will lose out, while those based in sectors with a comparative advantage will gain.

This simple prediction changes, however, once we allow for the fact that workers in sectors adversely affected by trade can look for new work elsewhere. In this case, the question of who gains and who loses becomes less clear. Workers who are relatively mobile between sectors may find they are better or worse off following reform: theory offers no unambiguous predictions. More specifically, in the basic specific-factors model of trade, the effect of trade reform on the real income of factors of production that are mobile across sectors is indeterminate.

This indeterminacy can be illustrated with a real-world example. In recent decades there have been some very large increases in employment in basic, labour-intensive manufacturing industries in several developing countries. Jenkins and Sen (2006), for example, estimate that the number of people employed in manufacturing during the 1990s increased by around 900,000 in Bangladesh, and by around 500,000 in Vietnam, and that in both cases the majority of the increase can be accounted for by increased exports.

Can these additional workers be described as winners from each country's trade reforms? Not necessarily, since to answer that question we need to know what level of earnings they were receiving in their previous employment, prior to the trade reform. This requires going beyond employment figures and looking more closely at earnings data.

The same point applies to workers who are displaced by competition from imports. Some argue that many developing countries are faced with a substantial decline in the number of workers employed in basic manufacturing, due to competition from lower cost suppliers in China and elsewhere. To what extent, however, can workers displaced for this reason be described as losers from trade reform? The answer is again uncertain: it depends on how long they remain unemployed after being displaced, and what level of earnings they receive when re-employed.

Unfortunately, there is relatively little evidence for developing countries on the length of time that workers displaced by trade remain unemployed, and on their earnings levels once re-employed.[4] Those studies cited in recent reviews by Matusz and Tarr (1999), McCulloch et al (2001) and Rama (2003) relate to workers displaced for reasons other than trade, such as public sector retrenchment. More evidence is available for developed countries, typically at the industry level (see Matusz and Tarr, 1999). Even in this case, however, most of the evidence does not relate specifically to workers displaced by trade, mainly because the reasons for displacement are difficult to establish.[5]

However, what evidence there is suggests that both the length of unemployment and the level of earnings on re-employment vary significantly according to workers' characteristics. Matusz and Tarr (1999), for example, argue that two important considerations are a) whether a worker has substantial specific human capital accumulated in their industry or firm; and b) whether a worker is earning a substantial wage premium, due for instance to high government wage scales. This is supported by evidence showing that reductions in earnings following displacement are usually greater than they are for workers with longer job tenure with their previous employers, and that reductions in earnings for workers displaced from the public sector are generally greater than they are for workers displaced from other sectors.

This evidence needs to be expanded, but what there is suggests we should be cautious about labelling all workers displaced from a sector as being losers from trade reform. At the least we need to go beyond employment figures and look at data on the duration of unemployment spells, and data on earnings. One plausible hypothesis, which appears to remain untested, is that both the duration of unemployment and the level of earnings on re-employment vary according to the more general, as opposed to industry or firm-specific, skills of displaced workers: their education level for example. This would suggest that workers' skill, rather than their initial sector, would be more important in determining whether they are among the winners or losers from trade reform.

Winners and losers by skill level

Another dimension according to which winners and losers from trade reforms in the labour market may be defined is skill, as measured for example by the amount and type of a person's education, training and on-the-job experience. Basic Heckscher–Ohlin (HO) trade theory suggests that, because of inter-sectoral factor mobility, the sector in which workers are initially based has no bearing on whether they gain or lose from a trade reform. Instead, it is their skills that matter, with those whose skills are in relatively abundant supply gaining, and those whose skills are in relatively scarce supply losing out.

Other models also regard workers' skill as being the main dimension according to which winners and losers from trade reforms in the labour market are defined. However, they allow for trade reforms to have more varied effects on workers with different skill levels, as compared with the basic HO model. This is mainly by allowing for the possibility that increased openness to trade also brings increased exposure to the latest technology. The effects of increased exposure to the latest technology can sometimes offset the standard HO effects of trade reforms on skilled and unskilled workers, even in low-income countries with highly abundant supplies of unskilled labour (see, for example, Wood, 2002).

Arguably the best evidence on the effects of trade reforms on the earnings and employment opportunities of workers with different levels of skill comes from studies of individual countries that have liberalized in recent decades, using household-survey evidence. Most of these studies are of Latin American countries. Examples include:

- Mexico, where the wages of non-production workers relative to production workers rose by 55 per cent between 1987 and 1995, while the average earnings 'premium' to an additional year of education doubled (Robertson, 2000);

- Brazil, where the wages of college-educated workers relative to primary or secondary-level educated workers rose by around 20 per cent between 1992 and 1999 (Green et al 2001);
- Chile, where the wages of college-educated workers relative to elementary-educated workers rose by about 80 per cent between the early 1970s and late 1980s (Beyer et al 1999).[6]

What was the contribution of trade reforms to these increases in the relative wages of more skilled workers? The answer to this question is somewhat uncertain. Nevertheless, Robertson (2000) finds that a reduction in the relative price of labour-intensive products following trade liberalization can account for 50 per cent of the rise in the relative wage of skilled labour in Mexico. Beyer et al (1999) also find that a fall in the price of labour-intensive products following trade liberalization helps explain the increase in wage inequality in Chile, although they do not provide an estimate of the share of the increase explained. Trade reforms do therefore appear to be playing a significant role in driving the relative wages of more skilled workers.

What about trends in the absolute earnings of workers with different skill levels? Not all of the above studies report this information, but those that do show that although the real wages of less-skilled workers did not actually fall over the periods considered, the magnitude of increase was marginal. Thus in Chile, Beyer et al (1999) find that the real average per-capita labour incomes of households headed by secondary-level educated workers rose by less than 1 per cent per year between 1970 and 1992, compared to a rise of 2.9 per cent per year for households headed by college-educated workers. In Brazil, Green et al (2001) find that the real wages of primary and secondary-level educated workers rose by less than 0.5 per cent per year between 1992 and 1999, compared to a rise of 2.5 per cent per year for college-educated workers.

Finally, to what extent, and how quickly, have supply-side responses tended to gradually counteract higher relative earnings of more skilled workers? Again, the evidence here is more limited, but what there is suggests that although the relative earnings of more skilled workers have stabilized at a new, higher level, they have not shown any tendency to return to their former levels. This is shown quite clearly by the most recent work on the Chilean case by Gallego (2006).[7]

Overall therefore, there is evidence to suggest that: a) trade reforms in at least some developing countries have widened wage differentials between skilled and less-skilled workers; b) less-skilled workers have seen only limited real wage increases in the process; and c) these effects appear to have persisted beyond the short run. We now consider whether trade reforms have had differential impacts on workers along another dimension, that of the geographical area in which they are initially based.

Winners and losers by geographical area

Workers in different regions of a country may be affected differently by trade reforms. One reason may simply be regional variation in the composition of the workforce by skills and/or sector. In Mexico for example, average nominal wages in northern regions increased faster than in other regions following trade integration (Hanson, 1996, 2003), which is partly explained by the rise in the wages of skilled relative to unskilled workers induced by the trade opening in Mexico, combined with a higher proportion of skilled workers in northern regions. Similarly, increasing regional earning inequality in the UK between 1982 and 1997 was driven mainly by differing regional compositions of the workforce: returns to education improved nationwide, causing average wages to rise by more in regions with higher proportions of more educated workers in the labour force, such as London (Duranton and Monastiriotis, 2002).[8]

Do trade reforms have differential impacts on wage levels in different areas, once we control for regional variation in the composition of the workforce? The broad answer is yes if we consider impacts on nominal wages, while differential impacts on real wages may occur only if internal labour mobility is constrained in some way. New economic geography (NEG) models help understand the channels involved, by adding transport costs and increasing returns to scale to the classical trade model.[9] The essential insight of such models is that interaction between increasing returns to scale and transport costs generates incentives for production to be concentrated in only a few places, ideally close to the market (to minimize transportation costs). As firms cluster in an industry centre, this becomes a larger market and thus the process self-reinforces. However, reductions in barriers to international trade extend the potential set of locations for production, and favour regions that have good access to foreign markets.

According to the model by Krugman and Livas Elizondo (1996) for instance, following trade liberalization firms will tend to relocate away from the industrial centre, towards regions with lower wages and better access to foreign markets. This raises the relative demand for labour in the regions in which firms relocate, and in turn tends to narrow nominal wage disparities across regions, other things being equal. They use the model to explain the decreasing share of population and gross domestic product in Mexico City following Mexico's entry into the North American Free Trade Agreement (NAFTA).

Some support for this hypothesis is provided by Hanson (1996), who tests whether the influence of distance from Mexico City on wages in the apparel industry differs before and after trade liberalization. He finds that wages in the apparel sector are a decreasing function of distance from the capital, but this influence diminishes after trade liberalization, and at the same time the influence of distance from the US border strengthens. These results are in line with those of Aroca et al (2005), who find that trade reform has disproportionately benefited northern regions in Mexico, at the expense of the capital city and the south, contributing to widening wage disparities across regions.

The case of Mexico suggests that the impact of trade reforms on the spatial distribution of nominal wages is likely to depend crucially on the spatial distribution of access to foreign markets. Hanson (2003) finds that differences in exposure to external trade, foreign direct investment and migration account for a large portion of current differences in wages across regions in Mexico. Similarly, Lin (2005) finds that between about 15 and 25 per cent of the real wage differentials among China's provinces can be explained by differential access to international markets. The possibility that trade integration may lead to a further polarization of earnings within countries may be substantial, as industrial centres in developing countries are often locations with better market access relative to the rest of the country (e.g. more developed infrastructure networks).

When seeking to assess the differential impacts of trade reforms across space, one major constraint is the availability of regional price data for the calculation of real wages. Of the studies reviewed, only Duranton and Monastiriotis (2002) and Lin (2005) measure the effects of trade openness on real as opposed to nominal wages, although the former are the more appropriate indicator of the welfare impacts of the reform. This makes it difficult to assess whether workers in different locations have benefited or lost out from trade reforms. At the same time, there is also evidence that real wage differentials across regions converge over time, most likely as a result of labour mobility. Duranton and Monastiriotis (2002), for example, show how regional real wage differentials in the UK converged over the period 1982–1997.

On balance, the empirical literature suggests that trade reforms do have differential impacts on wage levels across space, according mainly to the workforce composition of different regions and their access to international markets. The magnitude of these effects appear to be large in nominal terms but smaller in real terms, which is most likely due to inter-regional labour mobility. This is particularly the case when controlling for the composition of regions' workforces by skill level.

Policy implications

The previous section suggests that trade liberalization has in the past caused winners and losers in the labour market, and that workers' skill, rather than their initial sector or location, appears to be most important in determining whether they are among the winners or among the losers. The policy question for governments that have liberalized trade, and/or are considering further liberalization, is whether to compensate the losers from trade reform in some way.

The main arguments for and against compensation of this nature have been set out previously, for instance by Lawrence and Litan (1986) and more recently by McCulloch et al (2001, pp150–153). Before turning to these arguments, a prior question is whether it is possible to offset the adverse impacts of trade reforms on some groups in the labour market in some other way.

One potential option would be to alter the speed and/or sequencing of trade reforms. This would give workers adversely affected by trade reforms time to acquire new skills, relocate to different areas, and so on. However, it is doubtful whether this would benefit adversely affected groups to any great extent, without some form of financial support (e.g. subsidized training, relocation costs). With financial support, however, the policy would be more accurately described as a particular type of compensation, rather than an alternative to compensation. Another option would be to increase labour market flexibility. However, even in a world of perfect labour mobility and perfectly flexible wages, trade reforms are still likely to create winners and losers in the labour market. The only difference would be that the adverse impacts for losers would come purely in the form of lower earnings, as opposed to a balance between lower earnings and a higher (lower) probability of becoming unemployed (re-employed).

For these reasons, simply altering the sequencing or speed of trade reforms or promoting labour market flexibility is unlikely to benefit adversely affected groups by any great extent. What then are the arguments in favour of direct compensation for the losers? It is useful to group these arguments into three types, namely political, equity-based and efficiency-based.

Political arguments

The basic political argument is that compensating the losers from trade reform increases political support for the reform itself. This makes the reform more likely to be implemented and sustained, which may be desirable for the country as a whole, for instance because it raises social welfare. The argument applies to the extent that trade liberalization is considered desirable for the country as a whole, and to the extent that the losers from trade reform, or civil society groups who advocate on their behalf, are sufficiently cohesive and powerful politically to be in a position to block or reverse reform.

There are strong advocates of this rationale for compensation, and there is evidence suggesting that compensation for trade-displaced workers has reduced opposition to liberalized trade policies, at least in the US (Lawrence and Litan, 1986, p24). Nevertheless, it is recognized that there are limits to this justification for compensation (Lawrence and Litan, 1986, p25). In particular, compensation can only be partial, mainly because it is difficult and costly to raise the necessary public revenue (something which is aggravated in a developing country context by the fact that trade-related taxes may represent a high share of total public revenue). The constraint on the amount of compensation in turn means that the losers from trade reform may not reduce their opposition to reform to any great extent. In addition, if the losers from trade reform are among the more advantaged members of society, compensation to ensure their political support would tend to conflict with equity considerations.

Equity-based arguments

One equity-based argument is that, without compensation, trade reform would change the distribution of advantage within society in a way that would be regarded as unacceptable. For instance, it could be that, without compensation, the losers from trade reform would fall below some minimum level of income deemed acceptable.

This argument applies to the extent that the losers from trade reform are among the more disadvantaged members within society. Note, however, that societies may make different normative judgements about which particular yardstick – for example, income, opportunities or capabilities – to use when assessing distributional issues (see, for example, World Bank, 2005). Thus workers who experience a reduction in their wage level as a result of trade reform may not necessarily be considered worse off, if their opportunities – in terms of wage levels in other sectors or locations to which they have access – were to rise.

Another equity-based argument is that it would be unfair if a major government decision, such as a trade reform, was to have adverse impacts on certain groups of people. Put slightly differently, the argument would be that every effort should be made to ensure that all people share the benefits of collective social decisions. Of course, it may be unreasonable to require that every single policy reform does not have an adverse impact on any group of people. Nevertheless, it would arguably be reasonable to expect major policy reforms, such as trade liberalization, to meet this criterion.

Efficiency-based arguments

There are also various efficiency-based arguments for compensation. In the context of the labour market, arguably the main argument is that there is a tendency for people to underinvest in their education and skills. As a result, any trade reform that increases the return to skill raises the economic cost to society of that underinvestment (Wood, 1994). In such cases, government action that captures some of the benefits of trade enjoyed by skilled workers, and subsidizes basic education and training in return, can be economically efficient. Typically, however, the more prominent efficiency-based arguments have been against compensation, on the grounds that, in a second-best world, taxes and transfers are distorting and economically inefficient. Despite the increasing amount of evidence on the adverse effects that inequality has on efficiency and economic growth, this argument is still valid.

To summarize therefore, although there are various arguments in favour of compensating the losers from trade reform, there are various counter-arguments. Of the counter-arguments, the most prominent is that raising the revenues required for compensation, either through taxation or by reducing expenditure in other areas, would be too costly, particularly in developing countries where the capacity to raise revenues is lower and the returns to public expenditure in other areas is higher. For these reasons, the prevailing consensus, especially in the developing country context, is that direct compensation should not be sought. In the words of McCulloch et al (2001, p153):

> *Although identifying losers from a given trade reform is a key first step, public policy in most developing countries is probably best concentrated on the provision of social safety nets, targeted by the characteristics most likely to make people vulnerable to poverty from a wide range of possible shocks. In most countries, this will be preferable to compensation targeted at individuals suffering directly as a consequence of trade reform.*

The 2006 World Development Report argues along similar lines, stating that:

> *Permanent social protection can help reduce the need for special compensatory programs for each and every reform – all the more important because such programs are difficult to start and stop and are not always very efficient.* (World Bank, 2005, p149)

Are there any arguments to challenge this consensus? Here we make two points. First, without disagreeing with either of these quotations as general statements, there is still a need to assess the arguments for direct compensatory programmes on a country-by-country basis; there is no real basis for automatically ruling them out a priori. Secondly, we should be careful not to view a trade reform as another type of shock that households face. In fact, shocks and reforms are conceptually quite different: while the former are, at least to some extent, unavoidable events, the latter are, or at least should be, collective social decisions. The appropriate response when people are adversely affected by shocks is not necessarily, therefore, the appropriate response when people are adversely affected by reforms; different normative considerations are involved. For these two reasons, we consider in the next section the more technical issue of how a government could actually go about designing a policy of compensating the losers from trade reforms.

Policy design

There are various ways in which compensation for workers who have been adversely affected by trade reform can be provided. As with other government programmes, there are issues to be resolved around: a) who should be eligible for assistance; b) in what form assistance should be provided; and c) how assistance can be provided in such a way that does not undermine the benefits of trade reforms themselves.

As for the first issue, in the short term it may be appropriate to restrict assistance to workers in sectors or regions adversely affected by trade reform, since these are the groups of workers most likely to be adversely affected in the immediate aftermath of a trade reform. In the longer term, however, it will generally be more appropriate to restrict assistance to workers in skill groups adversely affected by trade. The reason for this difference is that adverse effects on workers with particular levels of skill are likely to persist for longer over time than adverse effects on workers in particular regions or sectors.

As for the second issue, it is again useful to distinguish between short and long term. In the short term, a combination of cash and in-kind transfers is likely to be appropriate. These may include for instance (Auer, 2001):

- early retirement and redundancy payments;
- relocation assistance or 'mobility grants', including repatriation grants;
- wage subsidies or 'wage insurance' for displaced workers willing to take up lower paid jobs;
- training and small business development schemes;
- enhanced cash payments during unemployment.

It is not unreasonable to expect that the 'in-kind' transfers among these (e.g. relocation assistance, training schemes) may be more feasible politically than pure cash payments. In the longer term, there may be other ways of assisting workers adversely affected by trade. For example, a combination of public works programmes and/or employment subsidies could be used to increase the demand for less-skilled workers on a longer term basis.

The third issue concerns the way in which assistance can be provided without discouraging those labour force adjustments that can greatly increase the benefits of trade (e.g. workforce retraining, movement of labour into more efficient sectors). This is a difficult issue, but there is a very large set of OECD country experiences on which to draw. In particular, there are positive experiences with 'active' labour market programmes from several OECD countries. In order to work effectively, these schemes provide relatively generous benefits, while at the same time minimizing potential moral hazard from the beneficiaries (e.g. through penalties for those who do not take up job offers).

A final issue concerns the possibility of establishing whether a reduction in earnings and/or employment opportunities experienced by a group of workers can be attributed to a trade reform, as opposed to some other factor such as technological change. The studies reviewed earlier in the chapter arguably do isolate the effect of trade on the labour market, as distinct from other influences. However, this does remain an area in which further work at the methodological level would be useful.

The largest direct compensatory policy for workers adversely affected by trade is the Trade Adjustment Assistance (TAA) Programme in the US, which was introduced in 1962 and has been expanded since. Since the early 1970s, approximately 2 million former workers in the textiles, electronics, autos and steel sectors have received benefits under the programme, out of an estimated 3 million eligible workers. The programme provides additional assistance over and above the normal unemployment system, and some assistance with training and relocation costs (Rosen, 2005).

Under the TAA, imports have to be shown to 'contribute importantly' to job loss in order for workers to access the funds. This means that imports must be as least as important as all the other responsible factors, though they need not necessarily be the sole reason. It also has to be demonstrated that the sales of the firm in consideration have declined in absolute terms, and that a significant number of workers have been or are threatened with being laid-off as a result. These issues are resolved by the US Department of Labour, although workers have the right of appeal.

The TAA programme is fairly unique among OECD countries, although towards the end of 2005 the European Commission called for a similar programme to be implemented throughout the European Union, under the proposed name of the Globalisation Adjustment Fund.[10] This Fund would focus on helping redundant workers move, set up new businesses, acquire new skills and so on, although no cash payouts would be involved since that is considered to fall within the responsibility of national welfare systems. It would complement the European Social Fund, which is a longer term initiative with a particular focus on building skills.

Programmes such as the TAA and the proposed Globalisation Adjustment Fund remain controversial, however. They face much criticism, both on the methodology for determining the causes of job loss, their cost in terms of public resources, and on the moral arbitrariness of differential treatment for workers displaced for different reasons.

Summary and conclusions

To summarize, this paper makes three main points. The first is that trade reforms have in the past produced winners and losers in the labour market, and will in all likelihood continue to do so in future. In the immediate aftermath of reform, winners and losers are defined by their sector or location of employment, but after this phase their skill is a more important and longer lasting determinant.

The second point is that there are various arguments as to why governments should compensate in some way the losers from trade reforms, but there are also important counter-arguments. The existing consensus is that direct compensation for the losers from trade reform should not generally be sought, and that instead policy makers should concentrate on providing broad-based social protection and/or insurance. This might be challenged, however, on the grounds that the appropriate policy response when people are adversely affected by shocks is not necessarily the appropriate policy response when people are adversely affected by reforms. Moreover, the arguments for and against compensation should be assessed on a case-by-case basis; there is no real basis for automatically ruling compensation out a priori.

The final point is that deciding on the appropriate level and form of any compensation to the losers of trade reforms is difficult, but useful and important lessons can be drawn from the experiences of OECD countries in this area, including the TAA Programme in the US, and the experience of 'active' labour market programmes in the US and Western Europe.

In terms of future research priorities, one area would be more time-series, household-survey based analyses of trends in the returns to education and skill in low-income countries, since most current studies relate to middle- and high-income countries. Similarly, research on the impact of trade reforms across geographical areas within countries is a further important area of investigation. This could usefully be accompanied by more research on the duration of job search and/or unemployment spells associated with trade liberalization, the size of the wage gains or wage losses associated with job mobility following liberalization, and how this varies across workers with different levels of skill.

Notes

1 Bannister and Thugge (2001).
2 For example, the recent World Bank report *Global Agricultural Trade and Developing Countries* emphasizes the impact of multilateral trade reform on food prices, and the differential impacts this is likely to have on net-food producing households (and countries) as compared with net-food consuming households (and countries).
3 See, for example, Kleen and Page (2005, pp100–101). This also includes recent debates surrounding 'aid for trade'; see, for example, www.odi.org.uk/iedg/aid4trade.html.
4 According to McCulloch et al (2001, pp147–148), 'there seems to be very little research directly on labour turnover in developing countries', and 'it is difficult to generalise about how deep and how durable transitional employment losses [from trade liberalization] may be'.
5 The one study reviewed by Matusz and Tarr (1999) that does focus specifically on trade-impacted workers is that by Bale (1976). It found the average duration of unemployment to be 31 weeks.
6 These and other recent studies are reviewed in more detail in Anderson (2005).
7 There is evidence that overall income inequality in Chile may have returned to its pre-reform level (see Winters et al, 2004, p101). This is not incompatible with the evidence of persistence in the relative wages of more skilled workers, however, since they are only one component of overall inequality.
8 Although the authors do not explicitly make the point, the period considered in the study coincides with a drastic trade opening of the UK economy.
9 Krugman (1991) was among the first proponents of such framework. See Fujita et al (1999) for an extensive exposition of the main NEG models.
10 For an enthusiastic endorsement of the Globalisation Adjustment Fund see www.number10.gov.uk/output/Page8381.asp.

References

Anderson, E. (2005) 'Openness and inequality in developing countries: A review of theory and recent evidence', *World Development*, vol 33, no 7, pp1045–1063

Aroca, P., Bosch, M. and Maloney, W. F. (2005) 'Spatial dimensions of trade liberalization and economic divergence: Mexico 1985–2002', *World Bank Economic Review*, vol 19, no 3, pp345–378

Auer, P. (2001) 'Labour market policy for socially responsible workforce adjustment', Employment Paper 2001/14, International Labour Organization, Geneva

Bale, M. D. (1976) 'Estimates of trade-displacement costs for US workers', *Journal of International Economics*, vol 6, pp245–250

Bannister, G. and Thugge, K. (2001) 'International trade and poverty alleviation', IMF Working Paper 01/54, International Monetary Fund, Washington DC

Beyer, H., Rojas, P. and Vergara, R. (1999) 'Trade liberalisation and wage inequality', *Journal of Development Economics*, vol 59, pp103–123

Duranton, G. and Monastiriotis, V. (2002) 'Mind the gap: The evolution of regional earnings inequalities in the UK, 1982–97', *Journal of Regional Science*, vol 42, no 2, pp219–256

Fujita, M., Krugman, P. and Venables, A. J. (1999) *The Spatial Economy: Cities, Regions, and International Trade*, The MIT Press, Cambridge, MA

Gallego, F. (2006) 'The skill premium in Chile: Studying the skill bias technical change hypothesis in the South', Unpublished Paper, MIT Department of Economics

Green, F., Dickerson, A. and Saba Arbache, J. (2001) 'A picture of wage inequality and the allocation of labour through a period of trade liberalisation: The case of Brazil', *World Development*, vol 29, no 11, pp1923–1939

Hanson, G. (1996) 'Localization economies, vertical organization, and trade', *American Economic Review*, vol 85, no 5, pp1266–1278

Hanson, G. (2003) 'What has happened to wages in Mexico since NAFTA? Implications for hemispheric free trade', NBER Working Paper No. 9563, NBER, Cambridge, MA

Jenkins, R. and Sen, K. (2006) 'International trade and employment outcomes in the South: Four country case studies', *Oxford Development Studies*, vol 34, no 3, pp299–322

Kleen, P. and Page, S. (2005) 'Making special and differential treatment work for development', Ministry for Foreign Affairs, Sweden

Krugman, P. (1991) 'Increasing returns and economic geography', *Journal of Political Economy*, vol 99, pp183–199

Krugman, P. and Livas Elizondo, R. (1996) 'Trade policy and the third world metropolis', *Journal of Development Economics*, vol 49, pp137–150

Lawrence, R. and Litan, R. (1986) *Saving Free Trade. A Pragmatic Approach*, Brookings Institutions, Washington DC

Lin, S. (2005) 'International trade, location and wage inequality in China', in R. Kanbur and A. J. Venables (eds) *Spatial Inequality and Development*, Oxford University Press, Oxford

Matusz, S. and Tarr, S. (1999) 'Adjusting to trade policy reform', Policy Research Working Paper No. 2142, The World Bank, Washington DC

McCulloch, N., Winters, L. A. and Cirera, X. (2001) *Trade Liberalisation and Poverty: A Handbook*, Centre for Economic Policy Research, London

Rama, M. (2003) 'Globalisation and workers in developing countries', Policy Research Working Paper 2958, The World Bank, Washington DC

Robertson, R. (2000) 'Trade liberalisation and wage inequality: Lessons from the Mexican experience', *World Economy*, vol 23, no 6, pp827–849

Rosen, H. (2005) 'Trade-related labour market adjustment policies and programs, with special reference to textile and apparel workers', Trade Adjustment Assistance Coalition, www.taacoalition.com

Winters, L. A., McCulloch, N. and McKay, A. (2004) 'Trade liberalization and poverty: The evidence so far', *Journal of Economic Literature*, 42, pp72–115

Wood, A. (1994) *North–South Trade, Employment and Inequality*, Clarendon Press, Oxford
Wood, A. (2002) 'Globalisation and wage inequalities: A synthesis of three theories', *Weltwirtschaftliches Archiv*, vol 138, no 1, pp54–82
World Bank (2005) *World Development Report 2006: Equity and Development*, Oxford University Press, Oxford

12

The Value of Value Chains: Spreading the Gains from Liberalization

Dirk Scheer

Introduction

Real globetrotters of the present are not individuals – as one might guess – but products, commodities and, albeit to a lesser extent, services. Even if the lion's share of producer and consumer trade is undertaken within regions (European Union (EU), North American Free Trade Association (NAFTA), Asia) supply chains more and more spread out between developed and developing countries. While in the past developing countries predominantly acted as raw material suppliers, for the time being finishing processes and knowledge-based work steps and services complement their portfolio. There is no doubt of ongoing processes of a globalizing economy.

While stepping further with liberalizing world trade with both multilateral and bilateral trade agreements, the perspective on consequences and future outcomes initiated through (free) trade policy gained momentum since the late 1990s. The European Commission (EC) has played a crucial role in the development and implementation of ex-ante world trade evaluations. This effort originates in a broader commitment to Impact Assessment, which 'introduced a comprehensive regulatory and assessment framework for all policy areas, including trade' (EC, 2004, p2). Trade-related evaluation has been labelled Sustainability Impact Assessment (SIA) and can be defined as 'a means of identifying and assessing the likelihood and scale of the economic, social and environmental impacts of a policy change or rule-measure. The purpose is to ensure that those charged with making policy have the most complete information possible to guide them in their decision-making' (George and Kirkpatrick, 2003, p3).

Product chain assessment is an emerging tool for understanding the dynamics of global economic transformations – and their sustainability impacts (Kuik and von Moltke, 1998). Instead of focusing on countries and their economic development as the ultimate units of account, product chain assessment takes markets, product and substance flows and the interlinkages of actors within the chain as its point of departure. In this manner product chain assessment offers the prospect of reflecting more accurately the dynamics of markets subject to liberalization and the relationship between producers and consumers, when these are in different countries

The methodological basis for product chain assessment is, however, still rudimentary. A significant effort to develop this methodology appears particularly promising from the perspective of SIA and will be attempted within this chapter, laying emphasis on integrating methods such as, for example, profit, actor and governance analysis as well as income/employment skill distribution and life-cycle assessment to meet sustainability assessment needs.

We argue that, with taking a product chain perspective, a more accurate view on the dynamics, transformations and sustainability impacts of globalizing product chains is possible. The objective of this chapter therefore is to give a better understanding and elaborate a generic but suitable framework for product chain analysis within SIA. The main thesis is to show that no methodological or research gaps prevent product chain approaches being used within SIA.

The first section of the chapter outlines the need for a product chain perspective when carrying out SIAs. The second section provides a short overview of what is a product chain perspective and depicts essentials for product chain analysis. The third section elaborates on integrating product chain analysis into SIA, while the fourth section draws conclusions.

Relevance of a product chain perspective

The world behind products

There is a complex world behind every product. Products and services are results of various combined activities of a multitude of actors at several product life-cycle stages. The final product can be seen as a result of 'a transactionally linked sequence of functions in which each stage adds value to the process of production of goods or services' (Dicken, 2004, p14). The transactions of processes are twofold in opposite directions. On the one hand, material and substance flows, semi-finished goods and final goods reach from cradle to grave – that is, from raw material extraction through manufacturing, retail, consumption and disposal/recycling. On the other hand, information flows, customer demands, demands of original equipment manufacturers (OEMs) towards their suppliers and so on, go backwards. The product chain describes the full range of activities from conception and production (involving a combination of physical transformation and the input of various producer services), trade and delivery to final consumers and the after use disposal/recycling. In short, product development and design, production, marketing, consumption and recycling are the most important phases. But besides the inner circle of the production chain there are several influencing factors determining the organizational and procedural development of the chain, namely the technological input, the financial system and the political framework. These input factors level the playing field of dynamics of product chain transformations.

However, there is rarely one single product chain; usually there is a multitude of parallel and interlinked chains. Taking the example of forestry (Kaplinsky and Morris, 2001), in a first product chain layer the forestry input gives stimulus to several chains: a) pulp and paper; b) sawmills with subsequent chains such as building and construction, furniture, biomass energy sector and so on; and c) mining. These product-determined chains develop individual upstream characteristics even though they rely on similar raw material. In our view, the development and singular characteristic of product chains depends to a great extent on product attributes and functionalities. In a first step it makes sense to categorize products and services according to their main product chain characteristics.

Gereffi (1994, p97) introduced a general distinction among product chains, that is producer-driven versus buyer-driven production networks. *Producer-driven* production networks are 'those industries in which transnational corporations (TNCs) or other large integrated industrial enterprises play the central role in controlling the production system (including its backward and forward linkages). This is most characteristic of capital- and technology-intensive industries like automobiles, computers, aircraft, and electrical machinery... What distinguishes producer-driven production systems is the control exercised by the administrative headquarters of the TNCs.' *Buyer-driven* production networks tend to occur in 'those industries in which large retailer, brand-named merchandisers, and trading companies play the pivotal role in setting up decentralised production networks in a variety of exporting countries'.

Kaplinsky and Morris (2001, p34) elaborated an overview of key aspects of these types of product chains. For producer-driven chains, drivers are industrial capital, core competences in research and development (R&D) and production, and investment-based network links. Typical industries are knowledge-based sectors such as automobiles, computers and aircraft providing markets with consumer durables, intermediate goods and capital goods. The chain organization is done by transnational firms with a high degree of vertical integration. In contrast, buyer-driven chains are driven by commercial capital with a crucial role of design and marketing. Typical industries are apparel, footwear and toys with local firms based predominantly in developing countries.

The globalization of product chains

Several economic indicators provide evidence of the global integration of commodity markets (homogeneous world market prices; increase of global volatility of commodities, capital and human resources; increase of world trade and foreign direct investment flows). These all reflect the dynamics of the on-going globalization process of product chains. While traditional patterns of world trade left developed countries producing and exporting industrial goods and developing countries exporting raw materials and foodstuffs, the landscape is fundamentally changing. Evidence of more heterogeneous spatial patterns of product chains can be observed in changing product information. While in the past, for instance, the label *made in Germany* indicated German-based product development and manufacture, current labels are more likely to have the meaning *designed and engineered in Germany* while assembly/manufacture takes place elsewhere.

Dicken lists several empirical observations backing the thesis of shifting contours of the geo-economy (Dicken, 2004, p38):

- Whereas the top three producers (the United States, Japan and Germany) account for 57 per cent of world manufacturing production the same three countries account for only 29 per cent of world manufacturing exports.
- The share of world manufactured imports accounted for by the top 15 importers increased dramatically between 1963 and 2000, from 46 per cent to 71 per cent.
- Whereas only four developing countries are in the top 15 producers of manufactures, there are six in the top 15 exporters. Only one of the six (Hong Kong) was in the top 15 exporters in 1963.
- Although the United States and Germany were the top two exporters of manufactured products in both 1963 and 2000, their combined share has fallen from 33 per cent to 21 per cent.

The increase of world trade has been accompanied by a considerable flow of materials and substances. Some research has been done on international material product chains related to different product categories (see for instance Vellinga et al, 1998; van Beukering et al, 2000; van Beukering and Bouman, 2000a), that is:

- **Primary commodities or virgin materials:** Raw materials that have been extracted from natural resources; examples are iron ore and wood pulp.
- **Secondary commodities or recyclable waste materials:** Raw materials that have been recovered after production or consumption; examples are iron scrap and wastepaper.
- **Final commodities or intermediates:** Intermediary products suitable to directly convert into consumer goods; examples are crude steel and printing paper. It is assumed that final commodities can be produced from both primary and secondary commodities.

- **Consumer products:** Final goods manufactured in the final production stage and used in the consumption stage; examples are cars and books.
- **Waste materials:** Residue materials that no longer can be converted in useful materials or products in an economically feasible manner; an example is municipal solid waste.

There is empirical evidence that major changes in world trade patterns have occurred. Primary, secondary and final commodity trade between North and South has increased considerably during the last 30 years. This pattern still dominates international trade by quantity within the so-called triade (US, Europe, Japan). About half of all commodity types are traded within the triade, while North–South trade counts for about 17 (primary) to 28 (secondary) per cent (see Table 12.1). However, what is striking is the fact of closer trading linkages between developed and developing countries. Considering the development from the early 1970s onwards, there has been a considerable decrease in North–North trade. Instead, North–South trade exploded for primary and secondary commodities. And even South–North trade developed for secondary products – even though from a very low level. Finally South–South trade increased for all commodity types considerably with high growth rates for secondary and final commodities.

Table 12.1 *Trade flows in the international material-product chain*

Trade flow		*Share in total trade (1995–97 average)*			*Change in share (relative to 1970–74)*		
From	*To*	*Primary commodity*	*Secondary commodity*	*Final commodity*	*Primary commodity*	*Secondary commodity*	*Final commodity*
North	North	45%	55%	54%	–22%	–36%	–15%
North	South	18%	28%	17%	207%	230%	15%
South	North	19%	6%	12%	–33%	106%	–33%
South	South	18%	11%	17%	120%	569%	299%

Note: The unweighted average share of commodities consist of aluminium, copper, lead, nickel, paper, iron, tin and zinc.
Source: van Beukering et al (2000, p5)

Product chains and the environment

Currently, there is a wide consensus that products and services are a source of considerable environmental impact. Obviously, past environmental policy with its process-oriented focus towards hazardous substances, waste quantity and emissions to air, water and land did not succeed in making products and services wholly environmentally benign. One can observe among policy makers and the scientific community a shift towards a more systematic and integrated approach based on product life-cycle thinking (Scheer and Rubik, 2006).

First, it becomes clear that environmental policy is challenged by so-called persistent environmental problems. Typically persistent environmental problems concern long-term and partly irreversible deterioration of the environment. Examples of these core global environmental challenges are climate change, loss of biodiversity, land erosion and contamination, health protection, and sustainable use of natural resources and waste management. Persistent environmental challenges are often linked to structural patterns of sectors, for example, transport, construction, agriculture or energy (Jänicke and Volkery, 2001).

Secondly, knowledge on the environmental impact caused by products and services has increased considerably. There is a wide range of methodologies – with Life-Cycle Assessment (LCA) being the most popular – available and in practise among policy makers, business and the scientific community to judge the product's impact on the environment. Empirical data show that business and industry is keen to apply a wide range of environmental product information methodologies with preferences for simple and smart tools (Konrad, 2005).

Thirdly, there are several arguments to emphasize a product focus in environmental policy. On the one hand, process-oriented environmental policy has been successful in bringing about considerable environmental media improvements – and obviously fails to cope with persistent problems. Compared with these process-related successes, environmental problems caused by products and services have gained in relative importance. Moreover, rebound effects in consumption patterns counteract efficiency gains. The rebound effect refers to the fact that efficiency gains made per (product/service) unit may be (over) compensated by the increased effective incomes of consumers. Paper consumption per capita, for instance, almost doubled between 1975 and 2000, despite very great gains in productive efficiency.

Scenario-based research on future trends concerning demographic developments and lifestyles (single household, emerging markets etc.) point to the fact of ever increasing consumption, while the shift towards knowledge-intensive products in Western economies introduces considerable environmental challenges: for instance, energy-intensive technical equipment components. Additionally, product chains tend to globalize leaving products and services as *globetrotters* out of the reach of traditional nation-based environmental policy.

To sum up, increasing knowledge on the environmental impact of products together with the need for continuing improvement in their environmental performance has stimulated a genuine product policy perspective. In the words of Carl Dalhammar: 'Products are seen as control points for the externalities occurring in product chains in all life cycle phases, and as the interface between producers and consumers' (Dalhammar, 2007, p31).

Analysing global product chains

As noted above, over several decades there has been a continuing globalization of product chains. Pushed by liberalizing international trade (e.g. through General Agreement on Tariffs and Trade/World Trade Organization (GATT/WTO)), advantaged by developments of the world political order (end of the cold war) and encouraged by technology-driven innovations (information and communication technologies), value chains speed up, reorganizing and relocating themselves worldwide. Against this background it becomes more and more difficult to understand and analyse global and dynamic product chains. A number of product chain assessment tools and methodologies have been developed to help with this.

In a first step to product chain characterization two aspects are of relevance: a multi-chain perspective and a governance perspective.

The multi-chain perspective

It seems to be essential to systematically focus on value chains with a **multi-chain perspective**. There is no single value chain but manifold linkages and interactions between upstream, downstream and parallel product chains. From an analytical perspective, one can distinguish a main product chain interacting with several peripheral chains. It is crucial to identify the dependencies and relationships between cross-cutting product chains. A main product chain might be defined as delivering essential goods and services, which relate to several needs that are indispensable in social lives. These will be supported by business-to-business and business-to-consumer service chains, which supplement the system.

This may be briefly illustrated by the textile chain (see Figure 12.1): the core chain is the textile product chain, which consists of yarn production with spinning techniques, textile production with weaving, knitting and dyeing industries, and textile finishing. Right of the textile chain output in Figure 2.1, further product chains are connected. The processed raw material serves as input into three different end manufacturing chains: the garment or clothing chain with about 50 per cent textile demand; textile for household goods such as furnishing and carpets with a demand of about 25 per cent; and textiles for industrial goods such as belting or upholstery for the auto industry, also with about 25 per cent.

Besides the main chain considered here, there are several peripheral chains interconnected at different stages of the textile chain. The most important is the natural fibre chain based on agriculture with support of the agrochemical product chain (seeds, fertilizers, pesticides, etc.). The chain can be divided into cotton and wool production. A parallel raw material input chain consists of man-made fibre production (synthetic fibre chain) delivering material such as nylon, acrylics and polyester with the latter accounting for about 50 per cent. Further supporting product chains address textile and clothing manufacturing stages delivering processing chemicals for spinning, weaving, dyeing and finishing procedures. In the use phase cleaning agents and cleaning infrastructure support customers.

Unlike the impression given above, the several chains are not uniform worldwide, but rather develop in particular ways due to their spatial, social and industrial context, even if they fulfil the same function. That accounts in particular for supporting product chains; for instance, the cleaning and

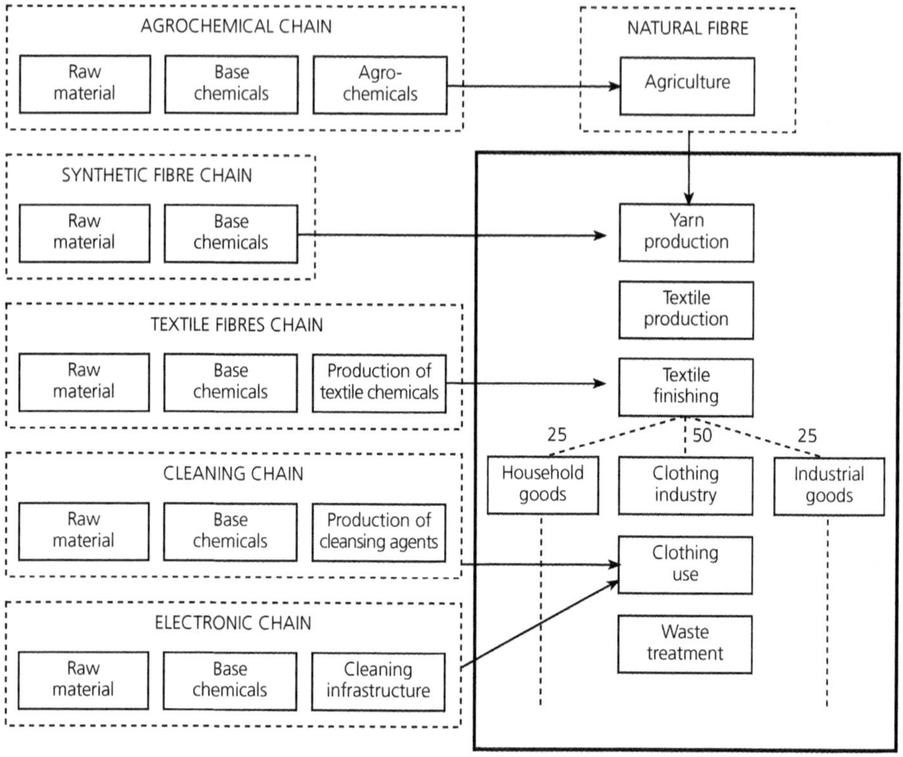

Source: Author

Figure 12.1 *The textile chain with peripheral chains*

electronic chain strongly is influenced by the diversity of social cleaning habits. Customers' cleaning procedures differ both within and between nations.

The governance perspective

The **governance perspective** is essential for analysing global product chains, since within production networks business actors (firms) play a leading role in organizing and regulating the value chain through a great variety of intra- and inter-organizational linkages. The varieties of firms ranges from public-sector based firms (state-owned enterprises) over national firms and transnational firms in the private sector. The business relationships may be 'arm's length' transactions, subcontracting or several forms of cooperation (joint ventures, industrial cooperation agreements, licensing, strategic alliances). In many product chains some key actors (lead firms) have a commanding position, and are able to exert upstream and downstream power and influence over the supply chain. Surrounding firms – and especially small and medium sized enterprises (SMEs) – are dependent on the management decisions of lead actors. A key management decision is, for instance, about externalized or internalized transactions leading to either market-ruled transactions (vertical disintegration) or hierarchally organized in-house transaction (vertical integration). Conceptually, market and hierarchy are at the opposite ends of the spectrum of international or global industry organization.

However, research on the international economy reveals great variety in product chain coordination. A key issue in the dynamics of product chain reorganization is fragmentation of value chains with the outsourcing paradigm as the most obvious trend of changing industry architecture. This trend has been labelled as 'turn-key production network' (Berger et al, 2001) or 'modular production network' (Sturgeon, 2002; Faust et al, 2004). Humphrey and Schmitz (2000, 2002) observed in particular the supplier's degree of competence and downstream relationship. They distinguished between suppliers in quasi-hierarchical relationships acting as so-called 'captive suppliers', and 'network relationships' between firms that cooperate because they have complementary skills and competences. Based on these empirical and conceptual approaches Gereffi et al (2005) developed a five-type governance model of current value chains (pp83–89):

- **Markets:** Market linkages do not have to be completely transitory, as is typical of spot markets; they can persist over time, with repeat transactions. The essential point is that the costs of switching to new partners are low for both parties.
- **Modular value chains:** Typically, suppliers in modular value chains make products to a customer's specifications, which may be more or less detailed. However, when providing 'turn-key services' suppliers take full responsibility for competencies surrounding process technology, use generic machinery that limits transaction-specific investments, and make capital outlays for components and materials on behalf of customers.
- **Relational value chains:** In these networks we see complex interactions between buyers and sellers, which often create mutual dependence and high levels of asset specificity. This may be managed through reputation, or family and ethnic ties. Many authors have highlighted the role of spatial proximity in supporting relational value chain linkages, but trust and reputation might well function in spatially dispersed networks where relationships are built up over time or are based on dispersed family and social groups.
- **Captive value chains:** In these networks, small suppliers are transactionally dependent on much larger buyers. Suppliers face significant switching costs and are, therefore, 'captive'. Such networks are frequently characterized by a high degree of monitoring and control by lead firms.
- **Hierarchy:** This governance form is characterized by vertical integration. The dominant form of governance is managerial control, flowing from managers to subordinates, or from headquarters to subsidiaries and affiliates.

This governance typology seems promising for analysing the key characteristics of a product chain. However, in any analysis of key actors and power distribution within a product chain, each chain step has to be taken into account, identifying the differing dynamics of the chain, notably market dynamics, technology dynamics and governance dynamics.

Sustainability Impact Assessment of global value chains

Objectives of SIA

Global value chains are in continuous dynamic and structural adjustment. These transformation processes are more and more market-driven, because of trade liberalization and reduced emphasis on regulation. In terms of classical economics, efficiency-driven factor allocation (natural capital, human capital, capital goods) determines the specification of particular value chains. However, the adjustment processes are not unitary throughout the whole product chain. While one product chain stage might remain in principle unaltered geographically over a long time, others might change considerably in the meantime with regards to location, technology and business characteristics. The main objective for product-chain analysis in SIA is to identify the key drivers for product chain transformations.

Taking the example of textiles, the main consumer market for textiles and clothing is within the triade, and in particular the US and the European markets. The worldwide relevance of textile consumer markets in developed countries goes back to early days of industrialization. With the upgrading of newly industrialized economies and the rise in consumption of East Asian countries such as China and India, a fundamental leapfrog in textile and garment final-consumer markets might occur in the near future. However, in contrast to the relatively 'static' consumption phase, the textile and apparel supply chain underwent radical geographical changes especially in the production phase. These differences should be reflected within SIAs.

In our view, SIAs should therefore deliver comparable results between and within sectors and branches. Following that argument Trade SIAs should bear in mind two general perspectives: the inter-sector perspective and the intra-sector perspective.

The inter-sector perspective

What is a sustainable sector? Are some sectors more sustainable then others? Is it possible to compare different sectors from a global value chain perspective with one another with regard to their sustainability performance? What are the sustainability performance effects when liberalizing international free trade for one or the other sector?

These are crucial questions when elaborating on SIA for free trade policies. The comparability of sustainability performances between sectors, that is the *inter-sector perspective*, is most relevant for policy makers when negotiating on trade policies, since assessment results give hints on which sectors to favour with regard to improving sustainability, for instance, with the design of flanking measures.

In order to get comparable results among sectors or products a classification system should be used. However, available classification systems of economic activities differ due to classification units. Existing classification may cover activity classification (e.g. ISIC Rev.4 – draft, ISIC Rev.3.1), product classifications (CPC Ver.1.1, SITC Rev.3) or classifications of expenditure according to purpose (functions of the government – COFOG, individual consumption of households – COICOP).

Taking the example of classification of expenditure according to purpose, the focus is on final consumption markets with a product-oriented bias. Some interesting studies have been carried out focusing on the environmental impact of products within the EU (e.g. Institut Wallon and Vito, 2002; Nijdam and Wilting, 2003; IPTS/ESTO, 2005). The IPTS/ESTO study (2005), for instance, aimed at identifying the products (or product groups) that have the greatest environmental impact from a life-cycle perspective. They identified an 80–20 rule where some 20 per cent of the product groupings appear to cause some 80 per cent of the environmental impact. Although these studies differ in scope, products considered and indicators used, the results suggest the priority relevance of agriculture and food, housing and construction, transport, packaging and electronic appliances. This research approach can be used to establish an inter-sector perspective within SIAs.

The intra-sector perspective

Is garment production in East Asian countries more sustainable than in Maghreb countries? Is vertical integration or disintegration along the value chain more favourable to sustainability performance? Similar garments may differ – when taking a sustainability perspective. There are considerable environmental, economic and social differences between products of the clothing industry. Some major differences are between:

- garments made out of natural fibre without using pesticides and garments made with extensive use of chemicals of plant protection agents. In 2003, worldwide production of cotton reached ca. 20 million tonnes with an input of ca. 40,000 tonnes of pesticides;
- garments made with the use of eco-efficient textile auxiliaries and garment production without environmental and social standards.

Empirical data on production and consumption pattern differences due to different geography, technology and so on, are rare and not systematically available. Concerning the primary production of cotton, Schmidt (1999, p71) gathered data through a literature review for several production steps. The data show that variables can differ by a factor of 2 to 8. Land use per kg raw cotton output differs from $6m^2$ to $69m^2$. The use of fertilizers (N, P, K) has been compared for Togo and the US with the latter using 4–5 times higher quantities than the African country. The same counts for energy, water and pesticide consumption within cotton production. As a result the transformation of product chains towards new localities can result in considerable changes in sustainability performance – an issue that SIAs should consider.

The intra-sectoral sustainability benchmarking should analyse existing differences of sustainability impacts within a sector. As shown above in the textile and garment sector, existing data suggest a great variety of input and output quantities depending on company, location, technology, products and so on.

There are several research initiatives that might help to establish a methodological framework for integrating intra-sector benchmarking into SIA. On the one hand, research findings analysing the sustainability performance within a sector; on the other hand research activities measuring national sustainability performance without explicitly considering industries and sector responsibilities.

When it comes to detailed industry sector analyses, Sorrell et al (2005) carried out a study in order 'to facilitate comparison of environmental and social performance between producers in these sectors and to investigate the reasons for the variations in performance between different producers and changes in this performance over time' (2005, p1) on basis of a total of 8884 performance measures for 479 'producers' (300 sites, 46 business units and 133 firms) located in 14 industrial sectors (aggregates, aluminium, cement, ceramics, electricity, glass, motor vehicles, paper, plaster, plastics, printing, steel, timber and water). The researchers found (Sorrell et al, 2005, pp36–37) that there is a huge variability in environmental performance across different producers. On some environmental indicators, the best companies or sites manufacture the same amount of output with 100 or 1000 times less resources, waste or emissions than the poorest performers. The great variety of performance benchmarking can be explained by basic differences in technology and products in most sectors.

Product chain analysis and SIA

As discussed in the following sections, product chain analysis can often shed light on the five core issues that may act as a counterweight to arguments for trade liberalizations. However, the first step that must underlie any product chain analysis is a mapping of the product chain itself.

Mapping product chains

Mapping the value chain aims at assessing the significance and relevance of each link within the product chain. It seeks to understand the simplicity/complexity of the value chain and specifies the transformation dynamics of global product chains. Assessment should identify the relevance of the main and peripheral chain segments and consider their relationship in terms of spatial dimension and environmental, economic and social significance. As a key result, the main product chain phases and input–ouput relationships should be identified. Input–output flows can be analysed on indicators such as, for instance, gross output values, net output values, the physical flow of commodities along the chain, the flow of services, consultants and skills along the chain, and imports and exports differentiated by region (Kaplinsky and Morris, 2001, p53).

At this stage it should be decided whether a deeper product chain assessment should be carried out in the following detailed SIA assessment. In our view this is most likely to be the case if the product chain is multi-chain in nature, and shows a fragmented and globally widespread picture with several intermediate stages within the life cycle (e.g. spinning, weaving, knitting, dyeing in the pre-manufacture stage of the textile industry). In addition, if the product chain is judged to be very dynamic with considerable transformations to be expected due to trade liberalization policies, a more detailed analysis should be carried out.

The economic dimension and the protectionist argument

The protectionist argument relies on the persistence of sectoral vested interests against structural and economic change. It is centred against free trade policy since this is seen as triggering market forces inducing economic structural changes. Protectionism resists the dynamic change of comparative advantages from one region (state) to another. When sectors benefit from comparative advantages and become strong, this strength can induce protectionism when comparative advantages change, due to dynamics in economic factors (labour, capital, technology, etc.). However, both the protectionist stands of economic actors, and their impact and weight on political decision makers are not always easy to identify – in particular when it comes to highly complex and fragmented product chains.

Against such a background a product chain SIA helps identify and better understand protectionist bias by analysing the governance architecture and economic power distribution within the chain. The governance perspective is essential, since within production networks business actors (firms) play a leading role in organizing and regulating the value chain through a great variety of intra- and inter-organizational linkages throughout the chain.

The main objective for assessing protectionist bias through the governance approach is to identify and locate the main actors, the relevance of peripheral chains and assess in general the type of markets for the product chain considered. Promising methods at hand relate to profit analyses, actor analyses and governance (power distribution along the chain) analyses. Indicators to be used centre on several indicators for market share (chain sales, chain value added, chain profit, chain buying power), control over a key technology, and holder of chain 'market identity', or brand names (see Table 12.2).

Table 12.2 *Economic dimension: Objectives, methods and indicators*

Objectives	*Methods/methodologies*	*Exemplary indicators*
• identify main actors • identify relevance of peripheral chains • assessing type of markets (buyer vs. consumer driven etc.)	• mapping value chains • Profit analyses (e.g. profit/revenue distribution) • actor analyses within main and peripheral chains • governance analyses of global value chains	• share of chain sales and share of chain value added • share of chain profits and relative rate of profit • share of chain buying power • control over a key technology and distinctive competence • holder of chain 'market identity' (e.g. brand name)

Source: Author

The social dimension and adjustment costs

Arguments relating to adjustment costs have been raised many times in the context of discussions about trade agreements. And there is no doubt that adjustment costs arising from trade liberalization are relevant. In that sense, adjustment costs are defined as short-term costs of transition from one (economic) state to another. Moreover, one has to differentiate between adjustment costs of the private sector (e.g. opportunity costs of unemployed labour, obsolescence of skills and skill specificity, lower wage levels or retraining costs) and the public sector (e.g. loss in tax revenue, social safety net spending, erosion of benefits from preferential treatment).

However, Rama (2003) pointed out that it is neither desirable nor feasible to separate out adjustment costs resulting from trade liberalization. He objected that it is globalization as a whole and not trade agreements by themselves that induce adjustment processes. Besides trade liberalization there is a great variety of input factors such as changing demand patterns and dynamics of input factors (labour, capital, technology) that determine structural adjustment processes. As a consequence, it is very difficult to isolate and measure adjustment costs caused solely by trade agreements.

Currently the measurement of adjustment costs is primarily done with either econometric tools (ex-post assessment) or with applied general equilibrium models (ex-ante assessment). The vast majority of adjustment cost studies for developing countries takes an ex-post perspective that is not very helpful for contributing to trade negotiation rounds.

Against that background a product-chain based SIA can contribute ex-ante via case-study approaches to estimate the adjustment cost impact. The main objective of a product-chain based SIA is to identify adjustment costs in highly complex product chains where liberalization policy affects not only the main players but to a high degree the 'hidden industries', that is peripheral chain segments. From a micro-perspective the distribution of adjustment costs along the product chain are of major importance (see Table 12.3).

Table 12.3 *Social dimension: Objectives, methods and indicators*

Objectives	*Methods/methodologies*	*Exemplary indicators*
• distribution of adjustment costs (both capital and labour costs) along the chain from a micro-perspective	• mapping value chains • income and employment skill distribution in value chains	• numbers, division of labour and rewards of different labour skills in each link in the chain; mobility of skilled personnel • gender, ethnicity (earnings per hour) • annual profits and wages at each chain stage

Source: Author

The environmental dimension and externalities

The externality argument refers to non-market products such as biodiversity, landscape or land preservation that are not reflected within market prices. The argument reflects the fact that further liberalization policies may give rise to both increased economic activities and negative environmental impacts.

Taking an environmental life-cycle perspective, it becomes clear that products differ according to their main environmental impact along the life cycle. On a generic level, one can distinguish products according to the categories consumable goods, durable goods and services. In a second differentiation one may further distinguish among consumable goods those which are recoverable (e.g. printing paper, packages) and which are not (e.g. foodstuff, detergents). Among durables, a distinction is made between energy-intensive (e.g. 'white goods', cars, housing) and energy-passive products (e.g. furniture, textiles). When it comes to services one might distinguish simple from complex ones. The crucial point is that the main environmental impact differs along the life cycle depending on the product groups considered. For instance, non-recoverable consumable goods (e.g. tissue papers, detergents, soil improvers, etc.) usually have their main environmental impacts during the production phase. More precisely, they might also have significant impacts during the end of-life, but the consumer cannot influence this process and avoid the impacts on the environment. In constrast, energy-intensive products (e.g. washing machines, refrigerators) have their main environmental impact during the use-phase.

Against that background, a product-chain based SIA can help identify empirically the environmental impact of product chains. Methods to be used relate to product-related information systems such as *life-cycle assessment* or *life-cycle costing*. This should be supplemented with an analysis of the sector's stance and activities towards sustainability – that is, voluntary and private action such as, for instance, voluntary agreements, level of quality and environmental standards, corporate procurement policies and so on (see Table 12.4 and Chapter 14 for further discussion).

Table 12.4 *Environmental dimension: Objectives, methods and indicators*

Objectives	*Methods/methodologies*	*Exemplary indicators*
• assess the sector's responses to sustainable development	• life-cycle assessment; life-cycle costing • analysis of existing responses to sustainable development impacts	• indicators as set out in the (standardized) methods such as LCA • government-based initiatives; voluntary consumer initiatives; voluntary producer initiatives

Source: Author

Conclusion

SIA for trade agreements is a promising pathway for a better understanding of the outcomes of policies for trade liberalization. The underlying assumption of a globalized and liberalized world economy is that free trade policy agreements support fast changing transformation processes of product chains worldwide due to simplification of market access. Regulatory policy restrictions lose weight against market forces as drivers for product chain dynamics, with efficiency-driven factor allocation (natural capital, human capital, capital goods) gaining importance. There are several economic developments assisting new location policy such as cheaper, faster and more efficient transport systems, efficiency of production processes with less raw materials needed, and growing knowledge-intensity of products with more R&D and service inputs to the disadvantage of material input. These transformations are judged to have considerable sustainability impacts.

A key challenge, therefore, is to elaborate SIA methodologies reflecting these product chain dynamics. As a contribution to this challenge, this chapter proposed a framework for considering the product chain perspective within SIAs. Several key aspects are relevant:

- First, methodologically SIAs should be based on a comparative benchmarking approach that is to allow comparisions within and between sectors and sub-sectors. In other words, there is a need to elaborate an inter-sector perspective and an intra-sector perspective.
- Secondly, the characterization of product chains should be based on a multi-chain perspective and a governance perspective in order to understand the complexity of value chains and their internal driving forces for transformations.
- Thirdly, attempts have been made to operationalize the product chain perspective for each dimension of sustainability (economic, social and environmental) with identifying objectives, promising tools and methods and exemplary indicators.

The framework proposed considered an alternative approach to current existing SIA based on the Global Value Chain Analysis. From a product chain perspective nothing prevents researchers, experts and policy makers from exploring the most promising and appropriate tools and methodologies. Thus, in our view there is no methodological or research gap preventing a product chain analysis based on alternative approaches from being used within SIA.

References

Berger, S., Kurz, C., Sturgeon, T., Voskamp, U. and Wittke, V. (2001) 'Globalization, production networks, and national models of capitalism: On the possibilities of new productive systems and institutional diversity in an enlarging Europe', SOFI-Mitteilungen, No 29, Göttingen

Dalhammar, C. (2007) 'An emerging product approach in environmental law: Incorporating the life cycle perspective', PhD thesis, University of Lund, Sweden

Dicken, P. (2004) *Global Shift: Reshaping the Global Economic Map in the 21st Century*, 4th Edition, SAGE Publications, London

EC (2004) 'Draft handbook for sustainability impact assessment', European Commission, DG Trade, Brussels

Faust, M., Voskamp, U. and Wittke, V. (2004) 'Globalization and the future of national systems: Exploring patterns of industrial reorganization and relocation in an enlarged Europe', in M. Faust, U. Voskamp and V. Wittke (eds) *European Industrial Restructuring in a Global Economy: Fragmentation and Relocation of Value Chains*, SOFI, Göttingen, pp19–81

George, C. and Kirkpatrick, C. (2003) 'Sustainability impact assessment of world trade negotiations: Current practice and lessons for further development', Impact Assessment Research Centre Working Paper Series 2, Institute for Development and Policy Management, University of Manchester

Gereffi, G. (1994) 'The organization of buyer-driven global commodity chains: How U.S. retailers shape overseas production networks', in G. Gereffi and M. Korzeniewicz (eds) *Commodity Chains and Global Capitalism*, Praeger, Westport, CT, pp95–122

Gereffi, G., Humphrey, J. and Sturgeon, T. (2005) 'The governance of global value chains', *Review of International Political Economy*, vol 12, 1 February 2005, pp78–104

Humphrey, J. and Schmitz, H. (2000) 'Governance and upgrading: Linking industrial cluster and global value chain research', IDS Working Paper 120, Institute of Development Studies, University of Sussex, Brighton

Humphrey, J. and Schmitz, H. (2002) 'How does insertion in global value chains affect upgrading in industrial clusters?', *Regional Studies*, vol 36, no 9, pp1017–1027

Institut Wallon and Vito (2002) 'Identifying key products for the federal product and environmental policy', Report for the Directorate-General for the Environment of the Federal Public Service for Health, Food Chain Safety and Environment, Brussels

IPTS (Institute for Prospective Technological Studies) and ESTO (European Science and Technology Observatory) (2005) 'Environmental impact of products (EIPRO): Analysis of the life cycle environmental impacts related to the total final consumption of the EU25', Full draft report for the European Commission, Brussels

Jänicke, M. and Volkery, A. (2001) 'Persistente Probleme des Umweltschutzes', *Natur und Kultur*, Jg. 2/2, pp45–59

Kaplinsky, R. and Morris, M. (2001) *Handbook for Value Chain Research*, prepared for the International Development Research Centre, Canada www.bdsknowledge.org/dyn/bds/docs/424/Value%20Chain%20Handbook%20Kaplinsky.pdf

Konrad, W. (2005) 'Product-oriented ecological information systems and life-cycle management: Quantitative and qualitative analyses in the German chemical and electrical industries', *Progress in Industrial Ecology*, vol 2, no 1, pp89–106

Kuik, O. and von Moltke, K. (1998) 'Global product chains: Northern consumers, southern producers, and sustainability. Part One: Global product chains and the environment', prepared for United Nations Environment Programme (UNEP), UNEP Trade and Environment Series #17, Geneva

Nijdam D. and Wilting, S. (2003) 'Environmental load due to private consumption', (Milieudruk consumptie in beeld), RIVM rapport 7714040004, RIVM, Bilthoven

Rama, M. (2003) 'Globalization and workers in developing countries', The World Bank Working Paper 2958, The World Bank, Washington DC

Scheer, D. and Rubik, F. (eds) (2006) *Governance of Integrated Product Policy: In Search of Sustainable Consumption and Production*, Greenleaf Publishing, Sheffield

Schmidt, K. (1999) Zur ökologischen Produktbewertung in der Textil- und Bekleidungsindustrie', Eigenverlag, Witten

Sorrell, S., Hertin, J. and Cirillo, M. (2005) 'Sustainability performance benchmarking: Statistical analysis of the PERFORM dataset', Science and Technology Policy Research, University of Sussex, Brighton www.sustainability-performance.org/results/outputs/PerformAnalysisReport.pdf

Sturgeon, T. (2002) 'Modular production networks: A new American model of industrial organization', *Industrial and Corporate Change*, vol 11, no 3, pp451–496

Van Beukering, P. J. H. and Bouman, M. N. (2000) 'Empirical evidence in international trade and recycling of secondary materials', World Bank Working Paper, Environment Department, The World Bank, Washington DC

Van Beukering, P. J. H., van den Bergh, J. C. J. M., Janssen, M. A. and Verbruggen, H. (2000) 'International material-product chains: An alternative perspective on international trade and trade theories', Tinbergen Institute Discussion Papers with number 00-034/3, www.tinbergen.nl/discussionpapers/00034.pdf

Vellinga, P., Gupta, J. and Berkhout, F. (eds) (1998) *Managing a Material World*, Kluwer Academic Press, Dordrecht

Part 4
International Cooperation

13
Collective Preferences and International Compensation

Tristan Le Cotty and Tancrède Voituriez

Introduction

How to reconcile collective preferences for non-trade concerns of exporting and importing countries is the question raised in this chapter. Focusing on agriculture, we show that, in some cases, tariff barriers that could help satisfy collective preferences for non-trade concerns in a given country may generate a net cumulative welfare that exceeds the level created through free trade. However, unlike free trade, which theoretically creates winners only at country level, 'collective preferences'-induced protectionism creates both winners and losers in comparison with free trade. Net cumulative welfare may be positive while domestic welfare is declining in one country. An international compensation mechanism is sketched out to address this issue, which could help both reconcile efficiency and cooperation and reveal the real value of collective preferences in any given country.

The economic rationale of the WTO's Agriculture Agreement

The World Trade Organization's (WTO) Agriculture Agreement was signed in Marrakech in 1994 with the aim of gradually removing agricultural support policies that modify market conditions, thereby restoring the allocative efficiency of the price signal. To do so, it classifies domestic support policies[1] according to whether or not they stimulate production (policies coupled to agricultural production) and aims to remove those that do.

This agreement can be interpreted from either a unilateral or a multilateral viewpoint. In unilateral terms, it represents a set of rules aimed at guiding states towards reforms that improve the efficiency of their agricultural policies, which they would gain from implementing in any event. In multilateral terms, these rules are essential to the reforms that states do not stand to gain from conducting alone, but rather collectively.

The unilateral approach has received more attention in economic literature on trade liberalization (Anderson and Blackhurst, 1992; Anderson, 2002) for two reasons: first, it falls within the traditional approach to public economics – finding the best policy to implement at the national level; second, most of the agricultural policies in the WTO's line of sight generate economic inefficiencies that are primarily national. In this sense, the WTO acts as an external constraint that states use when implementing reforms that are difficult to establish, due to domestic resistance, for example. Thus, in Europe, replacing production price support with income support decoupled from agricultural production is analysed as a unilateral reform (in other words beneficial to the European Union (EU)) that would probably not have occurred without WTO pressure. Anti-dumping measures can also be explained from this viewpoint: dumping policies are generally more costly than beneficial to the exporting countries that pursue them, but it is difficult to remove these policies unilaterally because of lobbies. External pressure therefore helps those countries that seek to improve the economic efficiency of their policies.

The multilateral interpretation suggests that a state signs an agreement because it needs other states to change their policies, rather than because it needs to change its own policies. It will only sign if doing so will improve its welfare and if such an improvement is unattainable without signing. Multilateral disciplines are a means of removing or reducing inefficiency caused by states acting as 'free riders' (meaning benefiting from a discipline without respecting it themselves). One example of this is the use of customs duties by the major importing countries: these duties increase the price of the goods imported into the country, and demand for these goods decreases creating surplus supply at the global level, which causes a drop in world prices; the terms of trade are modified in favour of the importing country that imposed the customs duties. This country initially benefits from the situation, but at equilibrium, if all countries follow suit, the trade volume of all goods is reduced and everyone loses out. However, it is not in any country's best interest to change behaviour unilaterally. A multilateral agreement is therefore required. By reducing customs duties through reciprocal exchange of market access, the General Agreement on Tariffs and Trade (GATT) can be seen as a multilateral agreement suited to limiting this kind of behaviour (Bagwell and Staiger, 1999).

The path advocated by the WTO for reforming agricultural domestic policies is a hybrid of these two approaches, both unilateral and multilateral.

For example, reducing export subsidies falls under the first interpretation. When a country stops subsidizing its exports, its welfare improves; in theory, it therefore has no need for an agreement to reduce or remove its export subsidies. Moreover, reducing export subsidies increases the price of goods for importing countries. The increase in the world surplus created by the agreement is therefore not mutually beneficial. The post-agreement situation cannot be deemed to be Pareto optimal.

At first glance, decoupling agricultural support from the volumes produced appears to belong to the unilateral approach. Indeed, the economic efficiency of support is increased (OECD, 2001) and countries that decouple improve their welfare without any need for a multilateral agreement to conduct this reform. However, a different analysis is possible. If a major importing country supports its production (support coupled with the volume produced), it reduces its imports. World prices fall, modifying the terms of trade in its favour at the expense of world trade volume. If, in response, the other major countries do the same for their imports, each country's surplus falls below the initial situation. In this case, a multilateral agreement that forbids or reduces production-linked support would prevent any manipulation of the terms of trade. This is the example we will develop in this paper.

Confusion between the two approaches to the agreement can be a source of difficulty for negotiators. In order to make progress in the international coordination of agricultural policies, it would be useful to make a distinction between the disciplines that are a matter of recommendation (the unilateral approach) and those that are a matter of cooperation (the multilateral approach). This implies defining good and bad policies not according to their nature (decoupled or not), but to their use (strategic or not), which in fact tells us about their objective (commercial or not). The aim of the following sections is to show that this distinction is possible, at least in theory, and that it broadens the spectrum of mutually beneficial reforms.

Optimal domestic support policy

Despite the surpluses of the 1980s and accession to the WTO's Agricultural Agreement, the major developed countries continue to provide considerable support for agriculture. There are several reasons for this: the political preference granted to farmers; the desire to maintain national production capacity in case of conflict; and the importance attached to the non-market functions of agricultural production.

This last reason for support was recently propped up by research on the multifunctional nature of agriculture, analysing the contribution it makes to public goods (Romstad et al, 2000; OECD, 2001; Vermersch, 2001; Paarlberg et al, 2002; Peterson et al, 2002; Randall, 2002; Vatn, 2002; Lankoski and Ollikainen, 2003). In order to ensure that farmers produce enough environmental public goods, the state must pay those farmers according to the social value of the goods produced.

For example, mountain livestock farming maintains pastures, thereby helping to prevent fires. If farmers are not paid for this public service as part of their professional activity, it would be economically efficient that they be paid for the service provided via the agricultural policy.

The optimal policy for promoting the non-market functions of agriculture (see, for example, Peterson et al, 2002; Vatn, 2002) implies paying farmers on an individual basis for each of these functions: maintaining pastures, protecting rare species and so on.

If there is a high level of complementarity between market and non-market goods, payments to farmers to supply non-market goods will encourage them to produce more agricultural goods (OECD, 2001). This effect of public policy on production levels is not a market distortion, but simply a consequence of the provision of public goods in conjunction with agricultural production.

In some cases it is difficult to measure – and thus pay for – these joint public goods. For example, biodiversity includes not only the species grown or reared, but also those species found in the habitats that farming maintains, such as grasses, birds that live in hedges and animals that live in meadows. In this case, public policy should subsidize agricultural production (Vatn, 2002) or a factor of production, such as the land (Peterson et al, 2002), but it does not generate any market distortion.

In these two examples, optimal public policy is coupled with production, since it increases it. For both reasons, the complementarity between market and non-market goods and the difficulty in measuring the production of certain public goods, states that seek to promote the non-market functions of agriculture cannot do so efficiently without modifying the level of agricultural production and domestic prices in relation to laissez-faire, the WTO's objective.

The fact that an environmental policy favours national producers should not therefore be seen as an economic inefficiency or a trade distortion. As long as the support paid by taxpayers does not exceed the value they attach to the environment, the environmental policy is justified from the viewpoint of welfare economics (see Corden, 1997, for example), whatever its effect on international prices. It should be noted that in the case of a public good provided on a large scale, such as food security or regional planning in areas suffering agricultural decline, the effects on production will have repercussions on trade. If the country in question is a major importer, its environmental policy will cause a fall in the world price for the imported good, and will improve its terms of trade, while reducing world trade volume. If it is a major exporting country, the environmental policy will increase supply and thereby reduce world prices, thus penalizing the country. This may explain why large countries give more support to imported goods than to exported goods (see Table 13.1).

As shown by Krutilla (1991) for environmental taxes and subsidies in large countries, to maximize welfare, an importing state will integrate a strategic motive into its domestic support policy – influencing world markets – along with other motives – promoting public goods.

The table below outlines the 'predatory' temptations of large countries, liable to use their national policy to influence world prices. At equilibrium, a

Table 13.1 *Public policy in large countries, with public goods and without coordination*

	Exporter	*Importer*
Amenities	$s^{nash} < s^{opt}$	$s^{nash} > s^{opt}$
Pollution	$t^{nash} < t^{opt}$	$t^{nash} > t^{opt}$

major importer would tend to subsidize its production beyond the level required to encourage non-market functions, allowing it to maximize the sum of national surpluses. A major exporter would tend to provide limited subsidies for its amenity-generating production in order to make world supply scarcer.

Here, t^{nash} and s^{nash} refer to taxes or subsidies chosen by countries in the absence of any coordination; s^{opt} and t^{opt} refer to globally optimal subsidies and taxes (corresponding to the environmental value).

If all countries behave according to theory (Table 13.1), the equilibrium reached in the absence of any international coordination is Pareto inefficient. Although mutual improvement is possible, it does not occur spontaneously, as each country can only gain more if the *others* modify their own policies at the same time. No country stands to gain from making the effort to change its own support policy, unless it is certain that the other countries will follow suit. In this case, a multilateral agreement would lead to mutual progress.

The optimal support level, s^{opt}, for each country depends on the national demand for public goods linked to agricultural production. In theory, this level could be revealed by negotiating a mutual reduction in support in importing countries. If countries are symmetrical – if they have equivalent support policies – the negotiations will end when the strategic component of support has been completely eliminated. In reality, this spontaneous coordination does not occur, as not all countries behave according to theory. For example, Southern countries will struggle to take a chunk of the public budget to finance domestic support. A centralized form of coordination may therefore prove necessary.

Let us take a closer look at the case of asymmetrical support.

The basis of international cooperation in the face of asymmetrical support

Let us take the example of the asymmetrical relations between the EU, which imports beef, and Argentina, which exports it, from the viewpoint of a trade agreement. The following assumptions apply: the marginal cost of production in Argentina is lower than in the EU; the quality of the agricultural product is identical in both countries; in Europe, there may be a local public good linked to the agricultural production, for which the EU may provide support; the EU may also provide strategic subsidy support to its agriculture; and the EU has not established import duties.[2]

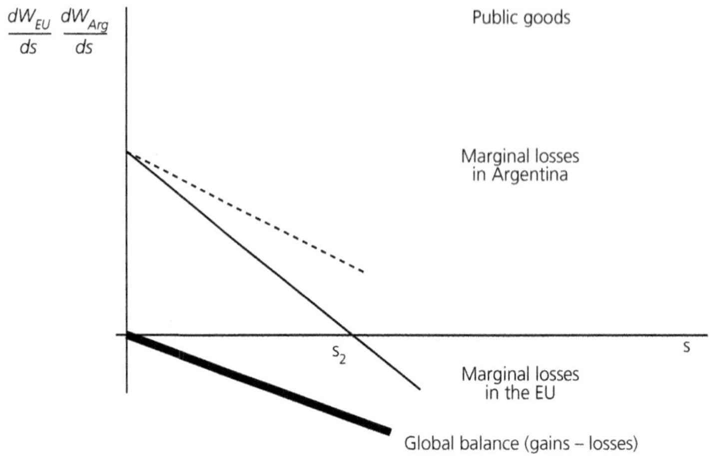

Figure 13.1 *Economic balance of a strategic support policy in a major importing country without public goods*

Let us now analyse the different support policies from the standpoint of maximizing welfare. In Figures 13.1 and 13.2 the horizontal axis gives the level of subsidy (s) to EU agriculture, while the vertical axis gives the marginal rate of welfare change in the EU and Argentina in respect of subsidy support. Let us imagine there are no public goods, and the EU subsidizes its agriculture by s_2 (Figure 13.1). The support policy is purely strategic, and the balance of the support is negative, in terms of the net welfare of both countries: the exporters' losses are not offset by the importers' gains. Indeed, the aggregate loss (bold curve) is equal to the sum of the global variations in surpluses in Argentina (gains for consumers and losses for producers, with net losses overall) and in Europe (gains for producers, losses for consumers and cost for taxpayers, with net gains overall). The surplus diminishes more quickly in Argentina than it grows in Europe when the subsidy is increased, as a result of the reduction in trade volume. In other words, as subsidies grow, the EU benefits from subsidies constitute a marginal gain that diminishes more quickly than the marginal losses in Argentina.

Thus, if there are no public goods, the maximum global surplus is reached when subsidy support is nil ($s = 0$). As the subsidy increases, the global surplus diminishes.

Figure 13.2 shows the case with a public good. Let us examine the different policies possible. In simple terms, the EU has the choice between three subsidy levels: $s = 0$, corresponding to laissez-faire, $s = s_1 = s^{opt}$, corresponding to the value of the public good associated with beef production, and $s = s_1 + s_2 = s^{nash}$, corresponding to the value of the public good plus the strategic subsidy. Initially, the EU may subsidize its beef production by $s_1 = s^{opt}$ to produce a public good. As its production increases, it imports less beef, causing a fall in world prices. Then, seeing that its terms of trade are improving, the EU may be

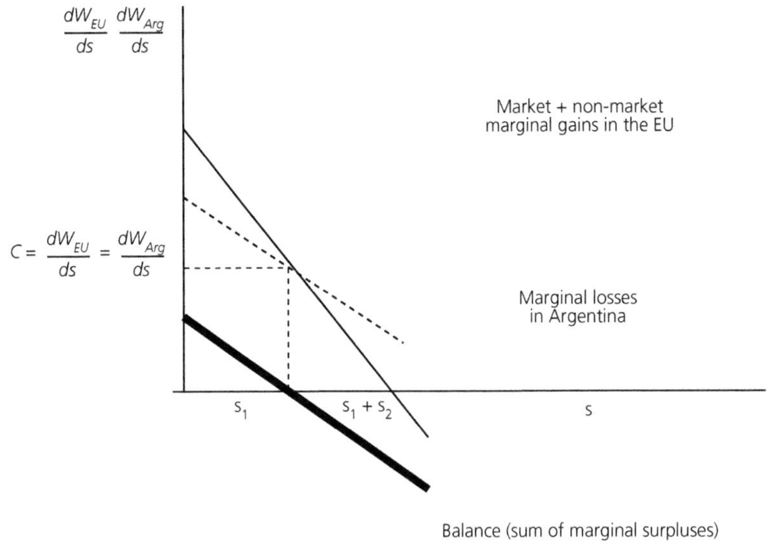

Figure 13.2 *Optimal domestic subsidy with public goods*

tempted to increase its subsidy in order to amplify this improvement. The new subsidy is thus established at $s_1 + s_2$, with s_2 being the strategic part. The additional s_2 domestic support increases the national surplus and lessens the global surplus (Figure 13.2), as it reduces the trade volume beyond the level required for the integration of the public good. The support policy adopted ($s = 0$, $s = s_1$ and $s = s_1 + s_2$) depends on the trade negotiation, which itself depends on the reference situation the countries consider legitimate. The $s_1 + s_2$ support level will be considered legitimate if countries recognize state sovereignty over their agricultural policy. Equilibrium without subsidies ($s = 0$) will be chosen if states recognize the right of countries to benefit from world prices that correspond to free trade and laissez-faire prices (an explicit reference to a world without externalities, distortion or market power, and, in some respects, an implicit reference to the WTO).[3]

From the EU's point of view, the subsidy that maximizes its surplus (where its marginal gain is greater than 0) includes both components, the public good and the strategic component ($s = s_1 + s_2$). The subsidy that maximizes the sum of both countries' surpluses is no longer nil, but s_1. s_1 support has an interesting economic property: the equilibrium it achieves is Pareto superior to the other two, as long as the losers are compensated, as one country's losses are lower than the other's gains in relation to both $s = 0$ and $s = s_1 + s_2$. If the subsidy increases above s_1, the marginal environmental gain linked to the subsidy diminishes (or remains constant), as the increase in production goes hand in hand with intensification, which generally means fewer public goods are produced (see, for example, Romstad et al, 2000). The environmental policy sees its economic efficiency diminish, while its effect on relative prices increases.

The subsidy level that defines the global optimum in terms of maximizing the sum of national surpluses is therefore s_1. But to reach this optimum, whether we start from a laissez-faire situation ($s = 0$) or from a free intervention situation ($s = s_1 + s_2$), there will inevitably be losers. In both cases, the losers can be compensated by the winners, while the latter retain some of their gains. This also shows that a mutually beneficial agricultural agreement (Pareto superior to the reference situation) cannot therefore be obtained without compensation.

If the reference situation is the real situation before negotiations begin ($s = s_1 + s_2$), the optimum s_1 can only be reached if the EU agrees to a reduction in its welfare. If the EU refuses to negotiate an agreement to reduce its domestic support, it is theoretically in Argentina's interest to pay the EU compensation to ensure it agrees to reduce its domestic support. This would produce a Pareto improvement in relation to the initial situation.

If the reference is the theoretical free trade and laissez-faire situation, implicitly adopted by the WTO as an objective to aim towards, it is the EU that should pay Argentina compensation to have the right to support its agriculture to s_1, a level it is not in its interest to exceed. Unlike the case without public goods, there is a positive s_1 support level that is mutually beneficial in relation to free trade, provided compensation is paid.

Indeed, when the subsidy level is lower than the surplus maximizing subsidy, the aggregate surplus is greater than the surplus in the free trade situation; the winner, the importer – the EU in our example – is thus encouraged to accept this situation, if it must pay the loser, the exporter – Argentina – compensation that is less than or equal to $\frac{dW_{EU}}{ds}$. In this left part of Figure 13.2, where $s < s_1$, we see that Argentina is also encouraged to accept this compensation provided it exceeds its reduction in marginal welfare $\frac{dW_{Arg}}{ds}$. As in this area the gains are greater than the losses, that is $\frac{dW_{EU}}{ds} > -\frac{dW_{Arg}}{ds}$, we can predict that both countries will want to agree on a mutually beneficial compensation.

If the amount is higher, the importer can continue to gain by increasing the subsidy, but will gain less than the exporter loses, $\frac{dW_{EU}}{ds} < -\frac{dW_{Arg}}{ds}$. If compensation is set up, the EU can no longer pay it with its welfare gains, and therefore has no interest in increasing its support. Compensation acts as a regulatory mechanism for support.

The optimal subsidy from a global viewpoint, s_1, makes it possible to obtain the environmental gains sought without generating external losses that cannot be offset by national gains. In theory, this optimal level can be reached through negotiations by production between two countries, as only the importing country knows its social demand for non-market public goods.

The choice between the two reference situations is open to debate. In the current situation, the first solution (Argentina pays the EU to reduce its support) is mutually beneficial *based on the existing situation*, which corresponds to a Pareto improvement. This is the kind of equilibrium that negotiations could lead to if the initial situation were considered legitimate. But given the asymmetrical budgetary means between Southern and Northern countries, the initial situation is seen as illegitimate by the WTO, which favours instead free trade and laissez-faire as a legitimate objective. This is why preference is given to finding a mutually improving agreement, not in relation to the existing situation, but in relation to a situation seen as 'legitimate' by most member countries – itself stemming from universal credence in the mutual gains from free trade.

Indeed, if the aim is to maximize the global surplus, the EU's natural attitude ($s_1 + s_2$ strategic support) can be deemed a go-it-alone policy (see above). This is why the second type of compensation corresponds more to the common idea of a legitimate instrument: it penalizes the country that goes it alone and not the one that 'lacked the budgetary means' to go it alone.

Indeed, if in the initial state the situation is asymmetrical (only some countries conduct strategic policies), these countries (the EU, in our example) have nothing to gain from reducing their strategic policy themselves to reach the equilibrium, $s = s_1$. Based on this observation, it seems reasonable to propose a reform leading to a reduction in strategic policies in major importing countries, *even if this reform is detrimental to the latter*, provided it increases global welfare. There are two main reasons for the major importing countries to accept this agreement, one economic and the other political. The economic reason is that the major importers are also major exporters (in particular the EU and the US), and their exports will benefit from the efforts made by the other major importing trade partners. The political reason is the desire of all large developed countries to reach agreements with the developing countries and to gradually consider their demands to reduce agricultural subsidies in Northern countries as legitimate. Hence the more realistic nature of the second type of compensation, which sees free trade and laissez-faire as a 'legitimate' reference.

To reach the optimum s_1, negotiations on compensation come up against three practical difficulties. First, coordination is only mutually beneficial if based on a theoretical free trade reference and not on the existing situation. This implies that the EU accepts a theoretical reference as legitimate grounds for negotiation, which is not in its interest, in theory. This is nevertheless the reference that seems to have been implicitly adopted at the WTO, particularly because the EU is also a major exporter.

Next, for positions to converge towards optimal compensation, states must accurately identify the potential gains, and therefore the preferences of stakeholders: producers, consumers and taxpayers with environmental demands. This is a classic difficulty in public economics.

Finally, current practices in multilateral negotiations, marked by bargaining between sectors, are not suited to the decentralized negotiation of compensation by each state for each product.[4] In negotiations as they currently stand, it is unlikely that the confrontation between states on negotiating grounds that remain mercantilist will reveal the non-market costs and benefits for each state and thereby define suitable compensation. This leads us to propose an international tax on subsidies, whose aim would be to regulate the use of support.

An international tax on support

An international tax on *all* production support instruments, whatever their justification within the country, would make it possible to restrict the use of support for non-market purposes and to eliminate the strategic part of the subsidy, s_2.

By penalizing production subsidies (and potentially, to a lesser extent, decoupled support), a general tax on support would limit the diversion of support towards purposes other than the production of public goods, as this tax would make the responsible country pay the external cost of its policy.

Ideally, this tax (*C* in Figure 13.2), which makes it possible to maximize the sum of surpluses in the world economy, makes taxpayers pay the external cost of support at the point where this support is optimal (s_1). But whether or not each country gains in relation to the current situation (or historic situation characterized by strategic support) or to a theoretical reference (free trade) depends on the redistribution of tax revenue.

If a tax is applied to support in an importing country and its revenue is redistributed within this country, it can be considered as a subsidy reduction that is self-imposed by the state. Let us return to our example: in relation to the existing situation, Argentina sees its terms of trade, and therefore its situation, improve. The EU loses the benefit of its strategic policy by bringing its subsidy back to s_1. Argentina will gain more (dashed curve) than the EU loses (black curve). If there is a global aggregate improvement (bold curve), it is not mutual as Argentina was not using strategic support.

If the rate of the tax is constant, C, the situation after the tax is imposed is less advantageous than free trade for Argentina. In Europe, the situation is still better than with free trade, as the subsidy policy, even limited, means the public good can be integrated to a certain extent. Such a tax improves the global surplus in relation to free trade,[5] but makes the situation in Argentina worse in relation to a total ban on EU support.

Whatever the reference chosen, theoretical or historic, a simple taxation (without compensation for the losers) of support cannot be mutually beneficial.

If the tax revenue is redistributed in Argentina, the tax is akin to compensation negotiated within a Coasian framework, and it is possible to restore the Pareto superiority of the post-agreement situation. In relation to the free trade situation, the international redistribution of the tax is mutually beneficial: in Europe, the EU maintains some of its subsidies (those that generate the most public goods); in Argentina as well, provided the tax compensates at least all Argentine losses to make the maintenance of a certain level of support acceptable. This is possible if the average tax rate is slightly higher than C, with C only partly compensating losses in Argentina (under the black curve).

In relation to the pre-agreement situation, it is also possible to achieve a Pareto improvement if the tax rate paid to Argentina is slightly below C.

To simplify matters, let us suppose that support coupled to production (the 'amber' box)[6] is subject to a certain tax rate and support that is supposed to have little impact on production ('green' box) to a lower rate (because green support is never completely neutral). The tax on coupled support is the cost that must be borne by those countries conducting strategic policies if they wish to derogate from the trade neutrality of support. An importing country that considers itself injured by s_1 support can lodge a complaint with the Dispute Settlement Body (DSB). The DSB pays it financial compensation, taken from the funds collected by the international tax on support (ITS). This compensation is mutually beneficial in the sense that it allows the importing country to maintain some of its support for production (s_1).

Conclusion

The distinction the WTO makes between support that modifies trade and production conditions and that which has no impact is not operational. It does not enable us to differentiate between strategic support that harms global welfare and support for public goods, which has a positive effect on global welfare. Yet the level of agricultural support that maximizes the global economic surplus is that which integrates the non-market functions of agriculture, but does not integrate the natural propensity of states to use support for trade purposes. As each country only stands to gain from reducing strategic support if its partners do the same, a multilateral agreement is needed. The difficulty is that as negotiations currently stand, there is a good deal of asymmetry in the initial situations of the countries that use strategic support and those that do not use support. Because of this asymmetry, the reform of support policies cannot be mutually beneficial without a compensation mechanism for the losers, which is incompatible with an agreement such as the agricultural agreement, as it is negotiated by consensus and must therefore be mutually beneficial to be accepted.

We propose coordination that is based on compensation that encourages the major countries to remove the strategic part of their support, and only this part, which corresponds to maximizing global welfare. When this optimum is reached, an additional increase in support would lead to greater losses in exporting countries than gains (in terms of trade) in importing countries. As long as this level is not reached, it is possible to compensate exporters' losses with importers' gains, but beyond this level, compensation for losses is no longer an option. The compensation mechanism increases the global economic surplus, whatever the reference situation – free trade with no intervention or free support policy (sovereignty of policies). Moreover, if the compensation is calculated by country and by product, it should improve the situation in both types of countries – importing and exporting – in relation to the two reference situations envisaged.

In practice, rather than a multitude of bilateral negotiations, compensation could take the form of an ITS in major importing countries, with tax revenue distributed to exporting countries or interest groups to offset the damages incurred.

The DSB could arbitrate the process, provided it is reformed on two major points: planning financial compensation, for example in the form of a drawing right on the funds provided by the revenue of the ITS; and granting non-state entities (producers' groups, etc.) the right to lodge a complaint and to reveal their own damages (Charnovitz, 2001).

Notes

1 Domestic support is a term used by the WTO to describe any agricultural policies that benefit farmers. It includes prices that are maintained at a higher level than world prices as well as agricultural subsidies. The WTO makes a clear distinction between support that is permitted, which states can use freely as it has no trade-distorting effects, and support that entails reduction commitments by states as it has an impact on trade. The main difference between the two is that the first type of support – though it represents a considerable sum – does not modify farmers' behaviour theoretically, just their standard of living.

2 This last point serves simply to remove the effect of customs duties from this analysis.

3 Note that these two extremes correspond more to distribution of wealth criteria than to welfare maximization.

4 In theory, a decentralized Coasian-type negotiation – where stakeholders find optimal compensation by themselves – does not require prior knowledge of all stakeholders' costs and benefits, as these are revealed during the negotiation. It only gives results in bilateral negotiations.

5 It has a low economic transaction cost, as it can be integrated into the support negotiated: rather than negotiating support at level x, taxed at y per cent, support can be negotiated from the outset at level $x(1-y)$.

6 Amber box support is support coupled to production, which incites farmers to produce more than they would if no support existed. The policies included are price support, input subsidies, production subsidies and so on. The countries have committed to bringing this support below a maximum level that depends on their past practices. Green box support is support to producers that is supposed to have little impact on production, and can be used without any quantitative limit.

References

Anderson, K. (2002) 'Peculiarities of retaliation in WTO dispute settlement', CEPR Discussion Paper Series no 3578, CEPR, London

Anderson, K. and Blackhurst, R. (1992) *The Greening of World Trade Issues*, Harvester Wheatsheaf, London

Bagwell K. and Staiger, R. (1999) 'An economic theory of GATT', *American Economic Review*, vol 89, no 1, pp215–248

Charnovitz, S. (2001) 'Rethinking WTO trade sanctions', *The American Journal of International Law*, vol 95, no 4, pp792–832

Corden, W. M. (1997) *Trade Policy and Economic Welfare*, 2nd Edition, Oxford University Press, New York

Krutilla, K. (1991) 'Environmental regulation in an open economy', *Journal of Environmental Economics and Management*, vol 20, pp127–142

Lankoski, J. and Ollikainen, M. (2003) 'Agri-environmental externalities: A framework for designing targeted policies', *European Review of Agricultural Economics*, vol 30, no 1, pp51–57

OECD (2001) 'Multifunctionality: Towards an analytical framework', OECD Publications, Paris

Paarlberg, P. L., Bredhal, M. and Lee, J. L. (2002) 'Multifunctionality and agricultural trade negotiations', *Review of Agricultural Economics*, vol 24, no 2, pp322–335

Peterson, M. P., Boisvert, R. N. and de Gorter, H. (2002) 'Environmental policies for a multifunctional agriculture sector in open economies', *European Review of Agricultural Economics*, vol 29, no 4, pp423–434

Randall, A. (2002) 'Valuing the outputs of multifunctional agriculture', *European Review of Agricultural Economics*, vol 29, no 3, pp289–307

Romstad, E., Vatn, A., Rorstad, P. K. and Soyland, V. (2000) 'Multifunctional agriculture, implications for policy design', Report no 21, Department of Economics and Social Sciences, Agricultural University of Norway

Vatn, A. (2002) 'Multifunctional agriculture: Some consequences for international trade regimes', *European Review of Agricultural Economics*, vol 29, no 3, pp309–327

Vermersch, D. (2001) 'Multifunctionality: Applying the OECD framework', A review of literature in France, mimeo

14
Reducing the Impacts of the Production and Trade of Commodities

Paul Ekins and Robin Vanner

International trading arrangements and the environment

As is clear from the discussion in Chapter 7, many of the critical trade and sustainable development issues and linkages actually have to do with commodity trade. The development dimension has been discussed in other chapters. This chapter starts by assessing how the current rules of the international trading system either do or do not take environmental issues into account. It then analyses the wide range of initiatives outside the formal trading system that have sought to make commodity production and trade more clearly aligned with the whole range of sustainable development objectives. From this analysis it identifies the major features of an institutional regime that really could ensure that the expansion of commodity production contributed to sustainable development, and therefore was able to address the sustainability impacts of trade liberalization, as identified in Sustainability Impact Assessments (SIAs), and help resolve the problems they raise in trade negotiations.

The environmental impacts of commodity production normally relate to how the commodities are produced, their process and production methods (PPMs). Now commodity markets are generally, though with some exceptions, (e.g. Organization of the Petroleum Exporting Countries (OPEC) and oil) intensely competitive. Pressures on production costs tend to rule out expensive modifications to PPMs, which may be desirable on social or environmental grounds, but which would raise those costs. The homogeneity of the final product means that there is usually little trace of how the commodity was produced, although such information might be useful for those consumers who wished to know the social and environmental impacts of production. Trade disciplines required under the General Agreement on Tariffs and Trade (GATT) make it difficult to prevent discrimination between physically like products (i.e. discrimination based solely on PPMs), as seen below.

Advocates of liberalized global trade believe that trade can still offer the prospect of an improved environment (via development) if properly regulated. (It is important to recognize that liberalization, concerned with removing discrimination between like products, is not the same thing as deregulation, although critics of trade liberalization believe that the former may lead to pressure for the latter.) The situation is expressed thus in a speech by the Director General of the World Trade Organization (WTO), Pascal Lamy, in respect of biodiversity:

> *There is no doubt in my mind that both trade and biodiversity policies* have the capacity to be mutually reinforcing ... *it is undoubted that completely unregulated trade can be harmful for biodiversity.* (Lamy, 2006, emphasis added)

It is therefore the challenge of the WTO to regulate trade to achieve the objectives of sustainable development, within the constraints of the present treaty, GATT 1994. In April 1994, a Ministerial Decision on Trade and Environment was adopted, establishing the Committee on Trade and Environment (CTE), with the aim of making 'international trade and environmental policies mutually supportive' (WTO, 2004, p6). The WTO therefore seems to perceive its role as being to continue to liberalize trade, while ensuring that environmental policies do not act as obstacles to trade, and that trade rules do not stand in the way of adequate domestic environmental protection. The WTO does not consider itself to be an environmental protection agency and does not aspire to become one (WTO, 2004, p6).

Environmental debate within the Doha Development Agenda

In November 2001 in Doha, ministers agreed to launch negotiations on certain issues related to trade and environment. The CTE and the Committee on Trade and Development were asked to act as a forum in which the environmental and developmental aspects of the negotiations launched at Doha could be debated (WTO, 2004, p5). Paragraph 32(i) of the Doha Declaration calls on the CTE to give particular attention to 'the effect of environmental measures on market access, especially in relation to developing countries, in particular the least-developed among them, and those situations in which the elimination or reduction of trade restrictions and distortions would benefit trade, the environment and development' (WTO, 2001a, p7). The original mandate has now been refined by work at Cancun in 2003, Geneva in 2004 and Hong Kong in 2005.

WTO (2004, p15) provides guidance for striking the appropriate balance between safeguarding market access and protecting the environment.

Environmental measures should be designed in a manner that 1) is consistent with WTO rules, 2) inclusive, 3) takes into account capabilities of developing countries, and 4) meets the legitimate objectives of the importing country.

The CTE Special Session (CTESS) was established to deal with environmental issues within the negotiations whilst the CTE continues to deal with the non-negotiating issues of the Doha Ministerial Declaration. In addition, paragraph 28 of the Doha Ministerial Declaration instructs members 'to clarify and improve WTO disciplines on fisheries subsidies, taking into account the importance of this sector to developing countries' (WTO, 2004, p9).

WTO case law to date makes clear that the environment debate within the WTO is largely being driven by the concerns of developed countries about the environmental impact of commodity production. Many developing countries are concerned that trade restrictions will be placed on their exports, even in cases where the products are physically indistinguishable from less environmentally impacting products and the environmental impacts of their production do not affect the importing country. The debate therefore centres on whether PPMs can be used as a justification for trade measures, and if so, to what degree these need to be implemented with international consent by the adoption of a multilateral environmental agreement (MEA). MEAs represent an additional challenge to the regulation of trade as they are often not signed by all WTO members, but the obligations accepted by participating countries potentially override the obligations they already have to maintain open markets for non-participating WTO members. These two issues are now discussed in turn.

Trade policy and MEAs

A lack of coordination has previously contributed to the negotiation of potentially conflicting agreements in trade and environmental forums (WTO, 2004, p8), although there have not yet been any adverse rulings by the WTO on an MEA trade measure. All environmental measures challenged to date in the WTO have been unilaterally imposed rather than implemented as the result of an MEA (reported in Knigge, 2005, p3). WTO (2004) makes clear the WTO's concern that unilateral solutions are often discriminatory, and frequently involve the extra-territorial application of environmental standards and that multilateral cooperation through the negotiation of MEAs constitutes the best approach for resolving transboundary environmental concerns. However, it also asserts that negotiations for MEAs should not prejudice the WTO rights of any member that is not a party to the MEA in question (WTO, 2004, p10).

Article 30(4b) of the Vienna Convention on the Law of Treaties states that if one of the two parties is not a signatory to one of the treaties, only the treaty to which both states are parties governs their mutual rights and obligations. However, the rights of WTO members not to have the extra-territorial application of environmental standards imposed on them would appear to be potentially undermined by one of the Appellate Body's compliance rulings in the shrimp–turtle case, which stated that 'the chapeau of Article XX does not necessarily require the conclusion of an international agreement but only the serious and good faith efforts for the conclusion of it' (this is discussed further below).

Article 30 of the Vienna Convention on the Law of Treaties[1] states that in cases in which both entities are parties to both regimes, the most recently agreed treaty prevails, implying that WTO members are not able to rely on their rights under GATT if they subsequently choose to be party to a MEA that limits these rights, although this would not be the case for any MEA that became binding before GATT was (re)signed in 1994. The effectiveness of some of the older MEAs might therefore be undermined. A CTE report adopted by the Ministerial Conference in Singapore recommends that, where two WTO members are in dispute and they are both parties to a relevant MEA, they should resolve the dispute though the dispute settlement mechanism available under the MEA rather than the Appellate Body of the WTO.

Process and production methods (PPMs)

PPMs refer to the way a product is produced rather than the characteristics of the product itself. The WTO (2004, p17) reports that countries are within their rights under WTO rules to set criteria for the way products are produced, if their production method leaves a trace in the final product (e.g. cotton grown using pesticides, with there being pesticide residue in the cotton itself). However, there is less agreement over whether measures based on PPMs that leave no trace in the final product (e.g. cotton grown using pesticides, with there being no trace of the pesticides in the cotton). As a general rule, international trading arrangements (i.e. the GATT) require that domestic and imported 'like products' be treated the same. This principle is central to discussions around trade in commodities and the environment.

There have been a number of disputes over alleged discrimination based on PPMs, and to a certain extent uncertainty remains over whether discrimination is permissible based on a product's PPMs. If taken at face value, all of these disputes stem from the desire of some countries (in this case developed) to maintain higher environmental standards of production for all products they consume, whether imported or domestically produced. However, any barriers to trade are considered with a great deal of suspicion by developing countries as it has the effect of maintaining developed countries' technological advantage and weakens the principle behind international trade, comparative advantage.

GATT Article XX(e) already provides for discrimination against physically like products where they have been produced using prison labour, which is therefore considered to be a *universal collective preference* in the terms discussed earlier in the book (Chapter 4). The PPM case law, however, deals with impacts of production that were not specifically set out in Article XX, but often rely on the more general exception '*relating to the conservation of exhaustible natural resources*' (GATT, 1994, Article XX(g)) or '*necessary to protect human, animal or plant life or health*' (GATT, 1994, Article XX(b)). The disputes that laid the foundations of much of the subsequent PPM debate were the so called 'Tuna–Dolphin' cases (case one between Mexico and the US taken in 1991 and case two between the EU and the US taken in 1994) and the 1998 shrimp–turtle case:

- **Tuna–dolphin one** was brought by Mexico in response to the US Government placing bans on imported tuna from countries whose 'incidental kill ratio' of dolphins was greater than its own. It placed embargoes on countries such as Mexico in order to restrict imports from countries that imported tuna from the Eastern Tropical Pacific and exported that tuna to the US. The subsequent ruling (never formally adopted by the GATT general council) ruled that the ban fell foul of Article III of the GATT (the national treatment requirement) and Article XI (quantitative restrictions on imports). Crucially, however, the ban was ruled not to be justified under Article XX(b or g) of the GATT as these exceptions could not be applied unilaterally or extra-jurisdictionally.
- **Tuna–dolphin two** was brought in 1994 by the European Commission (EC) against the US's secondary embargoes imposed on imports of tuna from countries that traded in tuna from embargoed countries. The panel ruled that the secondary embargoes were inconsistent with GATT. However, the panel ruled that Article XX exceptions could in principle be applied extra-jurisdictionally to protect global resources, but only when covered by an MEA. Dolphins were not so protected and it was ruled that the restrictions were not necessary and therefore the case was lost by the US.
- **The shrimp–turtle case:** In 1987 US legislation required domestic shrimp trawlers to use turtle-excluder devices in their nets to allow turtles to escape. Later potentially trade-restricting legislation required other shrimp-producing countries to show a regulatory programme, and incidental mortality rate, comparable to that of the US. A case was taken by Malaysia, Thailand, Pakistan and India based on both the environmental relevance and the extra-jurisdictional nature of the restrictions. The subsequent 1998 Appellate Body appeal ruling upheld the relevance of Article XX in the case but ultimately found against the US on the basis that the measure had been implemented in a discriminatory way contrary to the chapeau of Article XX as it had '*failed to engage shrimp exporting countries in serious negotiations with the objective of concluding an international agreement for the protection and conservation of sea turtles.*' However, within a later compliance ruling, the Appellate Body observed that '*the chapeau of Article XX does not necessarily require the conclusion of an international agreement but only the serious and good faith efforts for the conclusion of it.*'[2]

Other relevant GATT case law has been provided by rulings on beef hormones and asbestos:

- **The 1997 beef-hormone** case between the EU and the US/Canada over the EU's ban on cattle products produced using growth hormones centred on interpretation of the agreement on Sanitary and Phytosanitary Measures (SPS). The Panel found the EU measures to be inconsistent with the risk assessment procedures required by the SPS agreement as the precautionary principle continues to be a subject of debate. However, a later Appellate Body ruling failed to share the Panel's inference that the EU import ban was purely a 'protectionist' measure. Some (e.g. FOEI, 2001) interpret this ruling to suggest an acceptance that PPMs can be a basis for trade restrictions.
- **Asbestos:** The 2000 so-called asbestos case involved Canada challenging a French ban on asbestos in construction materials. The case involved Canada arguing that the asbestos it exports was a 'like product' to the substitute non-asbestos products used in construction in France, therefore deserving no less favourable treatment under the national treatment obligation of Article III:4 of GATT 1994. In assessing the 'likeness' between asbestos and the substitute products, the Appellate Body '*consider[ed] consumers' tastes and habits significant in determining "likeness"*' (WTO, 2001b, p123) even though the consumers of the product would be manufacturers of building materials. More particularly, it considered '*the extent to which consumers perceive and treat the products as alternative means of performing particular functions in order to satisfy a particular want or demand*' (WTO, 2001b, p101).

The legal status and the ultimate outcomes of these cases in terms of environmental protection are further complex issues not requiring further exploration here. However, in terms of discrimination on the basis of PPMs:

- The **tuna–dolphin (two)** case does demonstrate that the WTO's Appellate Body would be likely to rule in future cases that Article XX can in principle relate to extra-jurisdictional impacts as long as the measure is not implemented unilaterally.
- The **shrimp-turtle** case ruling demonstrates that the chapeau of Article XX does not necessarily require the *conclusion* of an international agreement (i.e. MEA) but only serious and good faith efforts for the conclusion of it.
- Some argue that the **beef-hormone** dispute may also provide guidance on the PPM issue as it provided implicit acceptance of PPMs as a basis for non-discriminatory measures, as long as it satisfies the scientific evidence requirements of the SPS annex of the 1994 GATT (the use of the precautionary principle was not accepted).
- The **asbestos** case provides for consumers' tastes and habits to *contribute* towards the determination of like products that are physically different. However, this case has not set a precedent for discrimination between physically like products driven *solely* by consumers' tastes and habits. This would need to be tested further by the Appellate Body and, based on a

detailed reading of the asbestos ruling, such attempts would likely fail as consumers' tastes and habits were not the dominant determinant in the judgement.

A certain level of ambiguity remains in the interpretation of these cases and what the likely outcomes would be for future such cases. At first sight, it would appear that in the absence of serious and good faith efforts for the conclusion of an international agreement, there is nothing in the present case law to support discrimination between physically like products based on PPMs that only impact the producer country. However, Lamy (2004, p6) interprets the shrimp–turtle case such that a country that is defending a PPM-type barrier to trade might win if they were able to provide proof that they are acting in good faith. Lamy is therefore arguing that the good faith engagement of trade partners in an MEA is merely an example of good faith and that all that is required is a demonstration that the action does not represent protectionism.

PPM case law assessed against motives to resist trade liberalization

These cases may be related to the motives to resist trade liberalization discussed in Chapter 4:

1 **Protectionist bias argument:** The detail of the application of trade restrictions shows that the shrimp–turtle and tuna cases were at least partially motivated by US attempts to protect their fishing industry from imports that did not comply with their own environmental standards. It is less clear whether the environmental standard was primarily motivated by environmental or protectionist interests. In any event, the rulings from these cases established that neither is justified on a unilateral basis.
2 **Adjustment cost argument:** None of these cases relate to the adjustment costs argument. It seems likely that the Appellate Body would permit restrictions motivated by reasonable attempts to manage any social adjustment to a trade liberalization.
3 **Externality argument:** On the face of it, the shrimp–turtle and tuna cases relate to environmental externalities that justified import restrictions for the importing country but not for the exporting country. The WTO preference is clearly to resolve such cases through negotiation and mutual agreement. Where this is not possible, the existing case law suggests that the validity of any trade restrictions depend on the situation and the motive for and detail of their implementation. The desire not to consume imported products that have been made using environmentally damaging PPMs might be considered to be a collective preference, the satisfaction of which may justify compensation.
4 **Collective preferences argument:** The beef-hormone dispute relates (in part at least) to a collective preference of the EU, based on the precautionary principle. However, as this principle was not *universally* accepted as part of

> the process of risk assessment as set out by the SPS agreement, the EU would still be subject to proportionate retaliatory measures by would-be exporting countries, or obliged to pay compensation to them. Only the asbestos case reflected a universal preference, acknowledged when the WTO Appellate Body agreed with the French case based on their right to set reasonable standards to protect their own population from health risks.

The earlier identification of the motives behind the resistance to free trade or trade liberalization, and the adoption of appropriate measures to reflect them (for example, compensation where collective preferences were involved), might have prevented them from developing into the protracted disputes that occurred, which have left an enduring legacy of suspicion that trade measures that purport to protect the environment are actually motivated by a desire to protect domestic industries. More broadly, however, it is clear that the WTO is not, and is most unlikely to become, a body that can systematically reduce the negative environmental impacts of commodity production, and of trade liberalization, which have been identified by SIAs. Some other means of international cooperation will need to be found for this to be achieved. There is in fact, outside the formal trade institutions, a wide body of experience from initiatives set up in response to the environmental and broader sustainable development impacts of commodity production, which will now be examined.

Initiatives to manage the sustainable development impacts from commodity production

Many initiatives have sought to manage the sustainable development impacts of commodity production. Some (especially the government-based initiatives discussed below) were introduced for purely economic reasons, sometimes before the objective of sustainable development was even on the policy agenda. Some have been initiated or supported by international institutions or governments in order to provide more stable commodity-producing environments. Others are private and voluntary in nature. These have been initiated by either producer groups, in order to manage the long-term viability and profitability of their business, or consumer groups in order to mitigate some of the sustainability impacts within the scope of their perceived responsibility. This section describes a range of these initiatives and assesses both how effective they have proved in meeting the negative impacts of commodity production and trade, as revealed by SIAs and discussed in Chapter 7, and whether they might be relevant to and help resolve some of the sticking points in trade negotiations.

The methods discussed in this section act merely as examples or case studies from a much larger number of initiatives within the commodity sectors. When considering any mitigating or price stabilizing measure, it is important to consider the wider or longer term impacts of the measure. Previous attempts to artificially increase or 'prop-up' commodity prices have resulted in misleading market signals. The result has often been greater price instability in the long term, thereby deepening the 'commodity trap' for poor producer-countries, and reducing the then economic growth.

Government-based initiatives

There have been a large number of attempts to mitigate the impacts of price fluctuations in commodity markets. Although they mainly pre-date the emergence of the idea of sustainable development as a major policy objective, and pay little or no attention to the environmental aspects of commodity production, their concern with ameliorating the economic and/or social outcomes of commodity production and trade mean that they can now be interpreted as efforts in some sense to make development more sustainable. UNCTAD (2004, p84) has reviewed the history of these initiatives, which include:

- In 1943, John Maynard Keynes proposed a world currency based on a price index of the 30 most-traded commodities. The idea was to link currencies to the index in order to automatically stabilize commodity prices.
- In 1963, the International Monetary Fund began offering a Compensatory Financing Facility that later became the Compensatory and Contingency Financing Facility.
- The Integrated Programme for Commodities set up an approach for an international policy framework that included the negotiation of a series of price-stabilizing agreements (referred to as commodity agreements) for commodities with very unstable prices.
- In 1988 the IMF introduced a Buffer Stock Financing Facility; this was discontinued in the early 2000s.
- The first Lomé Convention in 1975 gave birth to the STABEX (stablization of export earnings) system, which was designed to alleviate the effect of non-structural problems such as fluctuation in world commodity prices and unforeseen events such as natural disasters.
- STABEX was discontinued in 2000 with the signature of the Cotonou Agreement, and was replaced by the more narrowly focused FLEX (fluctuations in export earnings) programme.

Commodity agreements

Commodity agreements typically involve a pre-agreed intervention in the supply of a commodity to stabilize the price over the long term. This can either seek to involve all of the significant producers in an international agreement, or try to maintain agreement within a smaller group of producers at a national or local level.

The Sustainability Institute (2003, pp26, 29) explores national and sub-national collective agreements with reference to the Western Rock Lobster managed fishery in Australia, the main objective of which was to maintain local lobster stocks at sustainable and economically productive levels; and the

Burley tobacco agreement in the US, which seeks to manage the supply of tobacco through a price support system and quotas in order to stabilize prices and avoid overcapacity.

Both of these agreements are regulated and enforced within a government-run legal framework. It is, however, in the producers' interests to have the agreement, so long as there are not too many producers breaking the terms of the agreement. The allocation of property rights to incumbents and the restriction on technology and production may be considered acceptable interventions by local producers and populations. Such agreements can only hope to maintain prices so long as the production they support remains competitive with producers outside the jurisdiction of the agreement. This is therefore the greatest limitation of such agreements.

International commodity agreements have typically been managed in a similar way to the tobacco agreement in the US, via a 'buffer stock manager' who utilizes storage capacity to keep within a predetermined price band. Such agreements have been given international recognition. An Integrated Programme for Commodities was adopted by the United Nations Conference on Trade and Development (UNCTAD) at its fourth and fifth sessions. Its main objective was to stabilize prices within commodity markets through the negotiation of international commodity agreements and it was one of the main planks of the so-called New International Economic Order of the 1970s. The exceptions to trade discipline necessary for commodity agreements are permitted under Article XX(h) of the GATT treaty.

By the mid-1990s the commodity agreement movement was effectively dead, with only the International Commodity Agreement (ICA) on natural rubber maintaining the capability of active market intervention. The remaining agreements had either lapsed or collapsed (sugar, tin) or been replaced by agreements the role of which is primarily that of improving information (cocoa, coffee), at least partly due to a change in political climate and a 'lack of willingness of the parties to continue playing the ICA game'(Gilbert, 1995). ECA (2003) reports that buffer stock systems usually proved to be ineffective mechanisms for stabilizing commodity prices and that any modest price stabilization achieved was typically outweighed by the interest and carrying costs of the system. Van Groenendaal and Vingerhoets (1995) reported that the 6th Tin Agreement collapsed because it 'degenerated into an agreement for the defence of a non-competitive price floor'. More generally, they found the particular supply intervention method to be a significant factor in the success or failure of many of the main ICAs, concluding that 'buffer stock intervention should not go against the general tendency of the market, or more precisely, the structural development in the market' (Van Groenendaal and Vingerhoets, 1995, p259), and that, from a strict economic perspective, only the cocoa and rubber commodity agreements ever had the possibility to succeed. Even so, they noted that many of these agreements had in fact operated successfully for many years (e.g. 25 years for the tin agreements).[3]

Market-based initiatives

Another group of approaches used to reduce producer vulnerability to price instabilities are market-based contract and insurance mechanisms. These include a variety of insurance services and a range of capital market instruments such as future and option contracts, catastrophe bonds and weather derivatives. Insurance instruments, and forward and futures contracts have become more commonly used in developed countries as government-managed schemes such as buffer stocks have declined in use. However, small farmers in poor countries have limited access to insurance against price volatility, and markets are not fully developed in many developing countries in order to provide forward and futures contracts. ECA (2003, p10) identifies the market failures involved, which include a lack of enforcement as well as asymmetric information between small producers, which can often lead to exploitation. Governments might therefore have a role to play in ensuring enforcement of contracts, as well as regulating financial products in order to permit the economies of scale required to provide such services to small and vulnerable producers. One measure might be the establishment of a central institution such as a marketing board, which could enforce contracts and provide transparent information to market participants.

Marketing boards

An institution that is complementary to both commodity agreements and the provision of forward contracts is marketing boards. Marketing boards act as the sole purchaser of crops from farmers. Through pre-announced prices to farmers, marketing boards enable forward sales to occur between overseas buyers and the marketing board. The board can act as a single entity in entering into forward contracts and is normally backed up by government guarantees. This way it avoids enforcement problems. Asymmetric information problems are also minimized because marketing boards can afford to have a centralized unit of experts that monitors price developments for commodities. Therefore, these boards can successfully hedge risks arising from commodity price fluctuations. Apart from providing this type of hedging service, marketing boards also extend credit to producers, distribute agricultural inputs such as fertiliser and pesticides, and provide market information to farmers. Marketing boards have limited ability to maintain prices in the absence of some kind of supply restricting agreement.

Compensation finance mechanisms

There have been two major compensatory financing programmes for terms-of-trade shocks; the EC's STABEX mechanism, which has since been replaced by the FLEX mechanism, and the International Monetary Fund's (IMF's) Compensatory and Contingency Financing Facility (CCFF). The objective of the EC's instruments was to remedy the harmful effects of export earnings instability and thus to help sustained growth of the economies of the African, Caribbean and Pacific (ACP) countries. Although STABEX constituted a useful instrument for making transfers to a number of the ACP countries until it was replaced by the Cotonou Agreement (2000) and the FLEX mechanism, it was subject to many criticisms. ECA (2003, p9) describes the instrument's drawbacks as follows:

1 Coverage of only four products (coffee, cocoa/copra, groundnuts and cotton).
2 Coverage of only five countries.
3 Serious shortage of funding since the 1980s.
4 Delayed disbursement (of one to four years) to provide an opportunity to observe information on export earnings.

The FLEX mechanism is provided from the EU's European Development Fund under the Cotonou Agreement for ACP countries and provides general budget support instead of sector-specific assistance, which is likely to reduce delays in disbursements of aid as experienced under STABEX. To be eligible, applicant countries must experience a 10 per cent (2 per cent in the case of least developed countries (LDCs)) loss of export earnings; and a 10 per cent worsening in public deficits. It has been in place since 2000 and its objectives are to provide support in the case of short-term fluctuations in export earnings in order to safeguard reforms and policies at risk as a result of a fall in revenue, and to remedy the adverse effects of instability of export earnings in particular from agricultural and mining products. However, in 2004 the EC reported that, from 2000 to 2002, ACP countries were able to meet both criteria in only six out of 51 cases. Support from FLEX in the six cases totalled €35.65 million. Had the criteria been met in all the 51 cases from 2000 to 2002, ACP countries would have received €255 million through the FLEX system (EC, 2004). The EC proposed revisions to relax FLEX's eligibility criteria, in order to ensure that it responded more effectively to its stated objectives.

Giving greater international coverage, the CCFF was created in 1963 and provides financing to members experiencing balance of payments difficulties resulting from a temporary shortfall in export earnings or an excess in cereal import costs. There has been extensive debate within the IMF itself (see IMF, 1999) around the wisdom of providing finance in the absence of long-term adjustment plans. Adjustment is often considered necessary for the country to move away from and reduce its dependence on unstable or low profit commodities. IMF (1999) argues that timely financing to protect against temporary shocks is required as some members have little or no access to alternative sources of financing. It also goes on to report that, in practice, it is difficult to distinguish between temporary and permanent shocks and that commodity price shocks typically do not reverse quickly. Were this to be the case, such assistance might act to prolong low export prices, or prop up inflated cereal prices thereby further deepening the 'commodity trap' for the country's producers. There is therefore a balance to be struck between short-term relief and long-term adjustment. In reality, the CCFF has not appealed to low-income countries as such countries often already have borrowing ceilings in the absence of adjustments.

Voluntary consumer initiatives

What represents a fair share in the proceeds of trade, and the best mechanism used to achieve it, is the subject of extensive discussion. Least problematic from the point of view of the status quo would be endorsement as 'fair' of the international arrangements arbitrated by the WTO, whereby moves towards freer trade are the subject of multilateral agreement. However, disagreements with such a view come from at least two different directions, as the following two definitions show:

- Moore (2004) defines fair trade from a consumer initiative and developing country perspective: 'Fair Trade is a trading partnership, based on dialogue, transparency and respect, which seeks greater equity in international trade. It contributes to sustainable development by offering better trading conditions to, and securing the rights of, marginalized producers and workers – especially in the South.'
- Maseland and De Vaal (2002, p252) report how fair trade can be interpreted very differently, leading to 'calls for protectionist measures by developed countries against products that have been produced in poorer countries at prices developed countries cannot compete with because of their different economic circumstances'. They go on to argue that 'taken to the extreme, this would mean that all trade based upon comparative advantage should be abolished. In practice, the argument is mostly used to protect domestic industries in developed economies against cheaper imports from countries with low labour costs.'

Putting to one side the principles of a hypothetical fairer trading system, it is clear that some parts of the existing arrangements provide only a marginal existence for many small producers in developing countries, and can cause environmental impacts. A number of consumer labelling initiatives have sought to address this situation from various perspectives. However, consumer labelling has been a contentious issue within trade forums, especially when criteria have been linked to PPMs where no trace is left in the product that is imported. The WTO (2004, p17) advises that 'these schemes need to be non-discriminatory and not result in unnecessary barriers or disguised restrictions on international trade'. In 2000, the Technical Barriers to Trade (TBT) Committee agreed on a set of guiding principles for the development of standards, including environmental labelling standards. The principles are: transparency, openness, impartiality and consensus, effectiveness and relevance, coherence and, wherever possible, responsiveness to the needs and interests of developing countries (WTO, 2004, p19). However, there is little agreement on the application of these principles in the various schemes that have been developed, some of which are described below.

The Fairtrade mark

The Fairtrade mark is a consumer label that appears on products, and is intended to be an independently verified guarantee that 'disadvantaged producers in the developing world are getting a better deal'.[4] To carry the Fairtrade mark, the products' PPMs must meet international Fairtrade standards as set by the international certification body Fairtrade Labelling Organizations International (FLO). These social and environmental standards need to be met by all those in the product chain including producer groups, traders, processors, wholesalers and retailers.

The standards distinguish between minimum requirements, which producers must meet to be certified Fairtrade, and progress requirements that encourage producer organizations to continuously improve their performance (FLO, 2005).

There are a number of generic criteria that help define price premia that traders need to pay. Traders should:

- pay a price to producers that covers the costs of sustainable production and living and allows for investments in development;
- pay in advance, when producers ask for it;
- sign contracts that allow for long-term planning and sustainable production practices.

These criteria have led to a large number of products and sub-products being provided a specific price guarantee and price premium as defined by the FLO. The European Parliament reported that overall sales of fair trade verified goods totalled €660 million in 2005 (EP, 2006, p3). They also reported that in financial terms, the price premium provided over €23 million of benefits to coffee farmers, and the trade resulted in the empowerment of producers through capacity building and technical assistance, income security, direct trade and credit provision, improved levels of education, the preservation of indigenous cultures and potentially the break-up of monopolies on prices and transportation (summarized from EP, 2006, p6).

There are, however, a number of concerns for both producers and consumers raised by the introduction and growth of the Fairtrade mark.

First, retailers may take advantage of consumers' preparedness to pay a price premium by charging customers more than the Fairtrade price premium, to increase their profit margin (Webb, 2006). Secondly, any system that continues to pay farmers at a higher than market price will provide incentives for overproduction. The result is that certified production often needs to be sold onto the uncertified market in competition with such low-cost producers, leading to a concentration of price instabilities in the uncertified market. Moore (2004, p78) reported that 'in 1999 only 50% of the worldwide production of Fair Trade coffee was sold through Fair Trade channels, the remaining 50% being sold on the regular market'. ECF and CAOBISCO (2006, p3) reported that the fair trade market only absorbs 28 thousand tonnes of the 138 thousand tonnes certified coffee grown annually (i.e. an 80 per cent overspill).

Maseland and De Vaal (2002) tested[5] the effectiveness of fair trade initiatives to achieve their own objectives, by comparing fair trade against the two extremes of 'free trade' and 'protectionism' intended to protect the development needs of producer countries. The objective of fair trade was taken from the fair trade movement itself that: 'trade is fair when it comes to the advantage of the least well off in society'[6] (Maseland and De Vaal 2002, p268). They conclude: 'Fairtrade was found to be always superior to protectionism, but its superiority with respect to free trade depended on the price elasticity of demand of the product it targets at' (Maseland and De Vaal 2002, p269). The paper's overall conclusion was that 'it is by no means clear that fairtrade initiatives are always fairer than other options'.

Organic certified production

Not all organic verification schemes follow the same standards. There is, however a growing consensus on and convergence of standards. The International Federation of Organic Agriculture Movements (IFOAM) represents the worldwide body of organic agriculture and provides a platform for global exchange and cooperation but, as with the UK Soil Association, standards can be extended beyond this. In 1991, the EU produced Council Regulation 2092/91 (see EU, 2001), which regulates the sale and labelling of organic produce within the EU, but which was repealed and replaced by Council Regulation (EEC) No.834/2007 in June 2007, which now sets out the inputs and practices that may be used in organic farming and growing, and the inspection system that must be put in place to ensure this. This Regulation also applies to processing, processing aids and ingredients in organic foods. Very broadly, in order to be verified as an organic product, at least 95 per cent of the inputs must not have been:

- produced using a specified list of substances (i.e. Annex VI in Defra, 2005);
- subjected to ionizing radiation;
- produced or derived from any genetically modified organisms (GMOs)

There are also a number of animal welfare standards that need to be met.

Unless and until a joint organic–fair trade scheme is developed, organic production only limits the environmental impacts and fails to tackle the underlying drivers behind the 'commodity trap', noted in Chapter 7, or poverty in developing countries more generally. Perhaps one possible indirect poverty-reducing outcome of the increasing demand for organic produce might be the comparative advantage developing countries might have in a more labour-intensive system of production. Sustainability Institute (2003, p39) reports that China set aside 250,000 acres of unpolluted land in 2000 exclusively for production of organic food intended for the Japanese market.

Voluntary producer initiatives

Producers may have the incentive to improve their production practices in order to segment a commodity market and therefore achieve a rent through the use of product labelling and their brand. Such labelling is in no way contrary to WTO rules but is often met with scepticism by increasingly sophisticated consumers unless externally verified. It may well also make business sense for producers to engage in sustainable production techniques, irrespective of whether a price premium is available, as the long-term profitability of the company may be under threat if they endanger long-term levels of production or the communities on which they rely, or produce in ways that are inconsistent with the wider values of their consumers. Because of this many corporations are now considering what role their customers and stakeholders expect them to play in respect of all the components of sustainable development, or how they should exercise their 'corporate social responsibility' (CSR).

One result of this expansion of the traditional concern of business is that most large companies now have in place sophisticated systems to manage their environmental obligations to host governments, as well as manage stakeholder relationships. Such relationships include both those internal to their business (customers, employees, shareholders, suppliers) and those external to it (competitors, local communities, government, civil society). In addition, many companies are also seeking to measure and report on their environmental and social (as well as their economic) performance to a range of stakeholders, leading to the development of sector-specific (see for example Berkhout et al, 2001) and general reporting frameworks (see for example the Guidelines of the Global Reporting Initiative, GRI, 2002). Accounting approaches in these areas have also been developed and, in some cases, related to corporate financial accounts (see, among others, Bennett and James, 2000; Howes, 2000). At the same time, the social dimension of sustainable development has been treated in terms of its relationships with both internal and external stakeholders (see Steg et al, 2001 for discussion of this).

The concern with CSR has also led to a number of voluntary collective producer initiatives that have sought to define the principles and criteria for producer behaviour in respect of sustainable development issues that go beyond market success, a number of which are now briefly described.

Global Compact

The Global Compact sets out to bring companies together at the global level with UN agencies, labour and civil society to support ten universal environmental and social principles in the areas of human rights, labour, the environment and anti-corruption. The Global Compact is a purely voluntary initiative, which asks companies to embrace, support and enact, within their sphere of influence, ten principles derived from four different international agreements: the UN's Universal Declaration of Human Rights; The International Labour Organization's Declaration on Fundamental Principles and Rights at Work; the Rio Declaration on Environment and Development; and the UN Convention Against Corruption.[7]

Corporations that pledge 'to work towards implementation of the Global Compact principles through learning, dialogue, projects, process improvements or other such measures' (UNGC, 2006, p2) are listed on the Global Compact's website. However, it is not a compliance-based initiative and it does not permit its logo to be used in relation to any product or activities intended to solicit business (UNGC, 2006, p2). Since 2003, participants are required to communicate with their stakeholders on an annual basis about progress in implementing the Global Compact principles and make this available on the Global Compact website. Failure to do so, or failure to respond to a complaint of 'systematic or egregious abuse of the GC's overall aims and principles' (UNGC, 2006, p2) results in the organization being listed as a non-communicating company on the Global Compact's website.

Describing the Global Compact as 'a learning forum', Ruggie (2002, p27) discusses both pragmatic and principled reasons for adopting such a voluntary approach rather than regulation to induce corporate change. Pragmatically he argues that there would not have been the international or business consensus for a code, or the resources available for monitoring and verifying it. In addition he considers that:

- many of the Global Compact's principles cannot be defined at this time with the precision required for a viable code of conduct;
- the extraordinary pace of change in corporate strategies, structures and production processes makes it exceedingly difficult to specify ex-ante the full range of performance criteria and desired practices that a code should include;
- strategically, the accumulation of experience itself is likely to lead gradually to a desire for greater codification by industry leaders wanting to protect themselves against any possible competitive disadvantage.

As of 2004, only about 20 per cent of the world's 500 largest companies by market capitalization had become participants in the Global Compact (UNGC, 2007). Williams (2004, p757) reported that 'only six of the major U.S. companies joined as of June 2004', because a perceived lack of accountability (for example, the lack of a code and verification) might lead to its legitimacy being questioned in the US, and because unclear expectations in relation to human rights may lay companies open to litigation. The situation is different for European companies. Georg Kell, the Executive Director of the UN Global Compact has argued that European companies have not been deterred from joining either because their government regulatory environment has already mandated the substance of the Global Compact, or because they operate in a less litigious and adversarial context (reported in Williams, 2004, p758).

Sectoral initiatives: minerals and mining

MMSD (Minerals, Mining and Sustainable Development) (2002) reports on how the minerals and mining sector globally has responded to the challenge of sustainable development. In 2000, the mining and minerals industry faced some of the most difficult challenges of any industrial sector and was distrusted by many of the people it dealt with day to day (MMSD, 2002, pxiv). Against this background, and with the World Summit for Sustainable Development planned for 2002 in mind, nine of the world's largest mining companies decided to initiate a project to examine the role of the minerals sector in contributing to sustainable development. The World Business Council for Sustainable Development worked with the sector to achieve four broad tasks:

1 to assess the global mining and minerals sector in terms of the transition to sustainable development;
2 to identify how the services provided through the minerals supply chain can be delivered in ways that support sustainable development;
3 to propose key elements for improving the minerals system;
4 to build platforms of analysis and engagement for ongoing communication and networking among all stakeholders in the sector.

MMSD focused stakeholders' concerns into nine key challenges facing the sector, which emerged as the most pressing issues through various consultative mechanisms over two years, including: the viability of the minerals industry; its control, use and management of land; its contribution to national economic development and relationship with local communities; its impact on the environment; and its transparency and governance.

The nine large mining companies behind MMSD had a number of reasons for initiating this process. MMSD (2002) makes clear that the sector was suffering from mistrust among its own stakeholders and that a concerted collaborative effort was required to rectify this situation and maintain its 'social licence to operate'.

However, the advocacy by MMSD of voluntary initiatives and standards that go beyond national regulations pays little attention to what the Australian Government called 'the sovereign right of developing countries to attract foreign investment for, and create wealth from, their natural resources' (DMPR, 2002, p9), and highlights again the potential conflict between nationally and internationally imposed PPMs, especially if the latter benefits large transnational companies at the expense of local producers.

Sectoral initiatives: The Marine Stewardship Council (MSC) certified sustainable fisheries

The MSC initiative is an independent and voluntary certification programme intended to enhance the responsible management of seafood resources and ensure the sustainability of global fish stocks and the health of the marine ecosystem. Though operating independently since 1999, the MSC was first established by the Unilever corporation, which is the world's largest buyer of seafood, and the environmental NGO World Wide Fund for Nature in 1997. The initiative certifies fish that have been caught from so-called 'sustainable fisheries', and therefore relies upon all those involved in the product chain to meet specified 'Chain of Custody Traceability Standards'. This is a hybrid producer–consumer initiative, initiated and verified by producers, but with a consumer label.

MSC (2002) sets out the Principles and Criteria for sustainable fishing for the purposes of certifying that the fishing has been conducted in such as way that it:

- can be continued indefinitely at a reasonable level;
- maintains and seeks to maximize ecological health and abundance;
- maintains the diversity, structure and function of the ecosystem on which it depends as well as the quality of its habitat, minimizing the adverse effects that it causes;
- is managed and operated in a responsible manner, in conformity with local, national and international laws and regulations;
- maintains present and future economic and social options and benefits;
- is conducted in a socially and economically fair and responsible manner.

The scope for controversy over the implementation of such principles was illustrated by the criticism of the scheme by Greenpeace (2004), on the grounds that its operational criteria were insufficiently stringent. Yet a voluntary scheme depends for its take-up on consumers being prepared to pay a sufficient premium to compensate producers for forgoing some production opportunities, and it is not clear that the MSC would be viable if the criteria were made much more stringent.

Many of the same kinds of issues arise with the other major voluntary certification scheme for renewable resources, the Forestry Stewardship Council (FSC). For reasons of space this is not discussed in detail here.

Sectoral initiatives: The financial sector's 'Equator Principles'

The 'Equator Principles' are the financial industry's benchmark for determining, assessing and managing social and environmental risk in project financing. The 40 financial institutions (the Equator Principles Financial Institutions, EPFIs) around the world that currently apply the Principles have agreed not to provide loans to projects located in non-OECD (Organisation for Economic Co-operation and Development)[8] countries of total project capital costs greater than US$10 million unless the borrower complies with the first nine of the ten Equator Principles, relating to social and environmental assessment and standards; management systems and operational covenants; mechanisms for redress and review; and commitments to consultation, disclosure, monitoring and reporting. The tenth Principle concerns reporting by the EPFIs.[9]

Table 14.1 *Strengths, limitations and vulnerabilities of existing responses*

	Initiator	*Key strengths*	*Key limitations*	*Vulnerabilities*	*Status*	*GATT compliant?*
Regulated initiatives						
Commodity agreements	International consensus	Price stabilization	Limited environmental protection	Unsustainable price aspirations	Largely extinct	Yes, Article XX (h)
Market-based initiatives	Private	Provides resilience	Limited availability to small producers	Immature markets and lack of enforcement of contracts	Limited use in developing countries	Yes
Marketing boards	Producer governments	Tackles information market failures	Limited control over prices	Costs and politicization of production	Declining	Yes
Compensation finance	IMF & EU	Tackles short-term balance of payment difficulties	Fails to tackle causes of imbalances	Costs and politicization of production	Declining	Yes
Voluntary consumer initiatives						
Fairtrade	Consumer groups	Protection of vulnerable workers	Free riding and high cost	Oversupply and rent capture by retailers	Small but growing	Only when voluntary to consumers
Organic	Consumers Unilever &	Environmental protection	Fails to fully tackle 'commodity trap'			
MSC	WWF	Protection of fisheries	Might fail to provide incentives when fishery is severely depleted		Expanding	
Voluntary producer initiatives						
CSR	Companies	Promotes valuable relationships/'Licence to operate'	Limited by companies share of influence	Competition from less responsible short-term thinking companies/ organizations	Expanding	Yes
Global Compact	UN		Reluctance of US companies			
Sector initiatives (MMSD)	Sector		Dominance of large company interests			
Equator principles	Banks	Significant coverage	No guarantee of sustainable practices		New principles July 2006	

Clearly, at one level compliance with the Equator Principles provides lenders with a certain level of risk management against poorly managed projects that fail to comply with regulations and good practice or gain community consent. Such projects are less likely to fail or generate bad publicity for the lending organization. But even where they also generate wider benefits, they only apply to those activities financed by the EPFIs. And, in common with many producer-led initiatives, the Equator Principles fail to consider fully some of the wider challenges of sustainable development.

The government, producer and consumer initiatives described above vary greatly in terms of their priorities and therefore approach. Key to this will be who *initiated* the response and the objectives they had in mind. All of these responses have different *strengths and limitations* and will be *vulnerable* to different pressures over time. Table 14.1 summarizes these strengths, limitations and vulnerabilities and provides an assessment of their status and compliance with GATT trade disciplines.

Assessment of effectiveness of responses

Chapter 7 set out the underlying challenge faced by SIA practitioners and others when proposing measures to mitigate the impacts of commodity production. This chapter has explored some of the initiatives which have sought to mitigate the sustainability impacts of commodity production, and described the regulatory and political context within which they operate.

The effectiveness of these initiatives in contributing towards a more sustainable commodity-producing system may now be assessed, on the basis of the extent to which the initiative managed to:

1. **Stabilize markets:** Does the method reduce price volatility and promote stable markets?
2. **Promote development:** Does the method contribute towards achieving the Millennium Development Goals?
3. **Tackle the 'commodity trap':** Does the method tackle the capacity growth dynamic underlying the 'commodity trap'?
4. **Protect the environment:** Does the method reduce the environmental intensity of production to a level consistent with both local and global environmental capacities?
5. **Use resources sustainably:** Does the method either promote the sustainable management of renewable resources? Or ensure that sufficient profits from the extraction of non-renewable resources are invested in the development of renewable alternatives?

The assessment against these five objectives is set out in Table 14.2, which is explained in the paragraphs that follow.

Table 14.2 *Assessment of methods against the criteria of a sustainable commodity production system*

	Social objectives		*Both*	*Environmental objectives*		
	Stabilize markets	*Promote development*	*Tackle the commodity trap*	*Protect the environment*	*Sustainably use resources*	*Long-term viability*
Regulated initiatives						
Commodity agreements	■	▒	■	▒	▒	?
Market-based initiatives	■	▒	▒			■
Marketing boards	■	▒	▒ ?			■
Compensation finance						▒
Voluntary consumer initiatives						
Fairtrade	▒	■	■	■	▒	▒
Organic				■	■	■
MSC			■	■	■	▒
Voluntary producer initiatives						
CSR		▒		■	▒	▒
Global Compact		▒	▒	■	▒	■
Sector initiatives (MMSD)		▒		■	▒	▒
Equator Principles		▒		▒	▒	▒

Key:

■ Initiative explicitly sets out to and achieves objective
▒ Achieved in a limited way or only indirectly
(blank) Objective not achieved

Note: MSC is a joint producer/consumer initiative.
Source: Review of initiatives above

Regulated initiatives

All but one of the regulated initiatives managed to achieve market stability to some extent and therefore indirectly promote development. Only commodity agreements were assessed to be able to tackle the 'commodity trap' directly, and were therefore the only initiatives that could have been considered to have achieved any of the environmental objectives. However, the viability of commodity agreements is highly questionable and dependent on the economics of each particular commodity as well as the political will and trust among the participating countries to maintain prices at sustainable levels. Compensation finance did not achieve any of the objectives as set. Whilst it is hard to argue against assistance to the most vulnerable countries at times of commodity price shocks, finance as it is presently being provided may well actually be acting as a barrier to more long-term solutions. Its use should therefore be considered only where it is essential.

Voluntary initiatives

Overall, voluntary consumer initiatives performed well against the objectives, although organic-type initiatives failed to provide any of the social objectives, including tackling the 'commodity trap'. The MSC initiative also performed very well in many areas, although it failed to provide the more social objectives of stabilizing prices and promoting development. There is also some uncertainty associated with the ability of fair trade initiatives to promote macro-development or a wider sustainable commodity system, although it is likely to make a significant contribution towards the achievement of the Millennium Development Goals within participating communities. There is, however, some scepticism expressed within the literature whether such initiatives might in fact be holding back the kind of community-empowered development required for such communities to become self-sufficient. The literature also suggests that fair trade initiatives might in fact be destabilizing the uncertified commodity market. As for the explicitly producer-led initiatives, it is less easy to ascertain their direct market influence. Sectoral initiatives such as MMSD and the Equator Principles, businesses' involvement with the Global Compact and CSR more generally should perhaps be considered more in terms of the way they have affected the overall context for business activity.

A key issue in relation to Table 14.2 is the strength of consumers' preferences in relation to social and environmental values. If consumers desire sustainable commodity production, then consumers will be willing to pay a premium to achieve it and this premium will reflect their commitment to sustainable commodity production. Consumers may also want to know that their attempts to promote sustainable commodity production through a certified, segmented market are not having a detrimental impact on the non-certified producers. Also, many consumers will desire to achieve the objectives of a more sustainable commodity production in a cost-efficient way. Voluntary initiatives, and particularly voluntary consumer initiatives, therefore have limited potential for providing a more comprehensive sustainable commodity producing system, not least because the consumer surpluses associated with such objectives are prone to capture by suppliers and retailers so that they do not reach the producers who are their intended beneficiaries.

Designing a more effective mechanism for sustainable commodity production

From the discussion above, it is possible to identify the main characteristics of a mechanism that would promote the sustainable production of traded commodities. It is clear that the objectives of supply and price stability behind previous commodity agreements are still important. There is also a number of sustainable development challenges (such as environmental protection, sustainable resource management and development) that previous commodity agreements largely failed to tackle directly, but which would need to be dealt with better for commodity trade to be sustainable.

Any solution would need to be economically and politically viable. Arrangements would need to be acceptable to all producing and consuming countries, independent of any particular government, and include appropriate compensation to enable poorer countries to meet stricter environmental standards. Some of the government backed initiatives discussed above provide a form of impact mitigation and compensation, which might form part of a compensation package.

The general presumption of non-intervention in trade, and the mixed history of such intervention, might be thought to militate against any new institutional arrangements of this kind. However, it is possible that the 2007–08 crisis in the financial sector may have changed perceptions about the need for intervention in global markets. In addition, global concern with climate change has led, in a relatively short space of time, to the establishment of a whole new trading system in carbon, which, through the Clean Development Mechanism of the Kyoto Protocol, envisages very large transfers of funds to developing countries to enable them to shift to a less carbon-intensive form of development. The kinds of proposals described below would be far simpler, and cheaper, to implement and operate. Their introduction only requires an increase in global concern about the sustainable development impacts of commodity production similar to what has occurred with climate change. Such an increase is not inconceivable in the current climate of scientific anxiety about human impacts on environmental systems in general.

International Commodity-Related Environmental Agreements

Kox (1993, 1998) proposed International Commodity-Related Environmental Agreements (ICREAs) in order to regulate trade-related environmental issues with respect to primary commodities. ICREAs require producer and consumer countries to agree on measures to make the production of specific commodities for export (more) sustainable. A key issue explored by Kox when developing the ICREA was whether side payments or compensation were necessary. He explored the potential of using standards and norms in the absence of side payments, standards and norms combined with trade preferences or side payments via levies on imports or producer cartels. Kox concluded that some form of side payment from the importing country to the producer was both necessary and appropriate and concluded that a fund from import levies was the best payment mechanism. The proposed mechanism consisted of a fund that producer countries could draw upon in order to implement environmental measures that would otherwise not be possible. The fund was allocated to countries based on levels of production or environmental need, but remained separate and independent from producer governments. Kox argued that the fund may only need to be transitional as the adoption of new technologies would in time become the norm, and the price would accommodate the higher cost of production.

A new generation of sustainable commodity agreements (SCAs)

Kox's ICREAs could provide a useful foundation for a new generation of sustainable commodity agreements. If implemented in a non-discriminatory way as part of an international agreement they should be consistent with trade disciplines as set out in GATT (1994). They should also be a cost-effective mechanism as they are less prone to rent capture further down the product chain. Moreover, they could be linked to certification schemes (for example, MSC or FSC), such that only non-certified imports paid the levy, the funds from which were available to non-certified producers to achieve certification.

However, as proposed by Kox ICREAs do not tackle the wider sustainability challenges related to commodity production, which could be addressed by extending the principle of ICREAs to non-environmental issues. Moreover, SCAs could be set up such that private bodies including international corporations were able to compete for funds and win contracts to provide services (perhaps to smaller non-international companies) that lead to the achievement of a more sustainable commodity production. This should provide companies with a way of achieving their CSR goals whilst maintaining their competitiveness, as well as perhaps providing a cheaper way of achieving the sustainable development services. Such services and projects might include:

- **environmental** technological deployment as already described by Kox (1993);
- **social and development** projects associated with producer communities, which would not be possible without external funding;
- **one-off compensation funds** for capacity reduction in conjunction with sustainable resource and stock management initiatives (see for example MSC and fisheries);
- **research effort and marketing advice** in order to provide producers with information and share best practice;
- **supply and price management services** contracted by a buffer-stock type manager.

Although the supply management services such as storage capacity would typically be directly funded and independently managed by the fund's secretariat, there is no reason why fund managers could not outsource at least some of the buffer-stock services, as long as overall it remained in their control. This may well generate innovative supply management solutions throughout the commodity chain including better utilization of existing infrastructure and the increase in supply/demand flexibility. Such a decentralization of supply management services may provide greater long-term resilience in the system than the large-scale storage capacity typically used in buffer stock systems.

SCAs as proposed do not compromise the existence of voluntary consumer initiatives or certification schemes, such as MSC or FSC, or organic and fair trade. Indeed, these schemes could become the criteria that would provide exemption from the levy. Companies that have implemented voluntary producer initiatives would probably find it relatively easy to obtain certification for their production and therefore avoid the levy.

Table 14.3 *Mechanisms to promote sustainable commodity production and the arguments against trade liberalization*

	Responses to sustainable development challenges of commodity production									
	Government-backed initiatives				*Consumer initiatives*		*Producer initiatives*		*Proposed initiatives*	
	Commodity agreements	*Market-based initiatives*	*Marketing boards*	*Compensation finance*	*Fairtrade initiatives*	*Organic (verified) initiatives*	*Marine Stewardship Council*	*CSR motivated initiatives*	*ICREAs*	*SCAs*
1. Protectionist bias	+	+	+	+	+	+	+	++	+	+
2. Adjustment cost	+	+	+	++/–	++/–	.	.	++	++/–	++/+++
3. Externality	+	+	+	+/-	++	++	++	++	++/*	++/+++/*
4. Collective preferences	*	*	*	*	++	++	++	.	++/*	++/+++/*

Key:

+++	Mechanism directly addresses contextual reality and is not limited in scope
++	Mechanism directly addresses contextual reality to some extent
+	Mechanism only indirectly addresses contextual reality
–	Mechanism has the potential for negative impact on the contextual reality
*	Mechanism potentially provides a means of compensation
.	Mechanism does not address contextual reality

Source: Authors

There would need to be considerable assessment of the likely impacts of an SCA, and how it would be implemented, prior to its introduction. The models presently used within SIAs are well suited to study the implications of introducing an SCA, so that this could become an important additional part of SIAs as and when SCAs were introduced.

Revisiting the arguments against commodity trade liberalization

The question now arises as to whether the various initiatives discussed above to respond to the sustainable development impacts of commodity production can address the different motives and arguments to resist trade liberalization discussed in Chapter 4. Table 14.3 considers this in the table format proposed in Voituriez et al (2006).

Adjustment and externality arguments

Government backed methods. Neither adjustment capacity nor externalities are tackled directly by commodity agreements, market-based initiatives or marketing boards. However, they may provide a more stable environment for producers to operate in. Compensation initiatives do set out to provide support for adjustment to price instabilities that result from trade liberalization, but do not directly address externalities. There is, however, considerable doubt expressed within the international institutions themselves as to whether such finance in fact hampers long-term adjustments and might lead to further price instability. It might also have a positive or negative effect on externalities.

Consumer initiatives. Both fair trade and organic initiatives manage to address the issue of externalities in commodity production. However, they are limited by the voluntary nature of the initiatives. Organic initiatives would be unlikely to facilitate adjustment to trade liberalization and although fair trade initiatives help protect producers from free market pressures, they may also introduce vulnerability through excess supply in the certified market.

Producer initiatives. All of the initiatives that are motivated by CSR (UN's Global Compact, MMSD and the Equator Principles) have the potential to help with the social adjustments required after trade liberalizations, as well as tacking the externalities within the scope of the companies' operations.

The MSC (and FSC) initiative can be seen as a hybrid of all three types of method as it is essentially a voluntary producer-led commodity agreement that requires the support of consumers. While MSC manages to tackle the externality argument on a voluntary basis, it does not provide any adjustment capacity in the event of trade liberalization.

Collective preferences and protectionist bias arguments

Collective preferences. The initiatives led by consumers and producers may meet consumers' sustainable development preferences. However, in their present voluntary form, they could not express majority-held collective preferences because of their vulnerability to free riding. Any method that seeks to give expression to collective preferences will probably need to be backed up by some form of government regulation or other policy instrument.

Protectionist bias. As part of their CSR strategy, businesses might also refrain from lobbying for market protection motivated by their narrow interests, in favour of the longer term benefits of being perceived as a responsible business. None of the other methods have the capacity to motivate businesses in this way, though they may indirectly reduce disguised protectionism by addressing some of the other arguments against trade liberalization that lobbyists might otherwise employ.

ICREAs perform as well as or better than all the other mechanisms except for CSR initiatives in respect of protectionist bias, because only the producer-led CSR-oriented initiatives can respond to producer motivations of this kind. SCAs, as shown in Table 14.3, may be even more positive still. The degree to which SCAs would address adjustment costs, externalities and collective preferences would depend on how they are implemented. If SCAs were to be adopted by a significant proportion of producers and/or consumer countries, they would not be limited in their scope and could be assessed as the maximum, '+++', in which case they might be considered to reflect universal collective preferences. If, however, they are less widely agreed, then they could only be assessed to tackle these issues 'to some extent', and therefore be awarded a '++' assessment, as with many of the existing methods. They would still, however, be more effective than many of the voluntary initiatives as they could include all the commodity trade in different sectors within the scope of the agreeing countries.

Conclusion

Commodity production has considerable potentially negative implications for sustainable development, especially in respect of its environmental dimension, as a number of SIAs have made clear. Because these negative implications may be amplified by trade liberalization, and because trade negotiations have to date failed to propose credible ways of mitigating them, commodity production, especially in relation to agriculture, has been problematic in trade negotiations.

Governments, business and civil society have all introduced mechanisms to address the negative impacts of commodity production and trade, but so far these have been of only limited effectiveness in addressing the issues towards which they are directed. Building on earlier work by Kox, this chapter has proposed a new generation of SCAs, the principal feature of which is a levy on commodity imports that would generate a fund that could be used to make commodity production and trade more sustainable, especially in developing countries. Analysis in this chapter has showed that SCAs could combine many of the advantages of other mechanisms, without some of their limitations.

The multilateral negotiating climate in respect of trade and commodities is not currently propitious towards the setting up of the major new institutions that would be required to implement a system of SCAs in respect of different commodities. However, experience with the climate issue has shown that such institutions can be established when the level of public and policy concern about an issue reaches a high enough level, and it may be that market failure in the financial sector will make it easier for failures in other markets to be addressed. Global climate policy has effectively established a new currency (carbon) and detailed institutional arrangements for approving and verifying projects resulting in reduced carbon emissions. Such arrangements are considerably more complex than the kinds of institutions that would be necessary to implement SCAs. Perhaps therefore the time will come when the global community decides that it is time to take the sustainable development implications of commodity production and trade seriously.

Notes

1 See http://fletcher.tufts.edu/multi/texts/BH538.txt.
2 It should be noted that pre-1995, an Appellate Body ruling needed to be unanimously adopted by the GATT general council. This would not have occurred for observations made during compliance rulings and so this therefore represents an indication of how GATT 1994 might be interpreted by future Appellate Body rulings rather than actual case law.
3 It is also worth noting that OPEC and De Beers have successfully intervened in the world oil and diamond markets for many years.
4 See www.fairtrade.org.uk/about_what_is_fairtrade.htm.
5 This was done using a comparative-cost based Heckscher–Ohlin model of trade and a static version of a standard new economic geography model.
6 The other notion of fairness behind the fair trade movement – an absolute prohibition of certain types of behaviour in production – was acknowledged but not tested within the paper.
7 See www.unglobalcompact.org/AboutTheGC/TheTenPrinciples/index.html for articulation of the ten principles.
8 As well as OECD countries not designated as High-Income, as defined by the World Bank Development Indicators Database. Projects in High-Income OECD countries are required to show compliance with only a subset of the Principles.
9 See www.equator-principles.com/principles.shtml for full details of the Ten Principles.

References

Bennett, M. and James, P. (eds) (2000) *The Green Bottom Line*, Greenleaf Publishing, Sheffield
Berkhout, F., Hertin, J., Azzone, G., Carlens, J., Drunen, M., Jasch, C., Noci, G., Olsthoorn, X., Tyteca, D., Van Der Woerd, F., Wagner, M., Wehrmeyer, W. and Wolf, O. (2001) 'Measuring the environmental performance of industry (MEPI)', Final Report, SPRU, Science and Technology Policy Research, University of Sussex, Brighton, February, www.sussex.ac.uk/Units/spru/mepi/outputs/FinalReport.PDF
Defra (2005) 'Compendium of UK organic standards', Department for Environment, Food and Rural Affairs, www.defra.gov.uk/farm/organic/legislation-standards/compendium-july05.pdf

DMPR (2002) 'Mining, minerals and sustainable development (MMSD)', Executive Summary – comments, Australian Department of Mineral and Petroleum Resources, 17 April, www.poptel.org.uk/iied/mmsd/mmsd_pdfs/comments_carr.pdf

EC (2004) 'Developing countries: Commission adopts action plan to help developing countries fight agricultural commodity dependency and support the development of the cotton sector in Africa', European Commission, Brussels, 12 February, http://ec.europa.eu/trade/issues/global/development/pr120204_en.htm

ECA (2003) Session IV: 'Minimizing the impact of commodity shocks in Africa for debt sustainability', an Issues Paper (Session IV) 17–18 November, prepared by the Economic and Social Policy Division of the Economic Commission for Africa, www.uneca.org/debtforum/Commodityshocks%2003-12-03.pdf

ECF and CAOBISCO (2006) Comments by the European Coffee Federation and the Association of the Chocolate Biscuits & Confectionery Industry of the EU on the EP Draft on Fair Trade and Development (2005/2245 of 4.6.2006)

EP (2006) 'Why is a European policy framework for Fair Trade needed?', Explanatory Statement, Draft Report on Fair Trade and Development (2005/2245(INI)) Committee on Development, European Parliament, www.europarl.europa.eu/sides/getDoc.do?pubRef=-//EP//NONSGML+REPORT+A6-2006-0207+0+DOC+PDF+V0//EN, accessed 7 August 2008

EU (2001) 'Council Regulation no.2092/91 on organic production', European Union, Brussels, www.organic-europe.net/europe_eu/eu-regulation-2092-91.asp, accessed 13 August 2008

FLO (2005) 'Generic fairtrade standards for small farmers' organisations', Fairtrade Labelling Organizations International, December, www.fairtrade.net/sites/standards/sp.html

FOEI (2001) 'The citizens' guide to trade, environment and sustainability: Trade case study: Beef–hormone dispute', copyright Friends of the Earth, EWNI, 2001, last updated 24 January 2001, www.foei.org/trade/activistguide/hormone.htm

GATT (1994) *The Uruguay Round Agreements*, WTO, Geneva, www.wto.org/english/docs_e/legal_e/legal_e.htm, accessed 13 August 2008

Gilbert, C. (1995) 'International commodity control: Retrospect and prospect', Policy Research Working Paper 1545, International Economics Department Commodity Policy and Analysis Unit, November, The World Bank, Washington DC

Greenpeace (2004) 'Critique of marine stewardship council labelling scheme', Part of Greenpeace's Submission to the Royal Commission on Environmental Pollution: Environmental Effects of Marine Fisheries, prepared by Matthew Gianni, www.rcep.org.uk/fisheries/p2evid/P2-index.htm

GRI (2002) *Sustainability Reporting Guidelines*, Global Reporting Initiative, Amsterdam, www.globalreporting.org/ReportingFramework/G3Guidelines/

Howes, R. (2000) 'Corporate environmental accounting: Accounting for environmentally sustainable profits', in S. Simon and J. Proops (eds) *Greening the Accounts*, Edward Elgar, Cheltenham, pp223–245

IMF (1999) 'Review of the compensatory and contingency financing facility (CCFF) and buffer stock financing facility (BSFF)', Preliminary Considerations, prepared by the Policy Development and Review Department, International Monetary Fund, in consultation with other departments, 9 December, www.imf.org/external/np/ccffbsff/review/index.htm, accessed 7 August 2008

International Institute for Environment and Development (IIED) and World Business Council for Sustainable Development (WBCSD) (2002) *Breaking New Ground: Mining, Minerals, and Sustainable Development*, MMSD Final Report, Earthscan, London

Knigge, M. (2005) 'Public participation in the EU's sustainability impact assessments of trade agreements', Paper presented at the EASY-ECO Manchester Conference 'Impact Assessment for a New Europe and Beyond', 15–17 June

Kox, H. (1993) 'International agreements to deal with environmental externalities of primary commodity exports: With emphasis on international commodity-related environmental agreements', in L. Isaksson and C. Moorcraft (eds) *Striking a Green Deal*, Environment and Development Resource Centre (EDRC), Brussels, pp39–50

Kox, H. (1998) 'International commodity-related agreements: A way to promote sustainable production of primary commodities', *Bridges*, vol 2, no 7, October, International Centre for Trade and Sustainable Development, Geneva, pp17–18

Lamy P. (2004) 'The emergence of collective preferences in international trade: Implications for regulating globalisation', speech by EU Trade Commissioner Pascal Lamy at the Conference 'Collective Preferences and Global Governance: What Future for the Multilateral Trading System', 15 September, Brussels, www.trade-info.cec.eu.int/doclib/docs/2004/september/tradoc_118929.pdf

Lamy, P. (2006) Speech at the Ministerial Segment – Panel on Biodiversity and Trade, Convention on Biological Diversity, 8th Meeting of the Conference of the Parties (Cop-8), www.wto.org/english/news_e/sppl_e/sppl22_e.htm

Maseland, R. and De Vaal, A. (2002) 'How fair is fair trade?', *De Economist*, vol 150, pp251–272, Kluwer Academic Publishers, Dordrecht, The Netherlands, www.springerlink.com/(xlsksi45sa2aki55cjow5245)/app/home/contribution.asp?referrer=parent&backto=issue,2,7;journal,15,389;linkingpublicationresults,1:100260,1

Mining, Minerals and Sustainable Development (MMSD) (2002) *Breaking New Ground: Mining, Minerals and Sustainable Development*, Earthscan, London

Moore, G. (2004) 'The fair trade movement: Parameters, issues and future research', *Journal of Business Ethics*, vol 53, pp73–86, Kluwer Academic Publishers. Dordrecht, The Netherlands, www.springerlink.com/(0u35vq55znn0g245iqoomwua)/app/home/contribution.asp?referrer=parent&backto=issue,8,21;journal,44,337;linkingpublicationresults,1:100281,1

MSC (2002) 'MSC principles and criteria for sustainable fishing', Marine Stewardship Council Executive, November, www.msc.org/html/content_463.htm

Ruggie, J. G. (2002) 'The theory and practice of learning networks: Corporate social responsibility and the Global Compact', *Journal of Corporate Citizenship*, vol 5, pp27–36, Greenleaf Publishing, Sheffield

Steg, L., Vlek, C., Feenstra, D., Gerbens, W., Karsten, L., Kok, R., Lindenberg, S., Maignan, I., Moll, H., Nonhebel, S., Uiterkamp, T.S., Sijtsma, F. and Witteloostuijn, A. (2001) 'Towards a comprehensive model of sustainable corporate performance', Interim Report (revised), May, University of Groningen, The Netherlands

Sustainability Institute (2003), 'Commodity systems challenges: Moving sustainability into the mainstream of natural resource economies', Report, April, http://sustainer.org/pubs/SustainableCommoditySys.2.1.pdf

UNCTAD (2004) 'Development and globalization: Facts and figures', United Nations Conference on Trade and Development, New York and Geneva, www.unctad.org/Templates/webflyer.asp?docid=4848&intItemID=2364&lang=1&mode=downloads

UNGC (United Nations Global Compact) (2006) 'Global compact: Note on integrity measures', www.unglobalcompact.org/AboutTheGC/index.html, accessed 3 May 2006

UNGC (United Nations Global Compact) (2007) 'UN Global Compact Annual Review, 2007 Leaders Summit', UN Global Compact Office, United Nations, New York

Van Groenendaal, W. and Vingerhoets, J. (1995) 'Can international commodity agreements work?', *Journal of Policy Modeling*, vol 17, no 3, pp257–278, http://ideas.repec.org/a/eee/jpolmo/v17y1995i3p257-278.html, accessed 7 August 2008

Voituriez, T., Ekins, P., Blanco, H., Von Homeyer, I. and Scheer, D. (2006) 'Making trade sustainable impact assessment more relevant to trade negotiations', *Impact Assessment and Project Appraisal*, vol 24, no 4, December

Webb, A. (2006) 'How fair is Fairtrade?: More and more of us are prepared to pay extra to buy Fairtrade products, but is it really money well spent?', BBC *Money Programme*, 10 March, http://news.bbc.co.uk/1/hi/business/4788662.stm

Williams, O. F. (2004) 'The UN Global Compact: The challenge and the promise', *Business Ethics Quarterly*, vol 14, issue 4, pp755–774, http://ethicalbusiness.nd.edu/documents/Global%20Compact%20Article_final.pdf

WTO (2001a) Ministerial Declaration, adopted 14 November, Fourth Session of the Doha Ministerial Conference, 20 November, www.wto.org/english/thewto_e/minist_e/min01_e/mindecl_e.pdf

WTO (2001b) 'European Communities: Measures affecting asbestos and asbestos-containing products', Report of the Appellate Body WT/DS135/AB/R, 12 March, http://hesa.etui-rehs.org/uk/dossiers/files/Wto-appellatebody-report.pdf#search='WT/DS135/AB/R'

WTO (2004) 'Trade and environment at the World Trade Organisation: WTO's perspective on trade and the environment', WTO / (GATT), April, www.eldis.org/static/DOC15524.htm

15
The Trade and Environment Relationships Reconsidered: The Case of Regional Trade and Climate Change

Tancrède Voituriez

Introduction

The debates over the consequences of trade liberalization on the environment have been steadily growing throughout the 1990s, crystallizing over the identification of economic channels whereby trade effects are passed on to the environment, and over the appropriate institutional vehicles to make trade more sustainable. Outstanding academic researches provided clear-cut insights on the hypothesis upon which trade liberalization effects on the environment could be predicted to turn positive or negative. What has emerged from this body of literature is that no systematic effect could be predictable, and that the environmental impacts of trade eventually remained an empirical question.

In spite of this consensual finding, the trade and environment debate has regained momentum over the last couple of years, for at least three reasons. First, trade issues have taken up the lead in climate change debates, with flourishing contributions on food miles, and on the potential benefits, in carbon emission abatement terms, of short distance trade. Secondly, different carbon prices across Kyoto Climate Change Protocol signers and non-signers have raised the issue of competitiveness, particularly so in the European Union (EU) where the use of a 'carbon import tax' to restore the competitiveness of EU Emission Trading Scheme (EU ETS) constrained firms is now contemplated by some countries. Conversely, the environment is taking a high profile in trade talks once again, with a looming and already contested EU initiative on certified timber imports and more broadly with the ballooning issue of process and production methods (PPM) criteria to discriminate between 'clean' and 'dirty' imports. Thirdly, World Trade Organization (WTO) talks are stuck in the sand, and the skyrocketing number of regional trade agreements (RTAs) with heterogeneous environmental contents raise fundamental questions about the continuing validity of the empirical evidence on the trade and environment relationships, established almost exclusively with 1980s' and early 1990s' data – that is, within an outdated structure of markets and multilateral institutions.

The question we aim to address in this chapter is to what extent regional trade and RTAs modify the way we used to think about the trade and environment relationships, with a particular emphasis on carbon emissions.

To start with, we make a brief description of the analytical framework formalized in the early 2000s by international trade economists on the basis of researches developed throughout the 1980s and 1990s. In this first section, we wrap up the determining factors of environmental impacts that were then identified, as well as the main empirical evidence collected. Potential limitations of this international economics framework when contemplating recent developments in regional trade are described. The second section focuses on carbon emissions and the so-called carbon footprint at regional level, while the policy implications for members or potential members of RTAs are dwelt upon in the third section, before a conclusion.

The economic analysis of the environmental consequences of trade liberalization

The harsh debate between environmentalists and the trade policy community fuelled by the North American Free Trade Agreement (NAFTA) and General Agreement on Tariffs and Trade (GATT) negotiations in the 1990s crystallized around two antagonistic positions.[1] On the one hand, many from the 'deep green' environmental movement asserted that unfettered access to world markets was necessarily harmful to the environment because of trade-induced greater scale of economic activity. On the other hand, international trade economists underlined the positive environmental effect international trade could have thanks to income growth and higher willingness to pay for environmental protection, worrying at the same time that protectionism in the guise of environmental policy could obstruct efforts to open markets and integrate economies around the world.[2] Both views quickly appeared to be too simplistic. Other factors than trade, particularly innovation and capital accumulation, generate growth, and hence trade should not be blamed for all the environmental damages generated by output growth. On the other side of the argument, it was clear that political concerns about competitiveness could outweigh hypothetical increases in the willingness to pay for environmental protection, and prevent them from being translated into effective environmental policy.

In a further attempt to disentangle the complex links between trade and the environment, economists have developed and refined a conceptual framework in order to reconcile, or at least to create a dialogue between, 'deep greens' and 'free traders'.[3] In this framework, three channels through which trade is likely to have an impact on the environment are identified.[4] The first is the level or *scale* of economic activity. All else equal, and in particular the available technology and its distribution across sectors, the scale effect necessarily lowers environmental quality. The second channel is the change in economic activity caused by trade. Some countries may specialize in dirty productions and exports because of comparative advantages in those sectors. A change in the *composition* of their output can hence raise pollution, all else equal. Conversely, comparative advantages can lead a country to specialize in clean goods. In such a case the composition effect turns out to be positive. Contrary to the scale effect, no systematic sign is attached to the environmental consequences of liberalized trade related to changes in the composition of output. Last, changes in environmental regulation induced by income growth and higher environmental concerns in public opinion and among taxpayers are assumed to lower the dirtiness of production techniques for a so-called *technique* effect.

The 'all else equal' condition being invalidated in real world economies where the three effects occur in the same time, the uncertainty over the full environmental impact of trade has left many debates unresolved. In particular, the 'race to the bottom' or 'pollution haven' hypothesis, according to which dirty industries would leave tightly regulated countries and migrate to countries with lax regulations, found neither confirmation nor invalidation within the theoretical framework described above. Indeed, if developed and less developed countries differ in the stringency of their environmental regulations, they also differ widely in education levels, infrastructure and capital endowments, which are all determinants of production costs and ultimately of trade flows. The source of cost advantage does not lie in lax regulation alone. The root causes of comparative advantages matter. The full environmental impact of trade liberalization can only be resolved through careful empirical investigation (Copeland and Taylor, 2003).

In the most widely cited analysis – the case of concentrations of sulphur dioxide in air in over 100 major cities in the world – the above framework delineating scale, composition and technique effects of trade was confronted with empirical data.[5] Trade liberalization is defined as a gradual reduction in trade frictions (trade barriers, communication and logistical costs, shipment costs) that move domestic prices closer to world prices. The separation is further made between the impact of economic growth on the environment, modelled in either changes in technologies or endowments, and that caused by trade liberalization alone. We summarize below the main findings of this influential study as well as of converging research results, from general down to specific.[6]

Finding 1: While trade liberalization creates environmental impacts of no systematic sign across countries, capital accumulation favours the production of capital-intensive dirty goods, and hence creates an additional negative scale effect.

Finding 2: While economic growth fuelled by capital accumulation is likely to raise pollution levels, growth fuelled by technological progress will lower it.

Finding 3: The relative strength of scale versus technique effects depends on how government policy is formed and how quickly it changes in response to new conditions.

Finding 4: Even in a world where policy is flexible and responsive to trade-created income gains, the impact of freer trade still depends on the sources of a country's comparative advantages.

Finding 5: Among the potential sources of comparative advantages, conventional determinants of production costs – and particularly factor endowments – are empirically more important than are differences in environmental regulations. In short, human and physical capital as well as technology endowments in developed economies seem to more than outweigh developing countries' advantage stemming from less stringent regulation. Empirical evidence moreover shows that the share of production and exports coming from pollution-intensive products is growing in developing countries and falling in developed economies. Yet the largest producers of dirty pollution intensive goods remain OECD (Organisation for Economic Co-operation and Development) countries due to comparative advantages in capital intensive goods.[7] In the case of CO_2 emissions, and in spite of climate change mitigation policies such as the EU ETS, the EU and US export mixes contain a higher percentage of high carbon-intensity goods than the export mixes of China and developing countries (Delgado, 2007). And carbon emitting industry leakages toward countries not constrained by the Kyoto Protocol, though an obvious and potential threat for the global efficiency of the EU ETS, have still to be empirically assessed.[8] The empirical evidence for and against the pollution haven hypothesis thus remains limited.

Finding 6: Empirical evidence suggests that relatively rich developed countries have a comparative advantage in capital-intensive goods, and hence in dirty goods (labour-intensive goods are assumed to be 'cleaner' than capital-intensive ones). Freer trade shifts capital (dirty) goods production from labour well-endowed South to capital well-endowed North, meaning from lax-regulation countries to more stringent-regulation countries. Provided that such a result can be generalized to non-SO_2 cases, the global composition effect would hence lower pollution overall.

Finding 7: Combining estimates of scale, composition and technique effects created by trade liberalization leads to the conclusion – in the case of SO_2 at least – that freer trade is good for the environment.

All the above findings are not specific either to bilateral or multilateral trade. Still, cross-country econometric analysis upon which they are based basically takes into account different levels of pollution, trade openness and regulation across the widest range of countries. This makes such a framework identifiable with multilateral trade.

Are trade and environment linkages affected by the regional pattern of trade?

Regionalism is described in the Dictionary of Trade Policy Terms, as 'actions by governments to liberalize or facilitate trade on a regional basis, sometimes through free-trade areas or customs unions'. In the WTO context, RTAs may be agreements concluded between countries not necessarily belonging to the same geographical region.[9] Some 380 RTAs had been notified to the GATT/WTO up to July 2007 (Figure 15.1). Of these, 300 RTAs were notified under Article XXIV of the GATT 1947 or GATT 1994; 22 under the Enabling Clause; and 58 under Article V of the General Agreement on Trade in Services (GATS). At that same date, 205 agreements were in force. When taking into account RTAs that are in force but have not been notified, those signed but not yet in force, those currently being negotiated, and those in the proposal stage, we arrive at a figure of close to 400 RTAs that are scheduled to be implemented by 2010. Of these RTAs, free trade agreements (FTAs) and partial scope agreements account for over 90 per cent, while customs unions account for less than 10 per cent.[10]

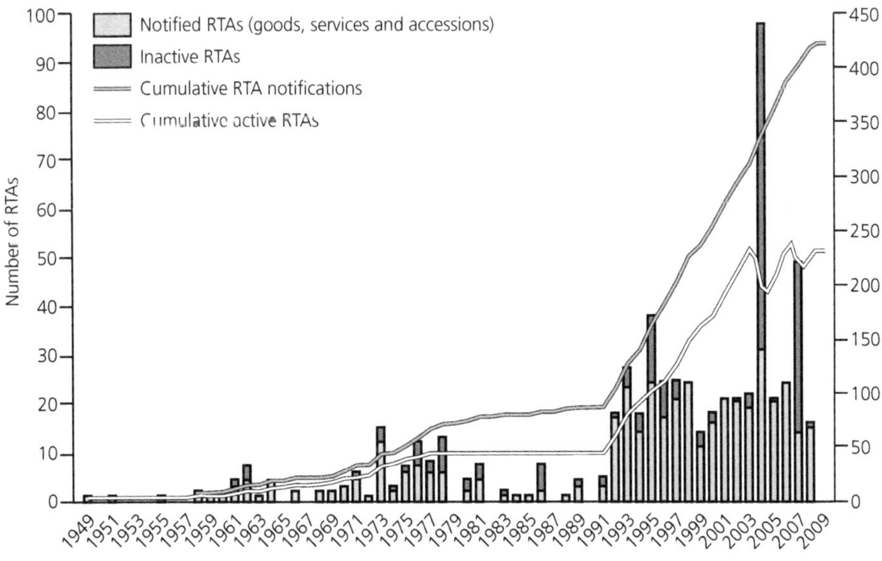

Source: WTO Secretariat, http://www.wto.org/english/tratop_e/region_e/regfac_e.htm

Figure 15.1 *Regional Trade Agreements notified to the GATT/WTO by date of entry into force*

Our literature review shows that the trade and environment linkages have not been conceptualized specifically in the case of regional trade and have been almost exclusively explored at the regional level from an institutional perspective.[11] A notable exception can be found in Ghosh and Yamarik (2007) whose modelling combines and connects RTAs, trade, growth and the environment, and tests for the existence of trade-induced economic growth and a Kuznets curve. However, their model does not explore regional-trade-specific channels of environmental impacts. The question as to whether potential changes in the 'Copeland and Taylor' trade and environment relationships described above could arise from regional trade and RTAs is hence left open.

To start to answer it, at least intuitively, let's recall first that in the Copeland–Taylor international economics framework of analysis, comparative advantages based on factor endowment were key determinants of trade flows in 'dirty' and 'clean' goods, and of the overall net environmental impact of trade. Restricting to industrial pollution, assuming that capital-intensive goods are 'dirtier' than labour-intensive goods as they do, we can define four hypothetical cases of RTAs, and derive for each a first set of implications on the trade and environment relationship at regional level.

North–South RTAs with poor South countries

The RTA with, in the Copeland–Taylor framework, the most predictable effects on the environment would be a North–South RTA with a rich, capital-intensive country trading with labour-intensive developing countries. This is the case for instance with EU Economic Partnership Agreements or US CAFTA (Free Trade Agreement with Central American States). Discrepancy in factor endowments is expected to bolster trade and shift capital (dirty) goods production from labour-abundant South to capital-abundant North where regulations are more stringent. As in the multilateral case, the competition from developed country exports of pollution-intensive goods should hinder developing countries' specialization in pollution-intensive goods, for an overall positive environmental impact.

North–South RTAs with emerging rich South countries

North–South RTAs including at least one emerging country could modify this straightforward analogy with freer multilateral trade. Assuming that emerging countries specialize in labour-intensive goods turns out to be erroneous in this case. Analysis of the composition of the exports of emerging countries such as China shows that their export basket is significantly more sophisticated than what would normally be expected for a country at a comparable level of income (Rodrik, 2006). Rodrik (2006) further demonstrated that what mattered for China's future growth was not the volume of its labour-intensive, mass-products exports, but whether China would continue to latch on to higher-income products over time as it did over the last decade. Consequently, no predictable composition effect such as those occurring in the labour-intensive scenario can be associated with China's exports at this stage – and very likely, with any RTA involving an emerging country – on the basis of its current export mix.

South rich – South poor RTAs

An even less straightforward case can be found in RTAs involving a rich developing country and low-income economies, such as the ASEAN Free Tradae Area (AFTA)–China, Southern Africa Development Community (SADC), or Mercosur trade agreements. Around 70 per cent of tariffs faced by developing countries are levied by other developing countries. First, the reduction of such tariffs thanks to South–South RTAs should in all likelihood foster trade and magnify the negative scale effect – this is indeed one of the core factual arguments supporting the trade-creation hypothesis of RTAs, when compared with the 'trade diversion' alternative hypothesis that has received, so far, much less empirical support. Secondly, if factor endowment remains a key driver of trade between, in this case, capital-abundant emerging countries and labour-abundant low-income countries, then the shift in dirty good production from the poor to richer developing countries may be less systematically accompanied by tighter regulation than in the multilateral scenario. Because policy response in relatively rich countries is quite income elastic, it was deemed possible in the multilateral freer trade case that pollution would fall in both the developed and the developing world. To what extent the policy response in rich developing countries is also income elastic so that environmental regulation would be tight enough to create a beneficial technique effect is an open question. The discrepancy between Beijing official targets set to protect the environment and the poor level of implementation by local officials who generally ignore them, preferring to concentrate on further advancing economic growth, has been repeatedly emphasized over recent years (Economy, 2007). Further, the pressure for tighter environmental regulation in countries such as China, conveyed by rich countries' public opinion, non-governmental organizations (NGOs), governments and even firms, could be much lower in the case of South–South RTAs, enabling policy makers to postpone the policy reforms needed to tackle the environmental damages associated with freer trade.

South poor – South poor RTAs

Then come RTAs among poor countries with relatively homogenous factor endowments such as the regional African unions, integrating labour-abundant countries with a budding manufacturing sector. The international economics framework of analysis does not help much in this case. Manufacture is not the most prominent source of pollution, when compared with natural resource extraction industries. A particular aspect of the pollution from natural resource industries lies in the difficulty, and costs, to establish and maintain property rights, and to control the extraction. As stressed by Taylor (2004), resource-abundant countries have both weak regulation and a cost advantage in these industries. The composition effect may hence be potentially damaging. This distinction actually applies for the four types of RTAs and maybe more prominently in the case of RTAs with a core emerging country tapping the natural resources of the poor countries at the periphery (South rich – South poor RTAs above).

These four types of RTAs provide as a first guess a rather negative picture of the trade and environment relationship at regional level. Such a relationship could be left unchanged in the case of North–South RTAs when compared with the multilateral case, should we set aside emerging countries as part of the South. But in all other cases, some possible negative effects, or uncertain effects at best, seem more likely to be either triggered or reinforced. The high South–South tariff level means a potentially huge scale effect. A shift toward natural resources exports in the poor South and a shift toward capital-intensive goods in the rich South could make the composition effect turn negative. Last, collective preferences for development and growth more than for the environment per se, in addition to non-systematic policy responses toward greener policy, may altogether dampen, not to say cancel, the positive technique effects underscored in the Copeland–Taylor multilateral case.

All these tentative estimates suggest that it matters what kinds of countries are involved in RTAs when considering the environmental consequences of trade. We now explore some complementary drivers for change in the trade and environment relationship at regional level, namely value chain motives for specialization, transport environmental costs and heterogeneous policy responses to environmental damages at regional level. These were not – or not fully – taken into account in the Copeland–Taylor international economics framework.

Global value chains, transport, and environmental policy at regional level

Global value chains

Providing a different perspective to, and rationale for, international trade when compared with the classical factor endowment motive, global value chains (GVCs) are defined as networks of production, distribution and marketing of particular products or groups of products. During most of the 1990s, the main components of value chains were defined as comprising an input–output structure or configuration; a specific geography; and an internal governance structure (Gereffi and Korzeniewicz, 1994). The notion of 'internal governance structure' was elaborated in relation to the distinction between 'buyer-' and 'producer-driven' commodity chains, the consequence being that it is the nature of specific categories of lead agent that determine input–output structures and chain geographies, instead of the conventional factor-endowment explanation found in economic textbooks (Gibbon, 2003). Many GVC case studies deal with apparel, an exemplary 'buyer-driven' chain.[12]

More recently, GVC approaches to international trade have come across environmental issues. For instance, the question, 'Who owns China's carbon emissions', originally raised by Chinese officials claiming that China's greenhouse gas (GHG) emissions were partly triggered by international demand-driven value chains is now raised in both climate change and trade community debates. The allocation of responsibility for the CO_2 emissions associated with world trade is still under scrutiny, especially in the case of US–China trade. Shui and Harriss (2006) have demonstrated that CO_2 emissions associated with the growth of Chinese imports into the US economy amounted to more than 700 million metric tons between 1997 and 2003. Had the US firms manufactured the products imported from China, American emissions would have been 6 per cent higher, while China's emissions would have been 14 per cent lower had it not produced goods for the US. Other studies, with a different accounting methodology, estimate that Chinese exports, whose major part goes to the US and EU, accounted for 28 per cent of China's energy consumption, against 6 per cent and 7 per cent respectively in the case of EU and US exports. In total, exports from China account for as much as 34 per cent of China energy-related emissions. Wang and Watson (2007) conclude that in 2004 – the most recent year in which comprehensive data is available – net exports from China accounted for 23 per cent of its total CO_2 emissions. In the same vein, Peters and Hertwich (forthcoming) assessed the balance of emissions embodied in trade (BEET) for a number of countries, and concluded that China's BEET (embodied emissions in exports less embodied emissions in imports) was 585.5 $MtCO_2$, compared to the US BEET of –438.9 $MtCO_2$ (see Table 15.1).

In general, as Keijun and Cosbey (2008) comment, Annex B countries – those with Kyoto targets – were found to be net importers of CO_2 emissions. But as a percentage of production-based emissions, variations are considerable. The highest impacts were for small trade-intensive economies. Though these figures deserve further research to support the discussion, they suggest that the positive composition effect outlined in the SO_2-factor endowment case did not occur for GHG emissions, at least for those embedded in EU and US trade with an emerging country like China.

Table 15.1 *Balance of emissions embodied in trade for selected countries*

	Annex B			*Non-Annex B*	
	BEET $MtCO_2$	*BEET as a % of production-based emissions*		*BEET $MtCO_2$*	*BEET as a % of production-based emissions*
Switzerland	–63.1	–122.9%	Singapore	–62.8	–128.2%
Latvia	–4.6	–60.7%	South Korea	–45.4	–11.4%
UK	–102.7	–16.6%	Morocco	–2.5	–6.3%
Germany	–139.9	–15.7%	Mexico	–17.6	–4.5%
Japan	–197.0	–15.3%	Brazil	+2.5	+0.8%
United States	–438.9	–7.3%	India	+70.9	+6.9%
Canada	15.5	+2.8%	China	+585.5	+17.8%
Australia	57.9	+16.5%	Indonesia	+58.1	+19.0%
Russia	324.8	+21.6%	South Africa	+123.5	+38.2%

Source: Peters and Hertwich, forthcoming; see also Keijun and Cosbey (2008, p4)

Embeddedness is also of concern when accounting for the environmental consequences of various transport modes. The specific issue of the amount of carbon embedded in air exports from long-distance supplying countries, and particularly remote developing countries, has received considerable attention within the so called 'food miles' debate. For each of these two aspects of embeddedness, RTAs have the potential to both reduce the embedded carbon content of exports by shortening distances, and to provide the appropriate policy framework for a closer cooperation between a restricted number of countries, at a time when progress on multilateral talks, whether the stalled Doha Round or the post-2012 climate change agenda, is proving difficult to achieve. By lowering environmental transport costs and enhancing environmental cooperation, RTAs may have the potential to act as a counterweight to the likely negative scale, composition and technique effects derived from the restrictive application of the international economics framework outlined above. To what extent such a potential is real remains worth examining on a case-by-case basis.

Transport

Growth in freight transport volume is strongly correlated with growth in world gross domestic product (GDP). Shortening the distance between importing and exporting countries could reasonably reduce the carbon footprint of exchanged goods, all else equal. Still, from a pure environmental perspective – and specifically, having in mind GHG emissions – long-distance commercial transport is not the top polluter. CO_2 emissions from the transport sector account for 20 per cent of the global total, with about three quarters coming from road vehicles. Seaborne transport, whereby most goods are exchanged over long-distance trade, is one of the lowest pollution modes and a marginal contributor to GHG per ton kilometre (Table 15.2). Maritime transport is currently responsible for approximately 13 per cent of the world's total transport GHG emissions (European Environment Agency, 2008).

Projections foresee an emission growth of 35–45 per cent in absolute levels between 2001 and 2020, based on expectations of continued growth in world trade and providing that no actions are taken to limit emissions per ton-kilometre.[13] This remains below air freight and inland transport projections (European Environment Agency, 2008). Further, the complete lack of environ-

Table 15.2 *CO_2 emissions of various transport modes*

Mode of transport	*CO_2 emissions (g/tkm)*
Lorry (12t)	110
Lorry (24t)	92
Lorry (36t)	84
Maritime shipping	14
Train	23
Plane	607

Source: Eurostat (2003); UBA (2006); Ecoinvent (2007); data collected by Kraemer et al (2007)

mental regulation – pertaining specifically to energy efficiency – in international maritime transport leaves room to make seaborne transport even more energy efficient and the 'less bad mode' of transport well ahead of air freight and road vehicles on a ton-kilometre basis.

Counter-intuitively, regional trade could also lead to an increase in transport-induced GHG emissions if road freight transport were to substitute for long-distance maritime transport. Inland freight transport (road, rail and inland waterways) in the European Economic Area (EEA) member countries indeed increased by 30 per cent (2.7 per cent per annum), with the road freight segment witnessing the greatest percentage increase (38 per cent). In China, the International Energy Agency estimates that transport-sector oil use would increase from 115Mt per annum in 2005 to 442Mt in 2030, roughly the same as is projected for the EU at that time (International Energy Agency, 2007). This is a 5 per cent annual increase, double the expected demand growth for energy as a whole. Currently, the transport sector accounts for a relatively small share of China's total oil demand (33 per cent), compared with the global average of 50 per cent. Although such domestic growth cannot be systematically associated with trade, and regional trade in particular, it underlines the uncertain nature of a hypothesis of a reduction in long-distance freight transport 'all else equal'.

The case for a reduction through RTAs in air freight-induced environmental cost is more straightforward. The Stern Review reports that emissions from aviation have been rising faster than other sectors in recent years, largely as a result of global trade. Nowhere are these concerns expressed more vocally than in relation to tourism and air freight.[14] Currently aviation accounts for 2 per cent of global GHG emissions and this proportion could double by 2050. Yet it is difficult to discern the driver for expansion, particularly in respect of air freight. Estimates in the case of UK show for instance that while accounting for an estimated 14–18 per cent of global air freight, the overwhelming majority of export horticulture is transported in the bellyhold of passenger planes, not in dedicated freighters – hence the wide error margin in the assessment. In spite of the difficulty of accounting accurately for the role of air-freighted food and agricultural products in the rise of aviation emissions, 'food miles' have taken a high profile in cross-cutting debates about climate, trade and development. The climate change debate for instance identifies air-freighted fresh produce from sub-Saharan Africa as the epitome of unsustainable consumption. The case of UK supermarket imported green beans from Kenya has probably been the most publicized. A joint study by the International Institute for Environment and Development (IIED), the Department for International Development (DFID) and the Natural Resources Institute (NRI) showed that when the energy consumed in transporting green beans from Kenya to the UK by plane is included, the difference in energy consumption between the Kenya and the UK domestic supply chain becomes considerable. Goods air freighted from Kenya are responsible for 200 times more emissions or 12 times more energy than goods that are shipped from Kenya (MacGregor and Vorley, 2006). When considering transport emissions alone, the case for shorter-distance trade or seaborne trade is compelling. Transport by sea would almost completely cancel the estimated energy consumption premium.

More controversial have been the policy aspects of food miles. To avert the potentially detrimental and unfair consequences for African producers of food miles labelling on their product in UK supermarkets, researchers and NGOs have reconsidered – and rebalanced indeed – the overall carbon cost of fresh food produce in sub-Saharan Africa and UK, while stressing the right for countries to emit a certain amount of carbon for development objectives when their emissions per capita are spectacularly low.[15] Policy implications widely differ depending on whether 'food miles' or 'fair miles' are considered. 'Food miles' arguments will urge for prioritizing short-distance value chains and domestic market protection through labelling initiatives, while fair miles will underscore a more balanced approach and the need to weigh environmental and social impacts, and to improve market access without restricting to short distance trade. From the latter perspective, the carbon cost of air freight has even been identified as a new pretext for protectionism (MacGregor and Groom, 2007).

Policies

The limited number of countries involved in RTAs – when compared to multilateral trade agreements – and the diversity of integration options for trade-related issues such as labour and environment make RTAs a scrutinized vehicle for sustainable trade. The proliferation of RTAs in addition to rising environmental and social concerns over the consequences of trade liberalization has somehow shifted expectations over RTAs from the early 2000s on. The original question, asking whether RTAs were building blocks or stumbling blocks to the world trade system, is now progressively replaced by questions revolving around the coherence of RTAs' rules and provisions on trade-related issues, and their effectiveness in delivering on particular environmental or labour aspects of trade. Having in mind that in our typology of RTAs, policy responses and flexibility were crucial determinants of the ultimate environmental impact of regional trade, to be empirically assessed in the particular case of emerging and developing countries, we examine the different modes of inclusion of environmental policy and commitments in RTAs, particularly when developing countries are involved.

We draw heavily upon a review undertaken by OECD on environment and regional agreements, which provides up-to-date insights on this issue (OECD, 2007). So far, the OECD study shows that, from an environmental point of view, the most ambitious agreements include a comprehensive environmental chapter, or are accompanied by an environmental side agreement, or both. At the other extreme are those agreements that deal with environmental issues only in the form of exception clauses to general trade obligations under the agreements. Between these two poles is a variety of more or less detailed handling of environmental issues. The most common environmental compo-

Box 15.1 Environmental provisions in North–South and South–South RTAs

North–South RTAs. The best-known example is the North American Free Trade Agreement (NAFTA), which includes detailed, legally binding environmental provisions, and has, in addition, a side agreement on environmental co-operation. All RTAs subsequently negotiated by the United States include environmental considerations both in environmental chapters and in separate instruments, focusing mainly on environmental co-operation. These agreements explicitly provide for an obligation by the Parties to effectively enforce their environmental laws, and include mechanisms to ensure enforcement of this commitment (e.g. dispute settlement and mechanisms for public submissions). They also provide for environmental co-operation between the Parties, and are accompanied by an environmental co-operation agreement or memorandum of understanding that establishes the framework for such co-operation. Under the Trade Act of 2002, the United States has a mandate by Congress to provide for detailed environmental chapters in all trade agreements, including certain binding obligations.

Within the Euro–Mediterranean Partnership, a wide framework of political, economic, and social relations between the Member States of the European Union and countries of the Southern Mediterranean region establish co-operation, aimed at preventing deterioration of the environment, controlling pollution, and ensuring the rational use of natural resources. The Partnership Agreement between the Members of the African, Caribbean, and Pacific group of States and the European Community (Cotonou Agreement) states that environmental co-operation should endeavour to mainstream environmental sustainability into all aspects of development co-operation, strengthen the scientific and technical human and institutional capacity for environmental management, and support specific measures and schemes aimed at addressing critical sustainable management.

There are also countries that do not consider the inclusion of environmental considerations in trade agreements to be a priority. An example, among OECD countries is Australia: while sustainable development and environmental protection is high on its agenda, it takes the view that environmental co-operation should generally be dealt with independently of trade negotiations.

South–South RTAs. Some RTAs which initially did not have an environmental chapter have evolved over time, and Parties have added on environmental commitments over the years, e.g. through a protocol to the agreement. Mercosur members, for example, adopted a Framework Agreement on Environment in 2001, ten years after the adoption of the main trade agreement. Parties to ASEAN have also gradually expanded co-operation on environmental matters. A few agreements also strive for harmonisation: under the Mercosur Framework Agreement on Environment, for example, Parties undertake to co-operate on the harmonisation of environmental standards. In Mercosur, environmental co-operation, detailed in the Framework Agreement on Environment, is defined quite broadly, not only addressing shared environmental problems related to trade, but also the sustainable management of natural resources, environmental planning, and environmental policy instruments.

The Common Market for Eastern and Southern Africa (COMESA) was established as an 'organisation of free independent sovereign states which have agreed to co-operate in developing their natural and human resources for the good of all their people.' As such it has a wide-ranging series of objectives, which necessarily include in its priorities the promotion of peace and security in the region. Its main focus is 'the formation of a large economic and trading unit that is capable of overcoming some of the barriers that are faced by individual states'. Other smaller regional integration agreements, such as the West African Economic and Monetary Union (WAEMU), also aim to co-ordinate sectoral policies, including policies related to the environment, though with less clear (or extensive) provisions or institutions.

Source: OECD (2007)

nent is an environmental cooperation mechanism. The areas of cooperation in different RTAs vary significantly, however, and depend on a range of factors, such as whether the trade partners have comparable levels of development or not (in which case, cooperation often focuses on capacity building), or whether they have common borders. Box 15.1 describes the various modes of environmental integration in RTAs depending on whether they are North–South or South–South RTAs.

Most RTAs reviewed deal with environment through environmental cooperation, and conceive environmental cooperation as capacity building with dedicated financial assistance. One example of an RTA including a pledge not to lower environmental standards in an effort to increase exports or to attract investment is the Trans-Pacific Strategic Economic Partnership, whose Parties agree that 'it is inappropriate to relax, or fail to enforce or administer, their environment laws and regulations to encourage trade and investment'. In some RTAs, parties pledge to raise or maintain high environmental standards. Under the North American Agreement on Environmental Cooperation, for example, Parties 'shall ensure that [their] laws and regulations provide for the highest levels of environmental protection and shall strive to continue to improve those laws and regulations'. In practice, however, it is very difficult to assess whether provisions aimed at raising environmental standards have been effective.

So far, the OECD report emphasizes, only a few trade agreements between developing countries or emerging economies include references to the environment. The main exceptions are RTAs including Chile, and Mercosur. It would be wrong to assume that including environmental considerations in trade agreements has become generally accepted or can even be taken for granted. On the contrary, negotiators have pointed out that it remains a challenge, first to convince their partners to accept the principle of including environmental issues at all in an RTA, and then to negotiate the details.

Further, while RTAs have contributed to better integration of trade and environment at bilateral and regional levels, this progress is not yet visible in the multilateral arena. Indeed, it is striking that a number of countries have been prepared to incorporate environmental provisions in RTAs, but are not prepared to countenance similar outcomes at the multilateral level. Last, with the current proliferation of RTAs, and the variety of environmental arrangements, some countries face an increasingly complex problem of managing various levels of environmental commitments and different types of environmental cooperation programmes under a range of RTAs. One example is Chile, which has entered into RTAs with a range of countries, including OECD members (Canada, Korea, Mexico, the US, New Zealand), the EU and developing countries (China, Colombia and Panama), all of which include at least some reference to the environment.

Globally, no clear-cut empirical evidence emerges on the effective commitment of developing countries toward enhancing environmental inclusion in RTAs. This said, the wide range of policy options and cooperation mechanisms at their disposal, along with the limited number of players, would seem to leave wider room for institutional innovation, targeting and flexibility in the making of accompanying policies when compared to the multilateral framework. Possible ways to use this policy space from an environmental and development perspective, so as to mitigate the likely negative scale, composition and technique effects possibly arising from RTAs are outlined in the last section.

Can RTAs be used as a lever for climate deals?

The trade and climate change nexus has been gaining momentum since 2005, under the increasingly convergent effort of the world community to craft the post-Kyoto and post-Doha agendas within a unified and global framework. Echoing the propositions of Stiglitz (2007) and Stern and Tubiana (2007) to instil extra-dimensionality in global deals by creating issue linkages between trade and climate change talks, international institutions, think tanks and NGOs have issued numerous reports and briefs on the subject, while official government-hosted workshops and conferences have multiplied.

The trade and climate change debate is now well established in the political arena. In Europe, propositions to tax imports from non-signers of the Kyoto Protocol have been discussed extensively within the European Commission (EC), with contrasted arguments and mixed support and opposition (Mandelson, 2006). President Sarkozy proposed to his Chinese counterpart during his official visit to Beijing on 27 November 2007 a New Deal for the climate, providing explicit support for a border tax adjustment (BTA) mechanism in Europe, while inviting China to become a proactive actor in the new global deal he was calling for. Should there be failure of UNFCCC (United Nations Framework Convention on Climate Change) talks on the definition of the post-2012 multilateral framework, the EU has cautiously envisaged resorting to border carbon adjustment (BCA) mechanisms for the post-2012 period to protect EU ETS constrained firms from import prices that do not reflect any cost of carbon, while sustaining unilateral efforts to further cut GHGs emissions within the EU by 2020 and 2050.

Debates inside and outside Europe over the post-Kyoto agenda have further highlighted that neither a unilateral commitment by the EU on GHG emission efforts, nor the accompanying measures envisaged such as a BTA or a BCA, would create the appropriate signal to gain other countries' support and make them join a global deal on climate change. This is particularly the case for emerging (so-called BIC) economies (see Box 15.2), which argue that the common and differentiated responsibility enshrined in UNFCCC allows them to postpone the setting of emission targets beyond 2050, while calling for an immediate increase in OECD market access for their 'clean products' (Brazilian biofuel for instance) and for improved technology transfer for energy-efficient goods (clean coal technology transfer to China for instance).

Against this background, the WTO official position remains that trade should be used as a carrot, not as a stick, contrary to the French BTA proposition. In a speech to the European Parliament in May 2008 the WTO Director-General Pascal Lamy asserted that:

> *the relationship between international trade, the WTO, and climate change, would be best defined by a consensual international accord on climate change... A multilateral agreement, that includes all major emitters, would be the best placed international instrument to guide other instruments, such as the WTO, as well as all economic actors on how negative environmental externalities must be internalized... Only such an accord could provide criteria for assessing when a measure at the country's border is environmentally sound... In the absence of such parameters, it will be hard, if not impossible, for the WTO to develop a coherent position on the matter. Each of its members will have a different interpretation to offer on how the playing field may best be levelled. And I would caution against such an outcome; the world could end up with a real spaghetti bowl of 'offsetting' measures that achieve neither trade nor environmental goals.* (Lamy, 2008)

Pascal Lamy's arguments cannot be disputed in a first-best policy perspective. But a reason why trade and climate have relentlessly come out as intertwined issues in climate and trade debates respectively stem from the mere fact that this first-best perspective might be unrealistic, and that non-multilateral trade and climate deals could actually replace the first-best solution Pascal Lamy delineated. Keeping in mind that a multilateral climate accord and a multilateral trade agreement altogether provide the first-best institutional framework to make trade and climate change policies mutually supportive, the second-best question is how to best use potentially inflating regional and bilateral deals or initiatives on both issues.

Focusing on the EU, some initiatives that are now being undertaken toward developing countries, and especially toward BIC countries, demonstrate the opportunities but also the limits of a bilateral approach to climate change. Hence the EU and Brazil met in their first-ever Summit in Lisbon on 4 July 2007 to launch a Strategic Partnership in a range of areas, including close cooperation on global challenges such as environmental issues (particularly climate change, forests, water management and biodiversity) and sustainable energy resources, as well as enhancing stability and prosperity in Latin America. Agreement was reached on an EU–Brazil Regular Energy Policy Dialogue, aiming at strengthening energy cooperation through bilateral action in the areas of biofuels and other renewable energy sources, low-carbon energy technologies and the improvement of energy efficiency. But in spite of all these efforts, the positions of the EU and Brazil in climate negotiations have not converged thus far.

This remains true in the case of India and China. Seven years before the first EU–Brazil summit, the EU and India launched the first EU–India summit.

Box 15.2 BIC (Brazil, India, China) countries and GHG emissions

When emissions from land use, land use change and forestry (LULUCF) are taken into consideration, Brazil is one of the top five producers of GHGs; and the country is unique in that three quarters of its emissions are due to deforestation (Osava, 2007). Brazil is also unique among the BICSAM (BIC plus South Africa and Mexico) nations in that 90 per cent of domestic electricity needs are met through hydropower generation (La Rovere et al, 2007, p78). Brazil lacks a national policy on climate change, but has adopted an action plan on the control of deforestation and a program on alternative energy sources. Key issues for Brazil are eliminating deforestation; correcting the direction of the country's energy base, which will become dirtier in future years; and maintaining leadership in the biofuels sector. Brazil has a long history of fuel ethanol use and a current government mandate of 25 per cent ethanol blending in gasoline. Brazil accounts for 17 per cent of global ethanol production, and has increased export levels (mainly to the United States) since 2000 (Nexant Chem Systems and Expetro, 2007).

In India, the National Council on Climate Change is in the process of developing a comprehensive national policy on climate change issues, including a "Green India" reforestation program. India's economy is growing at a rate of eight to nine per cent a year. It contributes four per cent of global GHGs, and these emissions are growing between two and three per cent annually (Mok, 2007). India suffers from higher rates of poverty than the other BICSAM nations, suggesting the need for different strategies of engagement. India's large rural population depends on climate-sensitive sectors (agriculture, fisheries, forests) and is extremely vulnerable to shifts in weather systems and ecosystems.

While the other BICSAM nations are influential, China is in a league of its own in regard to the magnitude of its economic growth, impact on global aggregate emissions and its ability to attract interest from the EU and other developed countries on climate change issues. With 20 per cent of the world's population and continued rapid economic growth (between eight and 12 per cent for the past decade), the expected rise in emissions could potentially dwarf any reductions made by developed countries. China has surpassed the United States in CO2 emissions to become the world's leader and with sustained high growth rates will open the gap even further.

Source: Murphy et al (2008)

There exists now a formal EU–India strategic partnership with a joint action plan (adopted in September 2005) including environment, climate change and energy. This includes an EU–India initiative on clean development and climate change, largely concentrating on practical yet voluntary measures such as the promotion of clean technologies in the context of the clean development mechanism. An EU–India energy panel inaugurated in June 2005 set up three working groups in coal and clean coal conversion technologies, energy efficiency and renewable energies, and fusion energy including India's participation in the International Thermonuclear Experimental Reactor (ITER) project.

EU annual summits are even older in the case of China – they date back to 1998. Bilateral sectoral agreements and dialogues have been struck that cover the environment, energy, standards and regulation for industrial goods, and science and technology (Murphy et al, 2008). At the conclusion of the 8th EU–China Summit in Beijing in September 2005, China and the EU signed a partnership on climate change focusing on clean coal technology with the aim of demonstrating, in China and the EU, advanced 'zero-emissions' coal technology by 2020.[16] Still in the area of energy policy, the EU and China established the Energy Environment Programme to promote sustainable energy use, with activities taking place under four components: energy policy development, energy efficiency, renewable energy and natural gas (Murphy et al, 2008). Still, China does not seem to value this partnership up to the point where it should accept binding commitments on emission cuts.

Can such partnership and cooperation initiatives mitigate the detrimental effects of North–South rich trade derived from our interpretation of Copeland and Taylor in a bilateral or regional framework? A rationale for second-best, climate-enhancing RTAs or Partnership Trade Agreements (PTAs) lies in the potential use of regional trade as a lever for a climate deal, and conversely in the potential use of climate policies as a lever or bargaining chip for market access – the so-called 'issue linkage' effect. Issue linking within RTAs in this case would provide an incentive for emerging countries to be further involved in curbing global warming and, conversely, a lever for emerging countries to be conceded greater market and technology access in OECD countries. In the case of EU–China trade for instance, alternative options to the envisaged BTA or BCA mechanisms could take the form of a mix of export taxes in China on key EU ETS constrained sectors such as cement and steel, in addition to technology transfers and investment flows. Such a mix should closely associate states and firms in the bargaining process, as RTAs with a limited number of players do permit. In the same vein, improved EU market access could be conceded to Brazilian products – and particularly to agricultural and agro-energy products – in exchange for Brazilian support of (some of) the EU's positions in the negotiation of climate change policies in the post-Kyoto period. The same rationale would apply to EU–India bilateral trade, conceived as a lever for a broader coalition around the EU's position on climate change.

Though linking trade and climate issues to bolster the fight against global warming seems reasonable and attractive on paper, there are drawbacks in the particular case of RTAs and PTAs involving emerging countries. The most serious one is the limited policy space that emerging countries and OECD (and particularly the EU) countries have managed to open jointly so far. Be it in the case of Brazil (Mercosur), India or China, no formal trade agreement links them to the EU, despite years of negotiations in some cases (EU–Mercosur). Table 15.3 gives an overview of RTAs notified to the GATT/WTO and in force that involve BIC countries.

Neither North – South rich nor South rich – South poor RTAs have been notified so far. This vacuum can even be filled by trade disputes in some cases. In a recent WTO dispute brought by India against the EU, complaining about the granting of additional preferences for particular countries on the grounds that they were assisting in the combating of drug production and trafficking, the Appellate Body clarified that 'non-discrimination' does not prohibit developed countries granting differential tariff treatment to developing country

Table 15.3 *Regional Trade Agreements involving BIC countries notified to the GATT/WTO and in force, as of May 2008*

Agreement	*Date of entry into force*	*Date notified by Parties**	*Related provisions*	*Type of agreement***
ASEAN–China	01/07/03	24/11/04	Enabling Clause	PS
Asia–Pacific Trade Agreement (APTA)-Accession of China	01/01/02	30/04/04	Enabling Clause	PS Accession
China–Macao, China	01/01/04	27/12/03	GATS Art. V	EIA
China–Hong Kong, China	01/01/04	27/12/03	GATS Art. V	EIA
Pakistan–China	01/07/07	18/01/08	GATT Art. XXIV	FTA
Chile–China	01/10/06	20/06/07	GATT Art. XXIV	FTA
India–Sri Lanka	15/12/01	17/06/02	Enabling Clause	FTA
India–Singapore	01/08/05	03/05/07	GATS Art. V	EIA
SAPTA	07/12/95	21/04/97	Enabling Clause	PS
APTA	17/06/76	02/12/76	Enabling Clause	PS
MERCOSUR	29/11/91	17/02/91	Enabling Clause	CU

Notes:
* Dates of WTO documents containing notification
** CU = Customs Union; EIA = Economic Integration Agreement; FTA = Free Trade Agreement; PS = Partial Scope
Source: WTO

members, provided that identical treatment is available to all similarly situated beneficiaries. BICs and the EU remain foes more than friends in trade talks. Exploiting linkages between trade and climate change in this context is not impossible – and it should even turn out reasonable as long as negotiations are stuck when restricted to either trade or climate change. But issue linking can work only if trade is used as a carrot for climate change, and conversely. Using climate policies – or foot-dragging – as a stick, as Brazil intended to do to hasten EU market opening, proves to be as inefficient as the EU strategy to use trade protection as a stick to hasten a global deal on climate change.

Conclusion

The broad question we have tried to address in this chapter is to what extent regional trade and RTAs provide effective opportunities to implement the environmental agenda. To answer, we have turned it this way: does regional trade affect the trade–environment relationship formalised by Copeland and Taylor in a multilateral framework, and if so, in what direction?

Our main findings are that the drivers of positive environmental change induced by freer trade in the multilateral case are very unlikely to be met in a wide range of regional trade patterns and agreements. South–South RTAs in particular could see the positive technique and composition effects we find in the Copeland and Taylor analysis either turn negative or counterbalanced by a huge and negative scale effect. Examining to what extent a shortening of distances between exporting and importing countries in the case of RTAs could reduce the pollution generated by transport, we find little evidence of significant pollution reduction. Last, the potential of RTAs to provide member states with the opportunity to link trade and climate change negotiation issues, and hence escape from the impasses of current multilateral negotiations, seems limited when compared with the range of issue linkages offered by multilateral talks, all the more so because existing trade agreements between the most polluting countries are much closer to loose partnership and cooperation agreements than RTAs per se.

Notes

1 See Esty (1994) and Bhagwati (2004).
2 On economic integration and environmental protection, see in particular Esty (2005).
3 This body of research culminated with the reference book of Copeland and Taylor (2003).
4 The terms scale, composition and technique effects were introduced by Grossman and Krueger (1993) in their study of NAFTA.
5 Antweiler et al (2001), with extension and comments in Copeland and Taylor (2003).
6 See Copeland and Taylor (2004) for a review of quantitative assessments. It may be worth noticing that the Trade Sustainability Impact Assessments (Trade SIAs) carried out by the European Commission since 1999 prior to any trade liberalization negotiation are not mentioned in this paper. This omission may be explained by the fact that most Trade SIAs use second-hand CGE model simulations from which they derive a systematic negative scale impact, with additional *qualitative* analysis of potential additional impacts. See for instance in the case of agricultural trade liberalization, Maltais et al (2002).
7 See Copeland and Taylor (2004) and Taylor (2004) for a review and comments.
8 This is indeed the objective of a current research project carried out by Climate Strategies, whose conclusions should be available at the end of 2008. See www.climate-strategies.org/
9 See the WTO website, www.wto.org/english/tratop_e/region_e/scope_rta_e.htm.
10 See also WTO website, www.wto.org/english/tratop_e/region_e/region_e.htm.
11 For a review of institutional patterns of environmental regulations in RTA see OECD (2007).
12 Appelbaum and Gereffi (1994), Bonacich and Waller (1994). See also Chapter 12.
13 The current climate framework (both United Nations Framework Convention on Climate Change (UNFCCC) and Kyoto Protocol) is built on a comprehensive rather than on a sectoral basis since it encompasses all sources and sinks of the six major GHGs from all sectors. The only exceptions to this comprehensive approach relate to: 'bunker fuels' used in international aviation and shipping, which are excluded from national emissions and then from national targets, land use and land use change and forestry (LULUCF), which are distinguished from other emissions sources and addressed by separate provisions.
14 Jones (2006). See also Wangler (2006) for a review of sub-Saharan horticultural exports to the UK.
15 Shifting hence from 'food miles' to 'fair miles', see MacGregor and Vorley (2006).
16 In March 2005, the Commission's Directorate-General for Transport and Energy and the Chinese Ministry for Science and Technology also signed an Action Plan on Clean Coal and terms of reference for an Action Plan on Industrial Cooperation on Energy Efficiency and Renewable Energies.

References

Antweiler, W., Copeland, B. R. and Taylor, M. S. (2001) 'Is free trade good for the environment?', *American Economic Review*, vol 91, no 4, September, pp877–908

Appelbaum, R. P. and Gereffi, G. (1994) 'Power and profits in the apparel commodity chain', in E. Bonacich, L. Cheng, N. Chinchilla, N. Hamilton and P. Ong (eds) *Global Production: The Apparel Industry in the Pacific Rim*, Temple University Press, Philadelphia, PA

Bhagwati, J. (2004) *In Defense of Globalization*, Oxford University Press, New York

Bonacich, E. and Waller, D. (1994) 'Mapping a global industry: Apparel production in the pacific rim triangle', in E. Bonacich, L. Cheng, N. Chinchilla, N. Hamilton and P. Ong (eds) *Global Production: The Apparel Industry in the Pacific Rim*, Temple University Press, Philadelphia, PA

Copeland, B. R. and Taylor, M. S. (2003) *Trade and the Environment*, Princeton University Press, Princeton, NJ

Copeland, B. R. and Taylor, M. S. (2004) 'Trade, growth and the environment', *Journal of Economic Literature*, vol XLII (March), pp7–71

Delgado, J. (2007) 'Why Europe is not carbon competitive', Bruegel Policy Brief 2007/05, November

Ecoinvent (2007) Ecoinvent database, version v1.3, Swiss Centre for Life Cycle Inventories (Ecoinvent Centre), Empa Dübendorf, Switzerland

Economy, E. (2007) 'The great leap backward?', *Foreign Affairs*, vol 86, no 5, pp38–59

Esty, D. (1994) *Greening the GATT*, Institute for International Economics, Washington DC

Esty, D. (2005) 'Economic integration and environmental protection', in R. S. Axelrod, D. L. Downie and N. J. Vig (eds) *The Global Environment. Institutions, Law, and Policy*, CQ Press, Washington DC

European Environment Agency (2008) 'Climate for a transport change', EEA Report 1/2008, http://reports.eea.europa.eu/eea_report_2008_1/en/EEA_report_1_2008_TERM.PDF

Eurostat (2003) *Transport and Environment Database System (TRENDS)*, Statistical Office of the European Communities, Brussels, Belgium

Gereffi, G. and Korzeniewicz, M. (1994) *Commodity Chains and Global Capitalism*, Greenwood Press and Praeger, Westport, CT

Ghosh, S. and Yamarik, S. (2007) 'What is the effect of regional trading arrangements on the quality of the environment', Mimeo

Gibbon, P. (2003) 'The African Growth and Opportunity Act and the Global Commodity Chain for clothing', *World Development*, vol 31, no 11, pp1809–1827

Grossman, G. M. and Krueger, A. B. (1993) 'Environmental impacts of a North American Free Trade Agreement', in P. Garber (ed) *The Mexico–US Free Trade Agreement*, MIT Press, Cambridge, MA

International Energy Agency (2001) *World Energy Outlook 2007: China and India Insights*, IEA, Paris

Jones, A. (2006) 'A life cycle analysis of UK supermarket imported green beans from Kenya', *Fresh Insights*, Paper 4, International Institute for Environment and Development, London

Keijun, J. and Cosbey, A. (2008), 'Embedded carbon in trade goods', Background Paper, Trade and Climate Change Seminar, 18–20 June 2008, Copenhagen, Denmark

Kraemer, R. A., Hinterberg, Dr. F. and Tarasofsky, R. (2007) 'What contribution can trade policy make towards combating climate change?', Study for the Policy Department External Policies, European Parliament

La Rovere, E. L., Pereria, A. O., Smioes, A. F., Pereira, A. S., Garg, A., Halsnaes, K., Schmidt Dubeux, C. B. and Cunha da Costa, R. (2007) *Development First: Linking Energy and Emissions Policies with Sustainable Development for Brazil*, UNEP Risoe Centre, Roskilde, Denmark

Lamy, P. (2008) 'A consensual international accord on climate change is needed', Speech to Temporary Committee on Climate Change, European Parliament, Brussels, 29 May, www.wto.org/english/news_e/sppl_e/sppl91_e.htm

MacGregor, J. and Groom, B. (2007) 'Air-freighted fresh food: Guilty pleasure or sustainable development champion?', *Fresh Perspectives*, issue 6, Department for International Development

MacGregor, J. and Vorley, B. (2006) 'Fair miles? Weighing environmental and social impacts of fresh produce exports from Sub-Saharan Africa to the UK', *Fresh Insights*, Paper 9, International Institute for Environment and Development, London

Maltais, A., Nilsson, M. and Persson, A. (2002) 'Sustainability Impact Assessment of WTO negotiations in the major food crops sector. Final Report', European Commission, Stockholm Environment Institute (SEI)

Mandelson, P. (2006) 'Trade and climate change', Speech delivered in Brussels, 18 December 2006, http://ec.europa.eu/commission_barroso/mandelson/speeches_articles/sppm136_en.htm

Mok, K. (2007) 'India announces new climate change strategy', *ExpressIndia.com*, www.expressindia.com/news/fullstory.php?newsid=89455

Murphy, D., Drexhage, J., Cosbey, A., Tirpak, D. and Egenhofer, Ch. (2008) 'Furthering EU objectives on climate change and clean energy: Building partnership with major developing countries', Climate Change and Foreign Policy Project, Phase II report, IISD

Nexant Chem Systems and Expetro (2007) *Brazil's Biofuels: Outlook for a Global Leader*, Nexant, New York

OECD (2007) *Environment and Regional Trade Agreements*, Organisation for Economic Co-operation and Development, Paris

Osava, M. (2007) 'Climate Change–Brazil: Once and future environmental leader', *IPS News*, www.ipsnews.net/news.asp?idnews=37827

Peters, G. P. and Hertwich, E. G. (forthcoming) 'CO_2 embodied in international trade with implications for global climate policy', *Environmental Science and Technology*

Rodrik, D. (2006) 'What's so special about China's exports?', Centre for Economic Policy Research (CEPR) Discussion Paper No 5484

Shui, B. and Harriss, R. C. (2006) 'The role of CO_2 embodiment in US–China trade', *Energy Policy*, vol 34, no 18, pp4063–4068

Stern, L. and Tubiana, L. (2007) 'New Deal pour le climat', *Le Monde*, 21 September

Stiglitz, J. (2007) *Making Globalization Work*, W.W. Norton and Company, New York

Taylor, S. (2004) 'Trade, development and the environment', Swedish International Development Cooperation Agency (Sida) Trade Brief, February

UBA (2006) *Luftschadstoffinventur Verkehr*, Umweltbundesamt, Vienna, Austria

Wang, T. and Watson, J. (2007) 'Who owns China carbon emissions?', Tyndall Briefing Note 23, October

Wangler, Z. L. (2006) 'Sub-Saharan African horticultural exports to the UK and climate change: A literature review', *Fresh Insights*, Paper 2, International Institute for Environment and Development, London

Conclusion

Paul Ekins and Tancrède Voituriez

'If it ain't broke, don't fix it!'

This reassuring piece of advice might have been taken as the watchword for the global institutional architecture since the last two great changes in that architecture: the establishment of the World Trade Organization (WTO) in 1995 and the agreement under the UN Framework Convention on Climate Change of the Kyoto Protocol two years later. The long boom in the world economy that followed over the next ten years, with the punctuation of the Asian financial crisis soon forgotten in the China-led Asian expansion that followed can now, in retrospect, be seen to have imparted a false sense of confidence in the governance arrangements for an increasingly complex, interdependent and environmentally challenged global economic and social system.

Writing this Conclusion as the global financial meltdown begins to bite into the 'real' economy, amid dire predictions of global recession and unemployment, it seems to us that there are two great dangers in this situation, on different timescales. The first is that the global institutions, world leaders and larger national governments do not do enough to stabilize the economic situation, so that the recession is longer, deeper and more damaging, especially to the relatively poor, than it needs to be. We leave it to those who have special expertise in this area to advise how to avert this danger.

The second danger is probably greater, certainly in terms of long-term impact. It is that global institutions and the rest will seek in their response to the global recession to return to the status quo ante. This would be a recipe for major disruption, and perhaps catastrophe, in the future, and it is here that this book has sought to make a contribution.

The stark reality is that the global system faces a number of serious, interlocking deficiencies and threats which have been gathering disruptive potential for some years but which global institutions have so far not been able to address adequately. The period of recovery following the recession offers an opportunity to seek to make good this deficit, starting with but going well beyond the governance of the international financial system, which was the proximate cause of the current global downturn.

The issues with which this book has been concerned are at the heart of the longer-term deficiencies and threats that now need to be addressed. They are summarized in that much used and abused term, sustainable development: a process of progressively meeting the needs of all the world's people (i.e. development) in a way that sustains rather than destroys the biosphere on which the present and future development depend (i.e. sustainability). This book has therefore been about development and the environment, and the role that trade can play in helping to achieve sustainable development.

This role is not obvious. GATT was originally created in 1947 with the relatively simple remit of progressively removing tariffs and liberalizing trade between a relatively small number of contracting parties. Over the years as the world has become more integrated, GATT has expanded its membership to cover the great majority of countries, and the agenda of multilateral trade liberalization has also expanded to cover and discipline an ever increasing range of policies (non-tariff barriers, subsidies, intellectual property) in an ever increasing range of sectors (agricultural and industrial goods, services). This process culminated in December 1994 with the creation of the WTO as a permanent organization, with objectives that far exceeded those of the GATT, its predecessor, with sustainable development appearing in the WTO preamble as the ultimate goal of trade liberalization itself.

The WTO has not yet begun to respond adequately to the lofty aspirations of its new mandate. Too many of its member governments, especially the powerful ones, continue to regard it as a forum to negotiate a form of trade liberalization that will be to their national advantage (the role of GATT), instead of a forum that will pioneer new kinds of trade that contribute to sustainable development.

As the first chapters of this book showed, we do not yet know enough about the contribution of simple trade liberalization to the development of the poorest people in the least-advantaged countries for negotiations so narrowly focused ever to satisfy those who were determined to see real development come out of the Doha Round, for which there now seem to be three possibilities. Either it will continue to focus on narrow trade liberalization for national advantage, and continue in deadlock; or it will continue to focus on narrow trade liberalization for national advantage, but the powerful countries will somehow push through a deal with which they feel comfortable but which offers little for the development of the least-advantaged, leaving a bitter taste of disappointment and disillusion that will do little for broader global cohesion; or it really will become a development round that includes the least-advantaged in those who benefit, for the greater future security and prosperity of the world as a whole.

One of the major means with which some major countries and blocs, most notably the European Union, have sought to get to grips with the WTO's new role as a promoter of sustainable development, and not just trade liberalization, has been the methodology of Trade Sustainability Impact Assessment (Trade SIA), which has been a major theme through this book. From one perspective Trade SIAs have been very successful. They have shown convincingly, as civil society had long come to suspect, that simple trade liberalization does not necessarily promote sustainable development. In fact, it can just as easily promote unsustainable de-development, by degrading natural environments and disrupting communities.

Unfortunately trade negotiators have not given this evidence the attention it deserves as they pursue their negotiations. Perhaps because the SIAs were not able to be specific enough in the downsides of trade liberalization; perhaps because their advice came at the wrong time; perhaps because the measures that they did recommend were inconvenient or did not appeal to the negotiators – for any or all of these reasons it is clear that they have not been as helpful to the process or influential in the outcome of trade negotiations as had been hoped. This book has identified another possible reason: it may also be that Trade SIAs failed adequately to seek to uncover the reasons why negotiators might not wish to come to a deal on trade liberalization.

The classic reason, of course, is the power of vested interests back home, generating the momentum to overcome, which is often considered one of the *raisons d'être* of trade negotiations. But this book has also explored the issue of adjustment costs, which are often not adequately addressed in the implementation of trade agreements, and which should be of special concern to a 'Development' Round, especially those that impact on poorer countries. Just as important is the issue of externalities, especially environmental externalities. While it may be welcomed that the Doha Round is the first ever to have paid any attention at all to the environment, its attention to and coverage of this critically important global issue leaves so much to be desired that it feels as if there is a fresh start to be made. However, there cannot be such a start until those countries that think that trade measures for environmental protection are actually a cover for trade protectionism are reassured both that it is not, and that attention to environmental issues will be matched by a comparable attention to development issues that has so far been conspicuously lacking, as has already been noted. Trade SIAs might have done more than they have to uncover these tensions between development and the environment in trade negotiations, and suggested how they might be eased. This remains an agenda issue for the future.

Finally the book has looked in some detail at the issue of collective preferences, raised some years ago by the current WTO Director-General Pascal Lamy when he was EU Trade Commissioner, but which have been an unacknowledged spectre at the negotiating table ever since. Collective preferences are simply valued aspects of national or transnational cultures, or just national or transnational values, which may be undermined or prejudiced by trade liberalization. It is clear that these cultural aspects and values exist, and that they influence attitudes and positions at trade negotiations, so that it cannot be helpful that they currently do so largely or completely unacknowledged. Perhaps if Trade SIAs did more to bring them out into the open, it would become more difficult to ignore them.

This book has sought to develop arguments and findings that lie at the crossroads of three branches of research whose respective communities – international trade economics, political sciences and environmental studies – too seldom exchange evidence and ideas on trade and sustainability issues, but all of whose contributions will be critical in finding a way through such that new trade patterns really can contribute to sustainable development. There is still an important role for research. For example, as this book has shown, the 1990s were characterized by a buoyant literature on the impacts of trade on the environment, the major conclusions of which were that no systematic effect of trade could be ascertained – the effect of trade on the environment remained an empirical question that had still to be adequately evaluated. The turn of the century marked a decline in the rate of production of new trade and environment literature, to be progressively replaced by researches on trade and poverty. Strikingly, the same conclusions prevail. The impact of trade on poverty also remains a largely undetermined empirical question.

However, what seems to be established with regard to poverty in particular is that, even though free trade remains theoretically the best available policy in situations of domestic market failure, average efficiency gains seem small and, when combined with large distributional effects across sectors and households, do not suffice to clinch adequate political support for freer trade among WTO member countries' constituencies. This leads to the intriguing question of why, if no substantial and systematic beneficial effect of trade on poverty can be ascertained either theoretically or empirically, the Doha Round was called the Doha *Development* Round, when such an appellation seemed bound to create aspirations and expectations that could not be fulfilled by trade liberalization alone, and would be bound therefore to lead to disillusion while trade liberalization remained the exclusive focus of the Round. By magnifying and overselling trade liberalization gains for poor countries and poor households without consensual scientific knowledge underpinning such gains, by further denying the 'trouble with trade' (as expressed by Paul Krugman), and particularly some job and wage losses attached to it in a world economy much more globalized than it was ten years ago, some influential institutions and economists, and particularly trade economists, have behaved as 'cheerleaders of globalization' (in Dani Rodrik's phrase) and, contrary to their intentions, have contributed to the Doha Round's current immobility and possible collapse.

Trade SIAs have an important potential role in helping to establish this new evidence based on trade, environment and development – in short, on trade and sustainable development. To do so, they will need to pay more attention to the dynamic and distributive effects of trade – economic, social and environmental – which have turned out to be a major complicating factor in the consideration of the consequences of liberalization for 'development'. Then, if they are to gain the attention of policy makers engaged in trade talks – on the basis of past experience, current expectations on the effective use of impact assessment by policy makers seem rather low – they should seek to be useful to trade negotiators by shedding light on the issues that bring negotiations to impasse, by illuminating the possible reasons why some countries wish to depart from free or freer trade.

A number of these reasons are mentioned above and dealt with in more detail in the book. Although methodological developments in the empirical investigation of motives behind resistance to trade liberalization remain uneven, their inclusion in current impact assessment processes seems promising enough to help bridge the gaps between negotiating parties. Further, integrating such motives in trade impact assessments well ahead of trade negotiations could help negotiators develop reflexivity in the formulation of their negotiation positions, improve their understanding of their partners' motivations to resist trade liberalization in specific sectors, and eventually identify an effective common liberalization agenda.

When asking what impacts should be assessed that could explain the failure of trade negotiations and provide policy targets liable to reconcile multilateral trade and sustainable development, we hope that we have highlighted in this book some converging areas of interest for researchers, NGOs and policy makers. We fully acknowledge that more research is needed to really reconcile the trade and sustainable development agendas, particularly with regards to the description of the current patterns of trade at firm level, the dynamic and distributive effects of openness, and the interaction between trade policies and public opinion in a democratic context. That is the importance of participation in Trade SIAs and indeed in trade negotiations themselves. The old certainties that trade liberalization was good for everyone except entrenched protectionist interests that needed to be faced down are gone. Participation is now needed not only to win support for new trade deals, but also to contribute to the actual substance of the deal in a new situation of still great uncertainty as to what kinds of trade really will contribute to sustainable development, and what will not. The ambiguous results of 'fair trade' initiatives in respect of commodities discussed in the book indicates the scale of the uncertainties: improved outcomes cannot be assured even when an altruistic motivation is unquestionable. How much more difficult will it be to determine positive outcomes when self-interest is also an important element of the motivational mix, as it is bound to be in mainstream trade forums.

Multilateral trade negotiations remain controversial, and for good reason in the current context. However, in our view they remain by far a more promising vehicle to harness globalization in support of sustainable development than the regional trade agreements (RTAs) that seem increasingly to be taking their place. This is because the evidence in this book suggests that the drivers of positive environmental change induced by freer trade in the multilateral case are very unlikely to be met in a wide range of regional trade patterns and RTAs. South–South RTAs in particular could see the positive technique and composition effects of trade either turn negative or counterbalanced by a huge and negative scale effect. Moreover, examining to what extent a shortening of distances between exporting and importing countries in the case of RTAs could reduce the pollution generated by transport, there seems to be little evidence of significant pollution reduction. Last, the potential of RTAs to provide member states with the opportunity to link trade and climate change negotiation issues, as a possible means of escaping from the current constraints binding both sets of negotiations, seems limited when compared with the range of issue linkages offered by multilateral talks, especially since existing trade agreements between the most polluting countries are much closer to loose partnership and cooperation agreements than RTAs per se.

The world now faces huge challenges of global governance across a range of issues, economic, social and environmental. New trading patterns and arrangements cannot address, much less resolve, all of these, of course. Just as important will be negotiations and agreements under the climate and biodiversity conventions, for example, and in the forums focused on the achievement of the Millennium Development Goals. There will also be a need for sector-specific arrangements such as the Sustainable Commodity Agreements that this book has proposed. Further moves towards trade liberalization will need to be taken in full recognition of these other agreements and initiatives, and be explicitly complementary and supportive of them, rather than at best ignoring them and at worst constraining their progress. Now that the 2008 global financial crisis has shown so spectacularly that, left to themselves, global markets implode through greed, short-termism and information failure, the way could be clear for a long-lasting recognition that global economic and environmental integration demands integrated global governance. It will be anything but easy to transform the current global institutions, and the relationships between them, so that they fit this bill. But nothing else will do. And current environmental imperatives mean that what needs to be done needs to be done quickly.

Index

Page numbers in *italics* refer to Figures, Tables and Boxes.

For Product Safety Concerns and Information please contact our EU representative GPSR@taylorandfrancis.com Taylor & Francis Verlag GmbH, Kaufingerstraße 24, 80331 München, Germany

Batch number: 10725973

Printed by Printforce, the Netherlands